FROM HOPE TO DESPAIR IN THESSALONICA

This ground-breaking analysis cuts to the heart of the critical debate surrounding the two Thessalonian Epistles. Colin R. Nicholl examines the situations giving rise to each letter with a view to determining how the two relate historically. His book presents an original and compelling hypothesis, arguing that reflected in the letters are two stages of a single crisis plaguing a recently formed Greek church, which spiralled from hope into despair on account of confusion about 'the end'. In addition to making a fresh case for the authenticity of 2 Thessalonians and resolving one of the most difficult problems in the Bible, the identity of 'the restrainer', this monograph is the most up-to-date and comprehensive analysis of the Thessalonian Epistles available today. It is an indispensable resource for scholars and pastors interested in the Thessalonian correspondence.

DR COLIN R. NICHOLL is Assistant Professor of New Testament at Gordon-Conwell Theological Seminary in Massachusetts. His writings have been published in a number of scholarly, religious and secular publications.

SOCIETY FOR NEW TESTAMENT STUDIES

MONOGRAPH SERIES

General Editor: Richard Bauckham

126

FROM HOPE TO DESPAIR IN THESSALONICA

From Hope to Despair in Thessalonica

Situating 1 and 2 Thessalonians

COLIN R. NICHOLL

CAMBRIDGE
UNIVERSITY PRESS

PUBLISHED BY THE PRESS SYNDICATE OF THE UNIVERSITY OF CAMBRIDGE
The Pitt Building, Trumpington Street, Cambridge, United Kingdom

CAMBRIDGE UNIVERSITY PRESS
The Edinburgh Building, Cambridge CB2 2RU, UK
40 West 20th Street, New York, NY 10011–4211, USA
477 Williamstown Road, Port Melbourne, VIC 3207, Australia
Ruiz de Alarcón 13, 28014 Madrid, Spain
Dock House, The Waterfront, Cape Town 8001, South Africa

http://www.cambridge.org

First published 2004

Printed in the United Kingdom at the University Press, Cambridge

Typeface Times 10/12 pt.   *System* LATEX 2_ε [TB]

A catalogue record for this book is available from the British Library

Library of Congress Cataloguing in Publication data
Nicholl, Colin R.
From hope to despair in Thessalonica: situating 1 and 2 Thessalonians / Colin R. Nicholl.
      p.   cm. – (Society for New Testament Studies monograph series; 126)
Includes bibliographical references and index.
ISBN 0 521 83142 3
1. Bible. N.T. Thessalonians – Criticism, interpretation, etc.   I. Title.   II. Monograph
series (Society for New Testament Studies); 126.
BS2725.52.N53   2004
227′.8106 – dc21   2004051554

ISBN 0 521 83142 3 hardback

For Sirscha

CONTENTS

Appendix

PREFACE

The title of this monograph encapsulates well not only its contents, but also a significant aspect of my experience in writing it. For, three years into my research, in March 1999, I travelled to Thessalonica and *environs* with my wife, Sirscha, to see the various sites of archaeological significance. On the evening of 16 March, we left Thessalonica for Philippi in our rental car. By the time we had reached Asprovalta, outside Thessalonica, the rain was coming down in torrents. As I was driving around a bend in the road, I saw a car stationary in the road in front of me and braked, only to skid into the other side of the road, as though on black ice. In spite of my efforts to manoeuvre the car into the ditch, we careered head-on into an oncoming lorry.

In the crash my wife sustained a terrible head wound and three fractures in her left arm, and I fractures in my sternum, ribs and right leg (tibia and fibula). Astonishingly an ambulance happened to be passing by with two empty beds. My wife was taken to the Hippokratia hospital and I to Saint Paul's hospital in Thessalonica. For sixteen hours I lay in pain and despair, wondering whether my wife would survive and, if she did, whether she would have her mental faculties. During that time, the gentleman in the bed opposite me died and I heard his wife's scream of despair as she heard the news. But I thank God that the life and mind of my spouse were preserved and that she was soon transported to be with me in Saint Paul's.

After five difficult days in Thessalonica (documented in *The Spectator*, 2 February 2002), we were airlifted to Addenbrooke's Hospital, Cambridge for surgery. Sirscha had metal plates inserted into her left forearm and I had a unilateral external fixator ('the mutilator') affixed to my tibia. Unfortunately, after four months with 'the mutilator' and two months in a cast, on the day when I was expecting to begin walking again, I was informed that my tibia had not united and that I required major surgery to rectify the problem. The feeling of abandonment by God at that time was very real. Needless to say, the palpable despair I experienced in Thessalonica (and Cambridge) has given me a greater empathy for what I believe was the predicament of the addressees of 1 and 2 Thessalonians.

In the wake of my experiences, I should thank certain key people, who gave me and my wife hope in the midst of our despair. I would like to thank Costas and the other ambulanceman who helped save my wife's life; the surgeons of Hippokratia Hospital who operated on my wife, and certain, regrettably anonymous, staff at Saint Paul's who showed kindness to my wife and me; Alison Haralimpidis, the representative of the British Consulate in Thessalonica, a very wonderful lady, who went far beyond the call of duty, making our stay in Thessalonica bearable and shorter than it otherwise would have been; Paul Stephenson, the US Consul General and his team, who also worked diligently on our behalf; and, most of all, missionaries Brian and Elizabeth Richards and their two children, who, upon receiving an e-mail about our predicament, left Skopje, Macedonia, and drove five hours to Thessalonica to serve us in a Christ-like manner for four days.

In addition, I am grateful to the members of Eden Chapel and some friends at Tyndale House, who for two months took turns to deliver home-cooked meals for my wife and me; and to the hundreds, even thousands, who prayed for us in Cambridge, Northern Ireland, Scotland, Germany, the USA, Canada and across the world.

My research has benefited greatly from access to the resources of the university libraries of Tübingen, Uppsala and Cambridge, as well as of the libraries of Corpus Christi College, the Faculties of Oriental Studies and of Classics, and Tyndale House. Friends particularly helpful to me include Wesley Olmstead, Steve Bryan, David Baer and John Hartmann.

A member of Corpus Christi College, I always appreciated the college's friendliness and warmth, particularly as expressed by the gracious Graduate Secretary, Margaret Cathie. The Student Awards Agency for Scotland are to be thanked for the three-year major Scottish Studentship which made this study possible, and for funding my 'study trip' to Greece. In addition, I wish to express my gratitude to Corpus Christi College and the Managers of the Bethune-Baker and Hort Memorial Funds (the Faculty of Divinity, Cambridge) for generous research grants.

Profound thanks are due to my supervisor, Professor M. D. Hooker, who never failed to offer incisive and rigorous criticism and valuable advice. At the same time, I must express my appreciation for the kindness, patience and sympathy she displayed in the face of my medical problems and those of my father, and for her sense of humour throughout the process. I feel honoured to have had her as my supervisor. I am grateful also to Dr. M. M. B. Thompson, who supervised me for one term when Professor Hooker was on sabbatical.

Thanks are also due to my doctoral examiners, Professor I. Howard Marshall and Revd John Sweet, for their constructive criticism of my work and their encouragement to publish my research. I am indebted to Professor Richard Bauckham for accepting this book as a part of the SNTS Monograph Series. In addition, I have been grateful to faculty, staff and students at the University of Cambridge's Faculty of Divinity, where I lectured for two years, and at Gordon-Conwell Theological Seminary, where I am now privileged to serve as an Assistant Professor, for helping to create congenial and stimulating academic environments in which theological research can truly thrive.

I am inestimably indebted to my parents, who first endued me with an appreciation for the Bible, and who sacrificed so much for me throughout my theological education, but especially in 1999, when, for a total of three months, they left everything to help my wife and me in the aftermath of the accident. They were consistently encouraging and supportive, as were my wife's parents, who also flew to Cambridge to assist my wife and me when we were so needy.

I dedicate this book to my wife, the most gracious, loving and patient person I have ever met. To see her with her head split open in the ambulance and then to lie in a hospital bed in Thessalonica thinking that she might be dead or brain-damaged were without doubt the worst moments of my life. But to hear that she had survived was undoubtedly the most joyful moment of my life. I cannot imagine life without her; she is my soul mate, whom I love to the very depths of my being. She has given so much of herself for me and for this book. I count it a privilege to be her husband.

Finally, I wish to thank God my Father and the Lord Jesus Christ for providing me with the opportunity and the means to study at Cambridge, for sustaining me throughout, for flashes of what seemed like inspiration and insight, and, most of all, for hearing the desperate cries of my wife and me for salvation on a road just outside Thessalonica.

ABBREVIATIONS

Unless specifically noted below, abbreviations follow the SNTS Monograph Series style and the *SBL Handbook of Style*.

1 Clem.	1 Clement
1 Esdr.	1 Esdras
2 Bar.	2 Baruch
ABS	Anvil Biblical Studies
ACNT	*Augsburg Commentary on the New Testament*
ACS	Ancient Culture and Society
Aeschylus, *Pr.*	*Prometheus Vinctus*
AGRL	Aspects of Greek and Roman Life
Apoc. Abr.	Apocalypse of Abraham
Apuleius, *Apol.*	*Apologia*
ARGU	Arbeiten zur Religion und Geschichte des Urchristentums
Aristotle, *Rhet.*	*Rhetorica*
Asc. Isa.	Ascension of Isaiah
ATLAP	*American Theological Library Association: Proceedings*
BAFCS	The Book of Acts in its First-Century Setting
Barn.	Epistle of Barnabas
BCBC	Believers Church Bible Commentary
BECGNT	Baker Exegetical Commentary on the Greek New Testament
BFCT	Beiträge zur Förderung christlicher Theologie
BLG	Biblical Languages: Greek
BPAA	Bibliotheca Pontificii Athenaei Antoniani
BS	The Biblical Seminar
BST	Bible Speaks Today
BTCL	Biblical and Theological Classics Library

BU	Biblische Untersuchungen
CB	Century Bible
CBSC	Cambridge Bible for Schools and Colleges
CC	Calvin's Commentaries
CCC	Christ and Culture Collection
CEB	Commentaires Evangéliques de la Bible
CECNT	Critical and Exegetical Commentary on the New Testament
CFTL	Clark's Foreign Theological Library
Cicero, *Rep.*	*De Republica*
COQG	Christian Origins and Question of God
CPNIVC	College Press NIV Commentary
CRS	Classical Resources Series
CUF	Collection des universités de France
Cyril of Jerusalem, *Cat.*	*Catechetical Lectures*
DBM	*Deltio Biblikon Meleton*
Did.	Didache
Diog. L.	Diogenes Laertius
EBC	*Expositor's Bible Commentary*
EBib	Etudes bibliques
Epictetus, *Diss.*	*Dissertationes*
Eusebius, *Hist. Eccl.*	*Historia Ecclesiastica*
FCCGRW	First-Century Christians in the Graeco-Roman World
Gen. R.	*Genesis Rabbah*
GLH	Greek Lands in History
GNS	Good News Studies
Gos. Thom.	Gospel of Thomas
Gr. Apoc. Ezra	Greek Apocalypse of Ezra
GTA	Göttinger theologische Arbeiten
GTJ	*Grace Theological Journal*
GTW	Grundriß der theologischen Wissenschaften
Herm. *Sim.*	Hermas, *Similitudes*
HFT	Helps for Translators
HNieT	Het Nieuwe Testament
HSL	Herald Scriptural Library
HSP	Halley Stewart Publications
HT	Harper Torchbooks
HTKNTSup	Herders theologischer Kommentar zum Neuen Testament Supplement-Bände
Irenaeus, *Adv. Haer.*	*Adversus Haereses*

JBS	Jerusalem Biblical Studies
Jerome, *Epist.*	*Epistulae*
JHC	*Journal of Higher Criticism*
JL	The Jowett lectures
Josephus, *Ant.*	*Antiquitates Judaicae*
Bell.	*De Bello Judaico*
JPentT	*Journal of Pentecostal Theology*
JProtT	*Jahrbücher für protestantische Theologie*
Jub.	Jubilees
KNT	Kommentar zum Neuen Testament
KVHS	Korte verklaring der Heilige Schrift
LaB	Old Latin text as found in Lat169 and Lat170 and as published by D. De Bruyne, 'Les Anciennes Versions latines du Cantique des Cantiques', *Revue Bénédictine* 38 (1926): 97–122
LaH	Jerome's Hexaplaric Emendation of the Old Latin as reconstructed by A. Vaccari, *Cantici Canticorum: Vetus Latina Translatio a S. Hieronymo ad Graecum Textum Hexaplarem Emendata*
LCBI	Literary Currents in Biblical Interpretation
McNTS	McMaster New Testament Studies
Malalas, *Chron.*	*Chronographia*
MC	Macmillan Commentaries
MSB	Monographien und Studienbücher
MTL	Marshall's Theological Library
MTS	Marburger theologische Studien
NCBC	New Century Bible Commentary
NClarB	New Clarendon Bible
NGS	New Gospel Studies
NHMS	Nag Hammadi and Manichaean Studies
NIVAC	NIV Application Commentary
NK	Natur och kultur
NLT	New Living Translation
NTM	New Testament Message
NTR	New Testament Readings
NTT	New Testament Theology
OBS	Oxford Bible Series
Obs.	Julius Obsequens
OCT	Outstanding Christian Thinkers

Origen, *In Mat.*	*Commentary on Matthew*
OTM	Oxford Theological Monographs
PCPSSup	Proceedings of the Cambridge Philological Society Supplementary Volumes
Peṣ.	*Peṣahim*
P. Flor.	D. Comparetto and G. Vitelli, *Papiri greco-egizii: Papiri fiorentini*
P. Hib.	B. P. Grenfell and A. S. Hunt, eds., *The Hibeh Papyri: Part 1*
Philo, *Leg. All.*	*Legum Allegoriae*
Leg. Gai.	*Legatio ad Gaium*
Mig. Abr.	*De Migratione Abrahami*
Mut.	*De Mutatione Nominum*
Plant.	*De Plantatione*
Praem. Poen.	*De Praemiis et Poenis*
Quaest. in Gen.	*Quaestiones in Genesin*
Sac.	*De Sacrificiis Abelis et Caini*
Spec. Leg.	*De Specialibus Legibus*
Pliny, *Ep.*	*Epistulae*
P. Lond.	F. G. Kenyon and H. I. Bell, *Greek Papyri in the British Museum*
Plutarch, *Public.*	*Publicola*
Pol. *Phil.*	Polycarp, *The Epistle to the Philippians*
Polybius, *Hist.*	*Histories*
P. Oxy.	The Oxyrhynchus Papyri
Ps.-Philo, *Ant.*	Pseudo-Philo, *Liber Antiquitatum Biblicarum*
Ps. Sol.	Psalms of Solomon
PTA	Papyrologische Texte und Abhandlungen
REL	*Revue Ecclésiastique de Liège*
SBG	Studies in Biblical Greek
SBibS	Sources for Biblical Study
SCBO	Scriptorum Classicorum Bibliotheca Oxoniensis
Sch. Eur. *Hec.*	W. Dindorf, ed., *Scholia Graeca in Euripidis Tragoedias ex Codicibus Aucta et Emendata.* 4 vols. Oxford: Academico, 1863
SEJC	Studies in Early Judiasm and Christianity
SENT	Schlatters Erläuterungen zum Neuen Testament
SFAC	South Florida Academic Commentary Series

SHCT	Studies in the History of Christian Thought
Sib. Or.	Sibylline Oracles
SJSJ	Supplements to the Journal for the Study of Judaism
SM	Studia Moralia
SMBCB	Supplements to Mnemosyne, Bibliotheca Classica Batava
SNTG	Die Schriften des Neuen Testaments neu übersetzt und für die Gegenwart erklärt
SNTW	Studies of the New Testament and its World
Sophocles, *Ant.*	*Antigone*
SVTG	Septuaginta: Vetus Testamentum Graecum
Tacitus, *Ann.*	*Annales*
TC	Theological Collections
TC	R. F. Collins, ed., *Thessalonian Correspondence.* BETL. Louvain: Leuven University Press, 1990
TED	Translations of Early Documents
TEH	Theologische Existenz heute
Tetrast. Iamb.	*Tetrasticha Iambica*
TG	*Theologisches Geschenkt*
T. Jud.	Testament of Judah
TSJTSA	Texts and Studies of the Jewish Theological Seminary of America
TTFL	Theological Translation Fund Library
TWAT	*Theologisches Wörterbuch zum Alten Testament*
TZT	*Tübinger Zeitschrift für Theologie*
UBS	United Bible Societies
VB	Verklaring van een Bijbelgedeelte
WesTJ	*Wesleyan Theological Journal*
Wis.	Wisdom of Solomon
WS	*Weidenauer Studien*
WSB	Wuppertaler Studienbibel
Xenophon, *An.*	*Anabasis*
Hell.	*Hellenica*

PART ONE

1

INTRODUCTION

Introduction

In this book we shall examine the situations underlying the Thessalonian correspondence with a view to determining points of continuity and discontinuity and whether a plausible course of development between these situations can or cannot be educed. Our special concern is the eschatological problems assumed by these letters.

The necessity of such an analysis comes into relief when we consider the critical problems relating to 2 Thessalonians that have repeatedly surfaced in the literature of the last two hundred years, and the breakdown of the scholarly consensus regarding the nature of the problems addressed in 1 and 2 Thessalonians. We shall examine each of these in turn.

The need for the study

Four critical problems concerning 2 Thessalonians

There are essentially *four* primary problems concerning 2 Thessalonians which have given rise to hypotheses of pseudonymity (and a plethora of other theories for relating 2 Thessalonians to 1 Thessalonians): (1) the unprecedentedly extensive literary parallels between 2 and 1 Thessalonians;[1] (2) the perceived contradiction between the eschatology of the second letter and the first, specifically between premonitory

---

[1] See especially W. Wrede, *Die Echtheit des zweiten Thessalonicherbriefs untersucht* (TU; Leipzig: Hinrichs, 1903), 3–36; W. Trilling, *Untersuchungen zum zweiten Thessalonicherbrief* (Leipzig: St Benno, 1972), 16–19; F. Laub, *Eschatologische Verkündigung und Lebensgestaltung nach Paulus* (BU; Regensburg: Friedrich Pustet, 1973), 96–110, 152–5; J. A. Bailey, 'Who Wrote II Thessalonians?', *NTS* 25 (1978–9): 132–6; R. F. Collins, *Letters that Paul did not Write* (GNS; Wilmington: Michael Glazier, 1988), 218–21; M. J. J. Menken, *2 Thessalonians: Facing the End with Sobriety* (NTR; London: Routledge, 1994), 36–40; E. J. Richard, *First and Second Thessalonians* (SP; Collegeville: Michael Glazier, 1995), 20–2; S. Légasse, *Les Epîtres de Paul aux Thessaloniciens* (LD; Paris: Cerf, 1999), 348–9.

signs in 2 Thessalonians and imminence/suddenness in 1 Thessalonians;[2] (3) the difficulty of interpreting 2 Thess. 2:2 and 3:17;[3] (4) the difference in tone between 2 and 1 Thessalonians, as suggested by the addition of ὀφείλομεν to the expressions of thanks in 2 Thess. 1:3 and 2:13, together with 2 Thessalonians' lack of personal remarks like those of 1 Thess. 2:1–3:10, and its perceived greater stress on authority.[4]

An initial examination of each of these problems highlights the significance of this study for their satisfactory resolution.

The problem of the literary affinities

To explain the literary parallels, seven main theories have been propounded: (1) while 1 Thessalonians is authentic,[5] 2 Thessalonians is pseudonymous;[6] (2) Paul kept a copy of 1 Thessalonians, which became the basis for 2 Thessalonians;[7] (3) the period separating the letters was so brief that 1 Thessalonians was still fresh in Paul's mind when he penned 2 Thessalonians;[8] (4) Paul had formed particular ways of thinking and

---

[2] While Wrede, *Echtheit*, 43–6 believed that the eschatology is a hint of (not an independent argument for) inauthenticity, but only after the case for pseudonymity has been established on other grounds (i.e. the literary parallels and 2 Thess. 2:2 and 3:17), most proponents of pseudonymity, including G. Hollmann, 'Die Unechtheit des zweiten Thessalonicherbriefes', *ZNW* 5 (1904): 29–38; C. Masson, *Les Deux Epîtres de Saint Paul aux Thessaloniciens* (CNT; Neuchâtel: Delachaux et Niestlé, 1957), 10–11; Laub, *Verkündigung*, 96–119, 147–50; G. Krodel, '2 Thessalonians', in *Ephesians, Colossians, 2 Thessalonians, the Pastoral Epistles* (ed. G. Krodel; PC; Philadelphia: Fortress, 1978), 75–7 and Bailey, 'Who?', 136–7 have insisted that the eschatology constitutes an important independent argument for inauthenticity.

[3] *Inter alios* Wrede, *Echtheit*, 54–61; Hollmann, 'Unechtheit', 38; Bailey, 'Who?', 138; Collins, *Letters*, 223–4; Menken, *Thessalonians*, 33–6; Légasse, *Thessaloniciens*, 352–3.

[4] Wrede, *Echtheit*, 74–6; Hollmann, 'Unechtheit', 38; Trilling, *Untersuchungen*, 63–4; Bailey, 'Who?', 137–8; Collins, *Letters*, 222–3; Menken, *Thessalonians*, 30–1; Richard, *Thessalonians*, 23–4; Légasse, *Thessaloniciens*, 349.

[5] That 1 Thessalonians is authentic is accepted by virtually all contemporary scholars.

[6] So *inter alios* A. Hilgenfeld, 'Die beiden Briefe an die Thessalonicher nach Inhalt und Ursprung', *ZWT* 5 (1862): 249–52; Wrede, *Echtheit*; Hollmann, 'Unechtheit'; Trilling, *Untersuchungen* and *Der zweite Brief an die Thessalonicher* (EKKNT; Zurich: Benzinger; Neukirchen-Vlujn: Neukirchener, 1980); Laub, *Verkündigung*, 149–57; A. Lindemann, 'Zum Abfassungszweck des zweiten Thessalonicherbriefes', *ZNW* 68 (1977): 35–47; Bailey, 'Who?'; Collins, *Letters*; G. S. Holland, *The Tradition that You Received from Us* (HUT; Tübingen: Mohr, 1988); F. W. Hughes, *Early Christian Rhetoric and 2 Thessalonians* (JSNTSup; Sheffield: JSOT, 1989); G. Krodel, '2 Thessalonians', in *The Deutero-Pauline Letters* (ed. G. Krodel; PC; Minneapolis: Fortress, 1993), 56–7; Menken, *Thessalonians*; Richard, *Thessalonians*; G. Lüdemann, *Heretics* (trans. J. Bowden; London: SCM, 1996), 108–19; Légasse, *Thessaloniciens*, 347–56.

[7] T. Zahn, *Einleitung in das Neue Testament* (2nd edn; 3 vols.; Leipzig: Deichert, 1900), 1: 161–74.

[8] J. Graafen, *Die Echtheit des zweiten Thessalonicherbriefs* (NTAbh; Münster: Aschendorff, 1930), 50.

feeling about his converts, and these paradigms remained frozen from 1 to 2 Thessalonians;[9] (5) Paul was employing stock words and phrases in both;[10] (6) 1 and 2 Thessalonians were written within a very short period of time, addressed to different sections of the same community, whether 1 Thessalonians to Gentile believers and 2 Thessalonians to Jewish believers,[11] or 1 Thessalonians to a 'special circle of the church' and 2 Thessalonians to the entire community;[12] (7) the situations addressed in the letters were similar.[13]

Option (1) is fast becoming the most popular explanation of the literary parallels.[14] However, we should be cautious about uncritically jumping through this particular escape hatch. For, closely scrutinised, the pseudonymous view is seen to be more vulnerable than most of its advocates concede. Two criticisms suffice to make this point: (a) Rigaux summarises succinctly the problem posed by the reference to the temple in 2 Thess. 2:4: 'un faussaire, après la destruction du temple aurait évité tout traite qui aurait pu mettre ses prédictions en contradiction avec la réalité de la destruction du temple' ('A forger, after the temple's destruction, would have avoided every trace which could have put his predictions in contradiction with the reality of the temple's destruction').[15] (b) The

---

[9] W. Bornemann, *Die Thessalonicherbriefe* (KEK; Göttingen: Vandenhoeck & Ruprecht, 1894), 460–3.

[10] E. J. Bicknell, *The First and Second Epistles to the Thessalonians* (WC; London: Methuen, 1932), xxx.

[11] A. von Harnack, 'Das Problem des 2. Thessalonicherbriefes', *SPAW* 31 (1910): 560–78.

[12] M. Dibelius, *An die Thessalonicher I, II* (HNT; Tübingen: Mohr, 1937), 57–8. A number of scholars have proposed that 1 and 2 Thessalonians were addressed to different cities. E. Schweizer, 'Der zweite Thessalonicherbrief ein Philipperbrief?', *TZ* 1 (1945): 90–105 suggested that 2 Thessalonians was written to the Philippians, on the basis of Polycarp's attribution of the citation from 2 Thess. 1:4 to a letter to the Philippians (Pol. *Phil.* 11:3). However, the lack of text-critical evidence for such an address remains a serious objection (E. Best, *The First and Second Epistles to the Thessalonians* (2nd edn; BNTC; London: A. & C. Black, 1986), 41). This criticism holds true also for the proposal of M. Goguel, 'L'Enigme de la seconde épître aux Thessaloniciens', *RHR* 71 (1915): 248–72, that 2 Thessalonians was originally sent to Berea.

[13] A. Jülicher, *An Introduction to the New Testament* (trans. J. P. Ward; London: Smith, Elder & Co., 1904), 62–3.

[14] This is largely due to the important studies of Wrede, *Echtheit* and Trilling, *Untersuchungen*.

[15] B. Rigaux, *Saint Paul: Les Epîtres aux Thessaloniciens* (EBib; Paris: Gabalda, 1956), 145. *Contra* Wrede, *Echtheit*, 112–13, it is implausible that an author writing after 70, drawing on a pre-70 tradition, might have avoided thinking of the serious problem posed by the destruction of the Jerusalem temple. Most proponents of pseudonymity conclude that the 'taking his seat in the temple of God' is a *metaphor* rooted in the OT. See chapter 5 for a consideration of this position. Note that M. Hengel, *Studies in the Gospel of Mark* (London: SCM, 1985), 131 n. 115 opts for a pre-70 date on the grounds that the ναός must be the Jerusalem temple.

lack of consensus regarding a date[16] and destination for the pseudonymous letter reflects a dilemma for this position: on the one hand, the date needs to be early enough for the letter to have been accepted as Pauline and included in the Pauline collection, and moreover to accommodate plausibly the reference to 2 Thess. 1:4 and 3:15 in Pol. *Phil.* 11:3 and 4 respectively (c. 107–17).[17] On the other hand, the date and destination need to be such that the author could be confident that no contemporary of 1 Thessalonians (especially no member of the original Thessalonian community) who might have known that Paul had dispatched only one letter to the Thessalonians could have exposed 2 Thessalonians as a rather deceptive forgery (note especially 2 Thess. 3:17). Whether a date and a destination exist which avoid these pitfalls has yet to be demonstrated. With regard to destination, Asia Minor certainly seems an implausible candidate,[18] since, given the communications between it and Macedonia, a pseudonymous author could hardly have been confident that his work would not have been exposed as inauthentic.

Whether 2 Thessalonians is pseudonymous has not been settled, and so we must give careful attention to the Pauline alternatives. Regarding

[16] Proponents of pseudonymity have suggested various dates for 2 Thessalonians: Wrede, *Echtheit*, 91–5, between 100 and 110; Lindemann, 'Abfassungszweck', 44, the close of the first century; Bailey, 'Who?', 143 and C. H. Giblin, '2 Thessalonians', in *NJBC* (ed. R. E. Brown, J. A. Fitzmyer and R. E. Murphy; London: Geoffrey Chapman, 1990; henceforth '2 Thessalonians'), 872, the last decade of the first century; W. Trilling, 'Literarische Paulusimitation im 2. Thessalonicherbrief', in *Paulus in den neutestamentlichen Spätschriften* (ed. K. Kertelge; QD; Freiburg: Herder, 1981), 154 (and his *Zweite Brief*, 28) and Menken, *Thessalonians*, 66, between 80 and the early part of the second century; L. Hartman, 'The Eschatology of 2 Thessalonians as Included in a Communication', in *TC* (ed. R. F. Collins; BETL; Louvain: Leuven University Press, 1990), 484, the late 70s, 'during the time, say, between Nero and Domitian'; W. Marxsen, *Introduction to the New Testament* (trans. G. Buswell; Oxford: Blackwell, 1968), 44, shortly after 70; F. H. Kern, 'Über 2 Thess 2, 1–12. Nebst Andeutungen über den Ursprung des 2. Briefs an die Thessalonicher', *TZT* 2 (1839): 200, between 68 and 70; and Hengel, *Mark*, 131 n. 115, between 62 and 70.
[17] Laub, *Verkündigung*, 157 and H. Braun, 'Zur nachpaulinischen Herkunft des zweiten Thessalonicherbriefes', *ZNW* 44 (1952–3): 156 acknowledged that Polycarp's *Phil.* 11:3 almost certainly alludes to 2 Thess. 1:4. However, J. Gnilka, *Der Philipperbrief* (HTKNT; Freiburg: Herder, 1968), 5–11; Trilling, *Untersuchungen*, 33 n. 69 and Holland, *Tradition*, 130 do not defer to the weight of the evidence, and consequently are forced to conclude that Polycarp is referring to a second Pauline letter to the Philippians. The extensive parallelism in such a confined space and the uncommon nature of the wording, combined with the abundance of references to the Pauline corpus in Polycarp, strongly suggest that he is here echoing 2 Thess. 1:4 and 3:15. The dating of Polycarp's letter is evident from 1:1 and 13:2: it must be very soon after Ignatius' death. The evidence from the Muratorian canon, Marcion's collection and the early versions also suggests that 2 Thessalonians was known and accepted as Pauline in the second century.
[18] *Pace inter alios* Trilling, *Zweite Brief*, 28; Giblin, '2 Thessalonians', 872; M. J. J. Menken, 'Paradise Regained or Still Lost? Eschatology and Disorderly Behaviour in 2 Thessalonians', *NTS* 38 (1992): 288 and *Thessalonians*, 65.

(2), while it cannot be outrightly dismissed that the apostle kept copies of his correspondence, several factors cast doubt on the plausibility of this suggestion: (a) It presupposes that Paul himself 'attached a greater importance to his own writings than their strictly occasional character warrants',[19] and (b) There is some doubt concerning whether the missionaries could have afforded to use papyrus so liberally as to keep copies of letters.[20] With respect to (3), although most would agree that the problem of the literary parallels is significantly eased if the two letters were written within a short time frame,[21] this hypothesis is independently insufficient to explain the full extent of similar material; moreover, without evidence that 2 Thessalonians did follow soon after 1 Thessalonians, it must remain no more than a hypothetical possibility. Concerning (4), while the psychological explanation does account for some of the literary affinities between the two letters, such as the two thanksgivings in each and the emphatic ἡμεῖς at the head of those in 2 Thess. 2:13/1 Thess. 2:13, it cannot explain the majority of the parallels, or why so much of the personal material in 1 Thessalonians (especially 2:17–3:10) is missing from 2 Thessalonians. With regard to (5), although the use of stock words and phrases may shed light on particular parallels (such as 2 Thess. 3:8/1 Thess. 2:9 and perhaps 2 Thess. 1:1–2/1 Thess. 1:1, the use of 'Lord/God of peace' in the benedictory prayers in 2 Thess. 3:16/1 Thess. 5:23 and the occurrence of αὐτός with 'God' or 'Lord' in prayers in each letter), it too is restricted in the help it offers. Suggestion (6) is unconvincing, for 1 Thess. 5:27 plainly indicates that 1 Thessalonians was addressed directly and primarily to the whole community, and, moreover, the prescripts of both letters, which are uncontested text-critically, suggest that the addressees cannot be restricted to groups within the community. Furthermore, 2 Thess. 2:15 most naturally implies that 2 Thessalonians was a *second* letter written to the same addressees, the Thessalonians.

All this highlights the importance of option (7). Can a significant number of the literary affinities be explained with reference to similarities in the situations? Much depends on our answer to this question. If it is affirmative, a crucial argument for pseudonymity is critically undermined. If

---

[19] G. Milligan, *St. Paul's Epistles to the Thessalonians* (MC; London: Macmillan, 1908), lxxxv.

[20] Laurent as cited by Wrede, *Echtheit*, 33 n. 2; Bailey, 'Who?', 135–6.

[21] Von Harnack, 'Problem', 574–5; Marxsen, *Introduction*, 40–1; Trilling, *Untersuchungen*, 43–4 and G. Friedrich, 'Der zweite Brief an die Thessalonicher', in *Die Briefe an die Galater, Epheser, Philipper, Kolosser, Thessalonicher und Philemon* (ed. J. Becker, H. Conzelmann and G. Friedrich; NTD; Göttingen: Vandenhoeck & Ruprecht, 1976), 257 maintained that the literary parallels could only be explained with reference to pseudonymity or Paul's having written 1 and 2 Thessalonians within a very short time span.

it is negative, the pseudonymous explanation becomes more compelling. Hence the importance of this investigation.

The problem of the apparently incompatible eschatologies

To overcome the problem of genuinely or apparently contradictory eschatologies centred on signs *versus* suddenness/imminence, defenders of the Pauline authorship of 2 Thessalonians have typically pointed to the fact that contemporary Judaism and indeed Jesus' eschatological teaching as recorded in the Synoptic Gospels (e.g. Mark 13:14–37) held signs and suddenness/imminence together.[22] Some have objected to this line of defence on the grounds that the coincidence in the eschatological discourses attributed to Jesus in the Synoptics may simply reflect use of two independent traditions[23] and that Paul and Jesus stand apart from the apocalypticists in rejecting signs.[24] However, the former objection merely pushes the coincidence to the time of the Gospels' redaction and composition. And the latter objection not only overlooks the fact that our access to Pauline thought is restricted to a number of occasional letters, which hardly constitute reliable grounds for such sweeping judgments concerning Paul's thought, but also the likelihood that Rom. 11:11–12, 23–4, 25–6 seem to anticipate that certain events will necessarily precede the eschaton (namely the fullness of the Gentiles and the salvation of 'all Israel'). Whether signs and suddenness/imminence are genuinely contradictory or not, it *is* surely significant that they could be held together by Jewish and Christian contemporaries of Paul. Moreover, it is remarkable that the majority of proponents of pseudonymity adopt the complementary hypothesis, which contends that 2 Thessalonians was intended to *complement* 1 Thessalonians, correcting the enthusiastic opponents' false eschatological notion (2 Thess. 2:2c), which was rooted in a *misunderstanding* of 1 Thessalonians' eschatological instruction, perhaps 1 Thess. 5:1–11.[25] That would mean that the author of 2 Thessalonians

---

[22] So *inter alios* J. E. Frame, *A Critical and Exegetical Commentary on Paul's Letters to the Thessalonians* (ICC; Edinburgh: T. & T. Clark, 1912), 43–4; Rigaux, *Thessaloniciens*, 140–1; W. Kümmel, *Introduction to the New Testament* (rev. edn; trans. H. C. Kee; NTL; London: SCM, 1975), 266; I. H. Marshall, *1 and 2 Thessalonians* (NCBC; London: Marshall, Morgan and Scott, 1983), 37; Best, *Thessalonians*, 55.

[23] Krodel, *Ephesians, Colossians, 2 Thessalonians*, 76–7; cf. Hollmann, 'Unechtheit', 31.

[24] Hollmann, 'Unechtheit', 31–2.

[25] So, for example, Wrede, *Echtheit*; Hollmann, 'Unechtheit'; Trilling, *Untersuchungen* and *Zweite Brief*; Bailey, 'Who?'; Collins, *Letters*; Holland, *Tradition*, 152; Hughes, *2 Thessalonians*; C. H. Giblin, '2 Thessalonians 2 Reread as Pseudepigraphal: A Revised

himself did not perceive the eschatology of the second letter to be ir-reconcilable with that of 1 Thessalonians. If the two concepts of signs and suddenness/imminence could indeed have been viewed as compat-ible by the author of 2 Thessalonians, the only plausible version of the argument for pseudonymity based on eschatological contradiction is that which contends that 1 and 2 Thessalonians could not have been addressed to the same community within a short period of time.[26] Hence the value of this argument from signs *versus* suddenness/imminence is also ulti-mately dependent on the analysis of the situations underlying 1 and 2 Thessalonians, which is the task of this book.

The problem of 2 Thess. 2:2 and 3:17

In their attempts to determine what 2 Thess. 2:2 and 3:17 (to which we might add 2:15) reveal about the relationship between 1 and 2 Thessa-lonians, scholars have come up with the following hypotheses: (1) the authentic 2 Thessalonians actually preceded 1 Thessalonians;[27] (2) the problem underlying the authentic 2 Thessalonians may have been caused by a misunderstanding or misrepresentation of 1 Thessalonians;[28] (3) the pseudonymous 2 Thessalonians was intended to complement 1 Thessa-lonians, a misunderstanding or misrepresentation of which had led to the problem giving rise to 2 Thessalonians;[29] (4) the pseudonymous 2 Thes-salonians was designed to discredit 1 Thessalonians as a forgery and to undermine what the author of 2 Thessalonians regarded as the heretical over-imminentist eschatological expectation of 1 Thessalonians, which

Reaffirmation of *The Threat to Faith*', in *TC* (henceforth 'Reread') and '2 Thessalonians'; Menken, *Thessalonians*, 34; Richard, *Thessalonians*.

[26] See Marxsen, *Introduction*, 40–2; Bailey, 'Who?', 137; Menken, *Thessalonians*, 29–30.

[27] So, for example, T. W. Manson, 'St. Paul in Greece: The Letters to the Thessalonians', *BJRL* 35 (1952–3): 437–47; R. W. Thurston, 'The Relationship between the Thessalonian Epistles', *ExpTim* 85 (1973–4): 52–6; C. A. Wanamaker, *The Epistles to the Thessaloni-ans: A Commentary on the Greek Text* (NIGTC; Grand Rapids: Eerdmans, 1990), 37–45; P. Trudinger, 'The Priority of 2 Thessalonians Revisited: Some Fresh Evidence', *DRev* 113 (1995): 31–5.

[28] For example, Marshall, *Thessalonians*, 187; R. Jewett, *The Thessalonian Correspon-dence* (FF; Philadelphia: Fortress, 1986), 181–91; F. Bassin, *Les Epîtres de Paul aux Thes-saloniciens* (CEB; Vaux-Sur-Seine: Edifac, 1991), 185; Fee, 'Pneuma and Eschatology in 2 Thessalonians 2.1–2: A Proposal about "Testing the Prophets" and the Purpose of 2 Thessalonians', in *To Tell the Mystery* (ed. T. E. Schmidt and M. Silva; JSNTSup; Sheffield: JSOT, 1994), 200 and *God's Empowering Presence* (Peabody, Mass.: Hendrickson, 1994), 72–4; A. J. Malherbe, *The Letters to the Thessalonians* (AB; New York: Doubleday, 2000), 355–6.

[29] So, for example, Wrede, *Echtheit*, 60–3; Bailey, 'Who?', 142–3; Trilling, *Zweite Brief*, 77; Menken, *Thessalonians*, 34.

was being employed by his opponents;[30] (5) Paul feared that a forgery in his name might have given rise to the community's new eschatological problem.[31]

Hypothesis (1) can probably be discounted since 2 Thess. 2:15's aorist ἐδιδάχθητε most naturally belongs with δι' ἐπιστολῆς ἡμῶν, indicating that the specified letter is almost certainly past rather than present,[32] and hence is probably 1 Thessalonians. That the 'letter' is indeed past seems to be confirmed by the observation that δι' ἐπιστολῆς ἡμῶν is paired with διὰ λόγου (note εἴτε . . . εἴτε), which can only refer to the missionaries' oral instruction passed on during the mission.[33] Concerning (2) and (3), 2 Thess. 2:2's μήτε δι' ἐπιστολῆς ὡς δι' ἡμῶν more naturally refers to a forged letter than a misunderstanding or misrepresentation of an authentic one, suggesting that 3:17 is intended to empower the readers to distinguish a possible forgery from Paul's authentic letters.[34] Proponents of option (4) have persistently failed to take seriously enough the problem that a pseudonymous author is almost certainly not going to base his composition of a Pauline epistle on a letter which he regards as a forgery. Moreover, not only have advocates of this view not given a satisfactory explanation of the Christian author's flagrant deception and hypocrisy as entailed in such a scenario, but they also have failed to respond adequately to the objection that 2 Thess. 2:15 most naturally refers to 1 Thessalonians as a part of the tradition which 2 Thessalonians is calling its readers to embrace. Furthermore, *contra* those who adhere to this view, it cannot be assumed that the mark of authenticity of 3:17, the handwritten greeting of Paul, is in fact absent from 1 Thessalonians,[35] nor can it be presumed that the three possible sources of the false claim in 2 Thess. 2:2 are more than *possible* sources. In the light of these critiques

---

[30] Hilgenfeld, 'Thessalonicher', 249–52, 262; H. J. Holtzmann, 'Zum zweiten Thessalonicherbrief', *ZNW* 2 (1901): 105–6; M. Rist, 'Pseudepigraphy and the Early Christians', in *Studies in New Testament and Early Christian Literature* (ed. David Aune; NovTSup; Leiden: Brill, 1972), 82–3; Lindemann, 'Abfassungszweck', 35–47, esp. 39–42, 47; W. Marxsen, *Der zweite Thessalonicherbrief* (ZBK; Zurich: Theologischer, 1982), 107–17; Krodel, *Deutero-Pauline Letters*, 56–7 and Lüdemann, *Heretics*, 108–19.

[31] So, for example, G. G. Findlay, *The Epistles to the Thessalonians* (CBSC; Cambridge: Cambridge University Press, 1894), 141.

[32] Wanamaker, *Thessalonians*, 40–1 suggests that the verb is either an 'epistolary aorist' or a 'perfective passive', but his proposal smacks of special pleading.

[33] Against the reversal-of-canonical-order view, see the case of Jewett, *Correspondence*, 26–30, which Wanamaker, *Thessalonians*, 39–45 fails to undermine.

[34] We shall substantiate this claim in some detail in chapters 5 and 8 below.

[35] See E. R. Richards, *The Secretary in the Letters of Paul* (WUNT; Tübingen: Mohr, 1991), 76–80 and 172–5. The change to the first-person singular in 5:27 would appear to endorse the claim of 2 Thess. 3:17.

and the lack of problems with hypothesis (5), it would seem that it is the most plausible explanation of these controversial verses. If so, the fact that the author of 2 Thess. 2:2 does not even consider the possibility that a misunderstanding of 1 Thessalonians could have been responsible for the problem, but only a forged letter (μήτε δι᾽ ἐπιστολῆς ὡς δι᾽ ἡμῶν), may mean that the false claim of verse 2c was made (and the community exposed to the possible forged letter) prior to reception of 1 Thessalonians.

Nevertheless, any hypothesis designed to elucidate the relationship of 1 Thessalonians to 2 Thessalonians must be rooted in an analysis of the situations underlying each letter. In this book we shall attempt to develop a fresh hypothesis which will better integrate 2 Thess. 2:2, 15 and 3:17 (Part 4) and be rooted in a rigorous analysis of the situations underlying 1 and 2 Thessalonians (Parts 2 and 3).

The problem of the perceived difference in tone

In response to the claim that the perceived difference in tone is a proof of pseudonymity, many proponents of authenticity have argued that any difference in tone is due primarily to the different situation being addressed in the second letter.[36] For example, Stepien attributes the differences between 1 and 2 Thessalonians to the change in circumstances of the Thessalonian community in the three months after 1 Thessalonians was written, especially the new idea reflected in 2 Thess. 2:2c and the worsening of the idleness problem.[37] He claims that this explains why Paul could not simply give thanks, as he did in 1 Thessalonians. Certainly Paul is perfectly capable of writing letters as different in tone as Philippians on the one hand and Galatians on the other. In the ensuing chapters we shall analyse both Thessalonian letters to determine whether the epistolary tones are as contrasting as is usually claimed and whether whatever difference in tone there is can or cannot be justified with reference to Paul's addressing different situations.

In conclusion, it can be seen that a study of the situations underlying 1 and 2 Thessalonians such as we shall attempt in this monograph is essential to a consideration of how the two letters are related and whether 2 Thessalonians is pseudonymous or authentic.

---

[36] For example, Milligan, *Thessalonians*, lxxxiii–lxxxiv; W. Neil, *The Epistles of Paul to the Thessalonians* (MNTC; London: Hodder & Stoughton, 1950), xxii–xxiii; Rigaux, *Thessaloniciens*, 150; J. Stepien, 'Autentycznosc listów do Tessaloniczan', *ColT* 34 (1963): 171–4; Jewett, *Correspondence*, 12, 17; Malherbe, *Thessalonians*, 351, 367.

[37] Stepien, 'Tessaloniczan', 171–4.

Are the eschatological situations underlying 1 and 2 Thessalonians incompatible?

A number of prominent scholars have argued that the eschatological situations presupposed by 1 and 2 Thessalonians are incompatible and cannot be explained except with reference to pseudonymity. Marxsen has claimed that the congregational situations are completely different[38] and cannot be accounted for with respect to the short time separation between 1 and 2 Thessalonians which is essential to the view that Paul wrote 2 Thessalonians.[39] Collins and Bailey develop their situational eschatological argument similarly: the readers of 2 Thessalonians have succumbed to the false teaching that the Day of the Lord has already come, in stark and irreconcilable contrast to the readers of 1 Thessalonians, who are troubled by the fact that the Day of the Lord has not yet come.[40] The goal of this book will be to determine whether a plausible line of development between the situations underlying the two letters can be drawn which does justice to the full range of data, or whether one is forced to opt for pseudonymity.

What are the situational criteria for 2 Thessalonians to qualify as a pseudepigraph?

In an important article on epistolary pseudepigrapha, Bauckham pointed out that pseudonymous letters are distinguishable from authentic letters in the way that they address their real readers. Since in a pseudonymous letter the supposed author and recipients are not the real author and recipients, the real readers 'must read it as a letter written to *other* people, in the past'.[41] Nevertheless, in order to ensure that the real readers understood that the religious instruction and/or ethical exhortation was also addressed to them, a pseudonymous author had two options. First, he could achieve relevance for the real readers by keeping his letter general. Second, if he sought to deal specifically with particular issues, he could write his letter to 'supposed addressees who were ancestors or predecessors of the real readers in a situation supposed not to have changed . . . up to the present, so that the real readers are still in the same situation as the supposed addressees once were';[42] or he could 'depict the historical situation of the supposed addressees as a kind of type of the similar present situation of

---

[38] Marxsen, *Introduction*, 38–40, 42; cf. Laub, *Verkündigung*, 147–9.
[39] Marxsen, *Introduction*, 40–2.   [40] Bailey, 'Who?', 136–7; Collins, *Letters*, 221.
[41] R. Bauckham, 'Pseudo-Apostolic Letters', *JBL* 107 (1988): 475 (italics his).
[42] Ibid., 476–7.

the real readers, so that what is said to the supposed addressees applies typologically to the real readers'.[43] If he chose the specific, typological option, he would have to describe the supposed situation sufficiently well for the readers to be able to identify it as analogous to their own.[44] Scholars who read 2 Thessalonians as pseudonymous must suppose that the author has sought to address his real readers either by establishing a typological situational connection between the supposed addressees and the real addressees or by keeping his letter general. But does 2 Thessalonians meet the criteria to qualify as a 'typological pseudepigraph' or as a general tract? We shall seek to answer this question after a detailed consideration of the situations underlying 1 and 2 Thessalonians.

The need for a situational study of 1 Thessalonians

In addition, there is a definitive need for a fresh study of the situation underlying 1 Thessalonians on its own terms. The consensus view in the twentieth century was that 1 Thessalonians portrays the Thessalonian community as joyfully excited at the prospect of the eschaton. However, over the past two decades this has been questioned by several scholars, and the seeds for a new understanding of the situation have been sown. In an essay in 1980 Hyldahl proposed that as a result of deaths in the community the converts had come to question whether the parousia would actually occur and indeed whether the Gospel was true; they were characterised by a hopelessness which threatened their continued perseverance.[45] While scholars have rightly pointed out that evidence is lacking that the Thessalonians thought that the parousia might not happen,[46] they have failed to take adequate account of the general direction pioneered by Hyldahl. In 1987 Johanson suggested that the primary exigency of 1 Thessalonians was an incipient worry of the Thessalonians concerning their status at the parousia, rooted in the unexpected deaths.[47] Although he did not satisfactorily integrate this idea with his reading of 1 Thess. 4:10b–12 and 5:14,[48] his study represents an important challenge to the predominant view that

---

[43] Ibid., 477.   [44] Ibid., 477.

[45] N. Hyldahl, 'Auferstehung Christi – Auferstehung der Toten', in *Die Paulinische Literatur und Theologie* (ed. S. Pedersen; Teologiske Studier; Århus: Forlaget Aros; Göttingen: Vandenhoeck & Ruprecht, 1980), 119–35.

[46] Marshall, *Thessalonians*, 122; Wanamaker, *Thessalonians*, 165.

[47] B. Johanson, *To All the Brethren* (ConBNT; Stockholm: Almquist & Wiksell, 1987), 129–30.

[48] Ibid., 116. Why would the author offer prophylactic paraenesis against conceivable side-effects of eschatological fervour and neophyte enthusiasm in a community so plagued with incipient doubt and anxiety?

the Thessalonians were joyfully excited at the prospect of the parousia. Kieffer has continued in this vein, arguing in an essay published in 1990 that the readers of 1 Thessalonians were anxious because of the deaths and needed to be reconfirmed in their faith.[49] In the light of these three studies, we propose that the time is right for a fresh examination of the situation underlying 1 Thessalonians, most specifically its eschatological aspect, to determine whether the community was characterised by enthusiastic eschatological excitement or hopelessness and anxiety in view of the imminent eschaton. It is this that we shall attempt in Part 2.

The need for a situational study of 2 Thessalonians

With regard to 2 Thessalonians, the consensus of the last two centuries has been that enthusiastic eschatological excitement was the predominant characteristic of the addressees. A foundation stone of this interpretation has been the problem of idleness in 3:6–15, which most presume must have been eschatologically motivated. However, this assumption has come under intense criticism over the last decade and a half. Russell's 1988 article, Aune's 1989 thesis, Winter's 1989 article (revised in 1994) and Wanamaker's 1990 commentary each proposed reading the problem of idleness in 3:6–15 as a social rather than an eschatological phenomenon. Aside from raising the need for a fresh study of that section, these writings have highlighted the necessity of a new analysis of the whole hypothesis of eschatological excitement/over-eager expectation. In Part 3 of this book we shall re-examine the situation underlying 2 Thessalonians to determine whether it is in fact best elucidated with reference to the paradigm of eschatological enthusiastic excitement.

Method and procedure

In this study we shall undertake an examination of the situations underlying 1 and 2 Thessalonians with a view to determining points of continuity and discontinuity, and whether or not a plausible course of development between these situations can be educed. Our special concern will be the eschatological problems assumed by these letters.

The methodological approach of our study will necessarily be eclectic, involving a wide range of critical exegetical methods (including socio-historical criticism, form criticism, tradition criticism, redaction

[49] R. Kieffer, 'L'Eschatologie en 1 Thessaloniciens dans une perspective rhétorique', in *TC*, 216, 218.

criticism and *Religionsgeschichte*). Leaving the matter of the authorship of 2 Thessalonians undecided, we shall draw inferences from explicit textual clues and the logic of the argumentation of each letter, reconstructing the situations underlying 1 and then 2 Thessalonians, before attempting to synthesise our results. The apparent author and recipients of 2 Thessalonians, whether Paul and the Thessalonians or pseudonymous constructs, shall be referred to as 'Paul' and 'the Thessalonians'. Our study will assume the authenticity of 1 Thessalonians, the *Hauptbriefe*, Philippians and Philemon, but not of Ephesians, Colossians or the Pastoral Epistles, although of course their contributions will be taken into account.

As regards procedure, having established the need, significance and method of our study with reference to recent scholarly discussion of 1 and 2 Thessalonians in Part 1 (chapter 1), we shall proceed to examine 1 Thessalonians in Part 2, giving attention first to the two eschatological sections 4:13–18 (chapter 2) and 5:1–11 (chapter 3), and then to the rest of the letter (chapter 4). In chapter 4 it will be suggested that the problem Paul is addressing in 4:13–18 is one of *hopeless* grieving for deceased community members, apparently on account of an unfamiliarity with the idea of the eschatological resurrection of dead saints. We shall postulate in chapter 4 that the reassurances of 5:1–11 presuppose that underlying the community's question regarding the times and the seasons (5:1) was a fear of sudden eschatological destruction. Such a fear, we shall submit, may be explained by the unexpected deaths, which may have undermined the believers' confidence in their eschatological status and even been perceived to be a *prodigium* of divine wrath. In chapter 4 it will be argued that this reading of the community's eschatological problems is supported and even developed by the rest of 1 Thessalonians.

In Part 3 our attention will switch to 2 Thessalonians, first the eschatological section 2:1–3:5 (chapter 5), then 1:1–12 (chapter 6) and 3:6–18 (chapter 7). In chapter 5 we shall contend not only that 2:1–3:5 is directly and explicitly confronting the erroneous eschatological idea that the Day of the Lord had in fact already come (2:2c), but also that 'Paul' is assuming that 'the Thessalonians' had responded to this message, not with joyful eschatological excitement, but with terror and despair. In chapter 6 it will be surmised that 2 Thessalonians 1 counters the view that persecution was an indication that God's judgment was unjust, and that this makes best sense in the light of our proposal concerning the inferred meaning and significance of the false claim. In chapter 7, evidence is presented that, contrary to the scholarly consensus, the problem of 'idleness' in 3:6–15 is unlikely to have been related to their eschatological confusion, but was merely *inertia vulgaris* manifesting itself in charitable abuse. Hence 3:6–15 has only a very limited significance for the study of the eschatological problem being addressed by 'Paul' in 2 Thessalonians.

Finally, in the light of this rereading of the situations underlying 1 and 2 Thessalonians, in Part 4 (chapter 8) we shall isolate the points of continuity and discontinuity between them before attempting to construct a case for situational development. It will be contended that the problem underlying 2 Thessalonians was probably closely related to that underlying 1 Thessalonians, that together they represented two stages of a *single* crisis ultimately rooted in a misinterpretation of the deaths as a phenomenon of eschatological significance – in the first stage the Thessalonians were asking a question concerning the timing of the Day of the Lord (1 Thess. 5:1), and in the second stage they have succumbed to what appears to be a particular answer to that question, the pronouncement that the Day had come (2 Thess. 2:2). We shall propose that 2 Thessalonians is essentially an appendix of 1 Thessalonians, written to reinforce 1 Thessalonians in the wake of that false claim, and we shall explore the possibility that the report underlying 2 Thessalonians was gathered before or at the same time as the first letter was delivered. It will then be argued that this revisionist rereading of 1 and 2 Thessalonians not only avoids the problems of the pseudonymous interpretation of 2 Thessalonians, but also is capable of overcoming the objections to Pauline authorship of 2 Thessalonians raised by proponents of pseudonymity.

PART TWO

2

GRIEVING WITHOUT HOPE

Introduction

In order to determine whether the situations underlying 1 and 2 Thessalonians can reasonably be regarded as compatible, we must reconstruct the eschatological dimension of the situation underlying 1 Thessalonians. That requires that we focus particularly on 1 Thess. 4:13–5:11, where Paul explicitly turns his attention to the community's eschatological concerns. In this chapter we shall examine 4:13–18.[1]

Paul has just received a report concerning the Thessalonian church from Timothy (1 Thess. 3:6), which presumably included an account of the situation underlying this section. Some members of the Thessalonian community[2] have unexpectedly died[3] and the others have apparently

---

[1] On the authenticity of 1 Thess. 4:13–18, see especially Bornemann, *Thessalonicherbriefe*, 301ff. and Rigaux, *Thessaloniciens*, 120ff. On the unity of the section, see especially Johanson, *Brethren*, 119 and H. Jurgensen, 'Awaiting the Return of Christ: A Re-Examination of 1 Thessalonians 4:13–5:11 from a Pentecostal Perspective', *JPentT* 4 (1994): 86. For defences of the unity of 1 Thessalonians, see Collins, *Letters*, 96–135; Jewett, *Correspondence*, 33–46; Wanamaker, *Thessalonians*, 29–37; R. Riesner, *Paul's Early Period* (trans. D. Scott; Grand Rapids: Eerdmans, 1997), 404–11 and Légasse, *Thessaloniciens*, 44–8, *contra* W. Schmithals, 'The Historical Situation of the Thessalonian Epistles', in *Paul and the Gnostics* (trans. J. E. Steely; Nashville: Abingdon, 1972), 123–218, esp. 126–35; R. Pesch, *Die Entdeckung des ältesten Paulus-Briefes. Paulus – neu gesehen: Die Briefe an die Gemeinde der Thessalonicher* (Freiburg: Herder, 1984), 20–121; Richard, *Thessalonians*, 11–19; J. Murphy-O'Connor, *Paul: A Critical Life* (Oxford: Clarendon, 1996), 105–14. The reading of 1 Thessalonians offered over the next three chapters constitutes a serious obstacle for those who maintain that it reflects more than one missive.

[2] *Pace* Lindemann, 'Abfassungszweck', 377–8 and 391. This is demonstrated by the fact that ἐν Χριστῷ in verse 16b most naturally belongs with οἱ νεκροί rather than ἀναστήσονται, and by the distinction between the 'sleeping' and οἱ λοιποί in verse 13b.

[3] *Contra inter alios* K. Donfried, 'The Cults of Thessalonica and the Thessalonian Correspondence', *NTS* 31 (1985): 349–51; J. S. Pobee, *Persecution and Martyrdom in the Theology of Paul* (JSNTSup; Sheffield: JSOT, 1985), 113–14; J. Chapa, 'Is First Thessalonians a Letter of Consolation?', *NTS* 40 (1994): 156; J. D. Hester, 'The Invention of 1 Thessalonians: A Proposal', in *Rhetoric, Scripture and Theology* (ed. S. E. Porter and T. H. Olbricht; JSNTSup; Sheffield: Sheffield Academic Press, 1996), 277 and Riesner, *Early Period*, 386–7, there is no substantial evidence that the deceased were martyred victims of the persecution (cf. 1 Thess. 3:3–4) endured by the community.

responded by 'grieving'.[4] Paul writes to comfort[5] the Thessalonians by removing the cause of their distress, which he presupposes is reflective of a defective eschatology. Precisely how their eschatology is deficient has been the *locus* of significant debate among exegetes. Gnostic, enthusiastic and chiliastic notions have all been proposed as keys to the Thessalonians' eschatological confusion; other explanations have included Jewish assumption theology and over-imminentist expectation. We shall attempt to mark a path through this labyrinthian puzzle by raising and answering questions of the text, thereby moving steadily to a clearer understanding of the nature of the eschatological confusion underlying 4:13–18.

Our initial three questions relate to verse 13.

Does οὐ θέλομεν δὲ ὑμᾶς ἀγνοεῖν indicate prior ignorance?

The section opens with a 'disclosure formula', οὐ θέλομεν δὲ ὑμᾶς ἀγνοεῖν. In spite of the fact that the most obvious implication of this is that the readers are presently unaware of the substance of verses 14–17, many scholars insist that οὐ θέλομεν δὲ ὑμᾶς ἀγνοεῖν is simply an idiomatic formula which underlines the importance of what follows and that one cannot infer that the letter's recipients are actually ignorant of the content of the ensuing verses.[6] The debate depends largely on Paul's usage of

[4] In an attempt to improve upon Schmithals' version of the Gnostic hypothesis, W. Harnisch, *Eschatologische Existenz* (FRLANT; Göttingen: Vandenhoeck & Ruprecht, 1973), 23–5 has proposed that 1 Thess. 4:13–18 is *prophylactic* rather than remedial, indicating a specific, concrete problem. However, how plausible is it that Paul would have anticipated that Gnosticism would be embraced by the community in such a way that it would cause distress when community members died? Moreover, we would surely have expected Paul to have had more fundamental objections to Gnosticism than we find in these verses. That a real and concrete problem underlies 4:13–18 is demonstrated by the command in verse 18, which is most probably authentic.

[5] To elevate consolation above instruction as the purpose of the section, as A. Malherbe, 'Exhortation in 1 Thessalonians', *NovT* 25 (1983): 254 does, is to construct an artificial and unhelpful dichotomy. The suggestion that 1 Thess. 4:13–18 conforms to the Greco-Roman 'letter of consolation' genre (so Malherbe, 'Exhortation', 254–6; K. P. Donfried, 'The Theology of 1 Thessalonians as a Reflection of its Purpose', in *To Touch the Text* (ed. M. P. Morgan and P. J. Kobelski; New York: Crossroad, 1989), 243–60) fails to take adequate account of the striking dissimilarities between 4:13–18 and consolatory letters, most especially the fact that the logic of the former is so distinctively Jewish and Christian and indeed eschatological in orientation and, as we shall argue below, the likelihood that 4:13–18 does not address grieving *per se* so much as erroneous grieving rooted in defective eschatological convictions.

[6] So, for example, E. von Dobschütz, *Die Thessalonicher-Briefe* (KEK; Göttingen: Vandenhoeck & Ruprecht, 1909), 186; Rigaux, *Thessaloniciens*, 239, 526–7; P. Hoffmann, *Die Toten in Christus* (2nd edn; NTAbh; Münster: Aschendorff, 1966), 208–9; P. Siber, *Mit Christus Leben* (ATANT; Zurich: Theologischer, 1971), 15 n. 8; Harnisch, *Existenz*, 22;

the phrase elsewhere, in (1) Rom. 1:13; (2) Rom. 11:25; (3) 1 Cor. 10:1; (4) 1 Cor. 12:1; and (5) 2 Cor. 1:8. The question which must be addressed is, are there any examples in Paul's letters where the expression does not imply prior ignorance? We suggest that a substantial case can be made that each of these instances implies previous ignorance on the part of the letter's recipients.

Concerning (1) and (2), there is no reason to question the formula's natural implication that the Romans had been ignorant regarding Paul's repeated, failed attempts to visit them (Rom. 1:13) or that they had lacked knowledge of the mystery regarding the salvation of 'all Israel' (Rom. 11:25–6). With regard to (3), Conzelmann has plausibly suggested that the prior ignorance relates to the new interpretation of or slant on the Old Testament texts which Paul is offering,[7] and, with respect to (4), there is nothing implausible about the suggestion that the Corinthians had been unaware that the decisive criterion of the Spirit's activity is whether Jesus is declared as Lord (12:3, itself introduced by another disclosure formula, γνωρίζω ὑμῖν) and perhaps more generally unaware of the instruction of chapters 12–14. Finally, regarding (5), it seems reasonable to understand the Corinthians as having been ignorant concerning the intensity of Paul's afflictions, as Plummer and Thrall have suggested.[8] We conclude then that in none of these instances is the natural implication of prior ignorance necessarily absent.

The fact that the formula in 1 Thess. 4:13a so sharply contrasts with 4:9's οὐ χρείαν ἔχετε γράφειν ὑμῖν (where what is known is already practised by them, although there is room for further development) and with 5:1's οὐ χρείαν ἔχετε ὑμῖν γράφεσθαι (where the implications of what is already known have not apparently been fully understood) strongly suggests that Paul is distinguishing between what his readers already know in 4:9 and 5:1 and what they do not yet know in 4:13. This is reinforced by the observation that throughout 1 Thessalonians Paul tends to refer to his readers' knowledge whenever applicable (1:5; 2:1, 2, 5, 11; 3:3, 4; 4:2; 5:2).

Z. I. Herman, 'Il significato della morte e della risurrezione di Gesú nel contesto escatologico di 1 Ts 4,13–5,11', *Anton* 55 (1980): 331; F. F. Bruce, *1 and 2 Thessalonians* (WBC; Waco: Word, 1982), 95.

[7] H. Conzelmann, *1 Corinthians* (trans. J. W. Leitch; Hermeneia; Philadelphia: Fortress, 1975), 165.

[8] A. Plummer, *A Critical and Exegetical Commentary on the Second Epistle of Paul to the Corinthians* (ICC; Edinburgh: T. & T. Clark, 1915), 15; M. E. Thrall, *A Critical and Exegetical Commentary on the Second Epistle to the Corinthians* (ICC; Edinburgh: T. & T. Clark, 1994), 1:114–15.

Therefore we conclude that the apostle's expression does seem to imply that the Thessalonians are unfamiliar with the essence of 4:13–18.

Does περὶ τῶν κοιμωμένων imply a future awakening?

Many scholars insist that κοιμάω in verse 13 (and verses 14–15) is simply a common euphemism for death (as it frequently is in the Old Testament), without any nuance of future awakening.[9] The fact that in 1 Cor. 7:39; 11:30 and 15:6 κοιμάω is not explicitly connected with the resurrection of the saints is viewed as proof that Paul never uses the verb in a specifically Christian sense. However, there are several reasons to question the supposition that κοιμάω in 1 Thess. 4:13–18 is simply a generic euphemism for death without implication of resurrection. (1) All but two uses of κοιμάω in Paul's letters occur in 1 Corinthians 15 or 1 Thess. 4:13–18, which both stress the eschatological resurrection of the saints (1 Cor. 15:6, 18, 20, 51; 1 Thess. 4:13, 14, 15). In particular, the remarkable appropriateness of this connotation of the verb in 1 Thess. 4:13–18, which highlights that the dead will be raised to participate in the parousia (1 Thess. 4:16–17a), strongly favours the view that Paul is consciously alluding to the awakening of deceased Christians at the eschaton. It is striking that outside 4:16–17a (which we shall argue below is the 'word of the Lord'), Paul consistently avoids his more common and concrete terms for death (e.g. νεκρός), choosing to employ κοιμάω in 4:13–15 and even καθεύδω in 5:9–10. Moreover, if, as we shall argue below, διὰ τοῦ Ἰησοῦ does not modify τοὺς κοιμηθέντας in verse 14b, then it is remarkable that, whereas in verses 13–15 Paul is content not to modify the appellation οἱ κοιμηθέντες, in verse 16 he is not content to do the same with οἱ νεκροί, to which he appends ἐν Χριστῷ. This would suggest that an unmodified οἱ κοιμηθέντες is equivalent not to οἱ νεκροί but to οἱ νεκροὶ ἐν Χριστῷ. (2) In every instance, even in 1 Cor. 7:39; 11:30 and 15:6, κοιμάω is employed to refer to Christians. (3) In later Christianity κοιμάω was regularly used where awakening at the resurrection was in view; indeed, κοιμάω in 1 Thess. 4:13–15 was interpreted in this way by early Christian interpreters such as Chrysostom. (4) Significantly, sleep language in LXX Dan. 12:2–3 (καθεύδω) and 2 Macc. 12:44–5 (κοιμάω) implies a future

---

[9] So, for example, F. Guntermann, *Die Eschatologie des Hl. Paulus* (NTAbh; Münster: Aschendorff, 1932), 37; Rigaux, *Thessaloniciens*, 529–32; Hoffmann, *Die Toten*, 186–206; H.-A. Wilcke, *Das Problem eines messianischen Zwischenreiches bei Paulus* (ATANT; Zurich: Zwingli, 1967), 114, 123; Herman, '1 Ts 4,13–5,11', 331–2; Best, *Thessalonians*, 185; T. Holtz, *Der erste Brief an die Thessalonicher* (EKKNT; Zurich: Benziger, 1986), 188.

resurrection (cf. 1 Enoch 91:10; 92:3; 100:5; 2 Bar. 21:24; 4 Ezra 7:32; T. Jud. 26:4). Dan. 12:2–3 is particularly relevant to our discussion not only on account of its importance in the development of the Jewish-Christian doctrine of the resurrection, but also because 1 Thess. 5:10's καθεύδω, which refers back to 4:13–18, seems to reflect dependence on LXX Dan. 12:2. (5) The use of the present tense in verse 13 may favour the idea of a future resurrection.[10] In the light of this evidence, it seems preferable to decide that Paul is employing κοιμάω in a particularly Christian sense here in 1 Thess. 4:13. The usages of κοιμάω in 1 Cor. 7:39; 11:30 and 15:6 can be interpreted as derivations of a particularly *Christian* usage; it is probable that κοιμάω became a standard Christian term for death to such a degree that it could be employed of Christian death even where the idea of resurrection was not primary (cf. Acts 7:60; 13:36).

We suggest that the portrayal of the Christian dead as 'asleep' in 1 Thess. 4:13–15 and 5:10 is a significant, if subtle, affirmation of Paul's main point in 4:13–18, that deceased Christians will rise from the dead to be with Christ at his parousia. It represents his first attempt to change the Thessalonian community's paradigm concerning Christian death, and thus render null and void what he regarded as illegitimate grief.

Does λυπῆσθε καθὼς καὶ οἱ λοιποὶ οἱ μὴ ἔχοντες ἐλπίδα imply that the Thessalonian community are lacking hope?

In 4:13b Paul expresses the purpose of his writing verses 13–18 to confront the community's ignorance: ἵνα μὴ λυπῆσθε καθὼς καὶ οἱ λοιποὶ οἱ μὴ ἔχοντες ἐλπίδα. Λυπέω in this context must refer to the Thessalonian community's emotional distress at the deaths of some of their community members: they are not to 'grieve' 'as also the others who do not have hope'. Οἱ λοιποί encompasses unbelieving Gentiles, but probably not unbelieving Jews,[11] in view of 5:6 and the predominantly Gentile constituency of the community (1:9–10; 4:1–8). As to the nature of the ἐλπίς which the pagans lack, Paul may be referring generally to expectation of an afterlife, or specifically to the *Christian* experience of hope or objective ground of hope.

The phrase καθὼς καί is extremely important in any discussion of the Thessalonians' eschatological confusion: is Paul implying that they are presently grieving *hopelessly*? This would be the case if the καθὼς καί

---

[10] Milligan, *Thessalonians*, 55.
[11] *Contra* Wilcke, *Problem*, 116–19; Laub, *Verkündigung*, 124 n. 105; J. Becker, *Auferstehung der Toten im Urchristentum* (SBS; Stuttgart: Katholisches Bibelwerk, 1976), 47; Holtz, *Thessalonicher*, 189.

clause indicates the manner of the grieving that Paul regards as illegitimate (hence 'so that you may not grieve like hopeless pagans').

However, Hoffmann rejected the view that the comparison of verse 13b is a source of information about the Thessalonian situation, specifically that it implies that the community is feeling hopeless.[12] He maintained that the first clues to the situation are found in verses 14ff., where Paul commences his argumentation.[13] He proposed that the comparative καθὼς καί clause here functions paraenetically, setting up what is essentially an *ad hominem* argument, intended to remind the Thessalonians of their distinctness from the pagans.[14] In this view Paul is rejecting grief *per se* as illegitimate.[15] The flow of thought would then be: 'pagans lack a parousia hope and so grieving is understandable for them, but you have a parousia hope and hence it is nonsensical for you'. Hoffmann justified this interpretation by appealing to the καί, which, he thought, adds to the comparative clause the character of an illustration, and, also, by appealing to the context.[16]

While initially plausible, Hoffmann's reading of 4:13b is ultimately unconvincing for several reasons. (1) It is difficult to imagine that the apostle who later wrote that God's sparing of Epaphroditus' life saved him λύπην ἐπὶ λύπην (Phil. 2:27; cf. Rom. 12:15; 1 Cor. 12:26) would have entirely spurned the legitimacy of grief for Christians here.[17] (2) The close parallel in Rom. 15:7 (Διὸ προσλαμβάνεσθε ἀλλήλους καθὼς καὶ ὁ Χριστὸς προσελάβετο ὑμᾶς εἰς δόξαν τοῦ θεοῦ) shows that καθὼς καί can be used as a strengthened form of καθὼς,[18] in an instance where the comparative particle is having a determining influence on the immediately preceding predicate. Another striking example of this is

---

[12] Hoffmann, *Die Toten*, 232; cf. Malherbe, *Thessalonians*, 264.

[13] Hoffmann, *Die Toten*, 211–12.   [14] Ibid., 210–11.

[15] The claim that Paul would have expected his readers to apply provisos which are obvious to 'thinking men' (J. B. Lightfoot, *Notes on the Epistles of St. Paul from Unpublished Commentaries* (London: Macmillan, 1895), 63; Milligan, *Thessalonians*, 56) is unsafe; given the nature of the problem Paul would probably not have been so categorical and insensitive to his converts (especially in a letter to vulnerable neophytes).

[16] Hoffmann, *Die Toten*, 210. He also appealed to von Dobschütz's argument that Pauline and early Christian thought necessitates understanding an absolute exclusion of grieving here (*Thessalonicher-Briefe*, 187).

[17] This refutes the erroneous claim of Hoffmann, *Die Toten*, 211 that Christianity's acceptance of grief arose from a loss of its early conviction. Note also that evidence for development in Paul's thought between 1 Thess. 4:13 and Phil. 2:27 in regard to the legitimacy of grief is lacking.

[18] See E. Best, *A Critical and Exegetical Commentary on Ephesians* (ICC; Edinburgh: T. & T. Clark, 1998), 417. Hoffmann (*Die Toten*, 210 including n. 15) was forced to acknowledge that a καθὼς particle can have a determining influence on the predicate verb (e.g. Phil. 3:17; 1 Thess. 2:4; 1 Cor. 8:2; 15:38; LXX 2 Chr. 30:7; Zech. 1:4; Num. 21:34).

found in Eph. 4:17 (τοῦτο οὖν λέγω καὶ μαρτύρομαι ἐν κυρίῳ, μηκέτι ὑμᾶς περιπατεῖν καθὼς καὶ τὰ ἔθνη περιπατεῖ ἐν ματαιότητι τοῦ νοὸς αὐτῶν). (3) The preceding introductory formula (verse 13a) probably implies that the Thessalonians are ignorant of the eschatological content of verses 14–17, and indeed the argumentation of these verses seems more fitting as a remedy for a problem of grief rooted in hopelessness rather than one of grief *per se*. If, on the one hand, proponents of the 'Hoffmannian' view understand the pagans' hopelessness for their dead as experiential, implying that the Thessalonian Christians are already hopeful, then Paul's focus on hope in verses 14–17 seems somewhat superfluous. If, on the other hand, they interpret the pagans' hopelessness as objective (i.e. they lack sound grounds for hope), implying that the Christians have an objectively sound basis for hope, such an emphasis might suggest that Paul is actually attempting to instil an experience of hope in a community lacking it. (4) The introductory purpose statement seems an eminently suitable place to look for clues regarding the situation. We conclude that Paul here is not rejecting grief as essentially pagan and rooted in hopelessness.

That leaves us with one exegetical possibility, the one favoured by the Antiochene School: the Thessalonians' grief is similar to the pagans' grief in that both are characterised by a distinct lack of experiential parousia-orientated hope (i.e. they did not *feel* hopeful). Against this conclusion it has been objected that οἱ μὴ ἔχοντες ἐλπίδα is a traditional catchphrase, which cannot bear the weight put on it by this explanation.[19] However, this objection is lacking in supporting evidence, especially if we judge that Paul is writing in AD 50. Moreover, in Rom. 15:7 and especially Eph. 4:17, the predicate immediately preceding the καθώς is defined by prepositional phrases following the subject and verb of the καθώς clause, and in LXX 2 Chr. 30:7 we find a prohibition followed by a καθώς particle followed by a subject without a verb, accompanied by a relative clause, which explicitly functions to define the prohibition (cf. Zech. 1:4).

It seems preferable to conclude that Paul wrote 1 Thess. 4:13–18 not so that the Thessalonian Christians would stop grieving *per se*, but rather so that they would stop grieving *hopelessly* in the manner of the pagans. Ἐλπίς here would appear to refer to the feeling of hope, in view of Paul's use of the term elsewhere in 1 Thessalonians (1:3; 2:19; 5:8) and the connection with grieving in this context.[20] It is a specifically

---

[19] Hoffmann, *Die Toten*, 211–12.
[20] However, in the light of the striking parallel in Eph. 2:12, it is possible to argue that there was an 'objective' dimension to the pagans' hopelessness.

Christian hope focused on the eschaton, as Pauline usage generally, and in 1 Thessalonians specifically, demonstrates.

Could the Thessalonians' confusion really be as acute as our exegesis of verse 13 suggests? We must examine verses 14–18 to see if they bear out our interpretation.

We turn first to verse 14, which is crucial for determining the nature of the eschatological confusion underlying the section, since it opens Paul's response to the situation and indeed represents the backbone of his argument.

Why do the protasis and apodosis of 4:14 not correspond?

In verse 14 Paul explains why (γάρ) the Thessalonian community should not grieve hopelessly for their dead. Whether or not Ἰησοῦς ἀπέθανεν καὶ ἀνέστη was an early ('pre-Pauline') Christian credal confession, it clearly was an important feature of the missionaries' kerygma during their Thessalonian ministry and a conviction which Paul assumed his readers embraced (πιστεύομεν). Upon this basis of common belief (verse 14a), Paul grounds his assurance regarding the future of the deceased Thessalonian Christians (verse 14b). However, it is notable that the apodosis does not correspond to the protasis in the way that we might have expected: (1) the formally conditional εἰ has become the formally comparative οὕτως καί; (2) πιστεύομεν has been dropped; (3) the expected subject, Ἰησοῦς or οἱ κοιμηθέντες, has been replaced with ὁ θεός; (4) instead of the anticipated ἀνίστημι we find ἄγω. The factors which led to such a striking set of changes must be fully explored.

Concerning (1), Wilcke argued that the apodosis is functionally more consecutive than comparative, and that Paul is viewing the belief in the protasis as a true condition for fulfilment of the apodosis.[21] However, it is hardly plausible that God's future intervention is being portrayed as contingent upon the belief of Paul and the Thessalonians. With regard to (1) and (2), it is possible that Paul's assertive apodosis is a concerted attempt on his part to avoid the impression of uncertainty which might be inferred from εἰ.[22] Certainly the apodosis does presuppose the truth of the protasis and communicates absolute certainty that God will in the future intervene on behalf of the deceased Christians. This may suggest that Paul is seeking to *assure* his converts that their deceased will be 'with Jesus'.

---

[21] Wilcke, *Problem*, 124–5.
[22] So Lightfoot, *Epistles*, 64 and von Dobschütz, *Thessalonicher-Briefe*, 190.

With regard to (3), it is possible that Paul had not worked out the wording of verse 14b before he penned verse 14a or that he got lost in the middle of his sentence, the unexpected change of subject springing from this. Plevnik has suggested that Paul's employment of a credal formula in verse 14a elucidates the unusual syntax in verse 14b,[23] but that presumes that verse 14a's Ἰησοῦς ἀπέθανεν καὶ ἀνέστη constitutes a credal formula, which is by no means certain. We suggest that there may be a greater continuity between the two parts of the verse than most suppose, if we understand διὰ τοῦ Ἰησοῦ as modifying the main verb, for that would suggest that the subject of verse 14b is in effect God-through-Jesus. In addition, οὕτως καὶ ὁ θεός may presuppose that God is the (implicit) subject of the resurrection of Jesus in verse 14a.

Change (4) is probably the most significant and certainly the most complex. Much hinges on what precisely Paul means by ὁ θεὸς τοὺς κοιμηθέντας διὰ τοῦ Ἰησοῦ ἄξει σὺν αὐτῷ. First, we must address the question of whether διὰ τοῦ Ἰησοῦ modifies (1) the substantival participle τοὺς κοιμηθέντας or (2) the main verb ἄξει. Those who adopt the first option do so for the sake of sentence balance and stylistic smoothness, since it avoids overloading ἄξει and allows both prepositional phrases to be read with what immediately precedes them. As to the question of how τοὺς κοιμηθέντας διὰ τοῦ Ἰησοῦ might be understood, four main opinions have been offered: (a) διὰ τοῦ Ἰησοῦ indicates that the sleeping died in relationship with Jesus, that is, that they died as Christians (essentially the equivalent of ἐν Χριστῷ);[24] (b) it is causal, alluding to their martyrdom;[25] (c) it is causal, suggesting that because of Jesus, the dead in Christ will certainly have a bright future;[26] (d) it refers to the fact that through the death of Jesus, death has been 'robbed of its terrors' and rendered mere sleep.[27]

---

[23] J. Plevnik, *Paul and the Parousia* (Peabody, Mass.: Hendrickson, 1997), 73 including n. 46.

[24] So *inter alios* J. Dupont, *ΣΥΝ ΧΡΙΣΤΩΙ* (Paris: Desclée de Brouwer, 1952), 42 n. 2; C. F. D. Moule, *An Idiom Book of New Testament Greek* (2nd edn; Cambridge: Cambridge University Press, 1959), 57; Richard, *Thessalonians*, 226; Plevnik, *Parousia*, 69 (including n. 20), 72; T. D. Still, *Conflict at Thessalonica* (JSNTSup; Sheffield: Sheffield Academic Press, 1999), 216.

[25] So *inter alios* K. Lake, *The Earlier Epistles of St. Paul* (London: Rivingtons, 1911), 88; P. Nepper-Christensen, 'Das verborgene Herrenwort. Eine Untersuchung über 1. Thess 4, 13–18', *ST* 19 (1965): 138; Pobee, *Persecution and Martyrdom*, 114.

[26] So *inter alios* Rigaux, *Thessaloniciens*, 535–7.

[27] G. G. Findlay, *The Epistles of Paul the Apostle to the Thessalonians* (CGTSC; Cambridge: Cambridge University Press, 1904), 97.

In the case of (a), however, we would have expected ἐν rather than διά. *Contra* (b), evidence for martyrdom is entirely lacking. Concerning (b) and (c), the causal use of διά is usually associated with the accusative rather than the genitive. Opinion (d) is too subtle to be valid; the fact that there is no contrast between death and sleeping in the preceding or succeeding context speaks strongly against it.

In the light of the lack of any convincing reading of διά τοῦ Ἰησοῦ with τοὺς κοιμηθέντας, it is worth noting that the major arguments adduced for this position, sentence balance and stylistic smoothness, are not particularly compelling, since Paul is perfectly capable of having more than one complement for a single verb (1 Thess. 1:5; 3:7; Rom. 2:16; 5:11, 21) and of writing stylistically awkward sentences, of which verse 14 is (regardless of one's interpretation of διά τοῦ Ἰησοῦ) a supreme example!

In conclusion, the problems resulting from taking the διά phrase with τοὺς κοιμηθέντας are such that even the most reluctant must seriously consider the alternative.

The majority of German scholars and a significant minority of Anglo-American scholars have opted for taking διά τοῦ Ἰησοῦ with the main verb which immediately follows it, ἄξει. In this view διά τοῦ Ἰησοῦ highlights Jesus as God's mediator of salvation – God acts through his intermediary agent, Jesus. It is notable that this reading evades the problems of the alternative view and allows διά with the genitive to keep its normal sense. And, as we noted above, this reading would also smooth the link between verse 14a and verse 14b, with Jesus the subject of the former and God-through-Jesus the subject of the latter (note the repetition of Ἰησοῦς).

Next we must examine the question of what Paul means by ἄξει. Scholars are sharply divided regarding whether the movement is upward or downward and what its *terminus a quo* and *terminus ad quem* are. Some think that ἄγω has the sense of *abducet* ('lead away') here, others that it has the sense of *adducet* ('bring'). Proponents of the former reading judge that the *terminus a quo* is the grave and that the *terminus ad quem* is the presence of Christ, whether the 'air' or heaven, on the grounds that verse 14b is anticipating verses 16–17a.[28] However, according to

---

[28] Dibelius, *Thessalonicher*, 24–5; J. Plevnik, 'The Taking Up of the Faithful and the Resurrection of the Dead in 1 Thessalonians 4:13–18', *CBQ* 46 (1984): 276 including n. 6; J. Delobel, 'The Fate of the Dead according to 1 Thessalonians 4 and 1 Corinthians 15', in *TC*, 345 n. 16 and E. Reinmuth, 'Der erste Brief an die Thessalonicher', in *Die Briefe an die Thessalonicher und an Philemon* (ed. N. Walter, E. Reinmuth and P. Lampe; NTD; Göttingen: Vandenhoeck & Ruprecht, 1998), 145 represent an extensive number who have argued that verse 14b is referring to the resurrection of the dead. Among those who

verses 16–17a the movement from grave/earth which has as its *terminus ad quem* the 'air' has as its goal the meeting of Christ (εἰς ἀπάντησιν τοῦ κυρίου), and so cannot possibly be accompanied by Christ, as the movement here in verse 14b clearly is (σὺν αὐτῷ). This observation also negates the suggestion of Rigaux that 2 Thess. 2:1's gathering language (cf. Matt. 24:31; Mark 13:27) elucidates ἄξει.[29] Finally, proponents of this position have yet to explain why Paul utilises such an enigmatic and potentially misleading verb, rather than his usual ἐγείρω, or even ἀνίστημι as in 1 Thess. 4:14a.

A significant group of scholars insists that the movement of verse 14b is best described as an 'assumption', the destination of which is heaven.[30] This position is largely dependent on verses 16–17 being interpreted as implying that the final destination of those 'caught up' is heaven, a position which we shall criticise below. Aside from this, the primary arguments for reading ἄξει as referring to an assumption are possible dependence on Dan. 7:13–14 (cf. 1 Cor. 15:23–4)[31] and a somewhat striking parallel in 2 Cor. 4:14.[32] However, the claim that Dan. 7:13–14 provides the conceptual framework in which the verse is to be understood cannot be substantiated. Also, evidence is lacking that Paul actually thought that Christ would return to heaven at or immediately after his parousia. Indeed, 1 Cor. 15:23–5 indicates that the handing over of the kingdom to God of Dan. 7:13–14 occurs after a reign of Christ in which he destroys 'every rule and authority and power' and which ends only when he has 'put all his enemies under his feet'. That this is a terrestrial reign rather than a celestial one is suggested by 1 Cor. 6:2; 1 Thess. 1:10; 5:2–3; Rom. 8:21 and 11:26. Hence it seems implausible that Paul believed that Dan. 7:13–14 would be fulfilled immediately at the point of the final resurrection or parousia. Furthermore, 2 Cor. 4:14 solves nothing, since proof of a *terminus ad quem* of heaven there is as lacking as in 1 Thess. 4:14b.

We turn now to the view that ἄξει here should be rendered *adducet*, referring to downward movement, with the *terminus ad quem* being the earth (*adducet in mundum*), 'those who sleep' coming in the company

---

have seen a destination of heaven are von Dobschütz, *Thessalonicher-Briefe*, 191; Frame, *Thessalonians*, 170–1 and P. Ellingworth, 'Which Way are we Going? A Verb of Movement, especially in 1 Thess 4:14b', *BT* 25 (1974): 426–30.
[29] Rigaux, *Thessaloniciens*, 550; cf. Malherbe, *Thessalonians*, 266–7.
[30] So, for example, Plevnik 'Taking Up', 76 and *Parousia*, 73–5; Johanson, *Brethren*, 121–2 including n. 581; Wanamaker, *Thessalonians*, 169–70.
[31] So W. H. Burkeen, 'The Parousia of Christ in the Thessalonian Correspondence' (Ph.D. thesis, University of Aberdeen, 1979), 129–30; Johanson, *Brethren*, 121–2 n. 581 (building on L. Hartman, *Prophecy Interpreted* (ConBNT; Lund: Gleerup, 1966), 186–7).
[32] Plevnik, *Parousia*, 74.

of Jesus at his parousia-descent. This interpretation becomes compelling when adequate attention is given to the parallel in LXX Zech. 14:5: καὶ ἥξει κύριος ὁ θεός μουκαὶ πάντες οἱ ἅγιοι μετ᾽ αυτοῦ. There we find the verb ἥκω used eschatologically of the coming down of Yahweh, where Yahweh is the subject and his 'holy ones' are said to accompany him.

If we consider 3:13, we note that there is significant disagreement regarding whether μετὰ πάντων τῶν ἁγίων αὐτοῦ refers to angels[33] or believers[34] or both.[35] Proponents of the angelic interpretation appeal to the possible echo of Zech. 14:5 and the perceived difficulty of understanding believers as coming with Christ at the parousia. However, this reading has the serious problem that every other Pauline usage of ἅγιος refers to believers, a problem made more acute by the fact that the context of 3:13 relates to eschatological holiness (ἁγιωσύνη). It is certainly true that 1 Thess. 3:13 (ἐν τῇ παρουσίᾳ τοῦ κυρίου ἡμῶν Ἰησοῦ μετὰ παντῶν ἁγίων αὐτοῦ) does seem to be echoing LXX Zech. 14:5 (καὶ ἥξει κύριος ὁ θεός μου καὶ πάντες οἱ ἅγιοι μετ᾽ αὐτοῦ). However, like Did. 16:7 (cf. Asc. Isa. 4:14), Paul may well have understood ἅγιοι to include believers. It could be that μετὰ παντῶν ἁγίων αὐτοῦ should be construed with στηρίξαι. In that case the displacement of the phrase to a final position in the sentence could reflect Paul's emphasis of it. However, the order of the sentence favours construing the phrase with παρουσίᾳ, and there are no serious problems with that view. It is a matter of creed to state that all 'saints' will be with Christ at his parousia; Paul's wish-prayer is apparently that the Thessalonians will be among them. Since the criterion to be among the 'holy ones' is, naturally enough, blamelessness in holiness, Paul prays that such will be theirs.

With regard to 1 Thess. 4:14, when we take into account that Paul has almost certainly alluded to the same part of LXX Zech. 14:5 just fourteen verses above, and that there he seemingly understood πάντες οἱ ἅγιοι to include believers as well as angels (cf. Matt. 27:52), the evidence for seeing an allusion to LXX Zech. 14:5 in 1 Thess. 4:14 becomes

---

[33] Dibelius, *Thessalonicher*, 30–1; von Dobschütz, *Thessalonicher-Briefe*, 152–3; Best, *Thessalonians*, 152–3; Wanamaker, *Thessalonians*, 145; Richard, *Thessalonians*, 177–8; Légasse, *Thessaloniciens*, 197–8.

[34] G. Wohlenberg, *Der erste und zweite Thessalonicherbrief* (KNT; Leipzig: Deichert, 1903), 82; Findlay, *Epistles of Paul*, 77; Owen E. Evans, *Saints in Christ Jesus: A Study of the Christian Life in the New Testament* (D. J. James lectures; Swansea: Penry, 1975), 89–90; J. M. Reese, *1 and 2 Thessalonians* (NTM; Wilmington: Michael Glazier, 1979), 41.

[35] C. J. Ellicott, *St. Paul's Epistles to the Thessalonians* (London: Longman, Green, Longman, Roberts & Green, 1880), 49; Lightfoot, *Epistles*, 50; Milligan, *Thessalonians*, 45.

strong. Confirmation, if it were needed, can be found in the enigmatic διά τοῦ Ἰησοῦ. Faced with the difficulty of ascribing to Jesus what in Zech. 14:5 is clearly ascribed to God, Paul was forced to add διά τοῦ Ἰησοῦ, thereby indicating that Jesus was God's eschatological agent, bringing his salvation. Recognition of the bearing of Zech. 14:5 on 1 Thess. 4:14b goes a long way to explaining its syntactical unorthodoxy.[36]

By ἄξει then Paul is apparently referring to the parousia-descent of Christ, when Jesus acts as the eschatological agent of God.[37] It seems that Paul has moved from the death and resurrection of Jesus in 1 Thess. 4:14a to the participation of the dead Christians in the parousia-descent of God's agent, Christ, in verse 14b. The logical relation of the two parts initially seems peculiar, for we might have expected verse 14b to parallel verse 14a, referring to the resurrection of dead Christians. The fact that it does not mention the resurrection of the deceased Christians requires explanation.

Paul has apparently omitted a step in his argumentation, and that step seems to be the resurrection of the saints and their ascending to meet Christ, which are needed to explain how the deceased Christians get from the grave to the company of the Lord at the parousia and why the death and resurrection of Jesus can serve as the grounds for confidence that the deceased will participate in the parousia. That this step is missing may well be because the community's worry was framed in terms of participation in the parousia of Christ, probably even in the language of Zech. 14:5, rather than in terms of the final resurrection.[38] That this may have been the case is perhaps reinforced by 1 Thess. 4:17b; there also

---

[36] Wilcke, *Problem*, 128–9 tried to refute the relevance of 3:13 on the grounds that 4:14b refers only to the 'sleeping'; however, we suggest that this argument lacks credibility, since Paul's point in 4:14b is specifically that the deceased Christians will be among the saints who accompany Christ at his parousia. Siber, *Mit Christus*, 30–2 has countered the Zech. 14:5 and 1 Thess. 3:13 parallels, not only by insisting that those texts refer to angels rather than believers, but also by claiming that in Zech. 14:5 the *terminus a quo* of the downward movement is heaven and pointing out that according to verses 16–17a the dead do not meet Christ until he gets to the air. However, evidence that 1 Thess. 3:13 or 4:14b interprets Zech. 14:5 as indicating a *terminus a quo* of heaven is entirely lacking when it is acknowledged that Paul probably did not understand πάντων τῶν ἁγίων to designate angels only.

[37] The choice of verb here may have been influenced by LXX Ezek. 37:12c.

[38] This speaks against the hypothesis of Schmithals, 'Historical Situation', 160–4, that Gnostic false teachers have undermined the Thessalonians' belief in the resurrection by spiritualising it, for in that case we would have expected Paul in verse 14b to speak in terms of the resurrection of the dead. *Contra* Schmithals, see U. Luz, *Das Geschichtsverständnis des Paulus* (Munich: Kaiser, 1968), 320–1 and J. P. Mason, *The Resurrection according to Paul* (Lewiston, N.Y.: Edwin Mellen, 1993), 73–6. Aside from the facts that (1) it is doubtful whether we can actually speak of 'Gnosticism' in AD 50 and (2) it is wrong to presuppose a unified understanding of resurrection among Gnostics (see M. L. Peel, 'Gnostic Eschatology and the New Testament', *NovT* 12 (1970): 141–65), this position cannot explain (3) why

the issue is conceived in terms of the dead being 'with Christ'. Clearly Paul assumes the resurrection of the deceased here; the question is only whether he assumes Thessalonian knowledge of it. This issue is of great importance to our study, and we shall deal with it below. For the moment, it is sufficient to note that, in the light of verse 13a and verse 13b, the idea that the Thessalonians were ignorant of the eschatological resurrection of dead saints cannot be dismissed.

Next we must consider verses 15–17. Determining the relevance of verses 15–17 for the underlying situation requires that we first discover where the λόγος κυρίου (verse 15a) is located.

Where is the λόγος κυρίου to be found?

Paul opens verses 15–17 with a striking appeal to authority: τοῦτο γὰρ ὑμῖν λέγομεν ἐν λόγῳ κυρίου. However, scholars are deeply divided regarding where exactly the word is to be found; two major proposals dominate the discussion: (1) verse 15b is the 'word' and verses 16–17 are an explication of it;[39] and (2) verses 16–17a are the 'word' and verse 15b is an anticipatory summary of it.[40] With reference to word statistics (the value of which is dependent on the supposition that Paul is not the originator of the λόγος, which we judge below to be a relatively safe assumption)[41] and stylistic features, we can perhaps conclude that verses

1 Thess. 4:13–18 lacks a polemical edge, and (4) why it is so different from 1 Corinthians 15. Harnisch, *Existenz*, 22–9 sought to improve on Schmithals' hypothesis by postulating that 1 Thess. 4:13–18 is dealing not with an existing situation, but with a potential one, and that Paul is simply anticipating the inevitable consequence of his converts' embracing Gnostic ideas about the resurrection. However, Harnisch's hypothesis also fails to convince, because of criticisms (1), (2) and (3), and because, as we have pointed out in n. 4 above, it is hard to imagine that Paul would have predicted that Gnostic ideas would be received by the community only to such a degree that they would cause distress. See also Hyldahl, 'Auferstehung', 124–6 and G. Lüdemann, *Paul, Apostle to the Gentiles* (trans. F. S. Jones; London: SCM, 1984), 206–9 against Harnisch.

[39] So, for example, von Dobschütz, *Thessalonicher-Briefe*, 193–4; J. Weiss, *Earliest Christianity* (trans. and ed. F. C. Grant; HT; 2 vols.; New York: Harper, 1959), 2:537 n. 24; U. Wilckens, *Die Missionsreden der Apostelgeschichte* (WMANT; Neukirchen-Vluyn: Neukirchener, 1961), 76 n. 1; Wilcke, *Problem*, 132–3; Holtz, *Thessalonicher*, 184–5; H. Merklein, 'Der Theologie als Prophet: Zur Funktion prophetischen Redens im theologischen Diskurs des Paulus', *NTS* 38 (1992): 410–11.

[40] So, for example, Hoffmann, *Die Toten*, 219–20; Luz, *Paulus*, 328–30; Siber, *Mit Christus*, 35–7; Harnisch, *Existenz*, 40–2; J. Plevnik, 'The Parousia as Implication of Christ's Resurrection: An Exegesis of 1 Thess 4, 13–18', in *Word and Spirit* (ed. J. Plevnik; Willowdale: Regis College, 1975), 230–1; Lüdemann, 'Apostle', 221–7; Mason, *Resurrection*, 89–91.

[41] Of course, as we shall point out below, we would expect Paul to redact his source so that it fits the epistolary context. Nevertheless, we would also anticipate that such redaction would be somewhat limited.

16–17a are more likely to contain the 'word' than verse 15b. Whilst verse 15b (apart from οἱ περιλειπόμενοι, which is also present in verses 16–17a) seems quite consistent with Paul's vocabulary and style, parts of verses 16–17a seem uncharacteristic for Paul, especially κέλευσμα and ἀρχάγγελος (both of which are hapaxes), καταβαίνω (which out of 82 uses in the New Testament is found in the Pauline corpus only in Rom. 10:7, where it is part of an Old Testament quotation, here, and in Eph. 4:9–10, where its use is dictated by the presence of ἀναβαίνω in an Old Testament quotation) and ἀνίστημι (which is arguably never used by Paul except in quotations: 1 Thess. 4:14 (possibly an early Christian credal tradition); Rom. 15:12 and 1 Cor. 10:7 (both Old Testament quotations); cf. Eph. 5:14 (probably a baptismal tradition)). Further, the more apocalyptic flavour of verses 16–17a sets them apart from the rest of verses 13–18. That verse 17b is not a part of the λόγος is rendered probable in view of the fact that its vocabulary is consistently Pauline without exception.

Therefore we suggest that the 'word' is located in verses 16–17a (introduced by a recitative ὅτι) and that verse 15b is an anticipatory summary (introduced by a declarative or epexegetical ὅτι), with verse 17b as a Pauline conclusion.[42] The few particularly Pauline elements of the λόγος κυρίου in verses 16–17a may be readily explained with reference to Pauline redaction.

Now we must determine the meaning of verse 15b, the anticipatory summary of the 'word'.

Does οὐ μὴ φθάσωμεν indicate relative disadvantage?

Φθάσωμεν in verse 15b has been for many scholars the determinative factor in deciding the nature of the eschatological confusion underlying 1 Thess. 4:13–18. In this context φθάνω must mean 'have priority over' or 'have precedence over', but it is unclear whether the priority/precedence is temporal or qualitative. A significant group of scholars claim that a temporal or a qualitatively *relative* disadvantage rather than an *absolute* disadvantage is presupposed.[43] According to this view, the Thessalonians were assuming that their deceased would rise from the dead, but only

[42] For a more detailed consideration of the word-statistical evidence that the λόγος is located in verses 16–17a, see especially C. R. Nicholl, '1 Thess. 4:15–17 as an Agraphon' (M.A. thesis, Trinity International University, 1996), 42–69; cf. Siber, *Mit Christus*, 35–9; Harnisch, *Existenz*, 41–2; H. Schade, *Apokalyptische Christologie bei Paulus* (GTA; Göttingen: Vandenhoeck & Ruprecht, 1981), 159–60.

[43] So von Dobschütz, *Thessalonicher-Briefe*, 193; Hoffmann, *Die Toten*, 232–4; Wilcke, *Problem*, 122; Luz, *Paulus*, 320–1; Bruce, *Thessalonians*, 99–100; A. F. J. Klijn, '1 Thessalonians 4:13–18 and its Background in Apocalyptic Literature', in *Paul and Paulinism* (ed.

after the parousia. The confusion, it is argued, is elucidated by a roughly contemporaneous intra-Jewish debate regarding whether the living or the dead would be better off at the parousia. Such Jewish texts concluded that, compared to the living, the dead would be at a disadvantage, rising after the eschaton (and the messianic kingdom) and thus incapable of beholding God's salvation and witnessing God's transformation of the world.[44] However, we judge this line of inquiry to be unhelpful. First, from where would the community have secured familiarity with such an idea? Although the Thessalonians are apparently aware of some apocalyptic imagery and Old Testament language, such facility probably derives from the missionaries' instruction, which cannot apply here, since Paul disagrees with the idea. And can we really presume that this community, which was so Gentile, would have been independently exploring 'contemporary' Jewish ideas regarding the resurrection and the eschaton and that they would have so firmly latched on to this particular strand of eschatological thought? Second, it is difficult to imagine that any genuine convert of Paul could have contemplated the possibility of salvation apart from the parousia; the idea that the parousia is the chronological locus of salvation was a fundamental tenet of the kerygma passed on to the Thessalonians by the missionaries (1 Thess. 1:3, 10a; cf. 2:19–20; 3:13; 4:14; see also 1 Cor. 1:7–8; 4:4–5; 11:23; 16:22; 2 Cor. 11:2; Phil. 3:20–1; cf. Col. 1:26–7; 3:4).[45] Third, since verse 15b is probably an anticipatory summary of the 'word' in verses 16–17a, it is essential to ask if verses 16–17a bear out this reading of verse 15b; we shall attempt to demonstrate below that they do not. Against the view that chiliastic ideas undergird the problem is the observation that Paul does not mention the kingdom in 4:13–18. In conclusion, then, we find that the argument that φθάνω is to be interpreted as indicating a temporal priority or relative advantage, and

M. D. Hooker and S. G. Wilson; London: SPCK, 1982), 69–72; J. Gillman, 'Transformation and 1 Thessalonians 4:13–18', *CBQ* 47 (1985): 270–1; Reinmuth, 'Erste Brief', 142; Malherbe, *Thessalonians*, 272–3, 283–5.

[44] Ps. Sol. 17:50; 18:7; 4 Ezra 6:25; 7:27; 9:8; 13:16–24; Sib. Or. 3.370. See especially Hoffmann, *Die Toten*, 233–4 and Klijn, '1 Thessalonians 4:13–18', 69–72. Similarly it is posited that Paul is like some other Jewish thinkers in judging that the dead would be at no disadvantage at the eschaton (2 Bar. 30:2b; 51:13; 4 Ezra 5:41–2; 6:20; Ps.-Philo, *Ant.* 19, 20; so J. J. Scott, 'Paul and Late-Jewish Eschatology – A Case Study, I Thessalonians 4:13–18 and II Thessalonians 2:1–12', *JETS* 15 (1972): 137; Klijn, '1 Thessalonians 4:13–18', 70–2); 2 Bar. 11:6–7 claims that it will be better for the dead.

[45] Note that, although the concept of the resurrection of dead saints had an important place in Paul's theology, there is no evidence that it constituted part of what was passed on to the Thessalonians during the mission; as we shall argue below, the Thessalonians may well have been unfamiliar with it. It seems plausible that the apostle, in teaching a community which had not yet experienced death, might have neglected to mention the resurrection of dead saints, focusing instead upon the fate of living Christians at the parousia.

therefore as implying that the Thessalonians still hold out some hope for their deceased, is implausible.

Finally, it is important to take note of the presence of γάρ in verse 15a, which suggests that Paul in verses 15–17 is not presenting a second proof or argument, but rather is confirming verse 14's compacted argument. Verse 15b, as the anticipatory summary of verses 16–17a, is explicitly deriving from the 'word' what reinforces the argument of verse 14. Hence it is necessary to see not just how verse 15b derives from verses 16–17a, which is not difficult in view of ἅμα σύν, but also how it confirms verse 14. Although the living are not explicitly mentioned in verse 14, Paul is plainly presupposing that they will accompany Christ in his parousia-descent, as 1 Thess. 3:13's interpretation of Zech. 14:5 verifies. It seems then that verse 15b reinforces verse 14 by stating that the 'word of the Lord' asserts that the dead will not suffer disadvantage *with respect to accompanying Christ at his parousia*. This would seem to confirm our conclusion that φθάνω does not indicate temporal priority or relative disadvantage, for verse 14b mentions only one eschatological event, the parousia. Recognising that verses 15–17 are a reinforcement of verse 14 rather than a second argument also highlights the point that verse 15b should not be the starting-point for those seeking to understand the situation underlying verses 13–18.

The alternative is that φθάνω here effectively refers to *absolute* advantage, which would imply that the Thessalonians hold out no hope of salvation for their deceased, no hope even that they will be resurrected. This coheres well with verse 13b's λυπῆσθε καθὼς καὶ οἱ λοιποὶ οἱ μὴ ἔχοντες ἐλπίδα. However, it is necessary to examine the plausibility of the idea that the Thessalonians are ignorant of the resurrection of the dead.

Did the Thessalonian community know about the resurrection of the dead?

The idea that the Thessalonians are unaware of the resurrection of the saints because it had been omitted from the missionaries' teaching during the mission at Thessalonica has come under particularly fierce attack on several fronts. Some have argued that Paul must have preached on the eschatological resurrection at the founding mission because it was inextricably linked to the resurrection of Christ,[46] a teaching with which Paul

---

[46] P. M. Magnien, 'La Résurrection des morts. D'après la première épître aux Thessaloniciens. Etude exégétique sur 1 Th. IV,13–V,3', *RB* 4 (1907): 351; Masson, *Thessaloniciens*, 54; Wilcke, *Problem*, 122; G. Friedrich, 'Die Bedeutung der Auferweckung Jesu nach Aussagen des Neuen Testaments', *TZ* 27 (1971): 323; Herman, '1 Ts 4,13–5,11', 330; Gillman, '1 Thessalonians 4:13–18', 270.

clearly does presuppose the Thessalonians' familiarity (verse 14a; cf. 1:10). However, the fact that the two concepts are closely, even inextricably, linked in Paul's mind (indeed, the resurrection of Christ is portrayed in 1 Cor. 15 as a bifurcation of the final resurrection) does not mean that for Paul the mention or thought of Christ's resurrection (and even the Christian's spiritual resurrection in Christ) always necessitated mention or thought of the final resurrection of the saints from the dead (as is demonstrated, for example, by Rom. 4:24–5; 8:34 and Gal. 1:1).[47] Others have suggested that Paul could not have taught on the parousia and judgment without also instructing on the final resurrection.[48] However, in the light of Paul's imminentist expectation,[49] it seems perfectly possible that, even though he almost certainly believed in the future resurrection of the dead saints, at the mission Paul could have preached on the resurrection

[47] Many have thought that the omission reveals that Paul did not at the time of the mission believe in the resurrection of the dead (because of the influence of *Naherwartung*) and that 1 Thessalonians testifies to a radical shift in Paul's theology in which he introduces the idea of a final resurrection into his eschatology (so, for example, C. H. Hunzinger, 'Die Hoffnung angesichts des Todes im Wandel der paulinischen Aussagen', in *Leben angesichts des Todes* (Tübingen: Mohr, 1968), 69–88, esp. 71–6; J. Becker, *Auferstehung*, 46–54; Schade, *Christologie*, 162–4; Lüdemann, *Apostle*, 212, 233–8, 259 n. 148). However, (1) if we accept the traditional dating of the second missionary journey, Paul would have had a decade and a half to encounter and process the phenomenon of Christian death before the Thessalonian mission. He can hardly have avoided coming to terms with death (indeed, see Acts 7:58–8:1); as Riesner, *Early Period*, 383 notes, 'according to the witness of grave inscriptions in the Roman empire, not even half of all people reached the age of twenty-five; hardly 5 percent reached fifty'. The problem is not entirely relieved even if we date 1 Thessalonians to the early forties AD (so Lüdemann, *Apostle*, 238 (c. AD 41); cf. K. Donfried, '1 Thessalonians, Acts and the Early Paul', in *TC*, 25 and *The Theology of the Shorter Pauline Letters* (NTT; Cambridge: Cambridge University Press, 1993), 9–12 (AD 41–4); C. Buck and G. Taylor, *Saint Paul* (New York: Scribner's, 1969), 146–9 (AD 46)). (2) It seems more natural to assume a line of continuity between Paul's Pharisaic belief in the resurrection of the dead and what he writes in 1 Thess. 4:16–17a and 1 Cor. 15 than to assume, as Schade, *Christologie*, 163 does, a hiatus of non-belief and to speculate that Paul abandoned the concept and then later grasped it again from his past. Certainly Paul in 1 Thess. 4:16–17a did not introduce the idea of resurrection of the dead to early Christianity; he does after all seem to be citing a tradition, which may even be dominical. Hence we conclude that Paul probably believed in the resurrection of the dead during the mission, as he clearly does in 1 Thess. 4:13–18. Indeed, in the light of 1 Thess. 4:14–17; Rom. 6:4; 8:11; 1 Cor. 6:14 and 2 Cor. 4:14, it seems difficult to think that Paul could have believed in the resurrection of Christ but not that of the saints.

[48] Von Dobschütz, *Thessalonicher-Briefe*, 189; Rigaux, *Thessaloniciens*, 526–7; Wilcke, *Problem*, 119–20.

[49] It is important to note that Paul's 'imminentism' consisted of the belief that the parousia would occur within the lifetime of his generation. Oἱ περιλειπόμενοι (verses 15b and 17a) probably issues from the common Jewish and Christian apocalyptic idea that the faithful will reach the end only by first passing through all kinds of eschatological tribulations, although this is undeveloped in this context (almost certainly because it is not strictly relevant). This should perhaps caution us against presuming that Paul adhered to a form of *immediate* imminentism.

of Christ and taught on the parousia and judgment, and yet still omitted to mention the future resurrection of physically dead Christians, presumably because of his premature, forced departure from Thessalonica (2:17; cf. verses 15–16; Acts 17:5–10).[50]

Certainly it seems that the Thessalonian community is not thinking in terms of a resurrection of the deceased. Although some claim that the author's silence regarding the saints' resurrection in verse 14b is evidence of the Thessalonians' familiarity with the concept, this is unconvincing. We suggest that the omission of any reference to the final resurrection of the saints is in fact evidence that they were *unfamiliar* with the concept. For if Paul could have assumed such knowledge on the part of his readers, it is difficult to see why he did not argue from that basis. Moreover, it is striking not only that κοιμάω in verses 13–15 and καθεύδω in 5:10 may well hint at the resurrection of the dead Thessalonian Christians, but also that the resurrection of the dead in Christ is the main point in verses 16–17a (probably 'the word of the Lord'), verses which justify the claim of verse 14 that the 'sleeping' will accompany Christ at his parousia. Hence the absence of any explicit reference to the *Totenauferstehung* in verse 14 cannot be taken as evidence that Paul is assuming that the Thessalonians were familiar with the idea.

In addition, it has been argued that since any Jewish Christians or former God-fearers in the community (cf. Acts 17:4) would have been familiar with the concept of the resurrection of the dead, the Thessalonians could not possibly have been ignorant of the final resurrection.[51] However, leaving aside the question of the historical value of Acts, this objection rests on several unsure assumptions: that the form of Judaism from which any Jewish Thessalonian Christians had been converted would have adhered to the resurrection of the dead; that in the absence of any specific instruction by the missionaries they would have assumed that belief in the eschatological resurrection of the deceased was a point of continuity between Judaism and Christianity; that God-fearers would have been familiar with Jewish eschatological ideas; and that those with a background in Judaism would have been sufficiently valued by the other

---

[50] It seems reasonable also to assume that Paul focused on the fate of the living at the parousia because all of his readers were alive (!) and because the issue of Christian physical death had not seemed relevant. Could it be that the Thessalonians had simply neglected to take note of what the missionaries had taught on this matter, on account of a strong *Naherwartung* and/or an inability to process and remember a complex of (what to them would have been) quite *unfamiliar* Jewish-Christian concepts? We are doubtful, because Paul assumes that the Thessalonians would have no problems comprehending and recollecting the concept of the resurrection of Jesus (1 Thess. 4:14a).

[51] Schmithals, 'Historical Situation', 163 n. 140; Best, *Thessalonians*, 181.

members of this predominantly Gentile community for the latter to defer to the former in theological matters.[52]

While some have objected that the reference to the resurrection in verse 16b is too brief to be a sufficient introduction to the idea of the resurrection of the dead for those previously unacquainted with it,[53] we suggest that for those already familiar with the concept of (Christ's) resurrection (cf. 1:9–10; 4:14 and 5:9–10) and already predisposed to accept Paul's instruction, the reference in verse 16b suffices.

In conclusion, we judge that there is nothing implausible about the proposal that the Thessalonians are ignorant of the resurrection of the dead and therefore are under the impression that their deceased will be at an absolute disadvantage at the parousia.

As we turn next to the 'word of the Lord' in 1 Thess. 4:16–17a, it is important to know from where Paul has drawn his source and how he has redacted it. Identifying the source of the λόγος is important, for if we decided that the word is a Pauline revelation or a Pauline summary of relevant Jesus tradition, we would anticipate that the 'word' was devised specifically for, and relates particularly to, the Thessalonian situation; but if we concluded that the logion is a quotation of Jesus tradition, then we would not expect the 'word' to address directly and explicitly the Thessalonian situation. Furthermore, the reconstruction of Paul's redaction is contingent upon one's identification of the logion's source (of course, if it is a Pauline revelation, redaction is virtually impossible). Discovering how Paul has edited his source is important in helping us deduce the emphasis and purpose of Paul in verses 15–17.

What is the source of the λόγος κυρίου?

With regard to the source of the λόγος κυρίου (verses 16–17a), there are two major options which subdivide into five possibilities: the word is either a word of the risen Lord, in which case it might be: (1) a Pauline revelation, possibly given in response to a prayer of Paul; or (2) a non-Pauline prophecy, which has perhaps come to be accepted by Paul as Jesus tradition; or it is a word of the earthly Jesus, in which case it could be: (3) a quotation which is present in the Jesus tradition represented in the canonical Gospels; (4) a general reference to Jesus' eschatological teaching; or (5) an agraphon. Concerning option (1), not only is

---

[52] The very fact that Paul writes 4:13–18 may constitute evidence that the Thessalonian community did not trust Timothy to teach them regarding these matters.

[53] Harnisch, *Existenz*, 22; Gillman, '1 Thessalonians 4:13–18', 270; Best, *Thessalonians*, 181; Delobel, 'Fate', 345 including n. 16.

there no evidence that Paul uses ἐν λόγῳ κυρίου as it is employed in the LXX (at least partly because of his use of κύριος for Jesus), but Paul arguably never uses λόγος of revelations or predictions. Option (2) has problems when studied closely. (a) In the light of the Thessalonians' apparently low opinion of prophecy as reflected in 1 Thess. 5:19ff., it is hard to believe that Paul would have considered it seemly to make an appeal to a (non-Pauline) prophetic word as a decisive authority for them. (b) In Acts prophetic words seem to be attributed primarily to the human speaker (e.g. Acts 11:28; 21:10–11). (c) Perhaps it is significant that in 1 Cor. 7:10 and 9:14, where Paul also uses κύριος in connection with a quotation of Christ's words, it denotes the earthly rather than the heavenly Lord. In addition to these points, it is worth noting that this hypothesis is largely untestable and must therefore be adopted only as a last resort. Moreover, the view that we have a word of the risen Lord communicated *via* a prophet which has been understood by Paul as a saying of the earthly Jesus is uncompelling: (a) historical evidence that prophetic words were integrated into Jesus tradition is lacking; (b) the fact that Paul finds it appropriate to instruct the Thessalonians not to despise prophecy (1 Thess. 5:19–20) and that he elsewhere seems to regard prophetic words as dispensable (1 Cor. 14:30–2) would suggest that prophecy may not have been quite so authoritative in the opinion of the early Christians as this view demands.[54]

Next we turn to critique the three primary proposals which hold that the 'word' is a saying of the earthly Jesus. *Contra* option (3), each of the Synoptic (such as Matt. 10:39; 16:24; 20:1, 16; 24:29–31; 25:6) and Johannine (such as John 5:25–6; 11:25–6) traditions which scholars have proposed are related to this 'word of the Lord' is so strikingly different from 1 Thess. 4:15–17 that Paul would virtually have had to falsify such traditions in order to use them in the way he does.[55] Specifically, no text in the Gospels indicates that the resurrection of the dead is an integral part of the parousia event, occurring in response to the descent of Christ and immediately before the catching up of living and dead believers to meet Christ.

A number of scholars have postulated option (4), that we have here a general representation of Jesus' eschatological teaching, Paul making free use of Jesus tradition to deal with the problem of the Thessalonian community. However, while this proposal does take account of the parallels noted above and cannot be altogether eliminated, λόγος is arguably

---

[54] For more against this hypothesis, see Nicholl, 'Agraphon', 70–87.
[55] Cf. Hyldahl, 'Auferstehung', 129–32.

more naturally understood as referring to a particular dictum.[56] Moreover, this reading faces the same problem as the position it seeks to improve, for according to it, although some parts of verses 16–17a (the language and conceptualisation) correspond to Gospel traditions, the thrust of the whole clearly does not, which raises the question, why would Paul appeal to such Jesus traditions when they do not contain the central point he is making?

That leads us to option (5), which sees the 'word' as a specific saying attributed to the earthly Jesus which did not make its way into the Gospels (cf. Acts 20:35). This position accommodates the extensive parallels which have been noted between the Gospel traditions and 1 Thess. 4:16–17a. Nevertheless, some objections have been raised against it. (1) No suitable dominical *Sitz im Leben* has been found in the Gospels.[57] (2) There is no reason why this 'word' would have been omitted from the Gospels' record of the eschatological teaching of Jesus.[58] (3) This view can never be more than an untestable hypothesis.[59]

Objection (1) is fallacious, since one perfectly feasible *Sitz im Leben* for the 'word' is Mark 8:34–8/9:1.[60] Concerning objection (2), when we observe the similarity of 1 Thess. 4:16–17a to texts such as Mark 13:26–7/Matt. 24:30–1/Luke 21:27, the Gospels' exclusion of a saying such as that in 1 Thess. 4:16–17a might credibly have been because it did not suit their purposes and because of their inclusion of other somewhat similar eschatological traditions. The force of objection (3) is defused when we take into account the greater plausibility of this position compared to the alternative hypotheses: its proposal of a common originator but distinct saying explains better than the other theories the many similarities and yet significant differences between 1 Thess. 4:16–17a and the eschatological Jesus traditions recorded in the Gospels.[61]

---

[56] So Dibelius, *Thessalonicher*, 25.

[57] Plevnik, 'Parousia', 232 n. 32; Best, *Thessalonians*, 190–1.

[58] E. Haack, 'Eine exegetisch-dogmatische Studie zur Eschatologie über 1 Thessalonicher 4:13–18', *ZST* 15 (1938): 559; Masson, *Thessaloniciens*, 63, who claimed that the text dealt with a burning issue of the entire apostolic age; Nepper-Christensen, 'Herrenwort', 150.

[59] A. L. Moore, *1 and 2 Thessalonians* (CB; London: Thomas Nelson, 1969), 69; R. E. H. Uprichard, 'Exposition of 1 Thessalonians 4,13–18', *IBS* 1 (1979): 153; R. H. Gundry, 'The Hellenization of Dominical Tradition and the Christianization of Jewish Tradition in the Eschatology of 1–2 Thessalonians', *NTS* 33 (1987): 164; Wanamaker, *Thessalonians*, 170.

[60] See Nicholl, 'Agraphon', 117–21; cf. J. Jeremias, *Unknown Sayings of Jesus* (trans. R. H. Fuller; London: SPCK, 1957), 66–7.

[61] Note also the view of Dibelius, *Thessalonicher*, 25 that the word is simply an apocalyptic tradition, perhaps attributed to Jesus by earlier Christians or by Paul.

We conclude that the 'word of the Lord', which we maintain is to be located in verses 16–17a, is most probably an agraphon. Paul, it seems, is appealing to a particular word of the earthly Jesus, the thrust of which is that the living have no advantage over the dead.

Possible Pauline redaction of the 'word of the Lord' (4:16–17a)

Verses 16–17a may show signs of Pauline redaction. Possible examples include the following: (1) adding αὐτός in verse 16a; (2) replacing ὁ υἱὸς τοῦ ἀνθρώπου with ὁ κύριος in verse 16a and verse 17a; (3) appending ἐν Χριστῷ to οἱ νεκροί; (4) inserting πρῶτον . . . ἔπειτα in verses 16b–17a; (5) affixing ἡμεῖς οἱ ζῶντες to οἱ περιλειπόμενοι and, accordingly, changing the third-person ἁρπαγήσονται to the first-person ἁρπαγησόμεθα; and (6) altering μετά to σύν and adding ἅμα to it.[62] Hence the original λόγος κυρίου may perhaps have read as follows: ὁ υἱὸς τοῦ ἀνθρώπου ἐν κελεύσματι, ἐν φωνῇ ἀρχαγγέλου καὶ ἐν σάλπιγγι θεοῦ, καταβήσεται ἀπ᾽ οὐρανοῦ καὶ οἱ νεκροὶ ἀναστήσονται καὶ οἱ περιλειπόμενοι μετ᾽ αὐτῶν ἁρπαγήσονται ἐν νεφέλαις εἰς ἀπάντησιν τοῦ υἱοῦ τοῦ ἀνθρώπου εἰς ἀέρα. If this suggestion is indeed reminiscent of the original word, the most significant of Paul's apparent changes would then be (4), which emphasises that the rapture of believers to meet Christ does not occur until the deceased believers have been restored to the realm of the living, and (6), which stresses that the catching up to meet Christ includes the risen dead.

This leads us to our next question, which relates to the logic and function in Paul's argument of verses 16–17a, particularly as elucidated by his redaction of the 'word'.

What do 4:16–17a contribute to the argument of the section?

In the light of the fact that Paul's focus in verses 13–15 has been on the deceased and that verses 15–17 function to confirm verse 14's assurance regarding the participation of the 'sleeping' in the parousia, we can probably presume that Paul quotes the 'word' because of how it elucidates the fate of the dead. The λόγος states that the dead in Christ will rise and

---

[62] It seems preferable to interpret the ἅμα and σύν, not independently, with the former functioning adverbially to indicate simultaneous action, but together, with the former strengthening the force of the latter (hence, 'together with'). This decision is strongly supported by the use of ἅμα σύν in 5:10.

then, together with the living, will be 'caught up' to meet Christ in the air. It does seem that, whether due to Pauline redaction or not, the emphasis in verses 16–17a falls on precisely these two aspects of the λόγος: πρῶτον . . . ἔπειτα functions to highlight the resurrection of the dead in verse 16b as the requisite for the rapture of the living and the dead to meet Christ in verse 17a, while ἅμα (σύν) stresses that the dead will be included along with the living in the 'catching up'.

Many have suggested that the three auditory attendant circumstances of the Lord's descent in verse 16a (ἐν κελεύσματι, (1), ἐν φωνῇ ἀρχαγγέλου (2) καὶ ἐν σάλπιγγι θεοῦ (3)) function here to wake the dead (verse 16b). The trumpet is directly associated with the resurrection in 1 Cor. 15:52b (cf. Ps. Sol. 11:1–3; Gr. Apoc. Ezra 4:36; א-ב midrash of R. Akiba 9; etc.). Moreover, in a prayer of the Jewish Falaschas of Ethiopia, Michael the archangel initiates the resurrection of the dead by blowing his trumpet.[63] When one considers the fact that Paul has included the three prepositional phrases in his quotation of the λόγος, that they are *noises*, that Paul has been speaking of the dead Christians as 'sleeping' in verses 13–15, and that the three noises are connected by καί to the raising of the dead, it is hard to deny that in some sense at least verse 16a is linked causally to verses 16b–17a. If indeed this is the case, Marxsen's proposal that verse 16b is a Pauline addition to the logion[64] can be dismissed as absurd, for verse 16b is seen to be an integral and particularly important part of the λόγος.

The second stage of the eschatological drama is described in verse 17a: having been resurrected, the dead are then caught up with the living to meet the Lord in the air. Although the subject of verse 17a is the living, verse 15b reveals that the Thessalonians were already quite familiar with the truth that the living would participate in the parousia, presumably by

---

[63] See Littmann as cited by W. Lueken, *Michael* (Göttingen: Vandenhoeck & Ruprecht, 1898), 50; Dibelius, *Thessalonicher*, 26. Probably, however, the significance of the auditory accompaniments to Christ's descent for believers cannot be limited to the raising of the dead alone. With regard to the trumpet in particular, in Matt. 24:31, which is particularly significant for our purposes if it is authentically dominical, the trumpet initiates the gathering of the elect (presumably the living as well as the dead) (cf. Isa. 27:13; Ps. Sol. 11:1–3; Apoc. Abr. 31:1; 1QM 3; note also that κέλευσμα is used in Philo (*Praem. Poen.* 117) in relation to God's gathering of the elect). More generally, the trumpet functions eschatologically in Jewish thought to commence *Yom Yahweh*, bringing salvation and judgment (e.g. Joel 2:1–12; Apoc. Abr. 31:1ff.; 4 Ezra 6:23ff.; Sib. Or. 4. 173ff.), and to announce the final battle (e.g. Zeph. 1:15–16; Zech. 9:14; 1QM). It is conceivable that the word's original context had more of a Divine Warrior dimension than 1 Thess. 4:13–18; such a conjecture may be supported by the observation that κέλευσμα is typically a military term.

[64] W. Marxsen, *Der erste Brief an die Thessalonicher* (ZBK; Zurich: Theologischer, 1979), 67–8.

being 'caught up' to meet Christ. It seems likely that Paul has formally preserved the subject of the logion (οἱ περιλειπόμενοι), although ἅμα (σύν) demonstrates where the primary focus is: on *the dead saints' resurrection* and *their* being seized upward to meet Christ. Verse 15b plainly anticipated verse 17a's ἅμα σύν: the dead would suffer no disadvantage compared with the living. Just as verse 15b is, in a sense, a 'commentary' on the 'word' of verses 16–17a, drawing out their relevance for verse 14, so also verses 16–17a shed light on verse 15b. Significantly for the interpretation of verse 15b, the λόγος (verses 16–17a) does not concern whether the living will *precede* the dead; rather, the 'word' reveals that the dead are raised and caught up and so the living do not have an *advantage over* the dead. Moreover, the probability that φθάνω in verse 15b concerns an *absolute advantage* rather than a temporal priority/relative advantage and that this perceived advantage of the living relates specifically to the events of the parousia rather than the question of the parousia vis-à-vis the resurrection of the saints is borne out by verses 16–17a.

Finally, we must address the vexed issue of what verses 16–17 imply about what happens after believers are united with Christ. According to verse 16a Christ is descending, but according to verse 17a the living and dead Christians are ascending. Since it is hardly plausible that Christ and those in him remain in the air,[65] there are but two serious possibilities: (1) that the Christians' upward movement is continued to heaven[66] or (2) that Christ's downward movement is continued to earth.[67] The decision depends largely on what one makes of ἀπάντησις. As Peterson demonstrated at some length, ἀπάντησις was often used in Greek papyri, epigraphs and literary texts in a technical sense of an important dignitary's reception (*Einholung*) by the inhabitants of a city, who come out of the city to greet and welcome in their honoured guest with much attendant

---

[65] *Contra* R. Kabisch, *Die Eschatologie des Paulus in ihren Zusammenhängen mit dem Gesamtbegriff des Paulinismus dargestellt* (Göttingen: Vandenhoeck & Ruprecht, 1893), 258; cf. J. W. Bailey, '1 Thessalonians', in *IB* (ed. George A. Buttrick; Nashville: Abingdon, 1955), 11:307.

[66] So, for example, Bornemann, *Thessalonicherbriefe*, 210; Milligan, *Thessalonians*, 61; von Dobschütz, *Thessalonicher-Briefe*, 191–2, 198–9; E. B. Allo, *Saint Paul: Première épître aux Corinthiens* (2nd edn; EBib; Paris: Gabalda, 1956), 451–2; Harnisch, *Existenz*, 43–4 n. 23; Plevnik, 'Taking Up', 281–3 including n. 29; Wanamaker, *Thessalonians*, 175; Richard, *Thessalonians*, 245–8.

[67] So, for example, Chrysostom; Theodoret; Theophylact; Augustine; E. Peterson, 'Die Einholung des Kyrios', *ZST* 7 (1930): 682–3; Dibelius, *Thessalonicher*, 28; Dupont, *ΣΥΝ ΧΡΙΣΤΩΙ*, 64–73; Lüdemann, *Apostle*, 226; B. Lindars, 'The Sound of the Trumpet: Paul and Eschatology', *BJRL* 67 (1985): 774–5; Holtz, *Thessalonicher*, 203 including nn. 299–302; Reinmuth, 'Erste Brief', 147; T. D. Still, 'Eschatology in the Thessalonian Letters', *RevExp* 96 (1999): 206 n. 35.

fanfare and celebration.[68] In the case of 1 Thess. 4:16–17a, ἀπάντησις
would conjure up a picture of the dead and living leaving their *polis*, the
earth, to form a reception party to welcome their Lord.[69] This proposal
is compelling. This technical usage of ἀπάντησις / ὑπάντησις[70] is found
elsewhere in the New Testament in Matt. 25:1, 6;[71] John 12:13; and Acts
28:15. That this technical sense of ἀπάντησις applies in the case of 1
Thess. 4:16–17a can hardly be doubted in view of close correspondences
between verses 16–17a and secular *Einholungen*, especially the presen-
tation of the Lord as a particularly important figure, as demonstrated by
the αὐτός. Some in the first centuries of the church seem to have read
ἀπάντησις in this way, most notably Chrysostom and the copyist(s) responsible for the ὑπάντησις variant reading of manuscripts D*, F and
G. Certainly it would have been difficult for the original Greek readers
not to read ἀπάντησις according to its technical usage, especially where
Jesus is being presented as κύριος, an imperial title, and his coming as
his παρουσία, a title for a dignitary's official visit to a city in his jurisdiction.[72] Moreover, it is more likely that the direction of the saints
would conform to the direction of their *Lord* than the converse.[73] Further,
since the context (esp. verse 15b) confirms that verses 16–17a refer to
the 'parousia' and since the παρουσία in eschatological contexts in the
New Testament is frequently used as a technical term for Jesus' future
coming to earth, it seems preferable to understand the next movement as
downward. Finally, as we shall see below, the evidence accumulated in
favour of the heavenward reading is unconvincing.

Therefore, we conclude that verses 16–17a function to point out how
Paul can be sure that the dead will suffer no salvific disadvantage, but will
be with Christ: they will rise from their graves and will be caught up with

---

[68] Peterson, 'Einholung', 682–702.   [69] Ibid., 698.

[70] This term is synonymous with ἀπάντησις. Indeed, as ibid., 693 noted, Oecumenius,
in his comments on 1 Thess. 4:17 in his Revelation commentary, used the two terms inter-
changeably.

[71] Matt. 25:6 demonstrates that ἀπάντησις used in its technical Hellenistic sense could
be attributed to the earthly Jesus, which is striking in view of the likelihood that verses
16–17a constitute Jesus tradition.

[72] With R. H. Gundry, 'A Brief Note on "Hellenistic Formal Receptions and Paul's Use
of ΑΠΑΝΤΗΣΙΣ in 1 Thessalonians 4:17"', *BBR* 6 (1996): 39–41, *contra* M. R. Cosby,
'Hellenistic Formal Receptions and Paul's Use of ΑΠΑΝΤΗΣΙΣ in 1 Thessalonians 4:17',
BBR 4 (1994): 15–34. Nevertheless, caution should be exercised to ensure that the comparison between verses 16–17a and a typical *Einholung* is not overdrawn. For instance, we are
unconvinced by Gundry's attempt ('Hellenization', 165 and 'Brief Note', 39–41) to read
the three auditory accompaniments of Christ's descent as contributing to the portrayal
of the parousia as an official *Einholung* in verses 16–17a.

[73] *Contra* Plevnik, *Parousia*, 95, it is an *Einholung* of *the Lord* and not, as he suggests,
an '*Einholung* of the faithful'.

the living to meet him in the air (before returning to the earth with him).
Thus it appears that verses 16–17a bear out the meaning of verse 15b that
at the parousia the living will not have an advantage over the dead, which
in turn reinforces the assurance in verse 14 that the 'sleeping' will be in
the company of Christ at his parousia-descent.

How do 4:16–17 relate to 4:14b?

Many scholars have despaired of integrating successfully the eschatological concepts of verse 14b and verses 16–17 on a literal level, claiming
that a literal interpretation of the language as it stands leads to 'anti-
nomies and contradictions'.[74] However, we suggest that such despair is
premature and that Paul might well have expected a historical, and indeed
somewhat literal, fulfilment of these words. It seems preferable to conclude that verses 16–17a function to fill in the missing step between verse
14a and verse 14b: in order to demonstrate that the deceased Christians
will be in the company of Christ at the parousia-descent, Paul explains
that there will be a resurrection of dead saints and a 'catching up' of the
dead (with the living) to meet Christ in the air. It is surely significant that
verse 14b and verses 16–17a, understood in the way we have proposed, fit
perfectly together: the saints rise to receive the descending Jesus (verses
16–17a) and then come down to the earth with him (verse 14).

On the one hand, Paul presupposes in verses 14–17 that the Thessalonians know about the parousia and indeed conceive of it in terms of
LXX Zech. 14:5 and that they are aware that living Christians will be
caught up to meet Christ at the parousia. On the other hand, in verse 14
he assumes that the survivors believe their deceased will not participate in
the parousia and so he assures them that they will. Presumably the living
think that their dead will not participate in the parousia because for some
reason they will not be caught up to meet Christ. But why might they
think that? The fact that Paul justifies his assurance of verse 14b with
reference to the resurrection of the saints (verses 15–17, especially verse
16b) may supply the answer: the readers seem not to know that the dead
will *rise* and so be in a position to be caught up and participate in the
parousia. This hypothesis would of course reinforce our explanation of
why Paul has omitted mentioning the resurrection of the saints in verse
14b, namely to express his assurance in the terms with which his readers
are familiar.

[74] Marshall, *Thessalonians*, 128; also Wanamaker, *Thessalonians*, 176; Morris, *Epistles*, 144.

The coherence of the scenario portrayed in verse 14 and verses 16–17 thus emerges: Paul assures the Thessalonians that their deceased ones will be among the holy ones at the parousia and then justifies this claim by appealing authoritatively to a saying of Jesus which makes it clear that dead believers will rise and so be caught up together with the living to meet the Lord and thus form his escort in the last stage of his journey to earth.

The close relationship between verse 14 and verses 16–17a is reinforced by verse 17b, which is almost certainly a Pauline conclusion to the 'word of the Lord'. It indicates that Paul's goal in quoting the 'word' in verses 16–17a is to elucidate how the deceased can be 'with Christ' at the parousia (note especially the οὕτως), which obviously picks up on the language of verse 14b (σὺν αὐτῷ). This seems to concur with our earlier judgment that verses 16–17a are designed to confirm verse 14, and appears to strengthen the suggestion that the Thessalonians' central concern was that the deceased would not be among those with Christ at his parousia.[75]

With regard to verse 18, in view of verse 17b and the tight cohesion of verses 14–17, ὥστε (here synonymous with διό) surely encompasses the whole section rather than just the 'word' of verses 15–17. Verses 13 and 18 together form an inclusio around the section, the former expressing the purpose of verses 13–18 negatively and the latter expressing it positively. Paul wants the members of the community to 'comfort' one another (which plainly alludes to the Thessalonians' hopeless grieving for their deceased (verse 13b)) by means of his eschatological instruction, particularly verses 14–17.

Is the source of the Thessalonians' confusion an erroneous theology of Jewish assumption?

Over recent years numerous scholars have suggested that the Jewish conception of assumption elucidates the eschatological confusion underlying 1 Thess. 4:13–18.[76] The hypothesis, which has been largely developed by Plevnik, depends on Lohfink's claim that in Jewish literature the dead are

---

[75] To Paul, and presumably his converts, being 'with Christ for ever' was the essence of salvation and the primary focus of Christian hope. That Paul is so concerned to assure the Thessalonians concerning the destiny of their deceased in these terms corroborates the view that the converts held out no hope for their dead. In the light of the link between verse 14b and verse 17b, Best's (*Thessalonians*, 200) claim that verse 17b is 'not strictly germane' to the Thessalonians' concern seems peculiar.

[76] So, for example, Plevnik, 'Taking Up', 274–83 and *Parousia*, 83, 95; Johanson, *Brethren*, 124–5; Wanamaker, *Thessalonians*, 166; Jurgensen, 'Awaiting', 85 n. 10.

never 'assumed'[77] (that is, with regard to their whole persons; note that
Lohfink argues that there are four distinct categories of assumption, of
which one is assumption of the whole person[78]). According to this view,
Paul had taught the Thessalonians about the parousia using the Jewish
concept of assumption and some of the converts had wrongly deduced, on
the basis of the observation that in Jewish literature the *dead* seemed never
to be assumed (*sc.* to heaven), that the deceased could not participate in
the parousia and so would not be with the Lord. For this reason, Plevnik
argues, Paul could not effectively reassure the faithful by verse 14 alone,
for he had to demonstrate graphically how the dead could be assumed (i.e.
by rising from the dead before the catching up occurs) (verses 16–17; cf.
Rev. 11:11–12).[79] Is this the key to the perplexing Thessalonian situation?
We think not. First, as we observed above, verse 14b suggests that the
ultimate *terminus ad quem* is earth rather than heaven. This conclusion is
probably confirmed by verse 17a's ἀπάντησις; there, where the *terminus
a quo* is earth and the meeting-place is the air, the *terminus ad quem* is
probably the earth.[80] As we argued above, Paul elsewhere (e.g. 1 Cor. 6:2
and especially 15:24–6) appears to believe that Christ will yet reign on
earth. Second, evidence is entirely lacking that Paul ever conceived of the
parousia in terms of an assumption. Third, it is implausible to suggest that
a recently converted community composed primarily of former pagans
would have been so familiar with intertestamental Jewish examples of assumption that they would have distinguished between assumptions of the
whole person and other kinds of assumptions, as Lohfink does, and then
so definitively drawn the conclusion that the dead could not be assumed
in this sense. Certainly no one could confidently draw such a conclusion
from the Old Testament alone. Furthermore, we cannot be sure that the
Assumption of Moses did not relate the story of the assumption of Moses'
dead body. If it did, the thesis of Plevnik collapses.

Conclusion

With the ultimate intention of determining whether the situations underlying 1 and 2 Thessalonians can reasonably be regarded as compatible,

[77] G. Lohfink, *Die Himmelfahrt Jesu* (SANT; Munich: Kösel, 1971), 37–71, 73–4
including n. 252 and n. 253.
[78] Ibid., 32–79, esp. 55–70.   [79] Plevnik, 'Taking Up', 281.
[80] That the movement immediately following the meeting is downward rather than upward has been recognised even by many who have questioned the applicability of the
technical meaning here (such as Dupont, ΣΥΝ ΧΡΙΣΤῼ, 64–73 and Masson, *Thessaloniciens*, 59–60). The dichotomy between Jewish and Greco-Roman usage presupposed by
many sceptics is unwarranted.

we began our investigation of the situation reflected in 1 Thessalonians by studying 4:13–18, where Paul deals explicitly with eschatological confusion in the Thessalonian community. Apparently, the deaths have brought to the surface a serious lack in the Thessalonians' eschatology. Ignorant of the resurrection of the dead (verse 13a, verses 16–17a), it seems that the Thessalonians have supposed that all Christians would necessarily be alive at the eschaton and so could participate in the parousia-descent of Christ and the salvation associated with it (verse 14b). (To that extent there may have been an 'over-realised' dimension to their eschatology.[81]) Hence when some of their number died, the community apparently concluded that the deceased would suffer an absolute disadvantage (verse 15b). The community members have lost hope for their deceased and have become greatly distressed by the unexpected deaths (verse 13b). If we are correct, this problem would have been acute and indeed potentially faith-threatening, for there must have been questions regarding the religious significance of these deaths for the community. Certainly the deaths seemed to declare that among the number of the converted were at least some whom God had not elected to salvation at the parousia, which meant that the elect status and eschatological destiny of the whole community was subject to suspicion. With this in view, we proceed to offer a reading of the situation underlying 5:1–11.

---

[81] Acknowledging this does not mean that we accept that the Thessalonians had a developed 'over-realised eschatology', as many scholars (such as W. Lütgert, 'Die Volkommenen im Philipperbrief und die Enthusiasten in Thessalonich', *BFCT* 13 (1909): 632; R. Jewett, 'Enthusiastic Radicalism and the Thessalonian Correspondence', in *SBLSP 1972*, 1:181–232 and *Correspondence*, 94–5; Murphy-O'Connor, *Critical Life*, 123) have supposed; we regard that as highly unlikely.

3

ANXIOUS AND FEARFUL

Introduction

With the ultimate goal of ascertaining whether the situations underlying 1 and 2 Thessalonians are compatible, in the preceding chapter we turned our attention to 1 Thess. 4:13–18. Although relatively neglected in comparison to that text, 5:1–11 is equally fundamental for understanding the nature of the eschatological confusion underlying 1 Thessalonians. On the basis of this passage it has been variously suggested that the Thessalonian community are expecting the parousia with deep imminentist excitement[1] or restless impatience,[2] that they are falsely secure,[3] that they are unwilling to live with the 'uncertainty' of a future eschatology,[4] and that they are worried that more might die before the parousia finally occurs[5] or worried that they might be unprepared for it when it does come.[6] Unfortunately, however, there has been a notable dearth of constructive scholarly interaction and debate regarding the situation of 5:1–11. In this chapter we shall attempt to cut a fresh path through this difficult terrain, all the while critically assessing previous contributions, with a view to establishing the background situation giving rise to this section.

[1] E.g. Jurgensen, 'Awaiting', 95, 96–7, 111–12; Still, 'Eschatology', 209 n. 49.
[2] E.g. J. M. G. Barclay, 'Thessalonica and Corinth: Social Contrasts in Pauline Christianity', *JSNT* 47 (1992): 52 and 'Conflict in Thessalonica', *CBQ* 55 (1993): 516–17, 527.
[3] E.g. W. H. Burkeen, 'The Parousia of Christ in the Thessalonian Correspondence' (Ph.D. thesis, University of Aberdeen, 1979), 167–8; cf. C. L. Mearns, 'Early Eschatological Development in Paul: The Evidence of I and II Thessalonians', *NTS* 27 (1980–1): 141–2 and 144.
[4] Jewett, 'Radicalism', 202 and *Correspondence*, 97.
[5] Findlay, *Epistles of Paul*, 106; Milligan, *Thessalonians*, 63; Laub, *Verkündigung*, 132 (cf. *1. und 2. Thessalonicherbrief* (NEchtB; Würzburg: Echter, 1985), 30); Burkeen, 'Parousia', 145; Marxsen, *Erste Brief*, 65; Best, *Thessalonians*, 203; Morris, *Epistles*, 149–50; Richard, *Thessalonians*, 249.
[6] Frame, *Thessalonians*, 178; Rigaux, *Thessaloniciens*, 552–3; Marshall, *Thessalonians*, 132 and 'Election and Calling to Salvation in 1 and 2 Thessalonians', in *TC*, 260; Johanson, *Brethren*, 129–30; M. W. Holmes, *1 & 2 Thessalonians* (NIVAC; Grand Rapids: Zondervan, 1998), 165.

Does idle speculation underlie the Thessalonians' question?

Paul opens 5:1–11 with περὶ δέ, which in 1 Corinthians is employed to demarcate the commencement of his response to specific questions posed by his addressees in a letter (7:1, 25; 8:1; 12:1; 16:1, 12). Given the improbability that Paul himself would raise a matter only to insist that his converts do not need to be written to regarding it since they already know 'very well' (ἀκριβῶς) the answer to it (cf. 1 Thess. 4:9), it seems safe to conclude that Paul is responding to a Thessalonian question. Nevertheless, it is unnecessary to suppose that the Thessalonians had written a letter to Paul,[7] since the data can be satisfactorily explained with reference to a question communicated orally *via* Timothy, who has reported to Paul, having just returned from visiting the community (3:6).

The question relates to 'the times and the seasons' (τῶν χρόνων καὶ τῶν καιρῶν), which in this context is almost certainly a hendiadys for the *timing* of the Day of the Lord (cf. Acts 1:7).[8] Scholars typically assume that the question is 'when will the Day of the Lord come?'[9] and that it relates to the date of the parousia,[10] and many contend that it is undergirded by idle apocalyptic speculation.[11] However, as Acts 1:6–7 ('Is this the time when you will restore the kingdom to Israel?') reveals, the range of possible questions which may be summarised by means of this expression is broader than that. Paul's response is the sole way to determine the precise nature of the Thessalonian query, and, as we shall

---

[7] *Pace* Frame, *Thessalonians*, 178; C. E. Faw, 'On the Writing of First Thessalonians', *JBL* 71 (1952): 221–2; B. N. Kaye, 'Eschatology and Ethics in 1 and 2 Thessalonians', *NovT* 17 (1975): 47; cf. Malherbe, *Thessalonians*, 76 (although he roots his case not in 5:1, but rather in the 'epistolary conventions' of 3:6–10). Note the conclusion of M. M. Mitchell, 'Concerning περὶ δέ in 1 Corinthians', *NovT* 31 (1989): 229–56 in regard to the use of περὶ δέ in 1 Corinthians: 'Although this formula *can* be used in response to information received by letter, it is surely *not restricted* to this use, even in letters which mention a previous letter' (p. 234, italics his).

[8] For the background of this combination, see LXX Dan. 2:21 (cf. Theodotion); 7:21; Wis. 8:8. E. Lucchesi, 'Précédents non bibliques à l'expression néo-testamentaire: "Les temps et les moments"', *JTS* 28 (1977): 537–40 has suggested that the New Testament instances are inspired indirectly rather than directly by Daniel, *via* philosophical or Gnostic usage (cf. Philo, *Quaest. in Gen.* 6.13).

[9] For example, von Dobschütz, *Thessalonicher-Briefe*, 202ff.; Frame, *Thessalonians*, 178, 179–80; Marshall, *Thessalonians*, 132; Best, *Thessalonians*, 204; Jewett, *Correspondence*, 96–7; Still, 'Eschatology', 199. Others (e.g. Morris, *Epistles*, 149) suggest that the question was 'What will be the signs which signal the coming of the Day of the Lord?'

[10] For example, Rigaux, *Thessaloniciens*, 552–3, 555; Laub, *Verkündigung*, 132; Marxsen, *Erste Brief*, 65, 68; Marshall, 'Election', 268–9; Jurgensen, 'Awaiting', 97; Richard, *Thessalonians*, 259, 260; Plevnik, *Parousia*, 101–2, 121.

[11] *Inter alios* Jurgensen, 'Awaiting', 97, 111; Plevnik, *Parousia*, 102.

see, that suggests that the question relates as much to 'who?' and 'how?'
as to 'when?'.[12] The idea that the Thessalonians have asked Paul for
the parousia's date fails at precisely this point: it does not satisfactorily
accommodate Paul's response. We shall postpone suggesting a suitable
candidate for the question until after we have completed our detailed
study of Paul's reply in 1 Thess. 5:1–11.

In spite of what the Thessalonians apparently think, Paul insists that
there is in fact no need for them to be written to (cf. 4:9) regarding
'the times and the seasons' (5:1), because they know well/accurately
(ἀκριβῶς), presumably from what had been imparted to them at the mission, that 'the Day of the Lord as a thief in the night, thus it comes'
(verse 2). Although the Thessalonians are aware of the thief simile, apparently they do not realise that it encapsulates the full answer to their
question.

The meaning of the 'Day of the Lord' in 5:2

The expression ἡμέρα κυρίου (יהוה יום) goes back at least as far as Amos'
time (5:18–20) and was used throughout the Prophetic era of the great
and terrible Day when Yahweh will intervene to punish his enemies and
the disobedient (e.g. Isa. 13:6–16; Ezek. 30:1–4; Joel 1:13–15; 2:1–11;
Obad. 15–20; Zeph. 1:14ff.; Zech. 14:1–21; Mal. 4:5) and also to save
the faithful (e.g. Isa. 27:2–13; Jer. 30:8–9; Joel 2:31–2 and 3:18; Obad.
21). It is essentially co-referential with παρουσία here, as elsewhere
in Paul's letters.[13] In the light of 1 Thess. 5:3 and 4, it is likely that
the parousia in its negative aspect (*qua* judgment) is in view here in
verse 2 (cf. 2 Pet. 3:10).[14] This is reinforced by the thief simile which
follows.

[12] This seems safer than assuming, with, for example, Reinmuth, *Erste Brief*, 148, that
Paul did not answer the question he was asked.
[13] Cf. L. J. Kreitzer, *Jesus and God in Paul's Eschatology* (JSNTSup; Sheffield: JSOT,
1987), 112–29; B. Witherington, *Jesus, Paul, and the End of the World* (Exeter: Paternoster,
1992), 152–69. It is enough to note that Paul's hope for his converts was that they will be
blameless 'in the day of our Lord Jesus Christ' (1 Cor. 1:8), 'until the day of Christ' (Phil.
1:10; cf. 2:15–16) and 'at the parousia of our Lord Jesus Christ' (1 Thess. 3:13; 5:23).
He longed to boast in his churches 'in the day of Christ' (Phil. 2:16) and 'at the parousia'
(1 Thess. 2:19). His converts could look forward to salvation at the parousia (1 Cor. 15:23)
and 'in the day of the Lord Jesus' (1 Cor. 5:5).
[14] Cf. Burkeen, 'Parousia', 150; G. Nebe, *'Hoffnung' bei Paulus* (SUNT; Göttingen:
Vandenhoeck & Ruprecht, 1983), 96–8; T. L. Howard, 'The Literary Unity of 1 Thessalonians 4:13–5:11', *GTJ* 9 (1988): 174–8; Wanamaker, *Thessalonians*, 179; Holmes,
Thessalonians, 166.

The import of the thief motif in 5:2

The thief simile[15] is used consistently in the New Testament to imply the unexpectedness and unwelcomeness of the Day of the Lord's coming upon those who will be judged by it (2 Pet. 3:10; Rev. 3:3; 16:15; Matt. 24:43–4; Luke 12:39–40).[16] That this nuance of judgment, which accords with the intrinsic negativity of the image of a thief (cf. Matt. 6:19–20; Luke 12:33; John 10:1, 8, 10; 12:6; 1 Pet. 4:15), is present here in 1 Thess. 5:2 is evident when we consider that verse 3 must unavoidably be interpreted as an explication of verse 2: in verse 3 the Day is pictured not only as unexpected, but also as painful, inescapable and destructive. As a thief comes 'in the night', with sudden destruction (αἰφνίδιος αὐτοῖς ἐφίσταται ὄλεθρος) upon the falsely secure, so also the Day of the Lord will come[17] upon its victims. Unfortunately, most commentators restrict the sense of the thief motif here to 'unpredictability', 'unforeseeability', 'suddenness' and/or 'unexpectedness', and judge that the answer in verse 2 amounts to 'no one knows when the Day will come'.[18] However, the negative dimension of the simile cannot be avoided just two verses later (verse 4), and there is no basis for distinguishing between the two usages.

If indeed this negative connotation of the Day of the Lord and of the thief image is pre-eminent here, it raises the question why. Some have suggested that Paul is directing his discussion at his readers' restless impatience as they wait for God's wrath to fall on their enemies[19] or that he is threatening his converts with the prospect of eschatological judgment to underline the necessity of obedience (cf. Matt. 24:42–4).[20] However, these hypotheses fail to take seriously enough the observation

---

[15] Probably this is an allusion to a saying of Jesus passed on to the Thessalonians at the mission. It seems implausible that the early church would have initiated the comparison between the coming of Christ and that of a thief. Note also the absence of the motif from contemporary Jewish literature.

[16] *Contra* most commentaries including Ellicott, *Thessalonians*, 69 and Best, *Thessalonians*, 205–6. Note that the Gnostic *Gos. Thom.* 21 has the thief motif describe the world's attack on the believer, a development consistent with the simile's negative sense.

[17] Note the proleptic/prophetic present, stressing the certainty (not the imminence) of the judgment (so also *inter alios* D. E. H. Whiteley, *Thessalonians in the Revised Standard Version with Introduction and Commentary* (NClarB; Oxford: Oxford University Press, 1969), 75).

[18] Holtzmann, 'Thessalonicherbrief', 97; Hollmann, 'Unechtheit', 33; Rigaux, *Thessaloniciens*, 557; Masson, *Thessaloniciens*, 67; Laub, *Verkündigung*, 132; Marxsen, *Erste Brief*, 68; Best, *Thessalonians*, 205; Holtz, *Thessalonicher*, 213 n. 346; Hughes, 'The Rhetoric of 1 Thessalonians', in *TC*, 105, 115; Jurgensen, 'Awaiting', 97 including n. 25.

[19] So, for example, Barclay, 'Social Contrasts', 52 and 'Conflict', 517, 527.

[20] So J. Plevnik, '1 Thess 5, 1–11: Its Authenticity, Intention and Message', *Bib* 60 (1979): 78; Wanamaker, *Thessalonians*, 180–1; Jurgensen, 'Awaiting', 97–8, 111.

that Paul strongly disavows the relevance of the thief simile (verse 4) and of divine eschatological wrath (verse 9) to the Thessalonian converts. Surprising as it may at first appear, it seems that the Thessalonian Christians' question concerns the Day *qua wrath* as it relates to *themselves.*

In view of the fact that ἐν νυκτί accompanies ἡμέρα here and of the sustained light–darkness and day–night contrasts in verses 4–7, it seems likely that ἐν νυκτί bears much weight in the argument of 5:1–11, probably implying the realm of evil and opposition to God, as in verses 5b and 7, as well as implying 'unsuspecting' and 'unprepared', and, moreover, indicating metaphorically the time when the parousia will occur. Paul was unprepared to rely on the Thessalonians correctly educing the necessary point from the thief simile; hence he proceeds to explicate it.

The relationship of 5:3 to the thief-in-the-night simile

The formula ὅταν . . . τότε in verse 3 connects sudden, inescapable destruction to a proclamation of 'peace and safety' (εἰρήνη καὶ ἀσφάλεια). Harnisch has claimed that this is the boast of Gnostics in their present realisation of salvation,[21] whilst Jewett has maintained that it refers to enthusiastic opponents' rejection of the possibility of future judgment.[22] However, to perceive such specific targets behind Paul's words here constitutes an illegitimate mirror reading which is tantamount to eisegesis – 5:1–11 lacks the required polemical thrust to justify such readings. Recently many scholars have postulated that this phrase alludes to imperial Roman propaganda for the programme of the early principate; the point would then be that the Day of the Lord would imminently shatter the false *pax* of the Roman establishment, in which the community's persecutors trusted.[23] This reading might establish a contrast between the false security of the contemporary Roman world and the insecurity of the Thessalonian community, strongly reinforcing the eschaton's imminence. Although it is uncertain whether a Roman political propagandising

---

[21] Harnisch, *Existenz*, 79–82.   [22] Jewett, *Correspondence*, 96–7.

[23] E. Bammel, 'Ein Beitrag zur paulinischen Staatsanschauung', *TLZ* 85 (1960): 837–40, esp. 837; Donfried, 'Cults', 344 (and *Shorter*, 16); Koester, 'From Paul's Eschatology to the Apocalyptic Schemata of 2 Thessalonians', in *TC*, 449–50; H. L. Hendrix, 'Archaeology and Eschatology at Thessalonica', in *The Future of Early Christianity* (ed. B. A. Pearson; Minneapolis: Augsburg, 1991), 109–14; T. R. Yoder Neufeld, *'Put on the Armour of God'* (JSNTSup; Sheffield: Sheffield Academic Press, 1997), 81–2 including n. 27; Holmes, *Thessalonians*, 166–7; Still, *Conflict*, 262–6. On pro-Roman sentiment in Thessalonica, see H. L. Hendrix, 'Thessalonicans Honor Romans' (Ph.D. thesis, Harvard University, 1984) and Donfried, 'Cults', 342ff.

slogan identical to this ever existed,[24] it would be unwise to dismiss this view too quickly.

However, in view of the scripturally resonant subsequent context, it is difficult to avoid understanding εἰρήνη καὶ ἀσφάλεια as alluding first and foremost (and perhaps exclusively) to the Hebrew text of Jer. 6:14 (cf. 8:11; Ezek. 13:10), on the basis of the conspicuous repetition of the idea of 'peace', together with the remarkably similar context (a false assurance of peace in the face of inevitable and devastating divine anger). Koester argues against such an allusion, appealing to the facts that καὶ ἀσφάλεια is not found in LXX Jer. 6:14, which translates the Hebrew שׁלום שׁלום as εἰρήνη εἰρήνη, and that in the LXX ἀσφάλεια never translates שׁלום.[25] However, Paul's ἀσφάλεια would seem to capture well the sense of the Hebrew שׁלום in Jer. 6:14/8:11, where it implies safety from the threat of divine wrath. The choice of term might have been intended to highlight the contrast between the falsely secure state of mind and the insecurity of the Thessalonian believers (or, possibly, to point more surely at the contemporary Roman establishment).[26]

That Paul is alluding to Jer. 6:14/8:11 here might suggest something of his view of the period immediately preceding *Yom Yahweh*: that people will be absolutely corrupt and yet feel a delusional sense of immunity from divine judgment, under the sway of false religion (prophets and priests, Jer. 6:13). This raises the possibility that verse 3's ὅταν clause is a specific reference to the state of the world on the verge of *Yom Yahweh* (cf. Matt. 24:23–4/Mark 13:21–2; Revelation 13).

Best and Richard have argued that verse 3 is proverbial rather than eschatologically specific on the grounds that we have ὅταν plus a present subjunctive rather than ὅτε plus a future indicative. However, they fail to do justice to the fact that ὅταν here is paired with τότε. Elsewhere Paul almost always uses this pair to refer to *specific* eschatological (1 Cor. 15:28, 54; cf. Col. 3:4) or non-eschatological (1 Cor. 16:2) events.[27] The emphasis seems always to rest on the content of the ὅταν clause (i.e. 'when . . . at that very time . . .'). Mark 13:4 and John 7:27 and 31 confirm that indeed ὅταν with the present subjunctive need not be

---

[24] While there were slogans such as *pax Romana/Augusti* and *securitas Augusti*, we have no evidence to suggest that a whole expression *pax et securitas* was used as Roman political propaganda in the contemporary world of Paul.

[25] Koester, 'Schemata', 449.

[26] It is unnecessary to follow Malherbe's bizarre proposal (*Thessalonians*, 304–5) that Paul has deliberately chosen an Epicurean word to inflict a stinging criticism of false prophets in the Thessalonian community, in spite of the fact that the Thessalonian confusion is blatantly eschatological.

[27] The sole exception is 2 Cor. 12:10.

iterative or proverbial.[28] Therefore we suggest that here the ὅταν clause is probably specific, referring to the era immediately preceding the Day of the Lord. In the light of the fact that Paul is responding to a question relating to the timing of the Day, it is difficult to avoid reading verse 3 as spelling out how verse 2's thief-*in-the-night* motif is the answer to their question.

If verse 3a can be regarded as the explication of the 'in-the-night' element of the simile, then v. 3b's τότε clause develops the 'thief' part: the destruction of the Day comes unexpectedly upon those living in false security. Paul reinforces the horror of the Day of the Lord by adding a birthpang analogy, this time almost certainly drawn from Isa. 13:8 (and perhaps Jer. 6:24; cf. Isa. 26:17; 66:8–9; Jer. 13:21; 22:23; 30:6; Hos. 13:13; also Ps. 48:6; 1 Enoch 62:4; 4 Ezra 4:40–2; 1QH 3:7–10; 5:30–1), which concerns the Day of the Lord *qua* judgment and destruction: it will be a painful and agonizing Day, coming without warning on its victims. Finally, he climaxes his description of the fate of the falsely secure by stressing[29] that they will not be able to escape the wrath due them on that Day (cf. Amos 9:1ff.), possibly educing that from the birthpang simile.

Thus it seems unavoidable that verse 3 is explicating verse 2's thief-in-the-night simile with a view to responding to the Thessalonians' question regarding the timing of the Day of the Lord *qua* judgment: it will happen when the world is supremely 'in the night', that is, falsely secure under the spell of pseudo-religion. Simultaneously, and more importantly, Paul has put the focus firmly on the identity of the victims of the Day of the Lord in preparation for verses 4ff.

Does 5:3 constitute grounds for judging the Thessalonian community to be guilty of false security?

Many scholars judge that the apostle is here countering real or potential false security within the Thessalonian community.[30] However, this

---

[28] Marshall, *Thessalonians*, 134.

[29] Οὐ μή is emphatic here (see W. W. Goodwin, *A Greek Grammar* (New York: St Martin's, 1894), 289; Best, *Thessalonians*, 208).

[30] Schmithals, 'Historical Situation', 164–6; B. Rigaux, 'Tradition et rédaction dans 1 Thess. V.1–10', *NTS* 21 (1975): 321; Plevnik, '1 Thess 5, 1–11', 78, 88 and *Parousia*, 106, 121; Collins, *Studies*, 163; Malherbe, *Thessalonians*, 302–5 (whose unrestrained mirror reading leads him to suppose that false prophets within the community were not only indulging their curiosity about the time of the end, but also were providing 'perspective for a life that, in Paul's estimation, is like that of "the rest"', ultimately dulling imminentist eschatological expectation with their message of 'peace and security', 'a security in their newfound community and relations with each other that did not sufficiently take into

hypothesis can be disallowed on account of the use of the third-person plural λέγωσιν in verse 3a, the confirmatory nature of the preceding section (4:13–18) and Paul's categorical disassociation of believers from unbelievers with regard to eschatological fate in the ensuing verses (especially verses 4–5 and 9–10). In order to uphold this view Plevnik is forced to the implausible hypothesis that the author threatens his readers in verses 2–3 (in what Plevnik regards as Paul's attack on *false security*) only to 'back off' and correct himself in verses 4ff. (which Plevnik regards as Paul's treatment of *insecurity*).[31] Jurgensen contends that Paul in verses 4–5 balances out the 'stern warning' of verses 2–3.[32] However, if verses 2–3 are a warning to the Thessalonian community, verses 4–5 do not balance them out as much as fatally undermine them. Collins and Wanamaker suggest that verses 2–3 function to impart a note of urgency to the subsequent paraenesis.[33] However, the paraenesis does not come until verses 6–8 and it is explicitly founded upon assurances regarding the converts' secure status and destiny (verses 4–5, 9–10).

What, then, is the function of these verses? We propose that they function quite simply to answer the Thessalonians' question regarding the timing of the Day of the Lord. First, Paul communicates his response in a nutshell, which encapsulates the fullness of his reply (verse 2). Then he explicates his summary response in such a way as to deal directly with the timing of the Day, whilst subtly shifting the focus onto the identity of the victims of the Day of the Lord in preparation for verses 4ff.[34]

---

consideration the eschatological dimension of their existence'). One of the fundamental bases of G. Friedrich's claim that 1 Thess. 5:1–11 is an interpolation is that it confronts addressees living in false security (implying a slackening of parousia expectation), which, he maintains, cannot be reconciled with 4:13–18 ('1 Thessalonicher 5, 1–11, der apologische Einschub eines Späteren', *ZTK* 70 (1973): 288–315 and 'Der erste Brief an die Thessalonicher', in *Die Briefe an die Galater, Epheser, Philipper, Kolosser, Thessalonicher und Philemon* (ed. J. Becker, H. Conzelmann and G. Friedrich; NTD; Göttingen: Vandenhoeck & Ruprecht, 1976), 206–7). Against this hypothesis, see Plevnik, '1 Thess 5, 1–11', 72–4; Collins, *Studies*, 110–13 and Légasse, *Thessaloniciens*, 280–1. Von Dobschütz, *Thessalonicher-Briefe*, 203, 209 has contended that Paul is here fighting on two fronts: against negligent unpreparedness and against extravagant eschatological expectations; but, as Schmithals, 'Historical Situation', 165 has pointed out, this makes the situation needlessly complex and difficult, and evidence of extravagant expectation is lacking.

[31] Plevnik, '1 Thess 5, 1–11', 78 and *Parousia*, 106, 121; A. Smith, *Comfort One Another* (LCBI; Louisville, Ky.: Westminster John Knox, 1995), 90 ('*epidiorthosis*').

[32] Jurgensen, 'Awaiting', 97–8.

[33] Collins, *Studies*, 166; Wanamaker, *Thessalonians*, 180–1.

[34] There is a sense in which verse 3 anticipates verse 4: since those on whom eschatological wrath falls will be living in false security, the Thessalonian community members, who are not so doing, can know that wrath will not fall upon them.

The function of 5:4

The contrast between verse 4 and the preceding verses (indicated by ὑμεῖς, δέ and ἀδελφοί) could hardly be more stark. In contrast to those 'in the night' (ἐν νυκτί) and those who are ill-advisedly claiming 'peace and safety' (λέγωσιν), Paul emphatically stresses that his readers are 'not in darkness' (οὐκ ... ἐν σκότει) (cf. Rom. 13:12–14; Eph. 4:17ff.; 5:8ff.). To be 'in darkness', here as elsewhere in the Pauline corpus (Rom. 13:12; 1 Cor. 4:5; 2 Cor. 4:4–6; 6:14; Col. 1:13; Eph. 5:3; 6:12; cf. 1 Pet. 2:9; also Job 22:9–11; Ps. 82:5; Prov. 4:19; Isa. 60:1–3; 1QS 1:9–10; 3:13–4:26; 1QM 1:1ff.), is to exist in the realm of sin, evil and unenlightenment, estranged from and opposed to God and his ways, which is the lot of humanity without Christ. Moreover, while the Day comes as a thief and with sudden, painful and inescapable destruction for those in the night according to verses 2–3, in verse 4 the Thessalonian converts are categorically assured that their fate is different: because they are not in darkness, the Day will not overtake them as a thief, that is, with sudden destruction.

Most scholars are reluctant to conclude that Paul is, in verse 4, completely withdrawing the relevance to his readers of the thief simile which he introduced in verse 2. Marshall speaks for many when he insists that, in spite of verse 4, a dimension of the thief motif remains relevant to the community, namely 'unexpectedness and unpredictability'.[35] Some of them root their case in the use of καταλαμβάνω in verse 4.[36] However, verse 3 indicates that a nuance of judgment is already present and so καταλαμβάνω is introducing nothing which is not already present in the text, and it is hard to imagine that verse 3 goes in a direction unanticipated by verse 2. Richard suggests that in verse 4 the meaning of 'darkness' shifts from being the cover for the thief's work to being the sphere of evil.[37] However, this artificially separates verses 4ff. from verses 2–3, and fails to consider that verse 2's 'night' also refers to the sphere of evil, as suggested by verse 3. Neither is Paul's point in verse 4 that believers *need not* be caught off guard by the Day of the Lord.[38] The fact that verse 4b is grounded in the converts' not being in the dominion of darkness, together with the content of verses 5 and 9–10, demonstrates the fallaciousness of that interpretation. His point is surely that the converts *will not* be overtaken as a thief. Verse 4 is an application of the thief simile

---

[35] Marshall, *Thessalonians*, 136; cf. Richard, *Thessalonians*, 252.
[36] *Inter alios* J. W. Elias, *1 and 2 Thessalonians* (BCBC; Scottsdale, Pa.: Herald, 1995), 195; D. M. Martin, *1, 2 Thessalonians* (NAC; Nashville: Broadman & Holman, 1995), 162 n. 105; Richard, *Thessalonians*, 252.
[37] Richard, *Thessalonians*, 252.   [38] Elias, *Thessalonians*, 195.

to the community, a stark rebuttal of the notion that the Thessalonian converts are under the threat of the thief, that is, of the Day of the Lord's sudden and destructive wrath.

But why would Paul introduce the image only to disavow its relevance to his readers? We suggest that verse 2's image must be understood on two levels, both drawn out in verse 3: on one, it serves to inform the Thessalonians regarding the timing of the Day of the Lord; on the other, it functions to identify the victims of the Day in a way that brings into relief the community's positive rather than negative eschatological destiny. It is Paul's way of answering the Thessalonian question and dispelling anxiety or fear that the Day of the Lord *qua* judgment will unexpectedly come upon the community.

The significance of the four pronouncements of 5:5

In verse 5 Paul founds (γάρ) the assertion of verse 4 on four more pronouncements relating to the converts' eschatological status and destiny. First, he asserts that all of the Thessalonians (πάντες . . . ὑμεῖς) are (1) 'sons of (the) light' (υἱοὶ φωτός) and (2) 'sons of (the) day' (υἱοὶ ἡμέρας). The former expression is found elsewhere in the New Testament (Luke 16:8 and John 12:36; cf. Eph. 5:8 (τέκνα φωτός)) and in Jewish literature (e.g. 1QS 1:9–10; 2:16; 3:13, 24–5; 1QM 1:1, 3, 9, 11, 13). As in those instances, so also in this context, where it contrasts with darkness, it reflects a notably Jewish dualism, demarcating those who belong to (υἱοί plus the genitive) the realm of God and his salvation, and possibly also portraying them as destined for God's eschatological kingdom of light.[39]

The latter expression 'sons of (the) day' is almost certainly a Pauline neologism, created to speak specifically to the Thessalonian community. Some have denied the future import of 'day' here,[40] on the grounds that it is unlikely that Paul would have added a temporal dimension to the spatial sense of the dualistic language employed in verses 4–5, that the present tense (ἐστε) is used in verse 5a, and/or that the arguably chiastic structure of verse 5 suggests that the apostle is not distinguishing between

[39] Holtz, *Thessalonicher*, 221 and Plevnik, *Parousia*, 110 maintain that 'sons of (the) day' interprets 'sons of light' in an eschatological sense. Perhaps it is preferable to conclude that 'sons of (the) day' has been partially inspired by a secondary eschatological nuance of 'sons of light'.

[40] For example, E. G. Selwyn, *The First Epistle of St. Peter* (2nd edn; London: Macmillan, 1946), 375, 379–80; E. Fuchs, *Glaube und Erfahrung* (Tübingen: Mohr, 1965), 334–63; Whiteley, *Thessalonians*, 78; Harnisch, *Existenz*, 117–31 and Koester, 'Schemata', 451. See R. W. Crown, 'The Non-Literal Use of Eschatological Language in Jewish Apocalyptic and the New Testament' (D.Phil. thesis, Oxford University, 1986), 281–303.

'light' and 'day' or 'darkness' and 'night'. However, (a) it is possible that 'sons of (the) light' has a (secondary) futurist eschatological dimension here, as in John 12:36; 1QM 1:1, 3, 7, 10, 16; 3:6, 9; 9:11, 13; 13:16 and 14:7. (b) The present tense in verse 5a functions to indicate that the converts' future destiny is already a settled matter in the wake of their conversion; it is not justification for an exclusively realised interpretation. (c) The argument from the chiastic structure of verse 5 is uncompelling: the lack of υἱοί in verse 5b undermines the suggestion of an intentional and meaningful chiasm. We freely acknowledge that in verse 5b 'night' is spatial rather than temporal, basically synonymous with 'darkness', referring to the realm of evil and opposition to God. Nevertheless, 'day' has otherwise consistently borne a temporal sense and hence is not necessarily synonymous with 'light' in this context. (d) In view of the facts that Paul has announced that this section (5:1–11) relates to the times and the seasons of the future Day of the Lord, and that both the preceding (verses 1–4) and succeeding (verses 8b–10) context relate to the final ἡμέρα (cf. Rom. 13:12 and possibly verse 13 also, although 'day' there may be spatial), it seems likely that 'sons of (the) day' refers to those who 'belong to, are inheritors of, and are destined for the eschatological day to come',[41] that is, the Day *qua* salvation. By means of πάντες Paul reveals his concern that none of the community members should think of themselves as exceptions to this rule (cf. 5:27).

Having emphasised the Thessalonians' status and destiny in positive terms in verse 5a, Paul proceeds to restate the same fundamental points in negative terms in verse 5b: (3) οὐκ ἐσμὲν νυκτός (4) οὐδὲ σκότους. Verse 7 almost certainly has metaphorical as well as literal significance, since it grounds verse 6's exhortation; if so, that strongly favours the proposal that νύξ in verse 5b is spatial rather than temporal (unlike Rom. 13:11–14). Probably it recalls the 'thief-*in-the-night*' simile of verse 2, picking up on its spatial aspect. Here in verse 5b the Thessalonian Christians are not 'of the night' in that they do not belong to the dominion of evil and enmity with God. Neither are the believers in Thessalonica 'of the darkness', which has essentially the same meaning as 'of the night'. By means of the notable shift from the second-person plural to the associative first-person plural in verse 5b Paul unites the missionaries with the Thessalonian community with regard to status, presumably primarily to reinforce the confirmation of verse 5b and secondarily to prepare for and soften the exhortation of verses 6–8.

---

[41] E. Lövestam, *Spiritual Wakefulness in the New Testament* (trans. W. F. Salisbury; LUÅ; Lund: Gleerup, 1963), 52–3.

The primary purpose of verse 5 is revealed in the γάρ: because the Thessalonian Christians are sons of light and of the Day and are not of the night or of darkness, they can be sure that they are not 'in the darkness' or 'in the night' and hence that the Day will not overtake them as a thief. That is, because they exist in the realm of God and his salvation and their destiny is to inherit the Day and because they do not belong to the realm of evil and Satan, they will not be unexpectedly destroyed.

The striking repetition within verses 4–5 reveals how important the message of reassurance is for the readers: they are not destined to become victims of the Day of the Lord's wrath. It is a crucial mistake to reduce verses 4–5's function to that of bridging the answer to the Thessalonian question in verses 1–3 and the exhortation of verses 6–8[42] or to view verses 4–5 as the commencement of the paraenesis.[43] The emphatic nature of verses 4–5 suggests that these are important verses if we seek to discover the intention of verses 1–11. This is confirmed by verses 9–10, where the same essential point is repeated: the Thessalonian believers are destined not to wrath but to the receiving of salvation. Jurgensen proposes that the apostle in verses 4–5 is simply diverting attention away from speculations regarding the date of the eschaton.[44] However, verses 4–5 are inextricably linked with verses 1–3 and indeed function as their climax, and so necessarily constitute part of Paul's response to the community's question about the times and the seasons, specifically the Day of the Lord *qua* wrath. Hence it seems that behind the Thessalonians' question stands a fear or anxiety that the Day of the Lord would come with sudden destruction upon them. We shall explore this further below.

The significance of 5:6–8

By means of ἄρα οὖν Paul moves on in verses 6–7 to dispatch somewhat general paraenesis based on the assurances of verse 5, perhaps most especially verse 5b, since it, like verse 6, is first-person plural (cf. Gal. 6:10; 2 Thess. 2:15). Paul's imperatives issue from his indicatives: the believers should walk in a manner consistent with who they are. First, since they are not 'in night' or 'in darkness', he exhorts them not to sleep (μὴ καθεύδωμεν) as 'the others' (ὡς οἱ λοιποί (cf. 1 Thess. 4:13), unbelievers). 'Sleep' probably refers to living in moral and spiritual disengagement, which is understandable for unbelievers since they exist in 'night' and

---

[42] So Best, *Thessalonians*, 211.

[43] So Hartman, *Prophecy Interpreted*, 191; Herman, '1 Ts 4,13–5,11', 341 and Wanamaker, *Thessalonians*, 181; cf. Still, 'Eschatology', 199.

[44] So Jurgensen, 'Awaiting', 98.

'darkness', the realm of evil and Satan, but which is not acceptable for the Thessalonian converts since they do not exist in these spheres. Some have suggested that by the concept of 'sleep' here Paul intends to imply living without a consciousness of the coming Day *qua* judgment[45] and/or living in false security,[46] supposing that Paul still has in mind the thief image of verses 2 and 4.[47] However, given that verses 6–7 are rooted in verse 5, especially verse 5b, and that verse 8 explicitly builds on verse 5a, such a proposal is uncompelling. Moreover, the claim of Marshall and Weatherly that Paul is exhorting the Thessalonian converts to be ready so that they are not taken unawares and so disqualified[48] is somewhat difficult to reconcile with the remarkably unqualified and categorical assurances in verses 4–5, 8a and 9–10 that all of the converts *will* definitely be saved on the Day of the Lord. In this section the motivation for obedience is not fear of judgment, but certainty of eschatological status. To the degree that the Day of the Lord is a motivation, it is that they are to live in the light of the Day *qua* salvation, not the Day *qua* judgment.

Instead of 'sleeping', Christians must be 'awake' (γρηγορῶμεν) and 'sober' (νήφωμεν). The former, as the opposite of 'sleep', probably refers to moral and spiritual engagement.[49] The latter probably refers to moral self-control and restraint.[50] In verse 7 Paul justifies his metaphorical exhortation of verse 6 with reference to literal reality: sleeping and drunkenness in the literal world are activities of the night. He implies that the same is true metaphorically: 'sleep' (living disengaged morally and spiritually) and drunkenness (indulgence in 'works of darkness' (cf. Rom. 13:12–13) or moral dissipation) characterise those who exist 'at night', in the sphere of evil. Hence it seems that verse 7 functions as an indirect exhortation.

In opposition to 'the others' described in verses 6–7, Paul contrasts (δέ) the Thessalonian Christians (ὑμεῖς): reiterating the essential point of verse 5a, he emphasises that they are 'of the Day', that is, they belong to the eschatological Day *qua* salvation. On this basis, he again exhorts them to 'be sober (νήφωμεν), putting on (ἐνδυσάμενοι) the breastplate of faith and

---

[45] *Inter alios* Best, *Thessalonians*, 211; Wanamaker, *Thessalonians*, 184; Martin, *Thessalonians*, 164.

[46] *Inter alios* Whiteley, *Thessalonians*, 78 and Best, *Thessalonians*, 211.

[47] The connection is most explicit in Bruce, *Thessalonians*, 111 and Best, *Thessalonians*, 211.

[48] Marshall, *Thessalonians*, 137; J. Weatherly, *1 & 2 Thessalonians* (CPNIVC; Joplin, Mo.: College Press, 1996), 173–4.

[49] Jurgensen, 'Awaiting', 100 seems to miss the point completely when he maintains that γρηγορέω refers to 'anxious waiting'.

[50] Findlay, *Epistles of Paul*, 114 and Best, *Thessalonians*, 212 have claimed without foundation that it is designed to challenge eschatological excitement.

love and the helmet of the hope of salvation'. Although some advocate giving νήφωμεν a meaning distinct from that in verse 6 on the supposition that ἐνδυσάμενοι is a participle of means/manner[51] or identical action,[52] that seems unnecessary since νήφωμεν can keep the same sense as in verse 6 if the participle is understood to be coordinate with it. Wanamaker has countered this proposal by claiming that aorist participles must refer to action prior to that of the main verb,[53] and some have even suggested that it must refer to an already past action such as baptism.[54] However, that aorist participles refer to prior action is not a hard and fast rule, as Acts 23:17; 25:13 and Heb. 9:12 demonstrate.[55] Hence it is probably best to read 'be sober and put on . . .'.

The participial clause undoubtedly alludes to LXX Isa. 59:17, where Yahweh is portrayed as a warrior wearing armour. However, here it is the Thessalonian believers who are called to wear Yahweh's armour. Yahweh's armour is the only suitable attire for those who will participate alongside the Lord, the divine warrior, when he comes to the earth to judge; hence the basis for the exhortation is ἡμεῖς δὲ ἡμέρας ὄντες. It is also important to note that Paul has modified LXX Isa. 59:17 by replacing 'righteousness' with 'faith and love' (the breastplate), and adding 'hope of' to 'salvation' (the helmet). So the armour appropriate for those participating as fellow-warriors of Yahweh on the Day of the Lord, and in the present age, consists of the familiar early Christian triad of faith, love and hope (which in 1 Cor. 13:13 Paul insists 'abide forever' (μένει), that is, beyond the coming of τὸ τέλειον (i.e. the parousia)). Together they represent for Paul the essence of eschatological existence, life in the light (cf. ἡ δὲ ἡμέρα ἤγγικεν . . . ἐνδυσώμεθα [δὲ] τὰ ὅπλα τοῦ φωτός, Rom. 13:12).[56] Therefore verse 8 accords well with verses 6–7: here as there the readers are to live in accord with their assured eschatological status. Moreover, as we noted in regard to verse 6 above, it is illegitimate to suppose that the purpose of donning the armour of verse 8b is that the Day *qua* judgment may not surprise them.[57]

---

[51] Findlay, *Epistles of Paul*, 114; Milligan, *Thessalonians*, 68.

[52] Frame, *Thessalonians*, 187; Best, *Thessalonians*, 215.

[53] Wanamaker, *Thessalonians*, 185; cf. R. A. Ward, *Commentary on 1 and 2 Thessalonians* (Waco: Word, 1973), 112; Richard, *Thessalonians*, 254–5.

[54] For example, Selwyn, *First Epistle*, 375–82; Richard, *Thessalonians*, 254; Yoder Neufeld, *'Armour of God'*, 90 n. 58.

[55] See S. Porter, *Verbal Aspect in the Greek of the New Testament, with Reference to Tense and Mood* (SBG; New York: Peter Lang, 1989), 385–7.

[56] It seems that 'the virtues as a whole correspond to the armour as a whole' (Whiteley, *Thessalonians*, 79), although hope as a helmet, protecting the head, is notably apropos.

[57] *Pace* Best, *Thessalonians*, 215.

In view of the addition of ἐλπίς ('hope', here 'confident expectation') and the usage of σωτηρία in the following verse, σωτηρία in verse 8 undoubtedly refers to future salvation inherited at the eschaton (cf. Rom. 13:11). The fact that Paul builds verses 9–10 upon this last piece of the armour (as we shall demonstrate below) suggests that it has a special significance in this context. Paul apparently thinks that it is particularly urgent that the Thessalonians live with hope in their salvation at the parousia. This reinforces the impression created by verses 2–5 that hope is an especial need of the converts.

This raises the question of what verses 6–8 as a whole indicate about the situation of the Thessalonian community. Some, especially those who see verses 6–8 as representing the essence of Paul's purpose in this section,[58] interpret each of the exhortations as a window on the specific Thessalonian situation. It is therefore variously proposed by scholars that verses 6–8 assume Thessalonian ignorance and indifference with regard to the eschaton, spurred on by parousia delay,[59] or a false sense of security induced by an over-realised eschatology[60] or an over-excited futurist eschatology.[61] However, even when we presume that verses 6–8 closely reflect the concrete situation of the community (we shall discuss this matter below), these hypotheses are found wanting. By grounding the exhortation in their eschatological identity (ἄρα οὖν, verse 6; ἡμεῖς δὲ ἡμέρας ὄντες, verse 8a), employing the hortatory subjunctive, explicitly distinguishing the readers from unbelievers (ὡς οἱ λοιποί, verse 6), urging them to live with hope in their eschatological salvation (verse 8b), and avoiding scrupulously even the appearance of threat or warning,[62] Paul indicates that his paraenesis is not to be construed as condemnatory or confrontational, which is difficult to imagine if he is responding to indifference or false security.

The function of 5:9–10

In the light of the fact that verses 9–10 relate to the objective hope of the converts whereas the exhortation to put on the helmet of hope in eschatological salvation (verse 8b) relates to the converts' experience of

---

[58] So *inter alios* Kümmel, *Introduction*, 256; Burkeen, 'Parousia', 156; Plevnik, '1 Thess 5, 1–11', 78; Wanamaker, *Thessalonians*, 146.

[59] Burkeen, 'Parousia', 145, 167; cf. Friedrich, '1 Thessalonicher 5, 1–11', 290.

[60] Jewett, 'Radicalism', 202 and *Correspondence*, 97; R. W. Stacy, 'Introduction to the Thessalonian Correspondence', *RevExp* 96 (1999): 187.

[61] Jurgensen, 'Awaiting', 112.

[62] The idea that verses 6–8 are a warning intended to induce urgency in the converts has been advanced by, *inter alios*, Whiteley, *Thessalonians*, 76ff. and Rigaux, 'Tradition', 321.

hope, and in view of the observation that the grounds of the exhortations of verses 6–7 and verse 8 have already been stated, it seems more natural to interpret verse 9's ὅτι as introducing the grounds of the specific exhortation to don the helmet of hope than the reason for the paraenesis of verses 6–8. Paul calls upon the Thessalonians to hope in their future salvation at the eschaton because God has not 'elected' (or 'predestined', ἔθετο) them to eschatological wrath (οὐκ . . . εἰς ὀργήν; cf. 1:10; 5:2–4) but rather to the περιποίησιν σωτηρίας.

Scholars are divided regarding whether περιποίησις here implies active human effort and so should be rendered 'acquiring' or does not imply human activity and so should be translated 'reception' or 'possession' (cf. 2 Thess. 2:14; 1 Pet. 2:9; LXX Mal. 3:17). Is Paul suggesting that the converts must persevere in order to be saved or is he stating *carte blanche* that they will receive salvation? The past couple of decades have seen a debate on this issue between Marshall, who has been a proponent of the former position, and Gundry-Volf, who has argued for the latter. In his 1983 commentary[63] Marshall acknowledged that the more common meaning of περιποίησις is 'possession', but insisted that Paul wished to 'bring out the need for Christians to play their part in receiving salvation. One might say that God's plan is that the readers should do what is necessary to acquire salvation.' He appealed to 'Paul's exhortations to vigilance' as evidence that Paul viewed the περιποίησις as embracing fallible human involvement.

In a published Tübingen thesis, Gundry-Volf responded to (*inter alios*) Marshall by (1) arguing that verses 4–5 and 8a suggest that περιποίησις here is a *nomen actionis* with a passive subject, as in Eph. 1:14; (2) pointing out that the immediately preceding context (οὐκ ἔθετο ἡμᾶς ὁ θεὸς εἰς ὀργήν) relates to divine rather than human action; (3) suggesting that Marshall is inconsistent since he also recognises that the following διὰ τοῦ κυρίου ἡμῶν Ἰησοῦ Χριστοῦ stresses that salvation depends solely on what Jesus has done; (4) insisting that verses 6–8 do not imply human activity toward the acquisition of salvation, but rather 'passive attentiveness in expectation of receiving salvation as a gift'. 'In summary, contextual considerations strongly discourage us from reading human effort into the term περιποίησις in 1 Thess. 5:9. The subject of this *nomen actionis* remains passive in their obtaining, for the obtaining is made possible through the effort of their Savior.'[64] Her case seems to be rather compelling.

[63] Marshall, *Thessalonians*, 139–40.
[64] J. M. Gundry-Volf, *Paul and Perseverance* (Louisville, Ky.: Westminster/John Knox, 1990), 21–7.

Marshall rejoined to Gundry-Volf's case in a paper published in 1990, asserting that what we have in 1 Thess. 5:9 is God *wishing* to see the Thessalonians saved, not actually bringing it about.[65] He argued that: (1) there is no evidence in the verse that the will of God will inevitably be accomplished; (2) 5:11 indicates that the purpose of God is achieved partly in and through human cooperation; (3) the idea that God will make obedient those whom he elects is absent from Paul's writings; (4) if the destiny of the salvation-bound is not contingent on free human response, that would suggest that the same is true of the destiny of the wrath-bound, but that idea is unsubstantiated in the Pauline corpus. According to Marshall, the onus is now on the Thessalonians to 'trust in [God]' and 'remain faithful and watchful'.[66]

So what do we make of Marshall's rejoinder? Without entering into the complexities of the broader *theological* issue, we venture to make the following comments. Concerning (1), contextual evidence that the elective will of God will certainly be accomplished may be found in 5:4–5, 10 and 24. With regard to (2) and (3), 5:11 is hardly evidence that in verse 9 Paul is conceiving of the purpose of God as contingent on human obedience; it simply indicates that the Thessalonian Christians should use the contents of 4:13–5:10, including 5:9, to encourage and edify one another. The New Covenant promise of Ezek. 36:26–7, so central to Paul's theology (see 1 Thess. 4:8; 2 Cor. 3:1–6; Gal. 5:16–25), suggests that God does effect obedience in his elected people by his Spirit.[67] Paul in Rom. 8:4 explicitly states that it is by the Spirit that Christians fulfil the righteous requirement of the Law. While it is true to say that the election of God to salvation is contingent upon human response, it may perhaps be truer to say that it is conditional upon a divinely effected human response (Rom. 8:1–9). Consequently Paul could say simply that believers, whose conversion attests to a call and hence election, have been elected to 'receive salvation', without feeling obligated to highlight the necessity of human cooperation. With respect to objection (4), according to Paul, the destiny of the wrath-bound is clearly contingent upon human rebellion, but upon human rebellion determined by divine 'handings over' (Rom. 1:18–32; cf. 2 Thess. 2:3–12) and divine 'hardenings' (Rom. 9:13–18; 11:7–10) and by a lack of the Spirit's resources to obey God's will (Gal. 5:17–21; cf. Rom. 7:13–25).

We conclude then with Gundry-Volf that Paul in 1 Thess. 5:9 is making an objective pronouncement regarding the assured destiny of the

[65] Marshall, 'Election', 266–9.   [66] Ibid., 269.
[67] See Fee, *Empowering*, 843–5 for a statement of the importance of these verses in Paul's thought.

Thessalonian converts: God has destined them to receive salvation (i.e. to be saved) rather than wrath at the eschaton.

This salvation is received διὰ τοῦ κυρίου ἡμῶν Ἰησοῦ Χριστοῦ, through the agency of Christ at his parousia, who died for (ὑπέρ) 'us'. Christ's death is the foundation of the Thessalonians' and all Christians' hope of eschatological salvation. The purpose (and result) of Christ's death on the believer's behalf is that 'whether we are awake (γρηγορῶμεν) or asleep (καθεύδωμεν), we may live together with him'. In view of verse 6, where γρηγορέω and καθεύδω are used ethically, a number of scholars have suggested that Paul is referring to holiness and unholiness: hence 'whether we are holy or unholy . . .'.[68] However, this reading is thoroughly incompatible with the logic of verses 2–8 and indeed more generally with Pauline soteriology. In the light of 4:13–18, it is likely that Paul is employing the language of sleep (κοιμάω there) to refer to the dead Christians in Thessalonica. The particular verb καθεύδω is used similarly in LXX Dan. 12:2 and Ps. 87:6, and it may well be that Paul's language is dependent on the former text, since there we also find ζάω employed of the eschatological destiny of believers. Hence it seems that καθεύδωμεν alludes to 1 Thess. 4:13–18 and the problem underlying it; it is worth noting that Christ's death and resurrection are the key to the problem underlying those verses, as here. 1 Thess. 5:10 then concludes 4:13ff. Who then are the living? We suggest that they must be those addressed in 5:1–11, who are also mentioned in 4:15b and 17a. Therefore it is unnecessary to interpret 5:10 as reflecting Paul's uncertainty about whether he would be alive or dead at the eschaton, as many do.[69]

Whether alive (i.e. the missionaries and the addressed community) or dead (i.e. the 'sleeping' of 4:13), Christians will 'live together with him' (ἅμα σὺν αὐτῷ ζήσωμεν). The use of the aorist subjunctive rather than the future indicative has led some to question whether Paul has future life in mind here and to wonder if in fact he does not simply have present life in view. However, in the light of the fact that ἅμα σύν (here almost certainly not meaning 'simultaneously with',[70] but simply 'together with') occurs in regard to Christ in 4:14 and 17, the possible dependence on LXX Dan. 12:2 and the point that the aorist subjunctive frequently has a futuristic or

---

[68] So Kaye, 'Eschatology', 51–2, esp. n. 27; R. L. Thomas, 'I and II Thessalonians', in *EBC*, 11:285–6; T. R. Edgar, 'The Meaning of "Sleep" in I Thessalonians 5:10', *JETS* 22 (1979): 345–9; Yoder Neufeld, *'Armour of God'*, 89–90, esp. n. 53; Koester, 'Schemata', 453; M. Lautenschlage, 'Εἴτε γρηγορῶμεν εἴτε καθεύδωμεν. Zum Verhältnis von Heilgung und Heil in 1 Thess. 5,10', *ZNW* 81 (1990): 39–59.

[69] For example, Moore, *Thessalonians*, 78.

[70] *Pace* Rigaux, *Thessaloniciens*, 573; Best, *Thessalonians*, 218.

potential sense, it is preferable to interpret 'life' here as eschatological. Living and dead Christians (at the parousia of Christ) will have eternal fellowship with Christ.

So, what is the function of verses 9–10? Contrary to Richard, who has detected an 'indirect, but clear warning' in οὐκ . . . εἰς ὀργήν in verse 9, we suggest that verses 9–10 are thoroughly affirmative and reassuring. First, verse 9 grounds the call for the converts to live in hope of eschatological salvation in the objective fact of divine election to salvation through Christ (which is itself rooted in the fact of Christ's death (5:10a)) rather than to wrath (note that the certainty regarding election has been grounded in an assurance concerning the authenticity of the converts' reception of the word and the missionaries' ministry in 1:4–2:16). This is strikingly reminiscent of 5:2–5, but stripped of the thief and night–day/light–darkness imagery. The converts can be assured that at the eschaton they will not face wrath, but rather salvation. In verse 10, Paul insists that Christ died for 'us' so that both living and dead Christians might have life with Christ. This verse functions to encapsulate the message of 4:13ff. and 5:1ff.: both the community members and their dead will have the supreme reward of life with Christ. Concerning verse 9, one might quote Calvin: 'There is no better assurance of salvation to be found anywhere than can be gained from the decree of God.'[71] Concerning verse 10, one might add: for early Christians there was no more solid rock upon which to build assurance than the death and resurrection of Christ.

Paul closes 4:13–5:11 with an exhortation to 'encourage one another' and 'build each other up', presumably with the content of 4:13–5:10, which is encapsulated in 5:10.[72] Here, as elsewhere, he avoids the appearance of criticism by acknowledging that the readers are already encouraging and edifying one another, although doubtless not with full knowledge of the teaching in 4:13–5:11.

The function of 5:1–11

First, we shall overview the content of 5:1–11. The Thessalonians have asked a question relating to 'the times and seasons' of the Day of the

[71] John Calvin, *The Epistles of Paul the Apostle to the Romans and to the Thessalonians* (ed. D. W. and T. F. Torrance; trans. R. MacKenzie; CC; Edinburgh: Oliver and Boyd, 1961), 370.
[72] *Contra* Wanamaker, *Thessalonians*, 189, who contends that Paul is picking up on the need for vigilance because the Day is coming as a thief in the night. As we have seen above and shall see below, the predominant thought is that the converts can be assured that they will be not be overtaken as a thief, but rather will be saved at the eschaton.

Lord *qua* wrath (verses 1–2). Paul insists that the Thessalonians are already familiar with the key to the answer to their question: the Day of the Lord (*sc. qua* wrath) comes like a thief in the night (verse 2). Paul explicates the thief-in-the-night image in verse 3, deriving from it that the Day's sudden, unexpected and inescapable destruction (the 'thief' dimension) comes at the moment when 'they' are living in supremely false security (the 'in-the-night' dimension). Thereby Paul has indicated the timing of the Day, while simultaneously focusing attention on the sphere of existence of its victims. In verse 4 Paul applies the thief-in-the-night concept to the Thessalonian community: since they are not 'in the darkness' (i.e. 'in the night'), they can be assured that the Day *qua* destruction will not overtake them as a 'thief'. Paul emphatically grounds this assurance regarding their destiny on the Day of the Lord in a series of brief pronouncements: they are 'sons of (the) light' (i.e. they exist in the realm of God and salvation) and 'sons of (the) Day' (i.e. they are destined to inherit the Day *qua* salvation); they ('we') are not 'of night' or 'of darkness' (i.e. they do not belong to the realm of evil and Satan). The thrust of verses 1–5 suggests therefore that Paul is reassuring the community members that they should not dread sudden destruction on the Day of the Lord.

In verse 6 Paul calls for the Thessalonians to walk in accordance with their assured eschatological status. They are to be 'awake' (i.e. morally and spiritually engaged) and 'sober' (i.e. ethically self-controlled): as those who do not belong to darkness they must put off the deeds of darkness. Verse 7 roots this exhortation in an observation of the literal world: just as moral sleep and ethical drunkenness belong to the realm of 'darkness', so literal sleep and drunkenness are characteristic of night-time. Then in verse 8 he reiterates the fact that the converts' destiny is the Day *qua* salvation and upon this basis calls for 'soberness' (i.e. ethical self-control) and for the donning of the armour appropriate for those who will participate in the Day of the Lord: faith, love and especially hope. They are to live in the light of who they are and who they will be.

Paul in verse 9 establishes his call for the Thessalonians to hope in eschatological salvation in the objective fact that God has destined them to receive future salvation rather than wrath at the eschaton, on the basis of Christ's death on their behalf. Then, summarising the essence of 5:1–11 and 4:13–18, he asserts that the living and the dead in Christ will, by virtue of Christ's death, enjoy eternal fellowship with Christ (5:10). As in verses 1–5, the function is clearly reassurance: their destiny is not one of destruction, but, on the contrary, salvation and all that it implies.

Verse 11 indicates that the purpose of 5:1–11 has been encouragement and edification.[73]

Were the Thessalonian converts over-excited?

Jurgensen represents a number of scholars who understand the problem presupposed by 5:1–11 to be 'eschatological over-excitement' manifesting itself in speculative preoccupation regarding the exact timing of the parousia.[74] According to this reading, Paul perceives in their fervour a false sense of security and warns that eschatological speculations will lead to the Day of the Lord's wrath coming upon them. However, this hypothesis cannot be substantiated. The section is strikingly devoid of warning and threat for believers; indeed, the apostle specifically disavows the possibility that the Day *qua* wrath might come upon the converts (verses 2–4) and could hardly have been more categorically reassuring regarding the salvific eschatological destiny of his readers (verses 5, 8–10).

Do 5:1–11 reflect a concrete situation?

Various scholars have proposed that this section is generic Pauline eschatological exposition rather than situationally specific.[75] Moore, for example, writes, 'There is no suggestion . . . of a crisis in the church, nor even of a problem, but Paul would be aware of the constant need under any circumstances for exhortation and pastoral care if slackness and apostasy were to be avoided.'[76]

However, there are indications that this section presupposes a concrete situation in Thessalonica. First, as we noted above, there is good reason to think that Paul is responding to a specific Thessalonian question. That he insists in verses 1–2 that the readers already know the answer to their own question in the form of the thief-in-the-night simile does not mean

---

[73] In the light of our analysis of 5:1–11, it seems misguided to interpret this section as primarily functioning to (re-)instil a sense of the parousia's imminence (*pace* ibid., 62, 177) or as a call for watchfulness or readiness (*pace*, for example, Kümmel, *Introduction*, 256; Wanamaker, *Thessalonians*, 146, 176–7, 189 and Jurgensen, 'Awaiting', 97). The message of 5:1–11 is not 'since the parousia's time is uncertain, believers must watch and be prepared' (*pace*, e.g., Hartman, *Prophecy Interpreted*, 190–1; H. Giesen, *Studien zum Neuen Testament und seiner Umwelt* (Linz, Austria: Fuchs, 1985), 145–6 and R. E. Brown, *An Introduction to the New Testament* (ABRL; Garden City, N.Y.: Doubleday, 1997), 462), for the paraenesis is not rooted in uncertainty regarding the parousia's time.

[74] Jurgensen, 'Awaiting', 95, 96–7, 111–12.

[75] For example, Marxsen, *Erste Brief*, 65, 68; Koester, 'Schemata', 448 and Weatherly, *Thessalonians*, 163.

[76] Moore, *Thessalonians*, 72.

that what follows is irrelevant to their question; on the contrary, Paul is explicitly addressing their question in the subsequent verses, as verse 3's ὅταν . . . τότε demonstrates, explicating the familiar thief motif and applying it to them. Second, the rarity of references to eschatological wrath in Paul's letters, together with the repetition and emphasis of the reassurances that the readers are not destined to wrath, suggests that Paul is confronting a specific problem (verses 4–5 and 9–10). There are actually *eight* explicit reassurances regarding the Thessalonians' status and destiny: verses 4, 5 (4x), 8a, 9, 10.[77] Third, 5:10's εἴτε γρηγορῶμεν εἴτε καθεύδωμεν unites 5:1–11 with the concrete situation underlying 4:13–18, thus suggesting that the concern of 5:1–11 is linked to that of 4:13–18, and is related to the fate of the surviving community members at the eschaton, just as 4:13–18 is related to the fate of the dead. Therefore there is good reason to think that underlying 5:1–5 and 9–11 is a concrete problem consisting of a lack of assurance of salvation. To what extent 5:6–8 are undergirded by a concrete Thessalonian problem is the issue to which we turn next.

Do 5:6–8 elucidate the specific situation of the Thessalonian church?

Why does Paul shift from reassuring the community to issuing paraenesis in verses 6–8? Are Paul's exhortations not to sleep but to be awake and sober (verse 6) and to be sober and don the armour of faith, love and hope (verse 8) indicative of the fact that he is now turning to address specific Thessalonian problems? The established tendency of Paul to transfer from the indicative to the imperative, and the naturalness of the transition from talk of day and night to paraenesis communicated in terms of light and darkness, as exemplified by Rom. 13:11–14, may suggest that verses 6–8 are not as situationally specific as the rest of the section. Indeed, in Rom. 13:12 we find a command to put off 'works of darkness', which is clearly the equivalent of metaphorical 'sleep' and 'drunkenness' (1 Thess. 5:6–7), and an exhortation to put on 'the armour of light', which is very similar to what we see in 1 Thess. 5:8. Hence the language of 'sleep'/'awake'

---

[77] Indeed, according to our reading of 5:1–11, verses 1–3 are the nutshell of reassurance: by defining the objects of divine wrath as 'in the night' and those living in false security, they function to indicate that the community is safe. Moreover, the call to don the armour of Yahweh (verse 8b) strikingly and reassuringly assumes that the converts have the right to wear it: only those eschatologically identified with the Lord are entitled to wear this armour. And verse 6's ὡς οἱ λοιποί is reaffirming in that it draws a fundamental distinction between the converts and the unbelieving world.

and 'drunk'/'sober' in 5:6–8 and the call to don armour in verse 8b look rather more general than situationally specific. Of course, it is possible that by means of this generic exhortation Paul is reinforcing his earlier attack on 'dark' features of community life (moral slackness and lack of self-control) that do not accord with the eschatological status and destiny of the community (cf. 4:6b–8).[78] Nevertheless, the idea that he is tackling community indifference or false security is implausible; the very fact that the community have raised the question concerning the Day's timing surely eliminates such hypotheses. By contrast, the stress on hoping in salvation in verse 8c would suggest insecurity and lack of hope. In view of how verses 9–10 build on verse 8c and in view of the preceding context (verses 2–5), it is probably wise to take seriously the possibility that the exhortation to put on the helmet of the hope of salvation is situationally specific, and indeed that it reveals why Paul is reassuring the community regarding their destiny: to ignite within them an experiential hope that they will be saved at the eschaton.

We conclude, then, that the safest places to look for situationally specific information seem to be in verses 1–5 and 8c–11, which are strikingly reassuring in function. Verses 6–8b do not constitute the essence of verses 1–11.[79] It is now necessary to examine the most important scholarly suggestions regarding why Paul might have needed to reassure his converts.

Was the delay of the parousia a factor in the problem?

A significant section of scholarship has explained the Thessalonians' concern about the parousia's timing with reference to the perceived delay of the parousia.[80] It has been proposed that the converts are troubled that the parousia has not yet come,[81] perhaps even wondering if it will ever happen,[82] or that their anxiety centres around the possibility of further deaths in the community because of the parousia's delay.[83] However,

[78] If the situation is one of overwhelmed fear and anxiety (as will be argued below), verses 6–8 may be intended to offset any ethical slackness which might conceivably emanate from this.

[79] *Contra* Plevnik, '1 Thess 5, 1–11', 78, 89 and *Parousia*, 100.

[80] For example, Bailey, 'Who?', 137; Burkeen, 'Parousia', 145, 157.

[81] Laub, *Verkündigung*, 132, 133; Thomas, 'Thessalonians', 280; Best, *Thessalonians*, 203, 208; Collins, *Letters*, 221.

[82] Bailey, 'Who?', 137.

[83] Findlay, *Epistles of Paul*, 106; Milligan, *Thessalonians*, 63; Laub, *Verkündigung*, 124, 131–3 and *Thessalonicherbrief*, 30; Best, *Thessalonians*, 203; Morris, *Epistles*, 149–50; Richard, *Thessalonians*, 249; cf. Marxsen, *Erste Brief*, 65.

as Koester has pointed out, a church which has been in existence for
only a few months is unlikely to be having problems with the delay of
the parousia.[84] Moreover, Paul's reassurances in 5:1–11 do not relate
to the certainty that the parousia would in fact come and come soon,
or the possibility that more may die (5:10's καθεύδωμεν is sufficiently
explained with reference to 4:13–18 alone), but rather to the fact that the
eschaton would be to their advantage rather than disadvantage. Further,
that more than a simple fear of dying is in view is suggested by: (1) the
fact that while in 4:13–18 the Thessalonians seem to have assumed that
the disadvantage of the dead would consist of their missing out on the
parousia, here in 5:1–11 the feared disadvantage apparently consists of
eschatological wrath; and (2) the observation that if the converts had
feared dying, 4:13–18 would have sufficed. The section 5:1–11 relates to
the fate of the living at the eschaton, not whether the converts will die
before it.

Were the Thessalonians worried that they might not be prepared for the Day?

A number of scholars have postulated that the converts were concerned
about their own worthiness to participate in the parousia.[85] According
to Marshall, since they did not know when the eschaton would occur,
they feared that they might not be morally and spiritually prepared for it
and so might be counted unworthy to be summoned to meet the Lord.[86]
However, if indeed the converts were so scrupulous and conscientious
about morality, we would not have expected the severe sanction of 4:6b–
8, the tone of which contrasts markedly with 5:1–11. Furthermore, it is
notable that the section on holiness, 4:1–8, which may well indicate that
this community was experiencing problems adjusting to the high ethical
standards of the Christian faith, seems to have issued from a concern of
Paul (following on the heels of his pastoral prayer of 3:13 as it does) rather
than from a concern of his converts, and is completely unrelated to the
eschatological material in 4:13–5:11. And the only reference to holiness
in 5:1–11 is found in the paraenesis of verses 6–8, which, as we observed
above, also seems to reflect *Paul's* concern more than the converts'. There
is in 1 Thessalonians no evidence that holiness was an exceptionally

---

[84] H. Koester, *Introduction to the New Testament* (FF; Philadelphia: Fortress, 1982),
2:113–14.

[85] For example, Frame, *Thessalonians*, 178; J. Stott, *The Message of the Thessalonians*
(BST; Leicester: IVP, 1991), 107; Holmes, *Thessalonians*, 165.

[86] Marshall, *Thessalonians*, 118, 132.

great preoccupation of the neophytes. Finally, this hypothesis does not give adequate explanation of the likelihood that the problems underlying 4:13–18 and 5:1–11 are linked.

The relationship between 4:13–18 and 5:1–11

The use of περὶ δέ in 5:1 and the shift of topic from the fate of the dead vis-à-vis the parousia to the timing of the Day of the Lord *qua* wrath indicates that 5:1ff. is a new section. However, that it is very closely linked with the preceding section 4:13–18 is clear when the following points are taken into consideration. (1) Both relate to the fate of believers at the eschaton and both reflect an 'apocalyptic' conceptual framework; (2) they have a similar structure: the topic statement with ἀδελφοί (4:13; 5:1), the essential reply (4:14; 5:2) and the paraenetic conclusion (4:18; 5:11); (3) 5:10's εἴτε καθεύδωμεν recalls 4:13–18, while εἴτε γρηγορῶμεν seems to allude to the problem underlying 5:1ff.; (4) Jesus' death and resurrection are the basis for confidence regarding eschatological destiny in both (4:14a; 5:9–10); (5) 'being with Christ' is the eschatological goal in both (4:17b; 5:10); (6) both have the same function of reassuring/encouraging the community members (4:18; 5:11), and indeed 5:11 may well function to conclude 4:13ff.[87] Any proposed situational explanation of 5:1–11 must acknowledge its close association with 4:13–18.

A new hypothesis

We saw above that Paul's primary purpose in 5:1–11 is to reassure[88] the community that they are not destined to wrath, but rather to salvation on the Day of the Lord. Behind the section we perceive an anxiety among community members that the Day of the Lord might overtake them with sudden destruction. In the light of our study, we suggest that the Thessalonians' question relates to the timing of the Day *qua* wrath, and that it was underlain by an anxiety or fear that they themselves might be victims of imminent eschatological wrath. We propose that their question might

[87] One might add that unbelievers are referred to as οἱ λοιποί in both (4:13; 5:6) and that ἅμα σύν is found in both (4:17a; 5:10).

[88] Cf. Johanson, *Brethren*, 129–30; Kieffer, 'L'Eschatologie', 216–18. Johanson, *Brethren*, 134 restricts the problem to one of 'incipient doubt'. Plevnik, '1 Thess 5, 1–11', 78–80, 89–90 and *Parousia*, 106ff. acknowledges the importance of reassurance in 5:1–11, although he judges verses 6–8 to be the essence and 'original intention' of the passage ('1 Thess 5, 1–11', 78, 87, 89 and *Parousia*, 100; cf. Harnisch, *Existenz*, 116) and suggests that the reassuring dimension of verses 4–5 and 9–10 may simply be Paul's attempt to counter any misinterpretation of verses 2–3 (Plevnik, *Parousia*, 100, 120).

have been something like 'Is the Day of the Lord about to come upon us?' Acts 1:6–7 make it clear that the expression 'the times and the seasons' can readily accommodate such a question. Our suggestion preserves the time element, while facilitating Paul's subtle shift of focus onto the matter of whether eschatological wrath would fall upon the readers. Moreover, the resultant reading of 5:1–11 is eminently feasible. Paul wants to move his readers from insecurity and fear in the face of God's wrath to security, confidence and strength in the assurance of God's salvation; he wants them to think and live in the light of their *settled* eschatological status and destiny.

It remains to consider *why* the converts are apparently wondering whether God's eschatological wrath might be about to fall on them. In view of the close connection between 4:13–18 and 5:1–11, we suggest that the unexpected deaths may hold the key to the answer.

From 4:13–18 it seems that the deaths had exposed a significant lack in the Thessalonians' eschatology: they had been under the impression that Christians would not die prior to the parousia, probably because the missionaries had failed to pass on the tradition concerning the eschatological resurrection of dead saints and perhaps, secondarily, because, in the light of their ignorance, it seemed to the Thessalonians that the missionaries had implied that the conquering of death by Christ's resurrection meant that death could not seize those in Christ. Consequently, the deaths were the catalyst for a considerable problem which related to the eschaton: in dying, the dead had been placed beyond the pale of parousia salvation. As Paul himself states in 1 Cor. 15:18–19, if there is no hope of an eschatological resurrection of dead saints, believers who have died have in fact perished and Christians are 'of all people most to be pitied'. We suggest that the destructive impact of the deaths on the community's hope could hardly have stopped there. For the deaths would rather inevitably have raised critical questions about the hope of the *entire* community, seeming to raise a question-mark over God's approval of it: if the faith of their brothers, who believed the same Gospel preached by the same missionaries, has proved unacceptable to God (as the deaths seemed to demonstrate), what right do the remaining members of the community have to expect salvation when Christ returns? And if survivors failed to pass God's eschatological test, they could only expect wrath. Since the hope which the Thessalonians had secured at the mission had been an imminentist one, it would make sense that they feared that this divine wrath might come very soon. In addition, one might also point out that the experience of bereavement can at the best of times be a chilling and disturbing challenge to faith. However, to a community lacking the belief in the resurrection of dead saints, the deaths may well have seemed to be hostile divine acts, especially frightening phenomena.

Indeed, we can perhaps propose a stronger link between the deaths and the fear that divine wrath was imminent: Christian deaths without the hope of a resurrection could readily have been perceived as an omen or portent of divine disapproval and imminent disaster. Such an interpretation of the deaths might have seemed particularly plausible to a community primarily consisting of former pagans (cf. 1:9b–10a) in view of the extent (at least *two* members seem to have died) and timing (shortly after their conversion) of the problem.[89] And one can imagine that this understanding of the deaths might have been promoted by any non-Christian friends and family of the deceased and by enemies of the church, both Jews and Gentiles.[90] Indeed, it is not inconceivable that those loyal to the Greco-Roman deities would have been looking for *prodigia* (τέρατα), expecting that their gods would soon express unhappiness concerning the apostasy of those who had converted to the new religious movement in Thessalonica.[91] Particularly in a context of conflict, the deaths might have seemed to demonstrate that the divine realm not only did not approve of the new community, but actually opposed it.

We propose therefore that the Thessalonians may have been inclined to view the deaths as *prodigia* (or 'omens' or 'portents'). Prodigies were essentially divine indications that the *pax deorum* had been disrupted and were warnings of imminent disaster.[92] Usually they consisted of 'striking and unusual phenomena – not necessarily miraculous',[93] such as lightning

---

[89] We simply cannot know whether there was anything unusual about the *manner* of the deaths.

[90] Cf. R. L. Fox, *Pagans and Christians* (Harmondsworth: Viking, 1986), 425–6; Barclay, 'Social Contrasts', 53 and 'Conflict', 515–16; C. S. De Vos, *Church and Community Conflict* (SBLDS; Atlanta: Scholars, 1999), 167.

[91] Tacitus, *Ann.* 15.44 and Pliny, *Ep.* 10.96 believed that Christians were such potential irritants of the gods that it was just to impose severe penalties on them.

[92] For more on prodigies, see R. Bloch, *Les Prodiges dans l'antiquité classique* (Paris: Presses Universitaires de France, 1963); J. H. W. G. Liebeschuetz, *Continuity and Change in Roman Religion* (Oxford: Clarendon, 1979), *passim*, esp. 9–10; B. MacBain, *Prodigy and Expiation* (Brussels: Latomus, 1982); J. North, 'Diviners and Divination at Rome', in *Pagan Priests* (ed. M. Beard and J. North; London: Duckworth, 1990), 54–5; D. S. Levene, *Religion in Livy* (SMBCB; Leiden: Brill, 1993), 17–37; M. Beard, J. North and S. Price, *Religions of Rome* (Cambridge: Cambridge University Press, 1998), 172–5. On prodigies in ancient Greece, see Bloch, *Prodiges*, 9–42. For a list of prodigies in AD 51–2, see Tacitus, *Ann.* 12.43.

[93] Liebeschuetz, *Roman Religion*, 9.

strikes,[94] exceptionally bad weather,[95] fire,[96] pestilence,[97] earthquakes,[98] rain consisting of stones,[99] miscarriages[100] and a statue being blown over by the wind.[101,102] 'It is not always easy to understand why some particular events were seen as prodigies, and others not.'[103] But timing and pre-existing anxiety were among the typical factors. Strikingly for our purposes, there is evidence that deaths could be viewed as *prodigia* (e.g. Livy 41.16.3–5; Obs. 9).[104] Prodigies played an important role in Greco-Roman life. In Republican Rome, when such phenomena were sighted, they were typically reported to the Senate, which consulted diviners to determine which gods were angry and how they might be expiated, and then proceeded to follow their advice carefully.[105] Liebeschuetz makes an interesting observation about this Roman official procedure of dealing with prodigies:[106]

> the institution was employed most intensely when public anxiety was at a peak and reassurance most needed. The ancients were helpless in many situations. Helplessness creates tension and fear, and since the world was thought to be governed by supernatural forces the tension took the form of religious fear – in fact it is precisely the situation described by the Latin word *religio*. In the circumstances sensational and dramatic ritual measures might bring relief . . . The combination of massive sacrifices, processions, and vows must have made a deep impression; something was being done. This would calm the emotions, reduce defeatism, and obviate the search for scapegoats.

---

[94] E.g. Livy 10.31.8; 22.1.8–20; 25.7.7–8; 42.2.3–7; Obs. 37; 56b.
[95] E.g. Horace 1.1.25–30 and 3.6.1–4; Livy 40.2.1–4; Obs. 5.   [96] E.g. Livy 22.1.8ff.
[97] E.g. Livy 38.44.7; 40.36.14–37.1.   [98] E.g. Livy 34.55; 41.28.2; Obs. 54.
[99] E.g. Livy 22.1.9, 36.7; 29.10.4–5, 14.5–14.
[100] Plutarch, *Public.* 21.1.   [101] Obs. 18.
[102] See MacBain, *Prodigy*, 82–106 for an extensive list of prodigies.
[103] Beard, North and Price, *Religions*, 173. Determining what precisely constituted a prodigy was a rather subjective enterprise. Certainly the event had to be distinctive on account of its grotesque, extraordinary or exceptional nature and/or its remarkable timing and/or its location and/or its extent or magnitude. Xenophon, *An.* 3.2.8–9 indicates that even a sneeze could be understood as an omen (in that case, a positive one), largely because of its timing.
[104] Apuleius, *Apol.* 92.8 indicates that a woman whose husband has died could be regarded as a person of ill omen (see Liebeschuetz, *Roman Religion*, 218).
[105] See Liebeschuetz, *passim*. On expiation, see especially F. Luterbacher, *Der Prodigien-glaube und Prodigienstil der Römer* (reprint of 2nd edn; Darmstadt: Wissenschaftliche Buchgesellschaft, 1967), 33–43; P. Händel, 'Prodigium', in *Realencyclopädie der classischen Altertumswissenschaft* (ed. A. F. von Pauly and G. Wissowa; Stuttgart: Druckenmüller, 1959), 23.2:2290–5; MacBain, *Prodigy*, 82–106 and 120–1.
[106] Liebeschuetz, *Roman Religion*, 9–10.

The parallel with the situation of the Thessalonian community as we have read it is striking – note that we concluded from 5:1–11 that its members were fearful and in need of reassurance.

Commenting on the psychological contexts in which prodigies tended to be perceived, Tacitus claimed that they tended to be characteristic of 'times of stress'.[107] Herein lies a further parallel, for the Thessalonian Christian community had clearly been experiencing stressful times. We have reason to think that its members may have felt abandoned on account of the missionaries' premature departure and Paul's failure to return to them (2:17–3:13). And we know that the experience of conversion itself would probably have rendered the (presumably) relatively small number of believers socially lonely and vulnerable, especially in view of the persecution that had plagued the community since its inception (3:3b–4a).[108] In such a context of helplessness, any apparently abnormal event was liable to be interpreted as a *prodigium*, and so might be expected to provoke fear and deep anxiety. Since the deaths had happened within the community, the portent could only have been perceived as negative, seeming to spell imminent disaster. As the Thessalonians had apparently been expectantly awaiting the imminent dawning of the eschatological Day of the Lord (1:9–10a; cf. verse 3; 4:14b–17), the nature of that disaster would have seemed plain to them: wrath on the Day of the Lord.

There remains the question of how precisely the situation underlying 5:1–11 is related to that underlying 4:13–18. How should the Thessalonians' grief concerning the fate of the dead vis-à-vis the living (4:13–18) be synthesised with our proposal that the survivors believed that their future was uncertain (5:1–11)? Does not 4:15 imply that the Thessalonians have hope for those still alive? We suggest that 4:13–18, on the one hand, assumes merely that the Thessalonian community members have a *belief* that *living Christians* will participate in the joys of the parousia, and that these verses do not presuppose that the believers have a *stable hope* that *they themselves* will enjoy these eschatological blessings. It seems that 5:1–11, on the other hand, does not imply that the Thessalonian believers have abandoned their belief that living Christians will enjoy the parousia's salvific benefits; rather, it seems to assume merely that they have lost hope that they themselves are destined to be recipients of those blessings. In other words, we are proposing that 4:13–18 reflects accurate knowledge

---

[107] See ibid., 195–6.
[108] See especially *inter alios* A. J. Malherbe, *Paul and the Thessalonians* (Philadelphia: Fortress, 1987), 36–52.

of dogma relating to the fate of living Christians at the parousia on the part of the Thessalonians, and 5:1–11 reflects a faulty application of dogma relating to the fate of living Christians at the parousia on the part of the Thessalonians.[109] Of course, it makes good sense for Paul to deal with the error relating to dogma (4:13–18) before dealing with the problem developing from that error (5:1–11).

The hypothesis that the deaths have been perceived to be an omen of imminent disaster and to have given rise to the question 'Is the Day of the Lord about to come?' seems historically plausible; while it may appear foreign to modern minds, it would have been all too real to early Christians, recently converted from first-century paganism. Propitiating the rather capricious Greco-Roman deities[110] had been a constant challenge for those who had previously paid homage to the temperamental pantheon and indeed had become used to interpreting undesirable events as portents of divine disfavour and imminent doom.

---

[109] In addition, 4:17 (a and b) may secondarily function to reassure the community regarding the fate of the living as well as the dead in Christ and hence to anticipate the thrust of 5:1–11. The use of the first-person plural in 4:15–17 unites Paul with the living Thessalonian converts and may be intended to reconfirm the surviving members of the community.

[110] Most religion in first-century Thessalonica was traditionally Greek, with Zeus, Pythian Apollo, Dionysus, Ianus, Nike, Cabirus, Asclepius and Hygeia being prominent. In addition, Egyptian gods seem to have been a notable feature of Thessalonian religious life, athough the fact that the only Thessalonian sanctuary yet discovered is the Serapeum means that we have to be careful not to exaggerate the importance of Egyptian religion in contemporary Thessalonica. The significance of the cult of Cabirus has been greatly overstated by Jewett, *Correspondence*, 127–32; Murphy-O'Connor, *Critical Life*, 118 and Stacy, 'Introduction', 187–8. For more on the predominantly Greek (and Roman) nature of religion at Thessalonica, see C. Edson, 'Cults of Thessalonica', *HTR* 41 (1948): 154–81, 188–204; F. Papazoglou, 'Macedonia under the Romans', in *Macedonia* (ed. M. B. Sakellariou; GLH; Athens: Ektodike Athenon, 1983), 204–5; Hendrix, 'Thessalonicans', 259ff.; J. L. Hill, 'Establishing the Church in Thessalonica' (Ph.D. diss., Duke University, 1990), 60–70; D. W. J. Gill, 'Macedonia', in *The Book of Acts in its Graeco-Roman Setting* (ed. D. Gill and C. H. Gempf; BAFCS; Grand Rapids: Eerdmans, 1994), 408 and De Vos, *Conflict*, 140–3, 176. See the Thessalonian coins listed by B. V. A. Head, *A Catalogue of the Greek Coins in the British Museum* (London: British Museum, 1879) and A. Burnett, M. Amandry and P. P. Ripolles, *Roman Provincial Coinage. Vol. 1: From the Death of Caesar to the Death of Vitellius (44 BC– AD 69)* (London: British Museum, 1992) and those in the Archaeological Museum of Thessalonike, Room 4, Area E, Case 21 (esp. the 'pseudo-autonomous' coins, nos. 22–51). Finds from late Hellenistic and Roman Thessalonica at the Archaeological Museum of Thessalonike suggest the importance of Heracles and Hermes (e.g. Room 4, Area C, Case 18, 9955–7), Aphrodite (e.g. Room 4, Area C, Case 18, 10263, 2931), Eros and Psyche (e.g. Room 4, Area C, Case 18, 10290, 10263, 2930; Case 20, 2449), Dionysus (e.g. Room 4, Area D, 11600), Athena (e.g. Room 4, Area D, 833) and Demeter (e.g. Room 4, Area D, 896). The importance of the Greek deities in Thessalonian religion is evident also in the wall paintings, marble revetments and mosaic floors of Room 4, Area G and Room 6 of the museum. See J. Vokotopoulou, *Guide to the Archaeological Museum of Thessalonike* (Athens: Kapon, 1996), 41–83 on Room 4 and pp. 88–95 on Room 6.

Conclusion

With the ultimate aim of determining whether or not the situations underlying 1 and 2 Thessalonians are compatible, we have been undertaking a situational analysis of 1 Thessalonians. In the previous chapter we concluded that the essential problem underlying 1 Thess. 4:13–18 was that the bereaved Thessalonians, ignorant of the Christian hope of a final resurrection, were grieving hopelessly, fearing that their loved ones would miss out on parousia salvation. We hypothesised there that such a problem might also have undermined their hope for surviving community members. In this chapter we have turned our attention to 5:1–11, arguing that it reveals first that the Thessalonian living were indeed insecure and fearful on their own behalf, anxious that eschatological destruction might suddenly come upon them, and second that their insecurity was likely to be rooted in the recent unexpected bereavements. As regards how the deaths might have given rise to this eschatological anxiety, we have surmised not only that the apparently failed hopes of the dead community members might have led survivors to question the legitimacy of their own right to expect salvation at the imminent parousia, but also that, given the lack of a resurrection hope and the extent and timing of the deaths, the Thessalonian believers might well have interpreted the deaths as a *prodigium*, i.e. omens that divine wrath would fall upon them imminently.

If our reading of the problem is correct and the Thessalonians did feel forced to consider the possibility that God's wrath might not have been successfully assuaged by their conversion to the Gospel of Christ died and risen as preached by the apostle, the resultant problem ('is the community destined to face imminent divine wrath?') would have threatened to unravel their neophyte faith. One would imagine that questions would have quickly surfaced relating to the cause of the divine displeasure: had their conversion been authentic? Had the missionaries preached the true Gospel of God? Were the missionaries, especially the chief figure Paul, authentic representatives of God? Was Paul's absence from them an indication that he was a charlatan or deceiver? With this in mind, let us examine the rest of 1 Thessalonians to see whether and how it confirms and develops or contradicts our reading of the situation in Thessalonica that gave rise to Paul's letter.

4

IN NEED OF REASSURANCE

In our quest to ascertain whether the situations underlying 1 and 2 Thessalonians are compatible, we have first turned our attention to 1 Thessalonians and specifically the eschatological section of the letter, 4:13–5:11. The hypothesis we formulated concerning the eschatological problems underlying 1 Thess. 4:13–5:11 must, of course, satisfactorily accommodate the data from the rest of the letter. In this chapter we shall examine the remainder of 1 Thessalonians to see whether and how it confirms and develops or contradicts our conclusions regarding the situation reflected in 4:13–5:11.

Specific features of the text confirming our hypothesis regarding the eschatological situation

1 Thess. 1:10b and c

In verse 10b and c there is a notable shift from the Greeks' report concerning events at Thessalonica (verses 9–10a) to dogmatic statements relating to the eschaton, the second-person plural being replaced by the first-person plural. It is worth asking why. Although many claim that verses 9–10 constitute a largely pre-formed, 'pre-Pauline' Jewish-Christian or Christianised Jewish tradition, whether missionary sermon, baptismal hymn or credal statement, this claim is built on weak foundations, as Hooker has demonstrated.[1] She rightly concludes, 'There are one or two unusual phrases, one unique verb – but any passage in Paul could easily provide as many oddities. The Pauline material we have available is too scanty for us to be able to conclude that certain words and phrases are

---

[1] M. D. Hooker, '1 Thessalonians 1.9–10: A Nutshell – but What Kind of Nut?', in *Geschichte – Tradition – Reflexion* (ed. H. Cancik, H. Lichtenberger and P. Schäfer; Tübingen: Mohr, 1996), 3:436–9.

non-Pauline.'[2] That verse 10b and c are Pauline (or at least that Paul has taken ownership of them) and that they serve a specific purpose in the letter's argumentation is suggested by the observation that verses 9–10a work well as Paul's report of what the Greeks were saying concerning the missionaries' entry to Thessalonica and the response of the Thessalonians ((verse 7) γενέσθαι ὑμᾶς τύπον πᾶσιν τοῖς πιστεύουσιν ἐν τῇ Μακεδονίᾳ καὶ ἐν τῇ Ἀχαίᾳ . . . (verse 9) αὐτοὶ γάρ . . . ἀπαγγέλλουσιν). For verses 9–10a function to confirm both proofs of the Thessalonians' election (verse 5 and verse 6), to justify Paul's claim that he did not need to tell the Greeks the story of the Thessalonians' conversion (verse 8c) and to explain how the spreading of the Thessalonians' faith can be equated with 'the word of the Lord' (verse 8a and b) and how the Thessalonians' conversion is a model for the Macedonians and Achaians (verse 7).

What, then, is the function of verse 10b and c? It has been suggested by some that Paul is anticipating 4:13–5:11.[3] The article τῶν in ἐκ τῶν νεκρῶν is probably original, as suggested by the external evidence (א B D F G I Ψ 0278.33.1739) and the plausibility of the proposition that a scribe conformed the text to Paul's usual anarthrous usage (Rom. 4:24; 6:4, 9, 13; 7:4; 8:11; 10:7, 9; 11:15; 1 Cor. 15:12, 20; Gal. 1:1; cf. Col. 2:12; Eph. 1:20; 2 Tim. 2:8). Its inclusion probably indicates that Paul's focus is on the particularity rather than the quality of the substantive; the sense is 'd'entre les morts' or 'from among the dead ones'.[4] As Collins has commented, there seems to be an implicit contrast not between a prior and a later state, but between those who are dead and Jesus who has been raised from among them.[5] This would favour the suggestion that 1:10b anticipates 4:13–18, where Paul discusses the fate of the dead Thessalonians. The fact that verse 10b is sandwiched in an eschatological context (verse 10a and c) would seem to confirm that this statement is

---

[2] Ibid., 439; cf. Wanamaker, *Thessalonians*, 85ff. The plural ἐκ τῶν οὐρανῶν is sometimes seen as un-Pauline since Paul elsewhere uses the singular twice (e.g. Richard, *Thessalonians*, 57); but that does not take into account that the plural 'heavens' is used in 2 Cor. 5:1 and Phil. 3:20 (cf. Col. 1:5, 16, 20; Eph. 1:10; 3:15; 4:10; 6:9) and that Paul seems to have utilised the concept of multiple heavens in 2 Cor. 12:2.

[3] J. Munck, '1 Thess i. 9–10 and the Missionary Preaching of Paul: Textual Exegesis and Hermeneutical Reflections', *NTS* 9 (1962–3): 107–8; Hooker, 'Nutshell', 444–5 (cf. G. F. Snyder, 'A Summary of Faith in an Epistolary Context: 1 Thess. 1:9, 10', in *SBLSP 1972*, 361–2).

[4] *Pace* Malherbe, *Thessalonians*, 122, who sees the article here as generic, its inclusion or exclusion being 'purely a matter of taste'.

[5] Collins, *Studies*, 341–2.

functioning to make an eschatological point. Moreover, the reference to God's eschatological (τῆς ἐρχομένης) wrath (ὀργῆς) in verse 10c favours the view that 5:1–11 is in view there.

The thesis of 1:10b, that God raised his Son from among the dead ones, excellently anticipates 4:13–18 as we have exegeted it above. For we argued that resurrection from among the dead ones is Paul's main point in 4:13–18: just as (and indeed because) Jesus died and rose again (4:14a), so also at the eschaton the dead ones in Christ, from the Thessalonian community, will *be resurrected* from among the dead and so be able to participate in the parousia-descent of Christ (4:14b–17a).

Furthermore, it is remarkable that verse 10c captures precisely the reassuring essence of 5:1–11 as we have interpreted it above: the Thessalonian believers will be rescued by Christ from the eschatological wrath of God (esp. 5:2–5, 9).

We therefore propose that verse 10b and c do indeed function to anticipate 4:13–18 and 5:1–11 respectively, much as Rom. 1:16–17 anticipate the main argument of Romans (cf. Aristotle, *Rhet.* 3.14.1), and that they accord with our situational readings of those eschatological sections.

1 Thess. 2:12b

The final clause of 2:12 (τοῦ καλοῦντος ὑμᾶς εἰς τὴν ἑαυτοῦ βασιλείαν καὶ δόξαν) is striking in that it represents a shift from a focus on the missionaries' conduct during the Thessalonian mission to a focus on the readers vis-à-vis God's kingdom and glory. The fact that δόξα (cf. Rom. 5:2; 8:18ff.; Mark 13:26; Matt. 25:31; 1 Pet. 4:13) accompanies βασιλεία shows that Paul's focus here is thoroughly eschatological (cf. 1 Cor. 15:24). Whether the original participle was the aorist καλέσαντος (e.g. ℵ A 104.326 and a range of versions; cf. 1 Thess. 4:7; Gal. 1:6; 1 Cor. 1:9; etc.) or (perhaps more likely in view of 1 Thess. 5:24 and the manuscript evidence) the present καλοῦντος (e.g. B D F G H K L P; cf. Gal. 5:8; Rom. 9:12), the clause seems to function to encourage and reassure the Thessalonians that their salvific eschatological destiny at the parousia remains valid and secure. This coheres well with Paul's purpose in 4:13–5:11: reassuring hopeless and insecure converts that they and their deceased will receive salvation at the parousia.[6]

---

[6] We see no evidence of an implicit threat here (*contra* Wanamaker, *Thessalonians*, 107).

1 Thess. 3:6

In 1 Thess. 3:6 Paul summarises Timothy's report concerning the situation in Thessalonica: the news is said to be good concerning their faith and love (εὐαγγελισαμένου ἡμῖν τὴν πίστιν καὶ τὴν ἀγάπην ὑμῶν). What is remarkable here, however, is the absence of the third member of the triad, hope. What are we to make of this? Many judge that the absence is of no significance.[7] Calvin and Rigaux[8] claimed that 'faith and love' here constitute the *tota pietatis summa*, while Holtz[9] has argued that both 'faith' and 'love' cover the entire religion of the Thessalonians from different angles. These are possible readings of the material (cf. Phlm. 5; Eph. 1:15). However, in view of the fact that the triad is conspicuous in 1 Thessalonians (1:3; 5:8), it is difficult to avoid interpreting the omission of hope as significant, reflecting a notable lack of good news regarding the Thessalonian community's hope in Timothy's report.

This accords well with our interpretation of the situation underlying 4:13–5:11, for at the core of our hypothesis is the proposal that the Thessalonian converts lacked hope, both for their dead and for themselves. In 4:13 Paul compares the grieving Thessalonians with 'the others who have no hope' (ἵνα μὴ λυπῆσθε καθὼς καὶ οἱ λοιποὶ οἱ μὴ ἔχοντες ἐλπίδα), and in 5:8b–10 Paul calls for the Thessalonians to don hope as a helmet on the grounds that they have a sound 'objective' hope. We suggest that Paul does not refer to good news of Thessalonian hopefulness because Timothy has reported to Paul that the Thessalonians were distinctly hopeless and indeed that they wished to know from Paul whether the deaths were a sign of eschatological wrath.

1 Thess. 3:10

Paul states that he wishes to return to the Thessalonian community to supply what is lacking in their faith (καταρτίσαι τὰ ὑστερήματα τῆς πίστεως ὑμῶν). If, as most scholars safely assume, Paul's letter *qua* substitute for his presence would have gone some way toward providing the necessary instruction which they lacked, then what in this letter might be τὰ ὑστερήματα? The eschatological problems of the community are

---

[7] So *inter alios* Ellicott, *Thessalonians*, 42; Marshall, *Thessalonians*, 94; G. L. Lyons, *Pauline Autobiography* (SBLDS; Atlanta: Scholars, 1985), 215–16 including n. 142; Best, *Thessalonians*, 140; Holtz, *Thessalonicher*, 132–3; Malherbe, *Thessalonians*, 206.

[8] Rigaux, *Thessaloniciens*, 478 and Calvin, *Thessalonians*, 354.

[9] Holtz, *Thessalonicher*, 132–3.

almost certainly covered by this designation. Indeed, they may well be uppermost in Paul's mind, for Paul does not seem to think that the Thessalonians are critically lacking in holiness (4:1) or brotherly love (4:9–10a), although on both counts he thinks that there is room for betterment (4:3–8 and 9–12). The likelihood that they are lacking in key aspects of their faith with specific regard to eschatology coheres well with our interpretation of 4:13–5:11: the Thessalonians seem to be without resurrection hope (4:13–18, esp. verse 13) and one piece of their spiritual armour, assurance regarding their salvific destiny (5:1–11).

1 Thess. 5:14

The second of the short exhortations in 5:14 is 'comfort/console (παραμυθεῖσθε) the faint-hearted/discouraged (τοὺς ὀλιγοψύχους)', which, like the preceding brief exhortation ('warn the ἄτακτοι'), is undeniably situationally specific. As to the possible source(s) of such faint-heartedness, the two most plausible suggestions are persecution (3:3–4) and the crisis provoked by the unexpected deaths (4:13ff.). The facts that this exhortation so perfectly describes what the apostle is himself doing in 4:13–5:11 as we interpreted it above and that the eschatological confusion resulting from the deaths is apparently a more urgent epistolary exigency than the persecutions form a strong case for understanding the 'faint-hearted' as those members of the Thessalonian community who, on account of their ignorance of the resurrection of the saints, are discouraged and anxious that the Day *qua* wrath may be about to fall upon them.

It is more difficult to determine the particular problem targeted by Paul's third brief exhortation 'help the weak'. One might seek to shed light on this 'weakness' with reference to (1) 1 Cor. 8–9 and Rom. 14:1–15:13; (2) 1 Thess. 3:3–4 or (3) 1 Thess. 4:3–8. Option (1) has for it Paul's usage in two of his other letters, but against it the silence of 1 Thessalonians regarding issues of conscience and perhaps the fact that Paul left the community prematurely, apparently with significant omissions in his teaching. Suggestion (2) is possible, although it is disputable whether Paul would have described those shaken by persecutions as being 'weak'. Position (3) faces the obstacle that those who may not have been sexually holy are not conceptualised as weak in 4:3–8, and indeed it is deeply questionable whether Paul would have thought of sexual sin in those terms; moreover, it is difficult to determine what 'help' would then mean.

There is perhaps one major alternative: that 'weak' is essentially co-referential with 'faint-hearted', referring to those in Thessalonica who are confused eschatologically. But could the addressees of 4:13–5:11 be regarded as 'weak'? It is striking that such a description coheres so well with our conclusions regarding the situation underlying 4:13–5:11, that the converts were emotionally and spiritually vulnerable and anxious in the wake of the unexpected deaths, fearful of imminent wrath.[10] Hence, while dogmatism should be avoided, a plausible case can be made for understanding the rather vague term 'weak' as referring to those addressed in 4:13–5:11.

1 Thess. 5:24

It is significant that Paul closes the main body of the letter on a note of strong eschatological reassurance: because God is faithful, he will ensure that the Thessalonians will meet the required standard (entire holiness and blamelessness) for participation in the parousia. That the apostle climaxes his letter to his converts thus accords well with what we saw in 4:13–5:11: the Thessalonians need to be reassured regarding their participation in the parousia's salvation.

Does the argumentation of the rest of 1 Thessalonians develop or contradict our hypothesis regarding the eschatological situation?

1 Thess. 1:1

Compared to the general pattern of Paul's prescripts, two features in 1:1 are notable for our purposes. First, the lack of any reference to the rank of the senders seems to accord with our judgment that there is no notable opposition to the missionaries in the Thessalonian community. Second, the presence of ἐν θεῷ πατρὶ καὶ κυρίῳ Ἰησοῦ Χριστῷ may function to underline the church's secure status (note ἐν τῷ θεῷ in Col. 3:3 and Paul's general usage of ἐν [τῷ] Χριστῷ) and may well anticipate themes important for resolving the eschatological difficulties (ἐν θεῷ πατρί = 1 Thess. 5:4–5, 9; cf. 1:4ff.; 5:24; ἐν . . . κυρίῳ Ἰησοῦ Χριστῷ = 4:14, 16–17a; 5:10).

1 Thess. 1:2–10

Faith, love and hope represent for Paul and early Christians the essential marks of the Christian life, evidences that the eschatological age is present

---

[10] Cf. D. A. Black, 'The Weak in Thessalonica: A Study in Pauline Lexicography', *JETS* 25 (1982): 316–18; Richard, *Thessalonians*, 277.

by the Spirit (1 Cor. 13:13; Gal. 5:5–6; Rom. 5:1–5; cf. Col. 1:4–5; Eph. 1:16–18; 4:2–5; Heb. 6:10–12; 10:22–4; 1 Pet. 1:3–8). By rooting his thanksgiving in the Thessalonian Christians' display of these qualities at the mission, Paul prepares the way for verse 4 and anticipates the argumentation of verses 6ff.

In verse 4 Paul indicates the ultimate grounds of his thanksgiving for the Thessalonian converts – his certainty regarding their election (εἰδότες . . . τὴν ἐκλογὴν ὑμῶν). Ἐκλογή is used four times elsewhere by Paul – Rom. 9:11; 11:5, 7, 28 (cf. Acts 9:15; 2 Pet. 1:10) – always of God's antecedent sovereign act of electing people, rather than the historical realisation of that election. There is no reason to deny that here also Paul is referring to the pre- (or a-)temporal election of God, inferring that from the events of the mission (1:3, 5–10). The reference to election is reinforced by the striking appellation ἀδελφοὶ ἠγαπημένοι ὑπὸ [τοῦ] θεοῦ (a New Testament hapax; cf. LXX Sir. 45:1).

Paul proceeds to justify his confidence regarding the Thessalonians' election by means of a causal ὅτι. First, he establishes his claim on the fact that the missionaries' Thessalonian ministry bore the hallmarks of authenticity: τὸ εὐαγγέλιον ἡμῶν οὐκ ἐγενήθη εἰς ὑμᾶς ἐν λόγῳ μόνον ἀλλὰ καὶ ἐν δυνάμει καὶ ἐν πνεύματι ἁγίῳ καὶ [ἐν] πληροφορίᾳ πολλῇ, καθὼς οἴδατε οἷοι ἐγενήθημεν [ἐν] ὑμῖν δι' ὑμᾶς. The Gospel preached by the missionaries[11] had not come to the Thessalonians only as speech communication; for it had come accompanied with 'power' (either miracles, or unction in preaching), with the 'Holy Spirit' (probably manifestations of the Spirit's presence) and with 'deep conviction'. Πληροφορίᾳ πολλῇ refers to the missionaries' proclamation rather than the Thessalonians' reception, since the immediately preceding and succeeding focus is the manner of the Gospel's coming, with the shift to the converts' response occurring only in verse 6. In verse 5b Paul appeals to the Thessalonians' knowledge of *what kind of people* the missionaries had been during the mission for their sake, in support of verse 5a, perhaps especially the assertion that their Gospel came with 'deep conviction'. We might well ask how verse 5 could serve as a reason for Paul's certainty regarding the converts' election, for it relates exclusively to the missionaries. The explanation seems to be that the elect can only be recognised by virtue of the historical actualisation of election (i.e. God's call): if the Gospel they

---

[11] That τὸ εὐαγγέλιον includes the content is demonstrated by 1 Thess. 2:2, 4, 8 and 9 (cf. Rom. 1:16–17; 2:16; 1 Cor. 15:1); that the proclamation (cf. 2 Cor. 2:12; 8:18; Phil. 4:3, 15) is in mind is clear from the rest of verse 5. Hence Best, *Thessalonians*, 73–4 is probably right to claim that both senses co-exist here (cf. Rom. 1:1; 1 Cor. 9:14, 18).

had received was not the authentic Gospel of God preached by authentic ministers of God, there could be no certainty regarding their election. Hence in verse 5 Paul is assuring his readers that with regard to the Gospel and its ambassadors, the hallmarks of authenticity were present during the mission, indicating that God had been actively calling the Thessalonians, and hence the true nature of the Gospel and its preachers constitute solid grounds for confidence.

Nevertheless, verse 5 alone does not remove all doubt, for certainty of elect status is a two-sided coin: unless they had also *received* that Gospel *in the appropriate manner*, there could be no certainty that they were genuinely elect. Hence Paul goes on in verses 6ff. to introduce this other side of the coin by means of a copulative καί.[12]

According to verse 6, the Thessalonians became imitators of the missionaries and of the Lord, receiving the word in affliction with joy from the Holy Spirit. The use of the imitation motif here and in 2:14 differs from Pauline usage elsewhere (1 Cor. 4:16; 11:1; Phil. 3:17; Gal. 4:12; 2 Thess. 3:7, 9) in that it is not exhortative, but confirmatory, since it views the imitation as having already been attained. That both Jesus and Paul are the objects of the imitation[13] makes it certain that the point of imitation is not the reception of the word, but the 'great affliction and experience of joy inspired by the Spirit' which characterised their reception of the word. For Paul, suffering affliction is the hallmark of authentic Christianity[14] (a participation in the sufferings of Christ (see, e.g., Rom. 8:17; cf. Col. 1:24) having been decreed for God's people before the end of the age[15]). Similarly for him joy in suffering was a characteristic of those genuinely justified (Rom. 5:3),[16] testifying to the presence of the eschatological Spirit and hence the salvific destiny of the people of God (Rom. 5:3, 5; 8:1–2, 9, 14–17, 23–4; 14:17; Gal. 3:1–2, 5; 5:22; cf. Eph. 1:13–14; 4:30; also Acts 2:33, 38–9). The converts' affliction and

---

[12] It seems unnecessary to conclude that καί is an example of the relatively rare phenomenon of parataxis (*pace* NA²⁷; UBS⁴; Jewett, *Correspondence*, 73). Understanding a comma or a colon to be present is preferable.

[13] Καὶ τοῦ κυρίου is probably not a self-correction (as in 1 Cor. 15:10) or an afterthought: 1 Cor. 11:1 and the order of the sentence speak against such construals of the data.

[14] This was the case in regard to both himself (1 Cor. 2:1–5; 4:9; 2 Cor. 1:9; 2:14; 4:11; 11:23–9; Phil. 1:30; cf. Acts 9:15–16) and his converts (1 Thess. 3:3–4; 1 Cor. 7:28; 12:26; Rom. 8:17; Phil. 1:29–30). Paul's sufferings were for him a mark of his legitimacy as an apostle, and he saw fit to boast in them (2 Cor. 11:23–30; cf. 12:10; Phil. 1:19–26; Gal. 6:17).

[15] See Col. 1:24; Eph. 6:13; Dan. 12:1; Mark 13:8; Matt. 24:8; 1 Enoch 47:1–4; 2 Bar. 30:2.

[16] Especially of Paul (2 Cor. 7:4; Phil. 3:20–1; cf. Col. 1:24).

paradoxical joy demonstrated the authenticity of their response to the divine call issued through the missionaries' ministry.

The result of their imitation was that they themselves became a model to the Macedonians and Achaians (verse 7). This is a weighty reinforcement of the second proof of the Thessalonians' election (verse 6): their embrace of the Gospel had been so manifestly genuine that Paul referred to it as exemplifying the ideal. Paul justifies his assertion that the Thessalonians are an example to the Macedonians and Achaians by explaining (γάρ) that 'the word of the Lord', here apparently equivalent to the Thessalonians' 'faith toward God' (since verse 8b seems to be synonymous with verse 8a), has so 'blasted forth' from Thessalonica throughout Macedonia and Achaia, and indeed everywhere, that the missionaries need say nothing about it (verse 8).

Why they need say nothing is explained in verses 9–10a: the Greeks themselves report (1) concerning the missionaries what kind of entry they had to the Thessalonians; and (2) how the Thessalonians had turned to God. The first part of the report (verse 9a) is a repetition of verse 5, and the second (verses 9b–10a) is reminiscent of verse 6; the testimony of the Macedonians and Achaians fortifies both proofs of the Thessalonians' election. In the light of the flow of thought in verses 6ff., with their emphasis on the manner of their reception of the Gospel, the apostle's focus is slightly more on the second part, that is, the example of the Thessalonians to the Macedonians and Achaians. Given the content of verse 6 and the presence of ὁποίαν in verse 9a, it is quite possible that πῶς in verse 9b preserves its usual sense of manner, referring to the context of affliction and the joyfulness of the Thessalonians' response (cf. Luke 8:36). The Greek believers reported that the Thessalonians had converted to serve God, who, in contrast to their former 'idols' (note that the community seems to have consisted primarily of former pagans), was living and true, and to wait for God's Son from heaven, who would save them (verses 9–10a). Finally, he concludes with two clauses which, as we saw above, seem to anticipate 4:13–18 and 5:1–11.

At this point the question must be asked, why does the apostle go to such lengths to justify his certainty that the Thessalonians are indeed elect on the basis that the Gospel they heard at the mission was authentic and divinely endorsed and on the basis that they embraced it in an exemplary manner? Verse 5b verifies that Paul is not merely expressing his personal thanksgiving, but that he also had a definite rhetorical agenda, persuading his readers of the veracity of his claim regarding their election. In the light of the fact that the only other reference to election is in 5:9 (which encapsulates the essence of Paul's thesis in 5:1–11), and in view of the emphasis on hope in 1:3 and 10, we propose that Paul is underlining the certainty of the Thessalonians' election in order to foster eschatological hope in his anxious and fearful converts. Moreover, if our reconstruction of the situation underlying 5:1–11 is correct, that the Thessalonians are wondering if the deaths are a sign that the Day of the Lord is about to come, we would expect that the community members would be seeking an explanation for God's inexplicable wrath. There would have been but two main alternatives: either there was a flaw in the Gospel as proclaimed by the missionaries or there was a fault in their reception of the word. For Paul to deal adequately with such a situation necessitated not only that he attest that the Thessalonians are elect, but also that he reassure them regarding the authenticity of the Gospel preached to them (1:5) and the acceptability of their response to that Gospel (verses 6ff.). This highlights the pertinence of Paul's address of the community as ἀδελφοὶ ἠγαπημένοι ὑπὸ [τοῦ] θεοῦ (verse 4) and his appeal to the testimony of other Christians (verses 7–10a), and elucidates Paul's conclusion of this section with an anticipatory glance at the hope he will develop in 4:13–18 (1:10b) and 5:1–11 (1:10c). It is therefore not incorrect to conclude that the section 1:2–10 prepares for the restoration of the converts' hope in 4:13–5:11 by building a solid foundation for the claim that God has not destined the Thessalonians to wrath but to salvation (5:2–5, 8b–10).

Some might object to our eschatological hypothesis on the grounds that since the apostle mentions their faith, love and hope in 1:2–3 and indicates in 1:10a that hope was a notable feature of the neophytes' new faith, it cannot be true that Paul regards the Thessalonians as lacking hope.[17] However, with regard to verses 2–3, Paul is referring to what he remembers from the mission, as indicated by ἀδιαλείπτως μνημονεύοντες,[18] since Timothy has only 'just now' (ἄρτι, 3:6) returned with the first update regarding the state of the Thessalonian church since the mission (cf. 2:17–3:8).[19] Indeed, the events of the mission dominate the letter until 2:17. With respect to verse 10a, there also the story of the Thessalonians' response to the Gospel at the mission is in view, as verse 9 makes clear. We suggest that neither of these two texts implies that the Thessalonian community is *currently* hopeful. Indeed, the facts that in both these instances hope is given the prominent, final position and that in both Paul

---

[17] So Légasse, *Thessaloniciens*, 186.
[18] The position of ἀδιαλείπτως and the difficulty of interpreting it with the preceding participle strongly favour taking it with μνημονεύοντες.
[19] Note that in 1 Thess. 2:9 (cf. 2 Thess. 2:5; Eph. 2:11; 2 Tim. 1:4, where μιμνήσκομαι is used) μνημονεύω refers to recollection of the past, specifically of events at the mission.

emphasises the *objectively* sound nature of their neophyte hope (note ἔμπροσθεν τοῦ θεοῦ καὶ πατρὸς ἡμῶν in verse 3[20] and ὃν ἤγειρεν ἐκ τῶν νεκρῶν, Ἰησοῦν τὸν ῥυόμενον ἡμᾶς ἐκ τῆς ὀργῆς τῆς ἐρχομένης in verse 10) suggest that his references to hope are part of a specific rhetorical strategy which does *not* assume that the believers are fine in regard to hope.

1 Thess. 2:1–12

Paul opens 2:1–12 by insisting that the missionaries' entry to Thessalonica was not κενή, here 'empty of substance and character', as the subsequent context indicates (2:2–12 with its focus on the behaviour and motives of the missionaries as preachers of God's Gospel, and particularly the antithetical 2:2, with its emphasis on their courage in their God to proclaim the Gospel of God). He develops his point with reference to the observable courage the missionaries displayed at Thessalonica in continuing to preach the Gospel of God in spite of having just faced fierce opposition in Philippi and indeed in spite of the hostility[21] they suffered in Thessalonica (verse 2). It is notable that in referring to the message proclaimed as 'the Gospel of God' (τὸ εὐαγγέλιον τοῦ θεοῦ) and highlighting the source of the missionaries' courage (ἐν τῷ θεῷ), Paul emphasises the Gospel's divine origin and the missionaries' divine empowering.

In verses 3–4 Paul states the thesis of verses 1–12, as indicated by the generality of verses 3–4 (note the use of the present tense and the lack of second-person plurals) in contrast to verses 1–2 and 5–12, which refer specifically to the Thessalonian mission. He is intent on stressing that the missionaries' ministry of the Gospel is not characterised by a faulty message/deception (ἐκ πλάνης), impure motives/uncleanness (ἐξ ἀκαθαρσίας) or dubious methods (ἐν δόλῳ) (verse 3). The preaching of the Gospel (οὕτως λαλοῦμεν) issues from missionaries who have passed the divine test and as a result are divinely approved (δεδοκιμάσμεθα) to be entrusted with God's Gospel; their sole motive in proclaiming the Gospel is to please God, as is verified by God himself, who continually tests their hearts. In verses 5–12 Paul proceeds to confirm this general point with specific regard to the Thessalonian mission.

---

[20] The final position of τῆς ὑπομονῆς τῆς ἐλπίδος and the apparent tendency of Paul not to use 'Lord' with 'faith' or 'Christ' with 'love' suggest that τοῦ κυρίου ἡμῶν Ἰησοῦ Χριστοῦ goes with 'hope'. This, together with 3:13, suggests that ἔμπροσθεν τοῦ θεοῦ καὶ πατρὸς ἡμῶν too may belong with 'hope', implying that their hope had validity before God.

[21] Ἀγών (2:2) in this context plainly refers to external opposition rather than an internal struggle in Paul's mind (*pace* Malherbe, *Paul and the Thessalonians*, 48).

In the negative part of the antithesis of verses 5–9, Paul insists that during the mission at Thessalonica the missionaries had not spoken as charlatans or false prophets, to gratify their own vanity (verse 5a) or line their own pockets (verse 5b) or gain (even legitimate) honour (verses 6–7a). In the positive part (verses 7b–9), by means of the metaphors of babes[22] and a nursing mother, he stresses the missionaries' guilelessness, sincerity and selfless and profound devotion toward the Thessalonian believers, extending beyond the call of duty, and then illustrates this with reference to the decision of Paul, Silas and Timothy to toil night and day rather than be a burden on their converts, as they preached the Gospel of God to them.

Paul then insists forcefully that the Thessalonians and God himself are witnesses of the missionaries' holiness, righteousness and blamelessness during the mission (verse 10). They had been impeccable and beyond reproach in their treatment of the Thessalonian believers, much as a father toward his children (verse 11). They had exhorted, encouraged and charged the new believers to walk worthy of God (verse 12), which revealed the true motivation of their proclamation. Finally, he assures the converts of God's calling of them into his eschatological kingdom (verse 12b).

Intense scholarly debate concerns whether 2:1–12 is paraenetical[23] or apologetic. That the latter is correct seems more likely in view of the following observations: (1) Paul explicitly appeals twice to God as a *witness* (verses 5, 10) and once to the Thessalonians in that capacity (verse 10). The so-called 'witness formula' is used in Paul only when he is especially concerned to affirm the truth of a given claim (Rom. 1:9; 2 Cor. 1:23; Phil. 1:8) and, as court language, is particularly at home in an apologetic context (e.g. 2 Cor. 1:23). (2) The notably dense concentration of references to the readers' knowledge (verses 1, 2, 5, 9, 11) is not a typical feature of Pauline paraenesis, but is suggestive of an apologetic purpose. It is worth noting that verse 5's καθὼς οἴδατε parallels θεὸς μάρτυς, suggesting that

---

[22] The decisive factor in favour of νήπιοι over against ἤπιοι is the external evidence. See G. D. Fee, 'On Text and Commentary on 1 and 2 Thessalonians', in *SBLSP 1992*, 175–9 (cf. J. Gillman, 'Paul's Εἴσοδος: The Proclaimed and the Proclaimer (1 Thess. 2,8)', in *TC*, 63 n. 4; B. R. Gaventa, 'Apostles as Babes and Nurses in 1 Thessalonians 2:7', in *Faith and History* (ed. J. T. Carroll, C. H. Cosgrove and E. E. Johnson; Atlanta: Scholars, 1990), 195–8. Cf. 2:17, where Paul uses the concept of a child being made an orphan to describe the missionaries.

[23] So *inter alios* A. J. Malherbe, 'Exhortation', 238–49 and *Thessalonians*, 79–81, 153–63; Lyons, *Pauline Autobiography*, 185ff., esp. 219–21 and 'Modeling the Holiness Ethos: A Study based on First Thessalonians', *WesTJ* 30 (1995): 187–211; Wanamaker, *Thessalonians*, 90–108.

each of the reminders may actually be a further appeal to the Thessalonians' own witness. (3) There is no evidence that 2:1–12 is presenting a model to be followed; even the references to imitation in the first three chapters (1:6; 2:14) cannot be paraenetic in function, since the imitation in these instances is an already accomplished reality; rather, in 1 Thessalonians imitation seems to function to reassure. Moreover, if 2:1–12 had been intended to be an *exemplum*, its relevance would have been restricted to a narrow band of church leaders and preachers (e.g. verses 3, 5–6, 11). The only place where a paraenetic purpose is conceivable is verse 12a, and even there, that is secondary at most. While we readily acknowledge that there are parallels between Dio Chrysostom's *Oration* 32 and 1 Thess. 2:1–12, these do not require that both texts share the same rhetorical function. (4) The surrounding context speaks in favour of an apology rather than paraenesis: since 1 Thess. 2:17–3:10 is most naturally interpreted as an *apologia pro absentia sua*, 2:1–12 is more likely to be an *apologia pro vita sua*. Further, 2:13 stresses that the word preached by the missionaries and received by the Thessalonians was not the word of men but the word of God, increasing the likelihood that 2:1–12 is not paraenetic, but soundly apologetic (cf. Gal. 1:1ff.).[24] But why would Paul launch into a defence of the missionaries' ministry of the Gospel?

Some have proposed that underlying 1 Thess. 2:1–12 are extra-community opponents.[25] However, if Paul is tackling opponents, why does he do so only on the level of some *ad hominem* charges they made against the missionaries? Could there have been opponents within the community? Evidence for such a claim is entirely lacking.

We suggest that the answer to the riddle may be found in the observation that verbally and logically 2:1 picks up on 1:9a and that just as 1:9a is rooted in 1:5 (perhaps especially verse 5b), so also 2:1ff. are manifestly an extension of the same verse, as indicated by the subject matter (the nature of the missionaries' Gospel ministry to the Thessalonians), by the appeals to the Thessalonians' knowledge in 1:5b and 2:1–12 (verses 1, 5, 9, 10, 11) and perhaps also by the use of γίνομαι in 1:5b and 2:5, 7 and 10. 1:5 and 9a constitute Paul's justification of his

---

[24] So also recently Riesner, *Early Period*, 368–70; J. A. D. Weima, 'An Apology for the Apologetic Function of 1 Thessalonians 2:1–12', *JSNT* 68 (1997): 73–99; Légasse, *Thessaloniciens*, 108–9; Still, *Conflict*, 141–8.

[25] Among those who have argued that Jewish opponents are in view are W. Horbury, '1 Thessalonians ii.3 as Rebutting the Charge of False Prophecy', *JTS* 33 (1982): 492–508, esp. 506–7 (reprinted in *Jews and Christians in Contact and Controversy* (Edinburgh: T. & T. Clark, 1998), 111–26, esp. 125) and K. O. Sandnes, *Paul – One of the Prophets?* (WUNT; Tübingen: Mohr, 1991), 198, 222–3. Still, *Conflict*, 143–8 argues that 2:1–12 reflects the detractions of Jewish *and* Gentile opponents in Thessalonica.

certainty regarding the Thessalonians' election (verse 4). Hence it is not unlikely that 2:1ff. functions similarly, to undergird 1:4. Further, since 1:5 and 9a were intended to assure the converts of their chosen, beloved status and to reassure the believers that they really had listened to and received exemplarily the authentic Gospel of God preached by ministers of integrity, it seems plausible that the section 2:1–12 also functions to discount one possible explanation of the unexpected deaths. For if those ministering the Gospel were in fact charlatans rather than God-endorsed preachers, then the wrath seemingly conveyed by the deaths would have become more explicable. The possibility that the missionaries might be charlatans received some credence from their (especially Paul's) speedy departure and failure to return, which seems to have been a sore point for the Thessalonians, judging by 2:17–3:13. The section 2:1–12 then, we suggest, is an apology intended to shore up the Thessalonians' shattered confidence in their own elective status before God, and ultimately in their salvific destiny at the parousia, as verse 12b seems to indicate.

1 Thess. 2:13–16[26]

In 2:13 Paul gives thanks that when 'the word of God' was transmitted to the Thessalonians by the missionaries, they embraced not 'the word of men' but 'the word of God', which 'it truly is'.[27] The emphatic point of this verse is that the missionaries had preached and the converts had embraced the genuine word of God (τοῦ θεοῦ, καθώς ἐστιν ἀληθῶς, λόγον θεοῦ). This refers back (note the first καί and the fact that διὰ τοῦτο in Paul seems always to be anaphoric rather than kataphoric) to 2:1–12

[26] Against the interpolation hypothesis of B. A. Pearson, '1 Thessalonians 2:13–16: A Deutero-Pauline Interpolation', *HTR* 64 (1971): 79–94 and *The Emergence of the Christian Religion* (Harrisburg: Trinity Press International, 1997), 58–74; H. Koester, '1 Thessalonians: Experiment in Christian Writing', in *Continuity and Discontinuity in Church History* (ed. F. F. Church and T. George; SHCT; Leiden: Brill, 1979), 38 (cf. 'Apostel und Gemeinde in den Briefen an die Thessalonicher', in *Kirche* (ed. D. Lührmann and G. Strecker; Tübingen: Mohr, 1980), 292 n. 16) and D. Schmidt, '1 Thess. 2:13–16: Linguistic Evidence for an Interpolation', *JBL* 102 (1983): 269–79, see Holtz, *Thessalonicher*, 27, 110–12; C. J. Schlueter, *Filling up the Measure* (JSNTSup; Sheffield, JSOT, 1994), *passim*, esp. 25–38; J. Holmstrand, *Markers and Meaning in Paul* (ConBNT; Stockholm: Almquist & Wiksell, 1997), 42–6 and Still, *Conflict*, 24–45.

[27] Concerning ἐδέξασθε οὐ λόγον ἀνθρώπων ἀλλὰ καθώς ἐστιν ἀληθῶς λόγον θεοῦ, many scholars unnecessarily interpret it as though there is a ὡς between οὐ and λόγον and so render it 'you accepted it not *as* the word of men, but rather, as it truly is, the word of God'. However, the text refers to what the word received by the converts actually is (i.e. divine), not the converts' estimation of that word. Hence it is wrong to link this verse to 1:6–7, as many have done (e.g. Moore, *Thessalonians*, 79; Friedrich, 'Erste Brief', 225–6; Johanson, *Brethren*, 94; Holmstrand, *Markers and Meaning*, 54–5).

(cf. 1:5, 9a), where Paul defends the missionaries' Gospel ministry as divinely endorsed. The final clause, ὃς καὶ ἐνεργεῖται ἐν ὑμῖν τοῖς πιστεύουσιν, proves the validity of Paul's assertion by pointing to God's (or possibly the divine word's) present work in the community. By stressing so vigorously (hence the tautology and the superfluous καθώς ἐστιν ἀληθῶς) that the Thessalonians had embraced the authentic word of God himself, Paul is reassuring them of the sound basis of their faith, and ultimately is assuring them of their election (1:4).

1 Thess. 2:14 indicates that the proof of the fact that the Thessalonians had accepted the genuine word of God[28] was their (passive[29]) imitation of the Judaean churches (τῶν ἐκκλησιῶν τοῦ θεοῦ τῶν οὐσῶν ἐν τῇ Ἰουδαίᾳ ἐν Χριστῷ Ἰησοῦ) in suffering at the hands of fellow-countrymen (τὰ αὐτὰ ἐπάθετε καὶ ὑμεῖς ὑπὸ τῶν ἰδίων συμφυλετῶν καθὼς καὶ αὐτοὶ ὑπὸ τῶν Ἰουδαίων). The Judaean churches were the original churches, the mother churches, which set the standard for what a church should look like, for all their daughter churches. By appealing to the precedent of the first, indisputably authentic, churches, Paul endues the Thessalonians' imitation with great significance, for the fact that the Thessalonian church bore the hallmark of the original churches meant that there could be no disputing the authenticity of their Christianity. This interpretation is apparently confirmed by τοῦ θεοῦ (when it accompanies ἐκκλησία in Paul, τοῦ θεοῦ is particularly weighty (1 Cor. 1:2; 10:32; 11:16, 22; 15:9; Gal. 1:13; cf. 2 Thess. 1:4), emphasising God's ownership) and ἐν Χριστῷ Ἰησοῦ (which stresses secure status). Together these highlight the authenticity of the Judaean churches and, by implication, of the Thessalonian church, since the latter is of the same pedigree as the former. 1 Thess. 2:14 therefore reinforces verse 13's thanksgiving that the Thessalonians received the authentic word of God by pointing to their suffering as proof of the genuineness of the community. In 1:6–7 the Thessalonians' imitation (of the missionaries and Christ) in regard to joy in suffering was the second proof of their election, with the divine nature of the Gospel proclaimed constituting the first proof (1:5). Here in 2:14 the Thessalonians' imitation (of the original churches of God) in regard to passive experience of

---

[28] That verse 14's γάρ gives the grounds for the whole of verse 13 and not just verse 13c is suggested by the fact that both verse 13b and verse 14 are in the aorist tense, apparently referring primarily to the time of the mission, while verse 13c, which functions further to substantiate verse 13b, is in the present tense. The passive character of the imitation in verse 14 also speaks against linking it with verse 13c's reference to the active working of God among the believers.

[29] *Contra* W. P. De Boer, *The Imitation of Paul* (Kampen: Kok, 1962), 100–8.

suffering is proof of the divine nature of the Gospel that they received (2:13; cf. 1:5, 9a; 2:1–12) and of their status as an authentic church of God (cf. 1:6–8, 9b–10). Possibly here, as in 2:1–12 and 1:5, Paul has in view the community's recovery from the insecurity induced by the unexpected deaths, combined with the missionaries' elongated absence.

In verses 15–16 Paul picks up on the reference to the Jews as persecutors, with which he concluded verse 14. They killed the Lord Jesus and the prophets and expelled (ἐκδιωξάντων) the missionaries themselves (ἡμᾶς)[30] from Thessalonica (cf. Acts 17:5–9); they do not please God and oppose all men by preventing the missionaries from speaking to the Gentiles so that they may be saved, thereby constantly filling up the measure of their sins and so inducing the wrath of God upon themselves. We might well ask why Paul has so highlighted Jewish opposition to the Gospel in verses 15–16, since it seems irrelevant to the readers, unless of course they too had experienced Jewish hostilities. Could it be that Paul is assuming that the group denominated by verse 14's συμφυλετῶν included, or was in collusion with, the Thessalonian Jews? Certainly Acts 17:5–9 and 13 suggest that the Jews of Thessalonica were notably anti-Christian and participated in persecution of the newly formed Thessalonian community. If we answer this question affirmatively, the purpose of 1 Thess. 2:15–16 emerges as a pedagogical one: since the Jews always displease God and consistently oppose his people, those whom the Jews oppose are shown to be divinely approved.[31] Since the Jews opposed the missionaries at Thessalonica and indeed have a track record of preventing the missionaries from speaking the message of salvation to the Gentiles, the Thessalonian believers can know that Paul, Silas and Timothy (and they themselves) are on God's side. Thus we see how verses 15–16 may function to reinforce the defence of the missionaries in 2:1–14 and 2:17–3:10.

By stressing that the Jews displease God and ultimately bring wrath on themselves by filling up the measure of their sin by their continual opposition of God's authorised representatives, Paul sharply contrasts the Jews' standing and fate before God with those of the Thessalonian community (1:10c; 4:13–5:11). The assurance that justly deserved eschatological wrath[32] is the destiny of the Jews *qua* persecutors would presumably

---

[30] The immediate and broader context indicates that ἡμᾶς here refers to Paul, Silas and Timothy.

[31] Cf. Schlueter, 'Filling Up', 73.

[32] We believe that wrath here is a future eschatological phenomenon rather than a past historical event. The logic of verses 15–16 suggests that the wrath is in response to sins up to and including the obstruction of the Pauline Gentile mission and specifically the

console the persecuted missionaries and their converts. Secondarily, the profile of a wrath-destined group as one which deliberately opposes God and his plan (thereby provoking divine wrath) would enable the Thessalonians to see themselves as separate from that group.

1 Thess. 2:17–3:10

From start to finish 2:17–3:10 is an apology[33] for the missionaries' absence; Paul is obviously concerned that the missionaries' premature departure from Thessalonica, the length of the period before the first post-visit contact and his own failure to return should not be interpreted by the converts as evidence of a lack of pastoral love and concern for them. In 2:17 he stresses that the separation was involuntary and distressing for the missionaries (ἀπορφανισθέντες), is now over in the light of Timothy's visit (note the aorist) and was in fact only brief (πρὸς καιρὸν ὥρας) and not reflective of a failure to remember the converts or of a lack of love (προσώπῳ οὐ καρδίᾳ); indeed, he emphasises that the missionaries made desperate efforts, inspired by deep longing, to revisit the community (περισσοτέρως ἐσπουδάσαμεν τὸ πρόσωπον ὑμῶν ἰδεῖν ἐν πολλῇ ἐπιθυμίᾳ). Then in verse 18 he repeats that they had wished to see the Thessalonians again, before insisting that he himself had personally tried to visit them more than once (ἐγὼ μὲν Παῦλος καὶ ἅπαξ καὶ δίς), but failed because Satan had prevented him (καὶ ἐνέκοψεν ἡμᾶς ὁ σατανᾶς). In verses 19–20 (τίς γὰρ ἡμῶν ἐλπὶς ἢ χαρὰ ἢ στέφανος καυχήσεως – ἢ οὐχὶ καὶ ὑμεῖς – ἔμπροσθεν τοῦ κυρίου ἡμῶν Ἰησοῦ ἐν τῇ αὐτοῦ παρουσίᾳ; ὑμεῖς γάρ ἐστε ἡ δόξα ἡμῶν καὶ ἡ χαρά) Paul inextricably links the missionaries' eschatological parousia hope with that of the converts. This functions to assure the community of the missionaries' love for and devotion to them, and perhaps as a guarantee that their destiny is as sure as the missionaries' (hence reinforcing the message of 4:13–5:11 as we interpreted it in the preceding chapters).

Thessalonian expulsion, which casts doubt on the proposal that Paul is referring to a past event, such as the riot and massacre in Jerusalem in 48–9, the expulsion of the Jews from Rome under Claudius in 49, the Judaean famine in 46–7 or the insurrection of Theudas in 44–6. These events are probably too local and insignificant to warrant the description of verse 16c, especially by someone writing in 50. The eschatological interpretation is therefore more likely; the proleptic/futuristic use of the aorist can be used to stress the certainty and/or imminence of events (e.g. Mark 11:24; John 13:31; Rom. 8:30; Heb. 4:10; Jude 14; Rev. 10:7; 14:8). The contrast with πάντοτε in verse 16b suggests that εἰς τέλος means 'at last' or 'in the end'.

[33] Wanamaker, *Thessalonians*, 119–20 has claimed that 2:17–3:10 is paraenetic, but evidence for this contention is entirely lacking. As we shall see, the tone throughout is reassuring and apologetic.

In 3:1–5 Paul fortifies the point that the missionaries have a deep pastoral concern for the community by appealing to the sending of Timothy, which, he claims, should be interpreted as a desperate measure motivated by agonising love which could not bear the separation (μηκέτι στέγοντες). Indeed, he implies that it cost him dearly in that it meant that he was left alone in Athens (verse 1). Moreover, he highlights that Timothy was no unimpressive deputy; he was in fact 'God's co-worker[34] in the Gospel of Christ' (verse 2a); hence dispatching him did not reflect a low view of the community on the part of Paul. Timothy had been sent because the missionaries had been anxious that the community should not be 'shaken' (σαίνεσθαι) by persecutions (verses 2b–3a). Indeed, Paul insists that the sending of Timothy should be understood as a proof of his pastoral anxiety and worry that the converts would not remain in the faith (verse 5).

Proof of Paul's pastoral concern is the fact that he writes this letter immediately (ἄρτι) upon hearing Timothy's report of good news (verse 6a). Timothy reports that the Thessalonians remember the missionaries with love and long to see them again (verse 6b). Paul declares that the feeling is reciprocal (καθάπερ καὶ ἡμεῖς ὑμᾶς) and then asserts that the news that the Thessalonians were standing strong (in spite of persecution, cf. verses 2–4) greatly cheered the missionaries, encouraging them in their affliction and distress, and was 'life' to them (verses 6b–8). In verses 9–10 Paul draws the section 2:17ff. to a close. Verse 9 underlines the missionaries' emotional commitment to the converts by means of a striking thanksgiving in the form of a rhetorical question, and accents the fact that a return visit to see and help the community is an urgent priority (verse 10).

Therefore in 2:17–3:10 Paul seems to be reassuring the community members concerning the missionaries' (especially his own (as indicated by the first-person singulars in 1 Thess. 2:18 and 3:5 and μόνοι in 3:1)) pastoral love of and commitment to them. And one can tentatively extrapolate that some converts were interpreting the period of the missionaries' absence, especially Paul's failure to return, as reflecting a lack of pastoral care. In the light of the likelihood that 2:1–12's defence of the missionaries during the mission ultimately functions to reinforce the genuineness of the Thessalonians' faith (2:13–14) and indeed election (1:4), it is not

---

[34] Cf. 1 Cor. 3:9. Συνεργὸν τοῦ θεοῦ is indisputably the best-attested and the most difficult reading, as well as the reading which best explains the others (see Rigaux, *Thessaloniciens*, 466; B. M. Metzger, *The Text of the New Testament* (3rd edn; Oxford: Oxford University Press, 1992), 240–2 and *A Textual Commentary on the Greek New Testament* (2nd edn; Stuttgart: Deutsche Bibelgesellschaft, 1994), 563; *contra* Findlay, *Epistles of Paul*, 62–3, 64–5).

implausible that 2:17–3:10's apology for the missionaries during their absence functions similarly. Since the authenticity of the Thessalonians' faith depends on the authenticity of its ministers, it is particularly urgent that Paul defend the missionaries, not only with respect to the mission, but also in regard to the absence. Otherwise the community might conclude that therein lay the explanation for God's wrath as apparently revealed in the unexpected deaths.[35]

In 3:3b–4, having stated that the motivation for sending Timothy was that the community would not be shaken by persecution (verse 3a), Paul digresses to assert almost defensively (note especially αὐτοί . . . οἴδατε and καθώς . . . καὶ οἴδατε) that the converts had been warned in advance by the missionaries that they were destined to suffer.[36] This may indicate that the readers thought that the missionaries had left them unprepared for the persecution they subsequently endured. And in the context of 2:17–3:10, it is possible that Paul thinks that this issue threatens to intensify the converts' doubts about the authenticity of the missionaries.

If Paul in 1 Thessalonians is reassuring his converts that they certainly will inherit eschatological salvation, how is 3:5b's reference to Paul's fear that the Thessalonians might have been tempted and the missionaries' efforts rendered useless to be explained? And further, how is verse 8's ἐὰν ὑμεῖς στήκετε ἐν κυρίῳ to be reckoned with? Concerning verse 5b, Paul's purpose is probably to stress that the missionaries' absence and his sending of Timothy reflected not the cold indifference of a charlatan, but the genuine worry of a concerned pastor. Since it reflects a past worry which has since proved to be unfounded, it does not undermine his reassurance.[37] The fact that verse 8's ἐάν is followed by the indicative discloses that their standing firm is a present reality (ἐάν for εἰ); hence ἐάν is 'if, as indeed you do'.[38] The worry of Paul is presented as no longer valid.

[35] It is also possible that the converts had deduced from Paul's apparent lack of interest in them that he did not consider them genuine Christians.

[36] Note also that in 3:7 Paul highlights the persecution the missionaries are going through, probably to imply that it is normal for Christians, so that the converts would not be shaken. Cf. 2:14–16.

[37] Nevertheless, one might wonder how Paul's argumentation in 1:5–2:16 holds up then, for how could the events of the mission guarantee the authenticity of their faith, if Paul is assured of their salvation only after Timothy's very recent report? There is a tension here, but it is not at the level of rhetoric, for Paul intends 3:5 and 8 to function to reinforce his love for the converts; rather it is at the level of Paul's thought: is it consistent for him to argue for their election based on their conversion if even he himself doubted that it was genuine? We suggest that the apparent inconsistency never occurred to the apostle. In the wake of Timothy's reports, any doubts that the apostle may have had seem to have been well and truly dispelled.

[38] Best, *Thessalonians*, 143; BDF §§371 (1a); N. Turner, *A Grammar of New Testament Greek. III. Syntax* (Edinburgh: T. & T. Clark, 1963), 115–16; NIV.

1 Thess. 3:11–13

That 3:11–13, which bring to a close the first major part of the letter, are especially closely related to 2:17–3:10, and motivated by the same concerns, is evident in that they express Paul's wish to return to the Thessalonians (3:11; cf. 2:17–18; 3:1, 5, 10) by means of a prayer that 'our God and Father himself' and 'our Lord Jesus' would make a visit possible (presumably by overcoming the obstacles of Satan, 2:18); in that they assure the converts of the missionaries' love (3:12b; cf. 2:17–20; 3:5, 6b, 7–10); and in that they reflect Paul's concern that the Thessalonians be strengthened (3:13; cf. verses 2–3). It seems that Paul, having reassured the converts that he and the other missionaries were deeply committed to them (2:17–3:10), opens the door of his heart to let them see the loving pastoral concern he has been talking about and to assure them that his commitment to them will endure until the parousia itself.

In addition, 3:11–13 point forward to 4:1ff., as is demonstrated by the observations that love (3:12) and holiness (3:13) become the themes of 4:9–12 and 4:1–8 respectively, and that the parousia (3:13) is the key concern of 4:13ff. and 5:23–4.[39]

One striking feature of this eschatological wish-prayer, in view of the emphasis on the Thessalonians' election and the security of their eschatological destiny in 1:4ff. (cf. 1:10b and c; 2:12b), is the apparent contingency of their eschatological salvation on their continued holiness. We shall seek to explain this below in regard to 5:23–4; it is enough to state here that this apparent contingency lends urgency to the ensuing instruction regarding holiness (4:1–8).[40]

---

[39] See chapter 2 above, where we argue that 1 Thess. 3:13b alludes to LXX Zech. 14:5b and that μετὰ τῶν ἁγίων αὐτοῦ refers to believers as well as to angels.

[40] The extended introductory thanksgiving of 1:2–3:13 is one of the most distinctive formal features of 1 Thessalonians (see esp. P. Schubert, *The Form and Function of the Pauline Thanksgivings* (BZNW; Berlin: Töpelmann, 1939), 16–27 and P. T. O'Brien, *Introductory Thanksgivings in the Letters of Paul* (NovTSup; Leiden: Brill, 1977), 144). We propose that its presence in the letter is intended to reassure the community by establishing the soundness of the grounds (1:4, Paul's certainty regarding their election) for his initial thanksgiving (1:2–3) in the face of the eschatological confusion and its ramifications and of Thessalonian concerns about the missionaries on account of their extended absence. Some have tried to restrict the introductory thanksgiving to (1) 1:2–5 (so Jewett, *Correspondence*, 72–3) or (2) 1:2–10 (so *inter alios* Donfried, *Shorter*, 6; Richard, *Thessalonians*, 88 and Hooker, 'Nutshell', 443–7) or (3) 1:2–2:16 (so *inter alios* Dibelius, *Thessalonicher*, 1 and Holmstrand, *Markers and Meaning*, 56). However, *contra* (1), as we have argued above, 1:6ff. seem to be closely related to verse 5 and ultimately verse 4, and verse 9a appears to be a recapitulation of verse 5 just as verses 9b–10a seem to recapitulate verses 6ff. Option (2) has in its favour that 1:10 could be viewed as an eschatological climax and 2:1–2 as a formulaic Pauline transition from the epistolary introduction to the main body. However, as J. L. White, *The Form and Function of the Body of the Greek Letter* (SBLDS; Missoula: SBL,

1 Thess. 4:1–12

The second half of the letter consists primarily of exhortatory material and subdivides into 4:1–12, 13–18; 5:1–11, 12–22, 23–4 and 25–8.[41] The first subsection, 4:1–12,[42] is introduced by verses 1–2. Paul urges the community to walk more and more so as to please God (verse 1), obedient to what the missionaries had taught them by the authority of Christ (verse 2). It is notable that Paul qualifies his exhortation with καθὼς καὶ περιπατεῖτε. By means of this Paul delicately avoids the impression that he is criticising the community or implying that God is displeased with them, which is understandable in view of the eschatological confusion of the converts as we have understood it. Then in verses 3–8 he calls for sexual holiness.

If, as we have argued, Paul is reassuring the Thessalonians in the face of doubts caused by the unexpected deaths, how do we explain (a) the apparent eschatological threat of 4:6b, underlining the need for holiness, and (b) what is, according to some, the challenge to the sexual ethic underlying 4:3–8?

Concerning (a), 4:6b's ἔκδικος κύριος περὶ πάντων τούτων represents 'the most powerful [sanction] available to [Paul]',[43] an unmistakably solemn warning (διεμαρτυράμεθα) of Christ's (eschatological) judgment

---

1972) and J. T. Sanders, 'The Transition from Opening Epistolary Thanksgiving to Body in Letters of the Pauline Corpus', *JBL* 81 (1962): 348–62 admitted, 2:1–2 is a quite 'irregular' example of a Pauline transition from epistolary introduction to main body, for γάρ replaces δέ, αὐτοί . . . οἴδατε substitutes for the usual οὐ θέλω ὑμᾶς ἀγνοεῖν or γινώσκειν ὑμᾶς βούλομαι or παρακαλῶ/ἐρωτῶ ὑμᾶς, and the verb is in the second person rather than the first person. Moreover, as we have argued above, 2:1–12 and 13–16 seem to be extensions of Paul's argument in 1:5 and 9a, reinforcing his certainty regarding the Thessalonians' election. While (3) has in its favour the cohesion of the argument in 1:2–2:16 and the lack of formal connections between 1:2–2:16 and 2:17ff., it does not take adequate account of the fact that 2:17ff. seem to function as an apology for the missionaries' conduct during the period since the mission, just as 2:1ff. seem to function as an apology for them during the mission, or of the observation that 2:17 seems to pick up where 2:1–12 and 15 leave off. We suggest that the eschatological climax is 3:13, which is more reminiscent of the climaxes which we find in 1 Cor. 1:8–9 and Phil. 1:10b–11 (cf. Col. 1:22–3) than is 1 Thess. 1:10, and we judge that the transition from 'introductory thanksgiving' to 'main body' is 4:1–2.

[41] The relation of the second section to the first hangs largely on how we interpret λοιπόν οὖν (4:1). It is difficult to deny the normal inferential value of οὖν; 4:1ff. would seem to be an inference from 3:13 or 1:2–3:13, but probably not 2:1–3:13. Concerning λοιπόν, it seems implausible that Paul intended 1:2–3:13 to be understood as the epistolary 'body'; certainly the subsequent material does not appear to be secondary. Probably it is best to take λοιπόν here as marking the commencement of a new section with an eye toward the close of the letter.

[42] For a defence of 4:1–12 as a pericope, see Johanson, *Brethren*, 112–13 and R. F. Collins, 'The Function of Paraenesis in 1 Thess 4,1–12; 5, 12–22', *ETL* 74 (1998): 404.

[43] Wanamaker, *Thessalonians*, 156.

for those violating the sexual ethic. It cannot be denied that it stands in sharp tension with Paul's reconfirmation of the Thessalonians regarding the certainty of their eschatological fate in 4:13–5:11 (cf. 1:4–2:16). Nevertheless, granted the importance of the holiness mandate in Paul's theology, as indicated by Rom. 6:19–23; 1 Cor. 5; 6:14–7:1; 10:8 and Gal. 5:19 (cf. Eph. 5:3, 5), and his conviction that those relating to God in terms of the New Covenant had an obligation to live holily, it is probable that the apostle is quite simply unwilling to compromise on the priority of this fundamental tenet of his kerygma, even when doing so seemed to undermine the major *raison d'être* of his letter. Notably Paul withholds from his wish-prayer in 3:13 confirmation that the Thessalonians will in fact be among the eschatological 'holy ones' until after he has remonstrated about the gravity of holiness for the young community (4:3–8), that is, until 5:23–4. There we see that the standard of holiness required for parousia participation will indeed be met by the Thessalonians.

Paul does reckon with the possibility that within the community are some individuals (ἕκαστον ὑμῶν and ἑαυτοῦ, verse 4) who might reject, or at least show some reluctance to embrace, the sexual ethic. To Paul a discarding of the sexual ethic is ultimately a rejection of God (verse 8a), his call (verse 7) and his will (verse 3), and particularly his gift of the eschatological *Holy* Spirit (verse 8b), which Paul regards as inexcusable and catastrophic (verses 6b, 8). Nevertheless, he clearly believes that the community as a whole is destined for salvation even in this section: it has been called by God (verse 7), generally conforms to the holiness ethic and pleases God (verse 1) and currently (διδόντα) experiences in its midst (εἰς ὑμᾶς) the work of God's eschatological Spirit of holiness as he creates a community of holy ones.[44]

Regarding (b), Jewett has followed Lütgert, Hadorn and Schmithals[45] in suggesting that 4:1–8 presupposes an active opposition in Thessalonica which advocates the abandonment of the Pauline sexual ethic. He claims that the ἄτακτοι are mounting a 'significant' intellectual challenge to Paul's traditional ethic, convinced that discarding his sexual ethic is the first stage of the coming of the new age.[46] However, first, far from pointing to a connection between Paul's exhortation to holiness in 4:3–8 and his eschatological instruction in 4:13–5:11, the evidence – the intervention of

---

[44] Verse 8b is of course strongly rooted in the concept of the New Covenant (LXX Ezek. 36:25–7), and indeed the wording is very similar to LXX Ezek. 37:6 and 14. Because of the Holy Spirit's divine power, the called community can and will be holy.

[45] Lütgert, 'Enthusiasten', 619ff.; W. Hadorn, *Die Abfassung der Thessalonicherbriefe in der Zeit der dritten Missionsreise des Paulus* (BFCT; Gütersloh: Bertelsmann, 1919), 54ff.; Schmithals, 'Historical Situation', 155–8; cf. K. Stürmer, *Auferstehung und Erwählung* (BFCT; Gütersloh: Bertelsmann, 1953), 48.

[46] Jewett, *Correspondence*, 105–6, 172–3.

4:9–12 between the two sections and, most especially, the aforementioned contrast between the reassurance of 4:13–5:11 and the threatening tone of 4:3–8 – suggests that there is no such connection. Moreover, it is difficult to imagine that Paul would have been content to avoid making any explicit mention of such a group of trouble-makers in 4:1–8 and using polemics to castigate them. Further, it is hard to imagine that he would then have so categorically assured the community that they are currently pleasing God in their 'walk' (4:1) and that he would then have cast Timothy's report in so positive a light (3:6).[47] Goulder has proposed, from reading σκεῦος as 'wife' and a consequent parallel between 1 Thess. 4:4 and 1 Cor. 7:3, that 4:3–8 reflects the presence of an ascetic movement in the Thessalonian community rooted in a realised eschatology, with Paul seeking to protect the believers from sexual immorality by stopping them from setting too lofty a standard.[48] However, this position depends on a dubious interpretation of σκεῦος, builds too much on the supposed Corinthians parallel, is unrestrained in its mirror reading and lacks support for the link with eschatology. Further, as Goulder himself admits, there is no 'apparent means of germination' for asceticism to have taken root so quickly.[49]

In the light of the connection between 4:3–8 and 3:13 and the sternness of the warning in verses 6b–8, it is probable that Paul has raised the issue of holiness because of the missionaries' anxiety rather than because of a specific concern of the community. All we need suppose is that Timothy has informed Paul that this predominantly pagan community is having problems adjusting to the high ethical standards of the Christian faith and resisting the pull of former ways.

In verses 9–12 Paul turns to the topic of 'brotherly love' (probably concerning the responsibility of the majority to the unemployed brothers), and immediately dismisses its pertinence for the Thessalonian believers on the grounds that they have been 'God-taught' to love (clearly affirming that they constitute a genuine New Covenant community of faith[50]) and indeed that they love not just each other, but also all the believers in the whole of Macedonia (verses 9–10a). Thus he again goes out of

---

[47] Καθὼς καὶ περιπατεῖτε is clearly Paul's tactful attempt to avoid conveying condemnation or blame where he regarded it as unwarranted (cf. Lightfoot, *Epistles*, 52); such diplomacy is particularly understandable if our reconstruction of the Thessalonian situation underlying 4:13–5:11 is correct.

[48] M. D. Goulder, 'Silas in Thessalonica', *JSNT* 48 (1992): 93; cf. Hester, 'Invention', 264–5.

[49] Goulder, 'Silas', 93.

[50] Cf. Isa. 54:13; Jer. 31:33–4 (LXX 38:33–4); Ezek. 37:6, 14; Lev. 19:18; Ps. Sol. 17:32; also John 6:45; 13:34; 15:12. See also 1 Thess. 4:8b.

his way, as in verse 1, to avoid the appearance of criticism of the young, insecure community and reveals that a Thessalonian question (probably communicated orally *via* Timothy), and indeed a concrete situation, underlies verses 9–12. Then in verses 10b–11 he issues four exhortations, that they abound even more in brotherly love, make it their ambition to live quietly,[51] tend to their own affairs,[52] and work with their [own] hands, which he underlines with καθὼς ὑμῖν παρηγγείλαμεν. Finally, in verse 12 two goals/purposes for these exhortations are presented: that the believers might 'walk properly (εὐσχημόνως) before (πρός) outsiders', and have need of no one (μηδενὸς χρείαν ἔχητε).[53]

Perhaps the majority of scholars believe that underlying 1 Thess. 4:9–12 is a problem caused by eschatological excitement.[54] With regard to internal evidence, the most common argument for this contention is that 1 Thess. 4:13–5:11 is sandwiched between admonitions which relate to the 'idleness' problem (4:11–12; 5:14).[55] However, it should be noted that there is no explicit connection of the two topics and that 4:13ff. and 5:12ff. are introduced as new sections; hence 4:13–5:11 is not necessarily related to the preceding or succeeding. Further, it is important to note that the admonitions of 5:12ff. do not primarily or initially refer to the idlers. Another argument in support of a link has been offered by Goulder: that 5:14 lists the idlers and the eschatologically confused together.[56] However, the ἄτακτοι are to be warned, while the faint-hearted are to be encouraged and the weak are to be helped. Some argue that the likelihood

---

[51] The suggestion of R. F. Hock, *The Social Context of Paul's Ministry, Tentmaking and Apostleship* (Philadelphia: Fortress, 1980), 46–7 that some members of the community had been involved in politics seems at odds with his judgment that the community was primarily composed of the urban poor. And, as Légasse, *Thessaloniciens*, 237–8 puts it, 'Mais on s'étonnerait que la toute nouvelle et chétive communauté ait pris le risque de s'attirer, en se mêlant de politique, une opposition dont elle n'avait que faire.'

[52] The suggestion of Barclay, 'Conflict', 522–5 (cf. 'Social Contrasts', 53–4) and Still, *Conflict*, 246–7 that the Thessalonians gave up work to prosyletise is, as Légasse, *Thessaloniciens*, 238 n. 5 asserts, without foundation.

[53] The masculine understanding of μηδενός seems more appropriate in this context than the neuter (*pace inter alios* Findlay, *Epistles of Paul*, 93 and Bruce, *Thessalonians*, 91 (cf. Lightfoot, *Epistles*, 61)).

[54] So *inter alios* Lightfoot, *Epistles*, 60; E. von Dobschütz, *Christian Life in the Primitive Church* (ed. W. D. Morrison; trans. G. Bremmer; TTFL; London: Williams and Norgate, 1904), 92; Frame, *Thessalonians*, 159–61; Rigaux, *Thessaloniciens*, 519–22; Mearns, 'Development', 141–2, 147, 151; Marshall, *Thessalonians*, 117; Best, *Thessalonians*, 175–6, 177, 178; De Vos, *Conflict*, 165 including n. 154 and n. 155.

[55] For example, Lightfoot, *Epistles*, 60, 62; von Dobschütz, *Thessalonicher-Briefe*, 182–3; Goulder, 'Silas', 88–9; J. A. D. Weima, ' "How You Must Walk to Please God": Holiness and Discipleship in 1 Thessalonians 4:1–12', in *Patterns of Discipleship in the New Testament* (ed. R. N. Longenecker; McNTS; Grand Rapids: Eerdmans, 1996), 113.

[56] Goulder, 'Silas', 89 n. 1.

of a connection between the 'idleness' problem and eschatology in 2 Thessalonians favours a similar link in 1 Thessalonians.[57] If there is such a connection in 2 Thessalonians, it will indeed favour a similar link here, even if 2 Thessalonians is regarded as pseudonymous (for 2 Thessalonians will then constitute evidence from an interpreter of 1 Thess. 4:9–12 writing within sixty years of its composition);[58] however, in chapter 7 we shall argue that a connection between eschatology and idleness there is implausible. Probably the simplest explanation of 4:10b–12 and 5:14's νουθετεῖτε τοὺς ἀτάκτους is non-eschatological: some from the manual labouring class were avoiding working for their own maintenance and instead were exploiting the brotherly love of fellow-community members and making a nuisance of themselves.[59] We conclude that the case for relating the problems underlying 4:9–12/5:14's νουθετεῖτε τοὺς ἀτάκτους and 4:13–5:11 is tenuous and unconvincing.[60]

1 Thess. 5:12–22

In 1 Thess. 5:12–13a Paul calls for the church to 'recognise' or 'respect' (εἰδέναι) its *de facto* 'leaders', who labour on its behalf, 'pastor'[61] it and admonish it,[62] and to esteem them very highly[63] in love on account of their work. Some have contended that these verses are closely related to the eschatological problems of the Thessalonians. Lightfoot maintained that they return to the matter of the community's 'restlessness' connected with an imminent parousia expectation.[64] However, such an interpretation not only depends on a dubious interpretation of the Thessalonians'

---

[57] *Inter alios* Frame, *Thessalonians*, 160–1 and Weima, 'Holiness', 113.

[58] *Contra* Hock, *Social Context*, 43.

[59] H. L. Hendrix, 'Benefactor/Patron Networks in the Urban Environment: Evidence from Thessalonica', *Semeia* 56 (1992): 40–1 makes the case that patronal networks were an important part of society in Thessalonica (*contra* De Vos, *Conflict*, 136–8, 296–7, who argues unconvincingly for a contrast between lack of social contact between different socio-economic groups at Thessalonica and extensive interaction between different socioeconomic groups at Corinth and Philippi). Acts 17:5–9 seems to portray Jason as a patron (not an *insula*-workshop owner, *pace* De Vos, *Conflict*, 147–9). And it cannot be assumed that the artisan status of the idlers is representative of the entire community (*pace* ibid., 150–4).

[60] Our refutation of the common argument from church history (e.g. Weima, 'Holiness', 114) in chapter 7 applies here too.

[61] This conveniently combines the two possible senses of προΐστημι: 'care for' (as in Rom. 12:8) and 'authority over'.

[62] Note the single article covering three participles. Whether the last two explain the first or whether all three are coordinate is difficult to determine.

[63] Note that the word order favours taking ἡγεῖσθαι with ὑπερεκπερισσοῦ rather than ἐν ἀγάπῃ.

[64] Lightfoot, *Epistles*, 78.

eschatological confusion, but also seems to read too much into verses 12–13a. Jewett has argued that these verses elucidate the eschatological situation of the community. According to him, the leaders had been unreceptive to the ecstatic/charismatic activities of the ἄτακτοι (who believed that the new age was realised in their enthusiastic activities), thus provoking insurrection within the community.[65] However, this hypothesis is based on numerous dubious and unnecessary suppositions: (1) that the problem of the ἄτακτοι and the apparent lack of respect for the pastors are rooted in a false eschatology; (2) that the leaders were anti-charismatic and those not submitting to them charismatic; (3) that some community members were *actively* resisting the leaders; and (4) that the leaders bore responsibility for any lack of acknowledgement of them or lack of respect shown to them.

As to possible formal links between 5:12ff. and 4:13–5:11, some have argued that the δέ in 5:12 is adversative,[66] but it is difficult to see what the contrast might be. It has been proposed by some that Paul is warning those who engage in mutual edification to beware of disrespecting their leaders.[67] However, this is an implausible hypothesis, for ἐρωτάω with ὑμᾶς, δέ and ἀδελφοί constitutes a generic transition to a new section. Some have suggested that verses 12–22 are an explication of verse 11, making its admonition concrete and specific.[68] If so, the case for verses 12ff. being very closely connected with the eschatological section would be strengthened, since verse 11 is clearly anaphoric. However, while verses 12–13a and 19–22 and perchance verse 14 might fit this hypothesis, verses 13b, 15 and 16–18 suggest that verses 12ff. are not primarily an expansion of verse 11.

It is unnecessary to suppose that the leaders' authority has come under attack from false teachers[69] or that the pastors provoked hostility by being tactless and officious,[70] a notion derived from interpreting verse 13b in the light of verses 12–13a, which we regard as precarious. It is probably enough to postulate that the problem stemmed from the fact that the leaders were as yet unestablished and did not yet command the community's full respect. It is notable that the eschatological problems would have made this problem of lack of respect for/recognition of the leaders more

---

[65] Jewett, *Correspondence*, 103, 175–6.
[66] So *inter alios* Chrysostom; Masson, *Thessaloniciens*, 71; NASB; NRSV.
[67] For example by Chrysostom.
[68] So, for example, Rigaux, *Thessaloniciens*, 575; C. J. Roetzel, '1 Thess. 5:12–28: A Case Study', in *SBLSP 1972*, 2:368, 369; Fee, *Empowering*, 56.
[69] So *inter alios* Schmithals, 'Historical Situation', 168–9.
[70] So *inter alios* Frame, *Thessalonians*, 191–2, 195.

critical, for a lack of deference to the leaders would have obstructed an important potential avenue of encouragement and correction.

Concerning verse 13b, ἑαυτοῖς is probably the correct reading, for if Paul had been expressing the thought conveyed by ἐν αὐτοῖς he would probably have written μετ' αὐτῶν (cf. Rom. 12:18). Read thus ('be at peace among yourselves'), verse 13b appears to be independent from its immediate context, being quite general, strikingly similar to paraenesis in Paul's other letters (Rom. 14:19; 2 Cor. 13:11; cf. Col. 3:15; Eph. 4:3; 2 Tim. 2:22; Heb. 12:14). If it had been situationally specific, we would have expected a more detailed, forthright treatment of the problem and its causes.

In verse 14 Paul calls on the whole community to 'warn the ἄτακτοι' (those who display an 'irresponsible attitude to the obligation to work',[71] mentioned in 4:10b–12), to 'encourage the faint-hearted' (those in view in 4:13–5:11), to 'help the weak' (possibly also those in view in 4:13–5:11) and to 'be patient with all'.

Verse 15 ('see to it (ὁρᾶτε) that none of you repay evil for evil, but always pursue what is good [both] to one another and to all') is traditional paraenetical material, occurring elsewhere in Rom. 12:17; 1 Pet. 3:9 and Matt. 5:43ff./Luke 6:27ff., and is probably generic rather than situationally specific, although it is relevant to a community enduring persecution (cf. 1 Thess. 3:3b–4a).[72]

In verses 16–18 Paul moves to issue a triad of terse instructions regarding the community's comportment before God: they are to 'rejoice always, pray continually and give thanks in everything'.[73] On the grounds that this triad is quite general, and that verses 16 and 17 are paralleled by Rom. 12:12a and c respectively (cf. 1 Thess. 5:18 and Eph. 5:20) and that 1 Thess. 5:17 and 18 are paralleled by Col. 4:2a and b respectively, many have concluded that 1 Thess. 5:16–18 are not motivated by situationally specific concerns.[74] However, the fact that Paul asserts that the triadic exhortations constitute 'God's will' *for them*, εἰς ὑμᾶς being emphatic, may cast some doubt on this conclusion.[75] The three exhortations

---

[71] G. Delling, 'Τάσσω, κτλ.', in *TDNT*, 8:48.

[72] In this respect verse 15 is like verse 13b, but unlike verses 12–13a, 14, 19–22 and quite possibly 16–18 also. Note that De Vos, *Conflict*, 160–1 (cf. Barclay, 'Social Contrasts', 53) infers from verse 15 that the Thessalonian believers were retaliating against their persecutors.

[73] Ἐν παντί as elsewhere in Paul seems not to be temporal; it should be rendered 'in all circumstances' here (*contra* Chrysostom and Wanamaker, *Thessalonians*, 200).

[74] E.g. Rigaux, *Thessaloniciens*, 588.

[75] Note the claim of Roetzel ('1 Thess. 5:12–28', 374) that 5:16–18 deals with the letter's 'central purpose and intent'.

do seem ideal for a discouraged community suffering persecution and needing to recapture the essence of Christian eschatological existence and relearning how to relate to God with confidence as those assured of salvation.[76] For example, joy in Pauline thought is rooted in the assured eschatological hope of future salvation (e.g. Rom. 5:2b–5; 12:12a) and empowers suffering Christians to persevere (Rom. 5:3–5; cf. 1 Pet. 4:13). Hence, although common in Paul's other letters, these exhortations may have a special significance in the Thessalonian context.

Concerning 5:19–22,[77] some propose that underlying these verses is a problem relating to prophets spreading eschatological excitement and/or enthusiasm and so causing or contributing to the problems of 4:13–5:11 and/or 4:9–12.[78] However, verses 19–20 read more like a single-pronged confrontation of a problem of quenching than a double-pronged confrontation of a conflict between quenchers and eschatological enthusiasts; and it is unnecessary to suppose that the apostle in verses 21–2 is doing anything other than establishing the alternative to outright rejection of the phenomenon of prophecy. Certainly if Paul had thought that prophets were proclaiming a false message which was confusing the community or that an opposition party was interpreting spiritual manifestations as evidence of the coming of the new age, we would have expected some fiery polemic and an explicit treatment of the deception at this point, or at least a direct textual connection between Paul's treatment of the eschatological problems and his treatment of prophecy.

Because despising prophecies (verse 20) is not something that we would have expected in an early Christian community and is absent from Paul's other letters, and possibly also because Paul employs present imperatives, it is likely that verses 19–22 are situationally specific, rather than general, exhortations. If eschatological enthusiasm did not give rise to the problem of quenching, what did? Verses 21–2[79] may suggest that inferior prophetic words had fostered scepticism within the community regarding the reliability of the phenomenon as a means of understanding

[76] Cf. ibid.

[77] Having just called for the community to conform to the content of God's will for them in verses 16–18, Paul encourages them to be open to the revelation of God's will by means of the prophetic Spirit in verses 19–22.

[78] *Inter alios* Schmithals, 'Historical Situation', 158–60, 172–5; Thomas, 'Thessalonians', 292; Jewett, *Correspondence*, 100–2; J. D. G. Dunn, *Unity and Diversity in the New Testament* (2nd edn; London: SCM, 1990), 326.

[79] The likelihood that δέ in verse 21a is original (it seems more plausible that a scribe removed the δέ, unaware of the link with the preceding verses) suggests that verse 21a is closely related to the preceding and adversative, introducing the positive alternative to despising prophetic utterances: 'but test everything'. Πάντα is therefore defined by verses 19–20 and means 'all prophetic manifestations'.

the divine mind[80] rather than that oracular speech had been used illegitimately to manipulate others.[81] In view of our situational hypothesis and specifically how much the community needed reassurance, encouragement and exhortation, it is little wonder that the apostle would have perceived this as an especial concern, for in Paul's view, rejecting out-of-hand oracular utterance was cutting off an invaluable avenue of divine aid. It is notable that Paul seems concerned that the community should accept its leaders (5:12–13a), Timothy (3:2; note also that Paul needs to write 4:13–5:11, even though Timothy has just visited Thessalonica) and genuine prophecies. It is perhaps worth noting that if indeed the converts were asking whether the deaths were a sign that the Day of the Lord was about to come, it would be understandable that they would be unwilling to trust the answer of unestablished leaders, a junior partner in the missionary band or a not wholly dependable phenomenon, for so much was at stake. Only the senior member of the missionary band, assuming that he was authentic, might be counted on to speak reliably for God.[82]

1 Thess. 5:23–4

Just as the first major section of the letter (1:2–3:13) concluded with an eschatologically focused wish-prayer, so also the second major section (4:1–5:24) climaxes with the same (5:23–4). As well as obvious parallels in form, the prayers have in common a striking wish that God would so work in the Thessalonians that they would be completely holy at the parousia of the Lord. However, verses 23–4 are distinctly different in that they culminate with a pronouncement of assurance (verse 24).

Verse 23 reads: 'And may the God of peace himself sanctify you through and through (ὁλοτελεῖς);[83] and may in entirety (ὁλόκληρον)[84] your spirit, soul and body be kept blamelessly at the parousia of our Lord

---

[80] It is not that the community, or a part of it, became 'anti-charismatic'; from 4:8b we gather that the Thessalonian community was still receptive to the Spirit's work in other areas.

[81] So Wanamaker, *Thessalonians*, 202–3, who contends that the leaders felt that their authority was threatened and so reined in prophecy; however, if the leaders were those quenching the Spirit, we would have expected 5:20 to read 'do not *forbid* prophecy'. Frame, *Thessalonians*, 191, 204 made the unsubstantiated claim that the ἄτακτοι were demanding money 'in the Spirit' from the church workers.

[82] Herein is a further reason for Paul's apologies in 1:5 (cf. verse 9a); 2:1–12 and 2:17–3:10: the community needed to know that they could indeed rely on him as an approved ambassador of God partly so that they might receive his assurances in 4:13–5:11.

[83] Although grammatically predicate, this adjective seems to function adverbially. We interpret it as quantitative/collective rather than qualitative/distributive.

[84] As with ὁλοτελεῖς, so also the adjective ὁλόκληρον seems to function adverbially. We regard it as qualitative/distributive.

Jesus Christ.' In the first part of Paul's prayer for his converts, verse 23a, God is conceptualised as the source of εἰρήνη, that is, final *shalom* (LXX: εἰρήνη), eschatological salvation (cf. Rom. 2:10; 8:6; 14:17; 16:20; Eph. 6:15); he alone can complete the process of making the Thessalonians holy (ἁγιάσαι). Verse 23b, apparently a synonymous parallel to verse 23a, reiterates this prayer wish that the converts would be *entirely* sanctified (note ὁλόκληρον and 'spirit, soul and body'). However, in it Paul speaks of being 'preserved blamelessly' (ἀμέμπτως, which seems to stress result rather than manner; cf. 3:13's στηρίξαι . . . ἀμέμπτους ἐν ἁγιωσύνῃ) and refers explicitly to the parousia (ἐν τῇ παρουσίᾳ τοῦ κυρίου ἡμῶν Ἰησοῦ Χριστοῦ, cf. 3:13). The importance of complete holiness and blame-lessness at the parousia is presumably so that the Thessalonians will be counted among the ἅγιοι (3:13; cf. 4:14b; Zech. 14:5). The apostle here, as in 3:13, presupposes that inheritance of eschatological salvation hinges on the standard of complete holiness and blamelessness being met. But here, unlike there, he does not leave his converts' salvation as a mere pastoral prayer wish.

In verse 24 he assures the Thessalonians that their meeting the eschato-logical standard for participation in parousia salvation is also a secure fact based on the faithfulness of God: 'Faithful is he who calls you who will also do it.' In this verse Paul skilfully synthesises the two major concerns of the second half of the letter: the need for holiness and the assurance of eschatological destiny. The latter does not mean the negation of the former, for God's faithfulness to his call of the Thessalonians ensures that the required eschatological standard will be satisfied in them. But why did the apostle omit such an assurance from the prayer of 3:11–13? We suggest that Paul in 3:13 postponed this assurance, simply presenting the required standard as the wish-prayer of a loving pastor, because he had yet to ground the Thessalonians' hope in the death and resurrection of Christ (4:13–5:11; although note 1:10) and, more importantly, because he was about to exhort them to sexual holiness (4:1–8) and did not want to undermine his paraenesis at this critical point. At the end of this second section, after he has underlined the urgent need for holiness and then re-assured regarding eschatological destiny, he moves to resolve the tension between his eschatological reassurances and his call for holiness.

In addition, 5:24 functions as the argumentative conclusion of the whole letter. The theme of election and calling is evident throughout 1 Thessalonians: the whole of 1:4–2:16 is essentially a testimony to the truth of the community's election (cf. 4:7). Just as 5:9 integrates assur-ance of eschatological hope with divine election, rooting the former in the latter, so also does 5:24 (cf. 1:4, 10); however, the latter adds an extra dimension: the reason why election guarantees salvation is that the one electing is faithful (cf. 1 Cor. 1:9). The God who called them and indeed still calls them (note the present participle, as in 2:12) will not rescind his call or reject them, because he is faithful; rather the call will be realised and so the Thessalonians will be among the ἅγιοι at the parousia.

The reassurance in 5:24 regarding eschatological destiny probably reflects the same problem as 5:1–11: extreme discouragement and anxiety on the part of the converts that they might not be saved at the parousia, apparently induced by the unexpected deaths. And so with the closing verse of the epistolary body Paul climaxes his treatment of the Thessalonians' lack of assurance concerning their eschatological destiny.

1 Thess. 5:25–8

In 5:25 Paul calls on the Thessalonian readers to pray for the missionaries, just as the missionaries pray for their converts (verse 23).[85] Then in verse 26 he instructs them to greet 'all the brothers' with a 'holy kiss', here probably a fellowship symbol of holiness among the 'holy ones'. The stress on 'all' in verses 26–7 (πάντας) is apparently motivated by Paul's desire to communicate his love to each member of the community. The use of the first-person singular in verse 27 indicates that it is no longer the amanuensis penning the letter, but Paul, who has taken over to write the last verses himself (verses 26–8, verses 27–8 or verses 25–8[86]). The fact that Paul uses ἐνορκίζω to underline his direction that the letter be read (aloud) to all (πᾶσιν) the brothers indicates strong feeling. It is unnecessary to conclude that he is anticipating the leaders' choosing not to read the letter to all sections of the community[87] or that he is worried about his name and authority being misused[88] or that he feared resistance from some within the community.[89] Much more plausible is the suggestion that Paul simply wished to ensure that the recipients knew what to do with his letter and specifically that all heard the letter, because the contents were relevant to all, especially to the faint-hearted and those wondering why Paul has not yet returned, but perhaps also to the sexually lax and the ἄτακτοι. For any members of the community to miss hearing

---

[85] This assumes that καί ('Αδελφοί, προσεύχεσθε [καὶ] περὶ ἡμῶν) is original (with P30 B D* 0278.6.33.81.104.326 *contra* ℵ A D¹ F G Iᵛⁱᵈ lat bo) (*pace* Richard, *Thessalonians*, 286).

[86] Rigaux, *Thessaloniciens*, 605. The plural in verse 25 does not necessarily undermine this view, since it would be expected that Paul would request prayer for the entire missionary band and not just himself.

[87] Cf. Theodore of Mopsuestia; Calvin, *Thessalonians*, 381.

[88] So Lightfoot, *Epistles*, 91, who extrapolated this from 2 Thess. 2:2.

[89] Frame, *Thessalonians*, 215, 217; Whiteley, *Thessalonians*, 86–7.

Paul's letter might have disastrous consequences and certainly could lead to unnecessary further anxiety, doubts, pain and even sin. Finally, in verse 28 Paul ends in a typical way: 'May the grace of our Lord Jesus Christ be with you' (cf. Rom. 16:20b; 1 Cor. 16:23b).

Conclusion to Part 2

With a view to the ultimate goal of determining whether the situations of 1 and 2 Thessalonians can reasonably be understood as compatible, in Part 2 we have commenced by undertaking an analysis of the Thessalonian Christian community's situation as reflected in 1 Thessalonians. What we have seen is a neophyte community moving from initial hope to hopeless grieving and nervous dread. One notes the following: (1) the believers in Thessalonica had during the mission accepted the Christian eschatological hope as an integral part of the Christian Gospel when they converted to the living and true God (1:3, 9b–10a). Indeed, their hope had inspired them to persevere in adverse circumstances (1:3), presumably because the eschaton promised to bring them blessing and their persecutors wrath. It had been a hope which was focused on the parousia, apparently conceptualised in terms of LXX Zech. 14:5 (1 Thess. 3:13; 4:14b), but one which did not include belief in the eschatological resurrection of dead saints (4:13–17). Moreover, it had been an imminentist hope (1:10a; 5:2–3). (2) When some members of their community died, the survivors grieved hopelessly for them, ignorant of the early Christian tradition concerning the final resurrection of dead saints. (3) Seemingly deducing that the anomalous deaths signified divine disapproval of the whole community and perhaps were an omen of imminent eschatological *Yom Yahweh* wrath, the Thessalonian believers were filled with anxiety and fear and could apparently only speculate what might be the cause of the divine disfavour. Nevertheless, the problem at the time of Timothy's visit seems to have been in its early stages, for Paul can still rejoice that they are characterised by faith and love (3:6ff.). That meant that Paul had to write to re-establish his converts' confidence in their own elective status before God, to refute the perceived possible causes of divine wrath (flawed missionaries or a flawed Gospel or a flawed reception of that Gospel), and to reassure the Thessalonians regarding the salvific eschatological destiny of their deceased and the whole community.[90]

---

[90] Although some have argued that 1 Thessalonians should be classified as a 'letter of consolation' (Malherbe, 'Exhortation', 254–6; Donfried, 'Purpose', 243–60; Smith, *Comfort*; De Vos, *Conflict*, 171–2), our study has demonstrated that it is more than a mere consolation

We conclude that the unexpected passing away of community members is the primary exigency of 1 Thessalonians, filling the survivors with despair both for their dead and for themselves.[91] We suggest that 1 Thessalonians was written to address Gentile[92] neophytes who, with regard to eschatological expectation, were not joyfully excited or enthusiastic, but, on the contrary, were lacking in hope and indeed anxious, insecure and fearful.

It now remains for us to consider the situation apparently reflected in 2 Thessalonians (Part 3) so that we shall be in a better position to deduce whether or not the two situations are compatible (Part 4).

in the face of death. As Chapa, 'Letter of Consolation', 159 concludes, 1 Thessalonians does not meet the thematic or literary criteria to be classified as a 'letter of consolation' (see also 'Consolatory Patterns? 1 Thes 4, 13.18; 5, 11', in *TC*, 220–8). Collins, 'Paraenesis', 404 made a valuable point when he wrote 'categories are always somewhat artificial. Letters, particularly, do not neatly fall into one category or another. A letter writer's authorial freedom generally implies that most real letters have a *Mischform*.'

[91] Why Paul does not treat the eschatological problems in the community directly until well into the letter (4:13–5:11) is explicable when we recognise that 1:2–3:13 is a necessary preparation for Paul's eschatological assurances, undergirding his claim that the community has been elected to inherit salvation at the eschaton.

[92] Regarding the constituency of the Thessalonian community, most rightly concur that the community was predominantly Gentile (1:9–10; 2:14). But what are we to make of Acts 17:1ff., which mentions Jewish converts in Thessalonica? We see no reason to deny that there was a population of Jews in first-century Thessalonica, as in Philippi and Stoboi (see Philo, *Leg. Gai.* 281; Josephus, *Bell.* 2.398 and *Ant.* 14.115; 1 Macc. 15:22–3). There is evidence from the third and fourth century that Jews did live in the largest city of Macedonia (see especially P. M. Nigdelis, 'Synagoge(n) und Gemeinde der Juden in Thessaloniki: Fragen auf Grund einer neuen jüdischen Grabinschrift der Kaiserzeit', *ZPE* 102 (1994): 297–306), and it seems a fair extrapolation that they had been there in the first and second centuries (so Hill, 'Establishing', 53–6, Sandnes, *Paul*, 187–9; I. Levinskaya, *The Book of Acts in its Diaspora Setting* (BAFCS; Grand Rapids: Eerdmans, 1996), 154–7; Riesner, *Early Period*, 344–8; Still, *Conflict*, 62–6, *contra* De Vos, *Conflict*, 130–2). In this regard, 1 Thess. 2:15 seems decisive. It seems wisest to give Luke the benefit of any doubt on the matter. But were there Jews in the community? If we were depending solely on the evidence of 1 Thessalonians, we would probably not conclude that there were. However, it is not necessary to discount Luke's evidence in this regard – a small number of Jews may have been a part of the community, but those to whom 1 Thessalonians is primarily directed were almost certainly Gentile believers (and not God-fearers, *pace* R. Russell, 'The Idle in 2 Thess 3:6–12: An Eschatological or a Social Problem?', *NTS* 34 (1988): 111). It is conceivable that the Thessalonian community was divided into different house churches, one or more of which was exclusively Gentile. Or the Jewish believers may have been largely confined to the band of leaders mentioned in 5:12–13, who it seems had not yet managed to command the community's full respect.

PART THREE

5

SHAKEN AND TERRIFIED

Introduction

Having offered a reading of the situation underlying 1 Thessalonians, we now turn to examine 2 Thessalonians in order to determine the nature of the eschatological problems it confronts. Our starting-point is 2 Thess. 2:1–3:5, which explicitly and directly confronts the eschatological idea which has gained currency among 'the Thessalonians' – namely ἐνέστηκεν ἡ ἡμέρα τοῦ κυρίου (2:2c). Unfortunately, what precisely 'Paul' and 'the Thessalonians' understood this claim to mean is unclear and has been much debated.[1] Most reject the literal meaning of the statement as impossible, choosing instead to avoid the perfective sense of ἐνέστηκεν and/or to soften the meaning of ἡ ἡμέρα τοῦ κυρίου.

How was ἐνέστηκεν ἡ ἡμέρα τοῦ κυρίου understood?

For 'Paul' and 'the Thessalonians', did ἐνέστηκεν mean 'is imminent'?

It has been suggested by some that ἐνέστηκεν should be translated 'is imminent' rather than 'has come'.[2] However, the perfect tense represents a present state resulting from a past action.[3] Moreover, the perfect of ἐνίστημι always seems to function perfectively. Certainly Paul used it thus, as indicated by Rom. 8:38 and 1 Cor. 3:22, where it contrasts with

---

[1] Our concern in this chapter is not with what the originator may have meant by this pronouncement (which we shall consider in chapter 8), but only with how 'Paul' and 'the Thessalonians' understood it.

[2] B. B. Warfield, 'The Prophecies of St. Paul. I – 1 and 2 Thessalonians', *The Expositor*, 3rd series 4 (1886): 37 including n. 1; Calvin, *Thessalonians*, 398; cf. Lightfoot, *Epistles*, 110 (but note his *Galatians*, 74).

[3] See, for example, M. Zerwick, *Biblical Greek* (Rome: Pontifical Biblical Institute, 1963), 96. As N. C. Croy, *A Primer of Biblical Greek* (Grand Rapids: Eerdmans, 1999), 83 put it, 'To say in the Greek perfect tense, "I have filled the cup", is equivalent to saying, "I have filled the cup and it is now full."'

μέλλοντα (see also Gal. 1:5; 1 Cor. 7:26; Heb. 9:9). And it was employed in this manner by Philo,[4] Josephus[5] and the Epistle of Barnabas,[6] and in the LXX,[7] classical literature[8] and the papyri.[9,10]

In spite of this overwhelming evidence, many scholars, unable to make sense of the reading 'the Day of the Lord has come', have chosen to render ἐνέστηκεν 'is [immediately] imminent',[11] judging that the statement is an example of rhetorical hyperbole[12] or that ἐνέστηκεν must be understood as a futuristic perfect.[13] Some have proposed that the present persecutions may have been interpreted by 'the Thessalonians' as the 'messianic woes' which would immediately precede the Day (Dan. 12:1b).[14] However, this reading of ἐνέστηκεν requires that no plausible alternative reading of 2 Thess. 2:2c can be achieved if the verb retains its usual perfective sense, and hence it is essentially a position of last resort.[15] We might then wonder

---

[4] E.g. *Leg. All.* 2.3.42; *Sac.* 6.47; *Plant.* 12.114; *Mig. Abr.* 43; *Praem. Poen.* 33.71.

[5] E.g. *Ant.* 3.24, 224; 7.391; 16.162; 17.185, 354; *Bell.* 2.280; 4.21.

[6] E.g. *Barn.* 1:7; 5:3; 17:2.

[7] E.g. *Est.* 3:13; 1 Macc. 12:44; 2 Macc. 6:9; 1 Esdr. 9:6.

[8] E.g. Aeschines 2.58; Aristotle, *Rhet.* 1.9.14 (1633b23); Xenophon, *Hell.* 2.1.6; Polybius, *Hist.* 1.18.48; 1.60.75; 2.26.3. See H. G. Liddell and R. S. Scott, *A Greek–English Lexicon* (rev. edn; Oxford: Clarendon, 1996), 568–9.

[9] E.g. P. Lond. 1164 [h]; P. Oxy. 1.37.1,11; 2.245.6; 82.4335.16 and 4338.2; 83.4356.2–3 and 4384.9 and 4390.7 and 4394.72; 85.4489.4, 11 and 4490.11; 86.4534.7; P. Flor. 1.1.6. See Milligan, *Thessalonians*, 97, George Milligan (ed.), *Selections from the Greek Papyri* (Cambridge: Cambridge University Press, 1912), 74 (29.6–7); 82 (32.10) and J. H. Moulton and G. Milligan, *The Vocabulary of the Greek Testament* (London: Hodder & Stoughton, 1930), 215.

[10] See E. D. Burton, *A Critical and Exegetical Commentary on the Epistle to the Galatians* (ICC; Edinburgh: T. & T. Clark, 1921), 432–3; A. M. G. Stephenson, 'On the Meaning of ἐνέστηκεν ἡ ἡμέρα τοῦ κυρίου in 2 Thessalonians 2,2', in *SE IV* (ed. F. L. Cross; TUGAL; Berlin: Akademie, 1968), 443–4; BDAG, 337. *Contra* Lindemann, 'Abfassungszweck', 41 n. 22, there is no reason to exclude 1 Cor. 7:26; 1 Macc. 8:24 and 12:44 (cf. *Barn.* 17:2) from this pattern.

[11] *Inter alios* von Dobschütz, *Thessalonicher-Briefe*, 267–8; Dibelius, *Thessalonicher*, 29; Rigaux, *Thessaloniciens*, 652–3; Stephenson, '2 Thessalonians 2,2', 449–51; Laub, *Verkündigung*, 138–40; Lindemann, 'Abfassungszweck', 41–2; E. Schweizer, *A Theological Introduction to the New Testament* (trans. O. C. Dean; London: SPCK, 1992), 99; L. J. L. Peerbolte, *The Antecedents of Antichrist* (SJSJ; Leiden: Brill, 1996), 73–4. Cf. Trilling, *Untersuchungen*, 126 and *Zweite Brief*, 78 including n. 280 and Wrede *Echtheit*, 41–2.

[12] Rigaux, *Thessaloniciens*, 653; Stephenson, '2 Thessalonians 2,2', 451; Légasse, *Thessaloniciens*, 383–4.

[13] A. Oepke, "Ἐνίστημι', in *TDNT*, 2:543–4, who (544 n. 2) proposed the rendering 'is in the process of coming'.

[14] Von Dobschütz, *Thessalonicher-Briefe*, 260–1, 267–8; Munck, 'Missionary Preaching', 100; Hartman, 'Eschatology', 471–2, 478, 484–5; U. B. Müller, 'Apocalyptic Currents', in *Christian Beginnings* (ed. J. Becker; trans. A. S. Kidder and R. Krauss; London: Westminster/John Knox, 1993), 307.

[15] Some (e.g. Wrede, *Echtheit*, 49–51; Laub, *Verkündigung*, 140 including n. 169; Friedrich, 'Zweite Brief', 263; Trilling, *Zweite Brief*, 78–80; Müller, 'Currents', 308) look to subsequent historical imminentist movements, especially the one recounted in Hippolytus' commentary on Daniel (4.18 and 19, G. N. Bonwetsch and H. Achelis, *Hippolytus Werke*

why ἐγγίζω[16] is not employed and why 'Paul', in refuting an idea that
he clearly regards as false, presents that idea in terms to which he himself technically subscribed (a concept of imminence is evident in 1:5–10
and 2:1). Moreover, there is nothing in the context which would suggest that we should interpret 2:2c as rhetorical hyperbole. Finally, if 'the
Thessalonians' perceived themselves as experiencing the messianic woes,
why then is there no *explicit* mention of the final tribulations of God's
people in the refutation of the false claim in 2:3ff.?

> For 'Paul' and 'the Thessalonians', what did ἡ ἡμέρα τοῦ
> κυρίου mean?

Many who accept the perfective sense of ἐνέστηκεν reject the literal sense
of ἡ ἡμέρα τοῦ κυρίου.

A complex of events?

It has been suggested by several scholars that 'the Thessalonians' think
that their own afflictions *qua* messianic woes are a part of the complex
of events which make up the 'Day of the Lord', culminating with the
parousia.[17] However, would any early Christian really have thought that
the 'Day of *the Lord*' would include persecution of those genuinely belonging to the Lord? Moreover, we might well ask why there is then no
categorical differentiation between the messianic woes and the Day in
2:1ff. Finally, it is difficult to imagine why 'Paul' would then argue in
1:5ff. that the afflictions of 'the Thessalonians' are an ἔνδειγμα of God's
just judgment of them, for that would risk exacerbating the problem.[18]

Holland[19] has argued that the addressees are perceiving signs that the
'Day of the Lord', a day of wrath distinct from and immediately prior to
the 'Day of Christ' (the parousia), is being revealed against the wicked,[20]
and moreover, that they are interpreting their persecutions as proof of this
Day's presence, since these afflictions demonstrate that God is purifying

---

(Leipzig: Hinrichs, 1897), 230–4), to elucidate the situation (where Hippolytus' rendition
of the eschatological claim (4.19) is a verbatim quotation from 2 Thess. 2:2c, apparently
reflecting an imminentist interpretation of the false claim). It is hard to avoid the conclusion
that too much weight is being given to Hippolytus' anecdote and that analogies are in fact
giving rise to eisegesis.

[16] D. J. Stephens, 'Eschatological Themes in 2 Thess. 2:1–12' (Ph.D. thesis, University
of St Andrews, 1976), 97.

[17] E.g. R. D. Aus, 'The Relevance of Isa. 66:7 to Revelation 12 and 2 Thessalonians
1', *ZNW* 67 (1976): 263–4 including n. 51; Gundry, 'Hellenization', 171; Wanamaker,
Thessalonians, 240; Still, *Conflict*, 283–4.

[18] Cf. Wrede, *Echtheit*, 53. For a defence of the view that ἔνδειγμα refers back to the
persecutions and afflictions of 1:4, see the following chapter.

[19] Holland, *Tradition*, esp. 96–105.   [20] Ibid., 105, 120–1.

them for the parousia.[21] Accordingly, 'Paul' stresses that the primary
event of the 'Day of the Lord' would be the appearance of the lawless
one,[22] thus demonstrating that the 'Day of the Lord' had manifestly not
yet come.[23] However, this distinction between the 'Day of Christ' and the
'Day of the Lord' seems artificial and undervalues the background Old
Testament use of the phrase for the ultimate intervention of God to punish
and to bring salvation. Furthermore, in 2:3b–4 'Paul' emphasises that the
ἀποστασία and the man of lawlessness's revelation *precede, rather than
characterise*, the 'Day of the Lord' (ἐὰν μὴ ἔλθῃ . . . πρῶτον[24]).

Spiritually present?

A number of scholars have argued that 'the Thessalonians' understood the
statement to mean that the 'Day of the Lord' was present *spiritually* and
that 2:2c refers to what is essentially an over-realised, pseudo-spiritual
Gnostic idea expressed 'apocalyptically',[25] their experience of the Spirit
causing them to conclude that the parousia had come spiritually and that
no further resurrection was therefore to be anticipated (cf. 2 Tim. 2:18),[26]
since freedom from the bondage of the world had already occurred.[27]
However, if 'the Thessalonians' had understood the pronouncement in
this way, we would have expected 'Paul' to defend the futurity of the resurrection[28] and to define the Day of the Lord and the parousia in opposition to the Gnostic position.[29] Moreover, ταχέως most naturally suggests that
the eschatological idea reflects a recent surprising 'turn of events' rather

[21] Ibid., 121.   [22] Ibid., 119–21.   [23] Ibid., 100–1, 120–1.

[24] Clearly temporal in this context, πρῶτον is unlikely to indicate the chronological
priority of the apostasy over the revelation of the man of lawlessness (*pace* ibid., 106;
Hughes, *2 Thessalonians*, 58), in spite of its position: verses 9–12 are unequivocal in
asserting that the culminative rebellion of humanity is accomplished *through the lawless
one*. Πρῶτον here therefore underlines the point that the Day will not have come until the
apostasy has first occurred.

[25] So *inter alios* R. M. Evans, 'Eschatology and Ethics: A Study of Thessalonica
and Paul's Letters to the Thessalonians' (Princeton: McMahon, 1968), 118–37; Marxsen,
Introduction, 39 and *Zweite Thessalonicherbrief*, 79–80; Bailey, 'Who?', 142–3.

[26] So, for example, Schmithals, 'Historical Situation', 166–7, 202–8.

[27] Marxsen, *Introduction*, 39 has argued that this position alone does justice to all relevant data, especially the force of the verb, and yet avoids the problems incurred by interpreting the phrase 'literally'.

[28] Stephenson, '2 Thessalonians 2,2', 450; Best, *Thessalonians*, 277; Menken, *Thessalonians*, 98.

[29] Several distinct features of Gnosticism appear to be absent from 2 Thessalonians:
the spirit–flesh dualism, christological speculation, speculation regarding Genesis 1–3, and
libertinistic behaviour (Jewett, *Correspondence*, 149). It cannot be assumed that there was
one particular eschatology common to Gnostics, as Peel, 'Gnostic', 141–65 pointed out.

than 'a developing theological tendency'.[30] Finally, the argumentation of 2 Thess. 2:3bff. seems particularly unsuited to a problem of Gnosticism. Similarly, verses 3bff. are inappropriate for a problem consisting of enthusiastic radicalist realised eschatologists[31] claiming that the kingdom had come spiritually on the basis of charismatic phenomena, such as is proposed by Jewett.[32] He claims that Thessalonian community members, on account of their experience of realised eschatology, were unwilling to live 'with the uncertainty of a future, incalculable parousia'[33] and so fell victim to radicals who proposed that in their ecstatic activities the millennium, including the Day and the parousia, had come.[34] His reconstruction of the situation seems too uncontrolled: the absence of polemic and harshness suggests that 'Paul' is not confronting a problem of intracommunal 'heresy', as the two thanksgivings and copious reassurances confirm.

A fresh analysis

So what are we to make of the phrase ἡ ἡμέρα τοῦ κυρίου in 2:2c? Particularly, how in the understanding of 'Paul' and 'the Thessalonians' did it relate to the parousia? Was the Day perceived to be a complex of events culminating with the parousia (i.e. 'the Day has come and the parousia is about to come')?[35] Was the 'Day' thought to be unconnected to the parousia?[36] Or was the 'Day' conceived of as co-referential with the parousia? In order to determine which of these is correct, it is necessary to examine the argument of 2:1ff.

Already in verse 1 we are given an important indication that the 'Day' and the parousia are co-referential in the view of 'Paul' and apparently also in the opinion of 'the Thessalonians' who embraced the false claim referred to in 2 Thess. 2:2c, for this section on the 'Day of the Lord' is introduced as relating to 'the parousia of our Lord Jesus Christ'.

---

[30] Barclay, 'Conflict', 527 n. 54 followed by Still, *Conflict*, 57 n. 44.

[31] *Contra* Lütgert, 'Enthusiasten'; B. Reicke, *Diakonie, Festfreude und Zelos, in Verbindung mit der altchristlichen Agapenfeier* (UUÅ; Uppsala: Lund, 1951), 243–5; Jewett, *Radicalism*, 202–3, 208–9, 215, 217; Reese, *Thessalonians*, 90–1; cf. Lüdemann, *Heretics*, 118 ('Gnostics or enthusiasts').

[32] Jewett, *Correspondence*, 161–78 and 'A Matrix of Grace: The Theology of 2 Thessalonians as a Pauline Letter', in *Pauline Theology I* (ed. J. M. Bassler; Minneapolis: Fortress, 1991), 63–6.

[33] Jewett, *Correspondence*, 97.   [34] Jewett, 'Matrix', 63 and *Correspondence*, 176–8.

[35] So Frame, *Thessalonians*, 248; Burkeen, 'Parousia', 316; Marshall, *Thessalonians*, 186; P. Müller, *Anfänge der Paulusschule* (ATANT; Zurich: Theologischer, 1988), 42–3; J. D. G. Dunn, *The Theology of Paul the Apostle* (Edinburgh: T. & T. Clark, 1998), 301 n. 37.

[36] Barclay, 'Conflict', 527–8.

Then in verses 3b–4 the false idea of verse 2c is tackled head-on, on the grounds that the ἀποστασία and the revelation of the rebel must yet transpire before the Day.[37] The former probably refers to the rebellion of humanity against God (cf. Eph. 6:13; 2 Tim. 3:1ff.(?); Mark 13:22/Matt. 24:24; Revelation 13; also 1QpHab 2:1–10; 1 Enoch 91:5–10; 93:9; Jub. 23:14–23; 4 Ezra 5:1–2; cf. Asc. Isa. 2:4; Ezek. 38–9). While Rom. 1:18–32 describes the *present* and unconsummated rebellion of humanity in Adam[38] and present divine 'handings over' (Rom. 1:24, 26, 28), 2 Thess. 2:3b and 9–12 concern *future* and ultimate rebellion (2 Thess. 2:3, 9–12) and eschatological divine wrath (2:11–12).[39] In Adam (cf. Rom. 5:12–21) humanity had an original relationship with God; hence its consummate eschatological rebellion can properly be conceived as an ἀποστασία. Hitherto it has rejected God's light in nature and the Old Testament Scriptures and the Gospel. But, while the supreme and ultimate eschatological act of apostasy may be rooted in previous acts of apostasy, according to 2 Thess. 2:3–12, it is still future (verses 10b–12). It is not difficult to see how the absence of such an apostasy might function as an unambiguous indication of the Day's futurity.[40]

---

[37] The temporal character of the argumentation is demonstrated by the copious temporal references (πρῶτον (verse 3); ὁ υἱὸς τῆς ἀπωλείας (verse 3); νῦν (? verse 6); ἤδη (verse 7a); ἕως (verse 7b); τότε (verse 8a) and perhaps τῇ ἐπιφανείᾳ τῆς παρουσίας αὐτοῦ (verse 8b)) and is accepted by the vast majority of scholars. C. H. Giblin maintained in 1967 (*The Threat to Faith* (AnBib; Rome: Pontifical Biblical Institute, 1967), 122–39) that the anacoluthon in verse 3 was qualitative rather than temporal, but he showed signs in 1990 ('Reread', 464 including n. 24) of backing down from that position.

[38] See M. D. Hooker, 'Adam in Romans 1', *NTS* 6 (1959–60): 297–306; J. Jervell, *Imago Dei* (FRLANT; Göttingen: Vandenhoeck & Ruprecht, 1960), 312–31; C. E. B. Cranfield, *A Critical and Exegetical Commentary on the Epistle to the Romans* (ICC; 2 vols.; Edinburgh: T. & T. Clark, 1975–9), 1:141–2; B. W. Longenecker, *Eschatology and the Covenant* (JSNTSup; Sheffield: JSOT, 1991), 173; Dunn, *Theology*, 91–3. The διό of Rom. 2:1, together with possible hints of the Adamic story (γνόντες τὸν θεόν, 1:21; εἰκόνος, verse 23; θανάτου, verse 32) and possible echoes of LXX Ps. 106:20 and Jer. 2:11 in ἤλλαξαν τὴν δόξαν τοῦ ἀφθάρτου θεοῦ ἐν ὁμοιώματι, verse 23) suggest that humanity in Adam may be in view in Rom. 1:18ff.

[39] It is perhaps worth noting that the worship of the creature (Rom. 1:25) takes on a new form (2 Thess. 2:10b–12). The characterisation in 2 Thess. 2:12 of fallen humanity destined to believe the lie as those who presently approve wickedness (εὐδοκήσαντες τῇ ἀδικίᾳ) fits well with the description of fallen humanity in their 'handed-over' state in Rom. 1:32 – 'they do these things' (τὰ τοιαῦτα πράσσοντες), including ἀδικία (verse 29), and 'they approve those who do [these things]', συνευδοκοῦσιν τοῖς πράσσουσιν.

[40] *Pace* Stephens, 'Themes', 141. That it is not a Jewish apostasy (*pace* B. Weiss, *Biblical Theology of the New Testament* (trans. D. Eaton; CFTL; 2 vols.; Edinburgh: T. & T. Clark, 1893), 1:306–7; E. Cothenet, 'Le Deuxième Epître aux Thessaloniciens et l'apocalypse synoptique', *RSR* 42 (1954): 38; W. D. Davies, 'Paul and the People of Israel', *NTS* 24 (1978): 8; Best, *Thessalonians*, 281–3; Wanamaker, *Thessalonians*, 244) is clear. (1) That is alien to the thought of the passage; (2) in Pauline, and presumably Paulinist, thought, the

Concerning the revelation of ὁ ἄνθρωπος τῆς ἀνομίας, scholars are largely united in taking ἀνομία to refer to rebellion and hostility to God and his revelation in a general sense[41] rather than to the Mosaic law.[42] Of what does this revelation consist? It is apparently defined by verses 4 and 9–12. The rebel will be revealed as the God-opposing, self-exalting rebel that he is, when he takes his seat in the temple of God, proclaiming himself to be God (verse 4). He will dupe unbelievers by means of Satanic miracles and deception and so cause them to 'believe the lie', that is, that he is worthy of worship (verses 9–12).

The majority of scholars think that the 'temple' is metaphorical and typological, based on Antiochus and Caligula.[43] However, neither Antiochus nor Caligula 'took his seat' in the temple; the former set up a statue of Zeus (1 Macc. 1:36–40, 54–9; 2 Macc. 6:2; cf. Dan. 11:31–5) and the latter merely ordered without effect a statue of himself to be erected in the temple (Philo, Leg. Gai. 188; Josephus, Bell. 2.10.1 §184–5 and Ant. 18.8.2 §261).[44] Hence it is hard to see how these historical analogies might serve as the basis for a metaphor of taking one's seat in the temple of God. Moreover, it is difficult to see why 'Paul' would appeal to a metaphor to describe the activity of the rebel when the situation called for a clear, concrete and unmistakable sign; it would have been pastorally unwise to give a sign which is so vague, especially in the light of Caligula's activities only a decade before. Further, he hardly needed to use a metaphor to suggest that this figure would be the supreme blasphemer, since that very point was already evident in verse 4a.[45]

Jews had already apostatised (Rom. 11:7–10, 17a, 20), and so their apostasy would have been of no value to 'Paul', who is arguing that the Day has not come. The view that it is a Christian apostasy (so Findlay, Epistles of Paul, 167; Friedrich, 'Zweite Brief', 263; Stephens, 'Themes', 145–7; Thomas, 'Thessalonians', 321–2; J. Y-S. Ahn, 'The Parousia in Paul's Letters to the Thessalonians, the Corinthians, and the Romans, in relation to its Old Testament-Judaic Background' (Ph.D. thesis, Fuller Theological Seminary, 1989), 232) ultimately founders on the contextual unsuitability of the concept. Not only is the church otherwise absent from verses 3–12, but it is also quite implausible that 'Paul' would rest a significant part of his argument on a future apostasy of believers in the same context where he unreservedly reassures believers of their election to salvation (verses 13–14).

[41] Note especially Giblin, Threat to Faith, 81–8 on this point.

[42] Pace M. Brunec, 'De "homine peccati" in 2 Thess. 2.1–12', VD 35 (1957): 22; Best, Thessalonians, 284; Jewett, 'Matrix', 66–7.

[43] So, for example, Trilling, Untersuchungen, 126–7 and Zweite Brief, 86–7; Friedrich, 'Zweite Brief', 264; Marshall, Thessalonians, 191–2; Richard, Thessalonians, 328–9, 351; Peerbolte, Antecedents, 77–8; Légasse, Thessaloniciens, 391.

[44] On Pompey's temple blasphemy, see Ps. Sol. 17:11–15.

[45] The referent of τὸν ναὸν τοῦ θεοῦ is much disputed. The suggestion that it refers to the church founders because (1) it cannot explain καθίσαι; and (2) the concept of the church is otherwise absent from verses 1–12. The view that τὸν ναὸν τοῦ θεοῦ refers to the

We judge that the temple is most probably the Jerusalem temple,[46] the reference being to the abomination of desolation referred to by Daniel (Dan. 9:27; 12:11; cf. 8:13; 11:31) and the Synoptic Gospels (Mark 13:14; Matt. 24:15).[47] This position pays due respect to the dependence on Dan. 11:36–7 in the preceding and succeeding context; 'Paul' apparently understood Dan. 11:36ff. as prophesying that a future figure (distinct from Antiochus IV Epiphanes, the apparent referent of the immediately preceding Danielic verses) would arise who would desecrate the temple, persecute the people of God and consummate world history (Dan. 9:27; 11:36–12:1), fulfilling Daniel's predictions and heralding the end.[48] Other supports for this reading of verse 4b include: (a) that the use of καθίσαι seems more fitting in a literal, physical place; (b) that the definite articles may suggest that we have here an allusion to a particular temple of the true God, namely the Jerusalem temple; (c) that the immediately preceding reference to σέβασμα in verse 4a favours understanding verse 4b to refer to a material temple.[49] Finally, as a clearly observable and concrete event, the rebel's taking his seat in the Jerusalem temple meets the criterion of being an unmistakably evident 'sign' which must transpire before the Day

heavenly temple is eliminated because it undermines verses 3b–4's perspicuity; further, the miracles and deception of verses 9–10a clearly occur on the earth. Also, if 2 Thessalonians is authentic, it is worth noting the lack of evidence that Paul ever thought in terms of an eschatological, heavenly temple.

[46] So also Irenaeus, *Adv. Haer.* 5.25.4; 30.4; Hippolytus, *On the Antichrist* 6 and *Commentary on Daniel* 4.49; Cyril of Jerusalem, *Cat.* 4.15; Jerome, *Commentary on Daniel* 9, 15; Origen, *In Mat. 24* (PG 13:1656–7).

[47] According to Mark 13:14 the 'abomination of desolation' stands 'where it does not belong'; according to Matt. 24:15 it is 'in the holy place'. These references seem to reflect the belief that a human person embodying rebellion is in view. It is perhaps worth noting that in LXX usage ναός could be used of the inner shrine of the temple (e.g. 1 Kgs. 6:5) as well as for the temple itself (e.g. Jdt. 4:2).

[48] Similarly, Hippolytus (*Commentary on Daniel* 4.48–9 and *On the Antichrist* 52–3) and Jerome (in his comments on Dan. 11:36) understood many parts of Daniel's prophecies to refer not to Antiochus but to the Antichrist. Josephus clearly thought that not all of Daniel's prophecies referred to Antiochus, for he states that Daniel wrote also about the Romans and the desolation which they would wreak in Israel (*Ant.* 10.11.7 §276).

[49] Giblin, *Threat to Faith*, 77; Stephens, 'Themes', 249 and D. Ford, *The Abomination of Desolation in Biblical Eschatology* (Washington, D.C.: University Press of America, 1979), 210 saw a theological problem in 'Paul' regarding the Jerusalem temple as the 'temple of God'. However, not only is it plausible that he is conceiving of the Jerusalem temple as fulfilling an important eschatological role regardless of its present status, but it is also worth noting that the separation of Christianity from Judaism was not yet final by 50. Whether Paul was open to the continuing validity (in some sense) of the Jerusalem temple for Jewish Christians is a matter of some debate. Acts 21:26–7; 22:17; 24:18; 25:8; 26:21 suggest that he may have been (although see R. J. McKelvey, *The New Temple* (OTM; Oxford: Oxford University Press, 1969), 124; J. D. G. Dunn, *The Partings of the Ways* (London: SCM, 1991), 75–86 and *Theology*, 543–8, 721–2).

can come.[50] 'Paul' implies that 'the Thessalonians' who succumbed to the erroneous claim referred to in verse 2c had forgotten that according to the eschatological schema the apostasy and rebel's revelation necessarily precede the Day.

Significantly, verse 3b refers to the rebel as ὁ υἱὸς τῆς ἀπωλείας. In the light of verse 10a, this almost certainly refers to the rebel's destiny of destruction. Undoubtedly it points forward to verse 8b, where Christ's parousia destruction of the rebel is highlighted. Just as πρῶτον functions to draw 'the Thessalonians' back to the chronological relationship between the apostasy and the Day, so ὁ υἱὸς τῆς ἀπωλείας indicates the connection between the rebel's revelation and the parousia. It is hard to avoid the suggestion that 'Paul' thinks that the Day and the parousia are co-referential and that he is presupposing that 'the Thessalonians' who have succumbed to the false pronouncement share his view.

Verse 5 and verses 6–8a, where the memories[51] of 'the Thessalonians' regarding the rebel's revelation (i.e. temple desecration) are refreshed by pointing to the celestial event which causes the rebel's revelation (the removal of the restrainer, probably Michael, LXX Dan. 12:1a[52]), imply that if 'the Thessalonians' had taken into account what they had been taught about the apostasy and the rebel's revelation, they would not have accepted that the Day of the Lord had come. In these verses he manifestly assumes that they understood the Day of the Lord to be the consummate event in their eschatological schema.

---

[50] Many proponents of Pauline authorship seem to abandon the view that the 'temple' is the Jerusalem temple because of the events of 70 (so, for example, Marshall, *Thessalonians*, 191). However, the exegete's task is not the reinterpretation of a text in the light of events twenty years later. Proponents of pseudonymity are divided regarding whether the Jerusalem temple is in view. On the one hand, in spite of the obvious problems for his post-70 dating of 2 Thessalonians, Wrede insists on the literal interpretation (*Echtheit*, 97–113). On the other hand, Trilling, *Zweite Brief*, 86–7 adopts the metaphorical view.

[51] Hartman, 'Eschatology', 473 argues that the supposedly familiar information must in fact have been new, since otherwise the readers would have viewed the false claim (2:2c) with a hostility similar to the author's. However, the expression of disbelief surely lends credibility to the statement; it seems perfectly plausible that 'the Thessalonians' may have suffered a memory lapse (even repeating teachings does not ensure remembrance, as any teacher could testify), and/or that the panic induced by the false claim and especially the apparent authority of its source combined to shake them to such a degree that they failed to take previous teaching into account.

[52] On the restrainer, see the appendix below; verses 6–7 are not designed to put the parousia off into the distant future, *pace* Trilling, *Untersuchungen*, 86, who argues that verses 5–7 constitute the key verses of verses 1–12 (*Zweite Brief*, 70; cf. M. J. J. Menken, 'The Structure of 2 Thessalonians', in *TC*, 381 and *Thessalonians*, 76, 108), maintaining that for pseudonymous authors, digressions turn into the primary sections (*Untersuchungen*, 90)!

This is reinforced by verse 8, where the reference to the rebel provokes another reference to his destruction, at the parousia (ὃν ὁ κύριος ['Iησοῦς] ἀνελεῖ). The point is once again that the Day cannot occur until the rebel is revealed, for that is a *sine qua non* of the parousia. Further, in view of the fact that ἐπιφάνεια in verse 8b can apparently only refer to the 'appearance' or 'dawning' of the parousia,[53] (cf. Polybius, *Hist.* 3.94.3), it is probable that τῇ ἐπιφανείᾳ τῆς παρουσίας αὐτοῦ also highlights the temporal coincidence between the parousia and the rebel's destruction. Finally, in verses 9–12 'Paul' stresses how the rebel's revelation leads to the apostasy of humanity: Satan will work with unrestrained power and deception through the rebel against those who reject the Gospel, and God will delude them so that they will be condemned (ἵνα κριθῶσιν) at the parousia (cf. verses 13–14). This seems to confirm what we observed above, that the parousia is being conceived of as the consummate event in this chronological sketch in which the Day of the Lord is the *terminus ad quem*.

Clearly, then, throughout verses 3b–12 'Paul' seems to be presupposing that the Day is co-referential with the parousia and is a single event rather than a complex of events and that 'the Thessalonians' share these assumptions. This is confirmed by 1:10 (four verses before 2:2), where the 'Day' is defined as 'when he [the Lord] comes'; 1:7b–10 (cf. 1 Thess. 4:14–17) explicitly states that the Day is the occasion of the 'revelation of our Lord Jesus from heaven'.

The nature of the argumentation of 2 Thess. 2:1ff. is elucidated when we understand that 'Paul' only needs to point to those most conspicuous, undeniably unfulfilled events in his eschatological schema which precede the Day, and indeed are prerequisites for it, since the Day cannot come until the antagonist of the parousia story is in place (after all, the coming of *Yom Yahweh* involves a battle between two sides). By focusing on the pre-parousia events yet to occur, 'Paul' also guards 'the Thessalonians' against further confusion.

We conclude therefore that the erroneous pronouncement that ἐνέστηκεν ἡ ἡμέρα τοῦ κυρίου is to be understood as implying that the Day of the Lord, and the parousia, had come.

But could any early Christian genuinely have believed such a bizarre claim as that in 2 Thess. 2:2c? As 2:15 asserts, the new idea came into conflict with what 'the Thessalonians' had already been taught. So why

---

[53] While ἐπιφάνεια in the Pastorals (1 Tim. 6:14; 2 Tim. 4:1, 8; Tit. 2:13) appears to be almost a *terminus technicus* for the second coming of Christ, virtually synonymous with 'parousia', here with παρουσία such a rendering would be pleonastic.

did they accept it? The answer is apparently found in the striking emphasis in verses 2–3a on the means by which the idea may have entered the community of 'the Thessalonians': μήτε διὰ πνεύματος μήτε διὰ λόγου μήτε δι' ἐπιστολῆς ὡς δι' ἡμῶν (verse 2) and κατὰ μηδένα τρόπον (verse 3a). The three suggestions have as a common denominator revelatory and/or authoritative status; they each might have been deferred to as accurately representing God's word. Whether 2 Thessalonians is authentic or pseudonymous, no original readers would have concluded that the 'spirit' (i.e. prophetic utterance) or 'word' (authoritative speech act) could have been 'Paul's', since 2 Thess. 2:15 implies that 'Paul' had not been present among 'the Thessalonians' during the period in which the idea had formed. As an absentee, he could only have been perceived as responsible for the claim if he had written a letter, an option which he apparently rules out in 2:2. Because it is somewhat unlikely that a prophet or teacher would have had sufficient weight to alter the established tradition, it is little wonder that 'Paul' apparently takes the possibility of a forgery most seriously (3:17).

We turn now to consider whether the idea that 'the Day of the Lord had come' was perceived by 'the Thessalonians' as good or bad news.

What were the implications of the false claim for 'the Thessalonians'?

The scholarly consensus is that 'the Thessalonians' were characterised by 'overheated eschatological enthusiasm'[54] or 'apocalyptic fanaticism'.[55] However, if we are correct in judging that the assertion was understood at

[54] Dunn, *Theology*, 301; cf. *Unity*, 326–8.
[55] Kümmel, *Introduction*, 266, 268. Others who have understood the letter to be addressed to those who are characterised by over-excitement and eschatological enthusiasm include Findlay, *Epistles of Paul*, 161–4; Milligan, *Thessalonians*, xxxviii and l, 94–5; Munck, 'Missionary Preaching', 100; Giblin, *Threat to Faith*, 226, 243–6; Trilling, *Untersuchungen*, 91, 124–5; G. Agrell, *Work, Toil and Sustenance* (trans. S. Westerholm and G. Agrell; Lund: Ohlssons, 1976), 122–3; Lindemann, 'Abfassungszweck', 41–2; Krodel, *Ephesians, Colossians, 2 Thessalonians*, 87–8 and *Deutero-Pauline Letters*, 57; Mearns, 'Development', 149, 152, 153, 154; M. D. Hooker, 'Trial and Tribulation in Mark XIII', *BJRL* 65 (1982–3): 95–6; Jewett, *Correspondence*, 97–105, 177–8; Müller, *Anfänge*, 47; Koester, 'Schemata', 455–6; Bassin, *Thessaloniciens*, 208; Reumann, *Variety and Unity in New Testament Thought* (OBS; Oxford: Oxford University Press, 1991), 125–7; Barclay, 'Conflict', 527–9; Müller, *Currents*, 307–8; Richard, *Thessalonians*, 342–4; Légasse, *Thessaloniciens*, 384–5; Still, *Conflict*, 282–5. Cf. *inter alios* Hollmann, 'Unechtheit', 34–5, 37; von Dobschütz, *Thessalonicher-Briefe*, 260–1, 265; Friedrich, 'Zweite Brief', 253–7; Marshall, *Thessalonians*, 20, 23–5, 43, 186, 205, 218–19; Holland, *Tradition*, 48, 99, 120–1; Donfried, *Shorter*, 87–9, 96; Menken, *Thessalonians*, 97 and Peerbolte, *Antecedents*, 66, although they hold that a section of the community responded less positively.

face value, there is good reason to think that it might have been perceived to be bad news, especially because those who accepted it presumably experienced no significant change in their circumstances. Indeed, we might anticipate that persecution (1:4, 5b, 6–7a) would then have presented them with a dire predicament and would conceivably have filled them with horror, confusion, disappointment and disillusionment, for it would have been difficult not to infer from the false claim that they had been abandoned by God and had no grounds for hope.[56] Is this the picture that emerges from 2 Thessalonians?

2 Thess. 2:2

In verse 2 'Paul' calls on 'the Thessalonians' μὴ ταχέως σαλευθῆναι ὑμᾶς ἀπὸ τοῦ νοὸς μηδὲ θροεῖσθαι by the false claim; this is the sole explicit clue to how they had responded to it.

Many of those embracing the view that 2 Thessalonians addresses a problem of over-excited eschatological expectation have claimed that θροεῖσθαι indicates joyful or enthusiastic excitement.[57] However, as our analysis will demonstrate, this interpretation is extremely dubious. On the contrary, this verb most naturally suggests fear or terror.

Searches of the *Thesaurus Linguae Graecae* and *PHI Greek Documentary Texts* databases demonstrate that the verb θροέω in the passive and causative consistently means 'frightened' and 'disturbed'.[58] The most striking parallel to 2 Thess. 2:2 is in the Synoptic eschatological discourses, where θροέομαι refers to the *frightened* reaction of people to wars and rumours of wars, perceiving them as signs of the eschaton. That the verb has this meaning in the Synoptics is reinforced by the parallel in Luke 21:9, where πτοέομαι ('be terrified, be alarmed, frightened, startled'[59]) replaces Mark's θροέομαι, a change to a more common,[60]

---

[56] Cf. Friedrich, 'Zweite Brief', 253, 262, who argued against a realised understanding of the false statement of 2:2c on the grounds that then 'the Thessalonians' would have been fearful.

[57] For example, Findlay, *Epistles of Paul*, 164; Mearns, 'Development', 149; E. Bammel, 'Preparation for the Perils of the Last Days: I Thessalonians 3:3', in *Suffering and Martyrdom in the New Testament* (ed. W. Horbury and B. McNeil; Cambridge: Cambridge University Press, 1981), 99; Barclay, 'Conflict', 526; Still, *Conflict*, 282.

[58] I conducted my search of *Thesaurus Linguae Graecae CD-ROM #E* at http://www.tlg.uci.edu in April 2002. An article presenting the results of my exhaustive word study of θροέομαι is forthcoming.

[59] BDAG, 895.

[60] As a search of *TLG* demonstrates. C. F. Evans, *Saint Luke* (TPINTC; London: SCM, 1990), 739 thinks that Luke's change is motivated by literary concerns. J. Fitzmyer, *The Gospel According to Luke* (AB; 2 vols.; Garden City, N.Y.: Doubleday, 1981–5), 2:1336 argues that Luke is reflecting his preference for Septuagintalisms. I. H. Marshall, *The Gospel*

synonymous[61] word. It is also worth noting that 𝔓75 and Vaticanus (cf. 1241) read θροηθέντες in place of πτοηθέντες in Luke 24:37.

It is doubtful, moreover, that the passive of the verb was, in our period, used of joyful emotion, as Liddell and Scott[62] maintain, appealing to LXX Song 5:4, where the Hebrew המה is rendered by θροέομαι. The Hebrew term designates an uproar or commotion, being used of, for example, groans of distress, the noise of the streets, the roar of the sea, the hostile roar of the enemy, the distress of a troubled soul and the raging of the heathens.[63] When it describes feelings, it refers to agitation, sometimes accompanied by distressed groaning, being used of 'anguish', 'mourning' and 'apprehensive uncertainty in the face of peril'.[64] MT Song 5:4 reads 'my lover moved his hand away from (מן) the door-hole and my bowels were—for him'. Some scholars, on account of normal usage and the immediate context as shaped by מן bearing its standard meaning 'away from', render המה here 'deeply disquieted',[65] although the majority of recent commentators take it to mean 'stirred with sexual passion',[66] translating מן 'in through',[67] in spite of the lack of evidence for such a rendering. Understanding מן in its normal sense necessarily endues the verb המה with a negative connotation.[68] Significantly, the LXX translation of this section of the Song of Songs, a word-for-word rendition of the MT,[69] renders מן by ἀπό plus the genitive. Further, the translator, whose knowledge of Hebrew was apparently somewhat limited,[70] may well have been influenced by the fact that המה elsewhere in the Old

---

of Luke (NIGTC; Exeter: Paternoster, 1977), 764 and L. T. Johnson, *The Gospel of Luke* (SP; Collegeville: Liturgical, 1991), 321 believe that the term πτοέομαι is 'stronger'; however, the use in *Tetrast. Iamb.* 4.1.2 seems to counter this suggestion.

[61] D. L. Bock, *Luke* (BECGNT; 2 vols.; Grand Rapids: Baker, 1994), 2:1666–7.

[62] Liddell and Scott, *Lexicon*, 807 (and Supplement, 153).

[63] See M. H. Pope, *Song of Songs* (AB; Garden City, N.Y.: Doubleday, 1977), 519; C. P. Weber, 'המה', in *TWOT*, 1:219.

[64] See A. Baumann, 'המה', in *TDOT*, 3:415–16.

[65] O. L. Barnes, *The Song of Songs* (Newcastle: Progressive Printers Ltd, 1961), 11–12, 27.

[66] So, for example, Pope, *Song*, 518–20; cf. J. M. Munro, *Spikenard and Saffron* (JSOTSup; Sheffield: JSOT, 1995), 131; NRSV and most translations and commentaries.

[67] Pope, *Song*, 518–19; D. A. Garrett, *Proverbs, Ecclesiastes, Song of Songs* (NAC; Nashville: Broadman, 1993), 411 n. 119; Munro, *Spikenard*, 130–1. R. Gordis, *The Song of Songs* (TSJTSA; New York: Jewish Theological Seminary of America, 1954), 88–9 maintained that the context suggests his withdrawal rather than the opening of the door.

[68] As Munro, *Spikenard*, 130 has noted; cf. Barnes, *Song*, 11–12, 27.

[69] J. C. Treat, 'Lost Keys: Text and Interpretation in the Old Greek "Song of Songs" and its Earliest Manuscript Witnesses' (Ph.D. diss., University of Pennsylvania, 1996), 18, 373–6.

[70] Ibid., 18, 385–7.

Testament tends to have a negative nuance as translated in the LXX.[71] Hence the LXX rendering should probably be translated 'my bowels were disturbed . . . ἐπ᾽ αὐτόν' (either 'for him', indicating sympathy,[72] or 'on account of him', indicating disappointment[73]). The fact that Philo of Carpasia, in his revision of the LXX, understood a negative nuance to be implicit here is clear from his choice of ταράσσω in place of the θροέομαι.[74] Hence Song 5:4 provides no sound basis for claiming that θροέομαι could be used of joyful emotion or for judging that its standard sense is neutral, with its joyful or fearful nuance contingent on the context.[75] Of course, some later exegetes of Song 5:4 cited the LXX whilst interpreting the verse positively in the manner that most scholars have understood the MT, including Theodotion. Theodoret, in *Explanatio in Canticum Canticorum* (PG 81, 152.52), justifies his positive interpretation, and implicitly acknowledges that the LXX's θροέομαι itself does not have a positive nuance, by citing Theodotion's ἐθερμάνθη. Gregory of Nyssa (fourth century), in *In Canticum Canticorum* (6.332.14; 6.337.3, 19[76]), cites the LXX's reading and interprets it negatively (ἔκπληξίν, 'Bestürzung' or 'consternationem') and positively (ξενισμόν, 'Befremdung' and 'admirationem'). In view of the fact that the negative meaning does not advance his christological interpretation of Canticles, whilst the positive sense does, it seems likely that the former is his acknowledgement of the LXX's ἐθροήθη, whilst the latter is his preferred (Theodotionic) interpretation of Song 5:4. We see the same pattern in

---

[71] See T. Muraoka, *Hebrew/Aramaic Index to the Septuagint* (Grand Rapids: Baker, 1998), 42 for a full list of Septuagint translations of המה.

[72] Baumann, 'המה', 416; Treat, 'Lost Keys', 489, who translates the LXX 'my belly was disturbed for him'.

[73] Barnes, *Songs*, 27; cf. Munro, *Spikenard*, 130.

[74] See Treat, 'Lost Keys', 231; cf. 45. Possibly this replacement was motivated by the desire to avoid an archaism. Cf. Philo of Carpasia, PG 40:101C. LaB (D. De Bruyne, 'Les Anciennes Versions latines du Cantique des cantiques', *Revue Bénédictine* 38 (1926): 97–122) rendered it 'turbata' (see Treat, 'Lost Keys', 231, cf. 37), while LaH (A. Vaccari, *Cantici Canticorum* (Rome: Edizioni di Storia e Letteratura, 1959)) translated it 'turbatus' (see Treat, 'Lost Keys', 231; cf. 38). Ambrose, *De Isaac* 44–57 (S. Sagot, 'Le "Cantique des Cantiques" dans le "De Isaac" d'Ambroise de Milan', *Recherches Augustiniennes* 16 (1973): 3–57) and *Expositio Psalmi* 118 (P. Sabatier, *Bibliorum Sacrorum Latinæ versiones antiquæ* (Rheims: Reginald Florentain, 1743)) translated it 'conturbatus' (see Treat, 'Lost Keys', 231, cf. 39–40). These readings reflect the same negative nuance and indeed may well indicate dependence on the LXX.

[75] *Pace* also Laub, *Verkündigung*, 137. Those who have argued that the verb is best rendered 'erschrecken' include Ellicott, *Thessalonians*, 107; Wrede, *Echtheit*, 47–50; von Dobschütz, *Thessalonicher-Briefe*, 265; Braun, 'Herkunft', 155 and Masson, *Thessaloniciens*, 93 including n. 7.

[76] H. Langerbeck, *Gregorii Nysseni opera* (Leiden: Brill, 1960).

the *Catena in Canticum Canticorum* (PG 87.2, 1681.38) of Procopius (sixth century).[77] BDAG's entry on θροέω includes the following: 'in the NT only pass. in the sense *be inwardly aroused* (cp. Tetrast. Iamb. 2, 1, 4 p. 286; Malalas 41, 12; SSol 5:4), *be disturbed* or *frightened* (TestAbr B 111,7 [Stone p. 70]) 2 Th 2:2. μὴ θροεῖσθε Mt 24:6; Mk 13:7; AcPl Ha 5, 25. θροηθέντες καὶ ἔμφοβοι γενόμενοι Lk 24:37 v.l.'[78] However, the evidence for the *general* meaning 'inwardly aroused' is unconvincing. In Malalas' *Chronographia* the verb is used of a pregnant woman's response to great lightning and thunder, which resulted in her going into labour immediately, at seven months; an editorial translation renders it appropriately as 'perterrefacta' ('to be thoroughly frightened/terrified').[79] Further, the context of *Tetrast. Iamb.* 2.1.4[80] makes it clear that ἐθρόεις there (active in form but passive in sense) is synonymous with, and perhaps even stronger than, ἐπτόει (a point noted in the editorial notes on the very page cited by BDAG[81]): the mule terrified (ἐπτόει) some goats because he acted superciliously, which prompted the lion to remind him: ἀλλ' ἐθρόεις ἄν μ', εἴπερ ὀγκοῦμαι μέγα, that is, if the lion were to raise himself up greatly, the mule in turn would be terrified (ἐθρόεις) of him. This leaves only the Song 5:4 text, which we have dealt with above.

Our conclusion therefore is that, far from demonstrating a general use of θροέομαι, these texts merely reinforce the point that in the passive and causative, the verb always denotes a feeling of terror, fear, alarm or disturbance. θροεῖσθαι in 2 Thess. 2:2 should therefore, we suggest, be translated 'frightened', 'terrified' or possibly 'disturbed', but certainly not 'excited'. The renderings of Hippolytus (θορυβῆσθε) and the Vulgate ('terreamini') capture the thought well.

---

[77] Note that elsewhere in his *Catena in Canticum Canticorum* (PG 87.2, 1684.5), Procopius uses the verb negatively.

[78] BDAG, 460.

[79] Malalas, *Chron.* 41.10–14: καὶ ἐν τῷ ἔχειν αὐτὴν ἐν γαστρὶ τὸν παῖδα χειμῶνος ὄντος ἐγένοντο ἀστραπαὶ μεγάλαι καὶ βρονταὶ καὶ ἐθροήθη ἡ κόρη Σεμέλη, καὶ τὸ μὲν βρέφος παρευθὺς ἐγέννησε μηνῶν ἑπτά, αὐτὴ δὲ μὴ ὑπενέγκασα τοὺς πόνους ἐτελεύτησε. Our English translation of 'perterrefacta' is derived from C. T. Lewis and C. Short, *A Latin Dictionary* (Oxford: Clarendon, 1896), 1358.

[80] Λέων, ὄνος θήρευον εἷς τί που σπέος
ὄνος δ' ἐπεισδὺς αἶγας ἔνδον ἐπτόει
ἐφ' ᾧ κατωφρύωτο· καὶ φησι<ν> λέων
ἀλλ' ἐθρόεις ἄν μ', εἴπερ ὀγκοῦμαι μέγα.

[81] BDAG, 460 cites O. C. F. H. Crusius, *Babrii Fabulae Aesopeae recognovit prolegomenis et indicibus instruxit Otto Crusius; accedunt fabularum dactylicarum et iambicarum reliquiae. Ignatii et aliorum tetrasticha iambica recensita a Carolo Fredrico Müller* (Teubner; Leipzig: Teubner, 1897), 286.

Those proponents of the view that enthusiastic excitement underlies 2 Thessalonians who acknowledge that θροεῖσθαι does not denote 'joyful excitement' explain the verb in various ways: some maintain that it is an echo of Jesus tradition (Mark 13:7 par. Matt. 24:6)[82] or stock apocalyptic language,[83] in which case it might be of limited usefulness in determining the situation underlying the letter. However, there are insufficient grounds for seeing an echo or stock language here; most notably, to the best of our knowledge, σαλευθῆναι ἀπὸ τοῦ νοός has no notable parallel in Jesus tradition or in Jewish apocalyptic literature. Furthermore, even if one were to grant that they echo Jesus tradition or reflect stock apocalyptic language, here in 2 Thess. 2:2, where the verbs have clearly been commandeered by 'Paul' and are intended to correspond with the situation of 'the Thessalonians', that would favour our proposal that they had responded negatively to the false claim.

Others maintain that there was not a united response to the false claim, but a mixed one, with some joyfully excited by it and others fearful/anxious regarding imminent judgment, perhaps worried that they might not be worthy of eschatological salvation.[84] However, this rests on there being other solid grounds for the presupposition of enthusiastic excitement, such as σαλευθῆναι ἀπὸ τοῦ νοός, a contention which we now examine.

With regard to σαλευθῆναι ἀπὸ τοῦ νοός, von Dobschütz spoke for many when he argued that this verbal phrase indicates that 'the Thessalonians' were enthusiastic in their reception of the false claim.[85] Σαλεύω is found only here in the entire Pauline corpus; elsewhere in the New Testament it occurs fourteen times.[86] It is used of the shaking of a reed (by the wind) (Matt. 11:7 par. Luke 7:24), of a measuring vessel (Luke 6:38), of a house (Luke 6:48; Acts 16:26) or room (Acts 4:31), of heavenly powers (Mark 13:25 par. Matt. 24:29/Luke 21:26), of the earth and the created world (Heb. 12:26–7), and of a crowd in agitation (Acts 17:13), frequently

---

[82] Wohlenberg, *Thessalonicherbrief*, 138 n. 3; von Dobschütz, *Thessalonicher-Briefe*, 265; Rigaux, *Thessaloniciens*, 649; Burkeen, 'Parousia', 310 and 389 n. 207; Bassin, *Thessaloniciens*, 208, 242–3.

[83] Trilling, *Untersuchungen*, 126 concluded solely on the basis of the use in the Synoptic eschatological discourses and 2 Thess. 2:2 that 'die Verben in 2,2f, besonders θροεῖσθαι, [gehören] der apokalyptischen Sprache [zu]'.

[84] Wrede, *Echtheit*, 47–50 (esp. 48), 67–9; Hollmann, 'Unechtheit', 34–5; von Dobschütz, *Thessalonicher-Briefe*, 260–1, 265; Frame, *Thessalonians*, 18, 22, 245, 246–7, 307; Masson, *Thessaloniciens*, 93; Friedrich, 'Zweite Brief', 256–7; Menken, *Thessalonians*, 97.

[85] Von Dobschütz, *Thessalonicher-Briefe*, 138 n. 159.

[86] One of these occurrences (Acts 2:25) is a citation of LXX Ps. 15:8: 'He [the Lord] is at my right hand, that I may not be shaken.'

with a violent connotation.[87] It denotes the 'restless movement of the sea with its rise and fall, whether from the standpoint of inconstancy suggesting transitoriness or of peril suggesting destruction' and has points of contact with words which 'express the inner emotion of fear, astonishment, or surprise'.[88] Σαλεύω ἀπό occurs in LXX 2 Kgs. 21:8 (οὐ προσθήσω τοῦ σαλεῦσαι τὸν πόδα Ισραηλ ἀπὸ τῆς γῆς), where it has the sense 'to shake so as to remove from'. The sense of σαλεύω ἀπό in 2 Thess. 2:2 is therefore most naturally 'to be [violently] shaken [by the false claim] to the point that one is removed from . . .'.

Νοῦς is unfortunately a rather vague term capable of a variety of senses.[89] It is used in the Pauline corpus twenty-one times. Behm perceives that these senses can be categorised into four distinct groups: (1) the inner orientation or moral attitude, views and convictions (Rom. 1:28; 12:2; 1 Cor. 1:10; Eph. 4:17, 23; Col. 2:18; 1 Tim. 6:5; 2 Tim. 3:8; Tit. 1:15); (2) the moral consciousness as it determines will and action (Rom. 7:23, 25); (3) the faculty of knowledge as state or act, understanding (Phil. 4:7; 1 Cor. 14:14–15 (3x), 19; cf. Rev. 13:18; 17:9; Luke 24:45); and (4) resolve, thought, the capacity to judge (Rom. 14:5; 11:34; 1 Cor. 2:16 (2x)).[90] In the light of 2 Thess. 2:5 and 15 with their stress on existing accurate knowledge which needs to be reactivated in the wake of the false claim, 'understanding'[91] or 'critical judgment'[92] would appear to be the most likely meaning of νοῦς in verse 2.

To be *shaken* from one's 'understanding' or 'critical judgment' more naturally describes a negative response to the false claim than a positive response. This corresponds with the meaning of θροέομαι for which we have argued above, and suggests that the two emotional responses are complementary: 'the Thessalonians' reacted with fear and mindless panic. The false claim apparently had a fundamentally destructive impact on those who heard it.

We conclude that θροέομαι and σαλεύω ἀπὸ τοῦ νοός should be interpreted as indicating that the false claim was frightening and violently shook those who accepted it. Rather than being enthused and positively excited, they were disorientated and terrified, needing stabilising and reassurance. This accords well with our earlier proposal that the idea that the Day of the Lord had come, literally understood, would naturally have been received by 'the Thessalonians' as bad news, undermining the essence of their Christian hope for judgment, both reward and vengeance.

---

[87] Cf. G. Bertram, 'Σαλεύω, σάλος', in *TDNT*, 7:65–70; *EDNT*, 3:224.
[88] Bertram, 'Σαλεύω', 7:65.   [89] Cf. J. Behm, 'Νοῦς', in *TDNT*, 4:958–9.
[90] See ibid.   [91] Stephens, 'Themes', 45, 88–9.
[92] Von Dobschütz, *Thessalonicher-Briefe*, 265.

Further, while ταχέως may hint that the problem is recent, the response indicated by the verbs would seem to be actual rather than merely potential; in view of the fact that the emotions denoted by the verbs are instinctive, it is difficult to conceive of a situation where 'the Thessalonians' might have been familiar with the false claim without experiencing 'shakenness' and fear.[93]

2 Thess. 2:1, 13–14

In the introduction to 2 Thess. 2:1ff., the section's content is specified as ὑπὲρ τῆς παρουσίας τοῦ κυρίου ἡμῶν Ἰησοῦ Χριστοῦ καὶ ἡμῶν ἐπισυναγωγῆς ἐπ' αὐτόν. Ἐπισυναγωγή is clearly an allusion to the event described in 1 Thess. 4:16–17a (cf. Mark 13:27; Matt. 24:30–1; also Did. 9:4; 10:5), as is confirmed by 2 Thess. 2:15's explicit reference to the eschatological teaching of 1 Thessalonians. It is the means by which Christians are able to participate in the parousia. The single article covering both 'parousia' and 'gathering' demonstrates that the two concepts are closely related; in 1 Thess. 4:14–17, the 'catching up' is the third stage of the parousia, following the descent of Christ to the air and the resurrection of dead believers, but preceding his arrival on the earth. However, it is striking that while the parousia is explicitly mentioned in 2 Thess. 2:8, the concept of 'gathering' is absent from verses 2–12. We might well ask why.

Possible explanations include: (1) the slavish dependence of the author on 1 Thessalonians[94] or on Jesus tradition; (2) 'Paul's' being subsequently side-tracked away from the 'gathering' onto a discussion of the rebel and his κατέχον/κατέχων;[95] (3) his asserting what is at stake in the ensuing discussion concerning the false eschatological claim for 'the

---

[93] Laub, *Verkündigung*, 150 suggested that the verbs did not have to be interpreted as reflecting a concrete problem of fear in view of an actual false claim, but could be understood generally as stereotypical responses to the near-expectation of the parousia (i.e. a post-apostolic author might not have been addressing a specific problem, but simply making a general comment about imminentist eschatological expectation). However, the specificity of the verbs is hard to evade, and one would have expected a general treatment of *Naherwartung* to warn against enthusiasm more than fear. Wrede, *Echtheit*, 47–50 and 67 considered the response of 'the Thessalonians' to be one of fear and consternation, but he explained that as a perfectly natural response of immature Christians (as distinct from the response of 'enthusiastic martyrs' or 'leading visionaries') to news of an *imminent* eschaton. But, as we have argued above, ἐνέστηκεν should probably be rendered 'has come' rather than 'is imminent'.

[94] For example, Wrede, *Echtheit*, 45–6; Trilling, *Zweite Brief*, 174.

[95] Von Dobschütz, *Thessalonicher-Briefe*, 265.

Thessalonians'.[96] With regard to (1), even if we were to accept the supposition of dependence on 1 Thessalonians or Jesus tradition, we cannot assume that any dependent vocabulary is devoid of significance in its new context; it is most natural to judge that an author has taken ownership of dependent materials. Option (2) faces a problem in that verse 8b refers explicitly to the parousia, also mentioned in the ὑπέρ clause; hence it seems that 'Paul' has not forgotten his point.

Option (3) seems the most natural and plausible explanation, given that the false claim is also eschatological in focus. Probably verse 1 serves to introduce the refutation of the false claim with special reference to its most serious ramification: if the Day had come, the question arises, what had happened to the parousia and more specifically the participation of 'the Thessalonians' in it (i.e. the 'gathering')? Apparently 'Paul' fears that the false claim might undermine the eschatological teaching of 1 Thessalonians. Of course, the focus on the judgment aspect of the end-time scenario in verses 3–12 renders an explicit reference to the ἐπισυναγωγή or participation of believers in final salvation inappropriate there.

However, in verses 13–14, which logically are an inextricable part of verses 1ff. (linked especially closely to verses 10b–12 and falling within the inclusio formed by verse 2 and verse 15 and before the 'concluding prayer' of verses 16–17), 'Paul' stresses his certainty that 'the Thessalonians' will participate in the eschatological salvation and glory of the parousia. It is notable that verses 9–12 emphasise the identity, character and story of the 'victims' of the parousia, τοῖς ἀπολλυμένοις[97] (verse 10a): they will perish because they rejected the opportunity to be saved by refusing the love of 'the truth' (i.e. the Gospel,[98] as indicated by the article and εἰς τὸ σωθῆναι αὐτούς) (verse 10b), and they do not believe 'the truth' but approve of wickedness (verse 12). And this group will be deceived by Satan and deluded by God and so will believe 'the lie' (the anti-Gospel concerning the rebel, as indicated by the definite article and the contrast with ἀλήθεια and also the context) and be condemned.[99]

The contrast between verses 13–14 and verses 9–12 is undeniable (hence δέ is contrastive): in distinction from those who perish at the

[96] J. Callow, *A Semantic Structural Analysis of Second Thessalonians* (Dallas: Summer Institute of Linguistics, 1982), 57 (who also notes that mention of 'the gathering', an event which had manifestly not happened, may also have functioned to reinforce 'Paul's' rejection of the false claim); Donfried, *Shorter*, 96.

[97] Evidence is lacking that those who waver in their Christian commitment are in mind here (*pace* Wanamaker, *Thessalonians*, 262).

[98] This presupposes that the Gospel will have been preached to the entire world by the time of the apostasy.

[99] Trilling, *Untersuchungen*, 87.

'Day of the Lord', 'the Thessalonians' have been elected to salvation and parousia glory, which is reached through the sanctification of the Spirit and belief in the truth. Ἡμεῖς δὲ ὀφείλομεν εὐχαριστεῖν τῷ θεῷ πάντοτε περὶ ὑμῶν is strikingly reminiscent of the thanksgiving report of 1:3 and, together with it, highlights the legitimacy (ὀφείλομεν) of continual thanksgiving to God for 'the Thessalonians', thereby reassuring those who are apparently reluctant to accept that thanksgiving to God for them is in order. The continual thanksgiving to God for 'the Thessalonians' is justified in the following ὅτι clause, ὅτι εἵλατο[100] ὑμᾶς ὁ θεὸς ἀπ' ἀρχῆς[101] εἰς σωτηρίαν. That God made a pre-historical choice that 'the Thessalonians' would receive eschatological salvation at the parousia[102] was undoubtedly intended to instil in them assurance concerning their salvific destiny. This is reinforced by ἀδελφοὶ ἠγαπημένοι ὑπὸ κυρίου, for in the Pauline corpus divine love is the foundation for Christian election and hence assurance of eschatological salvation (Rom. 1:7; 5:5–10; 8:35–9; 1 Thess. 1:4ff.; 5:9). This eschatological salvation is attained by (ἐν) a process of sanctification by the Spirit (ἁγιασμῷ πνεύματος)[103] and belief in the truth (πίστει ἀληθείας), which began for 'the Thessalonians'

---

[100] Αἱρέομαι is used of God's choice of Israel in LXX Deut. 26:18.

[101] *Contra* Findlay, *Epistles of Paul*, 160; Hughes, *2 Thessalonians*, 61; E. Krentz, 'Through a Lens: Theology and Fidelity in 2 Thessalonians', in *Pauline Theology I* (ed. J. Bassler; Minneapolis: Fortress, 1991), 57 n. 21; Fee, *Empowering*, 77 n. 142; UBS[4] (B. M. Metzger, *A Textual Commentary on the Greek New Testament* (2nd edn; Stuttgart: Deutsche Bibelgesellschaft, 1994), 568) and Elias, *Thessalonians*, 299, we join the vast majority of commentators in reading ἀπ' ἀρχῆς here. (1) It is hard to make any sense of ἀπαρχήν in this context (even Fee's suggestion (*Empowering*, 77 n. 142) that 'Paul' meant the first-fruits of Thessalonica seems distinctly inappropriate here; cf. P. Ellingworth and E. Nida, *A Translator's Handbook on Paul's Letters to the Thessalonians* (HFT; Stuttgart: UBS, 1976), 183 and Bruce, *Thessalonians*, 190 (firstfruits of humanity); E. E. Ellis, 'Coworkers, Paul and His', in *DPL*, 187 (the consecrated firstborn sons who were set apart to service for God, LXX Exod. 22:29); Dibelius, *Thessalonicher*, 51 and Krentz, 'Through a Lens', 57 n. 21 (a title of honour for Israel (Philo, *Spec. Leg.* 4.180)); Milligan, *Thessalonians*, 106–7 (firstfruits of Macedonia)). (2) It seems as likely that scribes, influenced by the fact that ἀπαρχήν is Pauline but that ἀπ' ἀρχῆς is not, might have opted to conform the text to Pauline usage (cf. von Dobschütz, *Thessalonicher-Briefe*, 298) or made a simple mindless slip (cf. LXX Sir. 24:9; Rom. 16:5; Rev. 14:4) (so Marshall, *Thessalonians*, 207). (3) If 2 Thessalonians is Pauline, it may be significant that ἀπ' ἀρχῆς fulfils the function commonly performed by πρό (Rom. 8:29–30; cf. Eph. 1:5, 11) or an adverbial phrase (1 Cor. 2:7; cf. Eph. 1:4) when Paul wishes to indicate the 'antecedent nature of God's action' (Best, *Thessalonians*, 312). (4) External evidence is arguably slightly stronger for ἀπ' ἀρχῆς. (5) Most importantly, the text unquestionably makes eminently good sense if ἀπ' ἀρχῆς is read.

[102] The futuristic sense of σωτηρίαν is certainly predominant here, as indicated by the preceding and succeeding context (esp. εἰς ὅ in verse 14) and the parallel in 1 Thess. 5:8–9.

[103] See Fee, *Empowering*, 78–9 for evidence that πνεῦμα is subjective, referring to the Holy Spirit, rather than objective, referring to the human spirit (*pace* J. Moffatt, 'The First and Second Epistles of Paul the Apostle to the Thessalonians', in *The Expositor's Greek New Testament* (ed. W. Robertson Nicoll; 4 vols.; New York: Hodder & Stoughton, 1897),

when they received the apostolic Gospel (note διὰ τοῦ εὐαγγελίου ἡμῶν in verse 14). While God acts to ensure that unbelievers will succumb to the supreme deception of Satan and will believe 'the lie' (verse 11), his activity in regard to 'the Thessalonians' is markedly different, for he works to produce holiness in them by his Spirit and to cause them to believe 'the truth'. God not only elects; he also supplies the grace necessary for the believer to be saved at the end.

The note of reassurance regarding eschatological fate continues into verse 14. Εἰς ὅ undoubtedly refers to the σωτηρίαν, hence 'toward which [eschatological salvation]'. Ἐκάλεσεν represents the effective historical actualisation of the choice indicated by εἵλατο in verse 13: God in history 'called' 'the Thessalonians' εἰς περιποίησιν δόξης τοῦ κυρίου ἡμῶν Ἰησοῦ Χριστοῦ ('unto the receiving[104] of the glory of our Lord Jesus Christ'; cf. 1 Thess. 5:9). The fact that they believed the apostolic Gospel demonstrates their election to a destiny of participation in their Lord's glory (cf. 2 Thess. 1:10; also 1 Thess. 1:4ff.).

2 Thess. 2:13–14 function to reassure, to root hope in God's love, election and call. Establishing the relationship between verses 13–14 and verses 1–12 has proved to be a rather difficult task for students of 2 Thessalonians, especially for those who maintain that the problem underlying verses 1ff. is one of eschatological enthusiasm and joyful excitement at the prospect of an imminent parousia. Why is there reassurance at this point? One suggestion is that verses 13–14 constitute an insincere confidence and thanksgiving, simply included because of slavish dependence on 1 Thessalonians, which also has two thanksgivings.[105] However, there are ample grounds for the thanksgiving in verses 13–14 (namely the contrast between the believers and the perishing). Hughes has postulated that verses 13–15 challenge the readers to stand firm in their relationships with 'Paul' and God so that they will be on the favourable side of things on the Day of the Lord.[106] But no such condition is attached to the reassurance. Further, we cannot restrict verses 13–14 solely to an outburst of praise to God on the part of 'Paul',[107] for verse 15 opens with ἄρα οὖν, which suggests that verses 13–14 constitute an important part of the

---

4:50; Findlay, *Epistles of Paul*, 189–90). The most decisive piece of evidence is the context's stress on divine activity.

[104] With Gundry-Volf, *Perseverance*, 19, we judge that, as in 1 Thess. 5:9, περιποίησις need not be understood as conceiving of salvation as having to be earned or purchased, *contra* A. J. Mason, 'The Epistle to the Thessalonians', in *A Bible Commentary for English Readers* (ed. C. J. Ellicott; 10 vols.; London: Cassell, 1902), 8:159; Müller, *Anfänge*, 156.

[105] Trilling, *Zweite Brief*, 118; Marxsen, *Zweite Thessalonicherbrief*, 91–2.

[106] Hughes, *2 Thessalonians*, 61; cf. Frame, *Thessalonians*, 278–9.

[107] D. Guthrie and R. P. Martin, 'God', in *DPL*, 354.

argumentation. Rather, it seems that 'the Thessalonians' are conceived of as in need of reassurance that they will yet participate in the salvation associated with the parousia.

In conclusion, then, verses 13–14 probably function as an essential and integral part of the rebuttal of the false eschatological claim. 'Paul' seems to regard 'the Thessalonians' as shaken, disappointed and scared by the notion that the Day had come (verse 2). Having established the parousia's futurity and the certainty that unbelievers will not escape condemnation at the eschaton in verses 1–12, he turns in verses 13–14 to assure 'the Thessalonians' that parousia salvation will be theirs. Hence verses 13–14 are not elucidated simply with reference to the persecution of 'the Thessalonians',[108] for that does not explain the close connection with verses 1–12; nor are verses 13–14 simply pre-empting their fears that they might apostatise on the day of evil.[109] Rather, verses 13–14 seem intended to rebuild hope in the face of the false eschatological claim: 'the Thessalonians' will not be victims of wrath, but will participate in eschatological salvation. This, of course, is the very concern anticipated in verse 1 (ἡμῶν ἐπισυναγωγῆς ἐπ᾽ αὐτόν).

2 Thess. 2:15

That verse 15 is based on verses 1–14 is indicated by ἄρα οὖν and the fact that verse 15 forms an inclusio with verse 2[110] – note that στήκετε (verse 15) is an antonym of σαλευθῆναι (verse 2) and that verse 2 and verse 15 make mention of means of communication (λόγος and ἐπιστολή) which 'the Thessalonians' are to distrust (verse 2) or trust (verse 15). Verses 1–14 represent a call of 'Paul' for 'the Thessalonians' to stand firm (στήκετε) and hold (κρατεῖτε) to the traditions (especially eschatological and confirmatory teachings) passed on to them (τὰς παραδόσεις ἃς ἐδιδάχθητε) orally (διὰ λόγου) or in 1 Thessalonians (δι᾽ ἐπιστολῆς ἡμῶν)[111] (perhaps especially 4:13–5:11 and 1:4ff.). The use of παράδοσις here is striking, apparently portraying the apostolic oral and

[108] Pace Gundry-Volf, Perseverance, 20.
[109] Calvin, Thessalonians, 408, 411; Friedrich, 'Zweite Brief', 269.
[110] Trilling, Zweite Brief, 124–6 makes the baffling claim that verse 15 introduces a new section of exhortations, in spite of his recognition that the positive verbs in verse 15 correspond to the negative verbs in verse 2 (Untersuchungen, 76).
[111] Against the implausible suggestion that the referent is 2 Thessalonians itself (so inter alios Lindemann, 'Abfassungszweck', 37, 39; Marxsen, Zweite Thessalonicherbrief, 94; Müller, Anfänge, 157; Wanamaker, Thessalonians, 268) or both 1 and 2 Thessalonians (so Holland, Tradition, 48–9), see chapter 1.

epistolary teaching as unchanging and authoritative, in contrast to the undependable eschatological idea which presently afflicts 'the Thessalonians'.[112] Verse 15 then functions to reinforce oral and written traditions of 'the missionaries' which have apparently been undermined by the false claim.

The unqualified 'word' and 'letter' here stand in tension with 'spirit', 'word' and 'letter supposedly by us' in verse 2. While some scholars regard them as having the same referents in both verses ('word' = 'Paul's' missionary teaching; 'letter' = 1 Thessalonians),[113] such a view is highly implausible since verse 2 concerns the source of the instability, whereas, by contrast, verse 15 relates to the source of stability. Hence while verse 15 denotes the missionary preaching and 1 Thessalonians, verse 2 presumably refers to the word of a resident or visiting prophet or teacher in Thessalonica and a forged letter in Paul's name. Only verse 15 refers to legitimate means of instruction regarding the Day of the Lord's coming; therefore any other sources of eschatological information can be unequivocally eliminated. By holding only to legitimate means of instruction regarding the Day of the Lord, 'the Thessalonians' can be steadfast and unshakeable.

Verse 15 calls for 'the Thessalonians' to stand firm in the light of the facts that the Day of the Lord/parousia is still future (verses 3b–12) and that it will bring condemnation to the unbelievers (verses 9–12) but salvation to themselves (verses 13–14), and to look only to the oral instruction of 'the missionaries' and to 1 Thessalonians for guidance on eschatological matters. Verse 15 suggests that the purpose of the preceding section is the fortifying of vulnerable believers against the false claim that the Day had come, by reinforcing earlier teaching. The use of στήκετε and κρατεῖτε seems to confirm that 'the Thessalonians' are perceived to be shaken and in a state of turbulence rather than excited and joyful.

2 Thess. 2:16–17

Verses 16–17 seem to have been intended to bring the section verses 1ff. to a close with a prayer (cf. 1 Thess. 3:11–13) which not surprisingly

---

[112] Proponents of pseudonymity argue that παραδόσεις is indicative of the special authoritative status of the apostle in 2 Thessalonians (e.g. J. Beker, *The Heirs of Paul* (Minneapolis: Augsburg Fortress, 1991), 74, 81). However, the term is adequately justified with reference to the epistolary situation.

[113] For example, Fee, 'Pneuma', 203, 208 and *Empowering*, 72 and Menken, *Thessalonians*, 97–8.

reflects 'Paul's' main concerns in the foregoing verses. Αὐτὸς δὲ ὁ κύριος ἡμῶν Ἰησοῦς Χριστός is emphatic, possibly because the central under-lying problem relates to the Day of *the Lord* and because 'our Lord Jesus Christ' is the focus of the Christian hope in verse 14. The unique ὁ θεὸς ὁ πατὴρ ἡμῶν underlines reassuringly the status of 'the Thessalo-nian converts' together with 'the missionaries' as the children of God, in a manner similar to verses 13–14. The relative clause which modifies it re-inforces this note of reassurance: ὁ ἀγαπήσας ἡμᾶς καὶ δοὺς παράκλησιν αἰωνίαν καὶ ἐλπίδα ἀγαθὴν ἐν χάριτι. That God loved them presumably alludes to verse 13's theme of election in love unto salvation (cf. ἀδελφοὶ ἠγαπημένοι ὑπὸ κυρίου). God also gave 'the Thessalonians', along with 'the missionaries', 'eternal' comfort (παράκλησιν αἰωνίαν), that is, com-fort which is permanent and unfailing. Both it and 'good hope' (ἐλπίδα ἀγαθήν)[114] seem to pick up on verses 13–14's note of reassurance. Ἐν χάριτι is most naturally taken with δούς alone: 'who graciously gave us . . .': the hope is rooted in the grace of God. This relative clause's strong note of consolation and reassurance with regard to hope is par-ticularly significant, coming as it does in the concluding prayer of the section. If the underlying problem had been excessive joyful enthusiastic excitement about the false claim, we would hardly expect such an em-phasis. Like the verbs of verse 2 and the assurances of verses 13–14, this relative clause suggests that 'Paul' is seeking to counter discouragement on the part of 'the Thessalonians', even the thought that God did not love them and that Christian hope was not 'good' or its encouragement 'eternal', which would quite naturally have resulted from their believing that the Day of the Lord had come. The substance of the prayer (that God and Jesus[115] παρακαλέσαι ὑμῶν τὰς καρδίας καὶ στηρίξαι ἐν παντὶ ἔργῳ καὶ λόγῳ ἀγαθῷ, verse 17) indicates the process through which 'the Thessalonians' must go if they are to recover from the false claim: their hearts must be encouraged and they must be strengthened in every good work and word. This reinforces the impression that 'Paul' conceives

---

[114] 'Good', like αἰωνίαν, is adjectival, describing the nature of the 'hope'. Those who have argued that this phrase refers to life after death, as in contemporary Hellenistic usage (e.g. P. Otzen, '"Gute Hoffnung" bei Paulus', *ZNW* 49 (1958): 283–5; cf. F. J. Cumont, *Lux Perpetua* (Paris: P. Geuther, 1949), 240–3, 401–5), have introduced an idea alien to the context, overlooking the conspicuous parallel παράκλησιν αἰωνίαν (which relates to the same participle), and have missed the connection with verse 2c and the probable correlation between this and the absence of hope from the triad in 1:3–4 (see the following chapter): 'the Thessalonians' need to know that they have an objectively sound basis for hope.

[115] As in 1 Thess. 3:11–13, a singular verb is used when God and Jesus are the subject, because they are so closely related, or else because the duality of the subject has been forgotten on account of the intervening relative clause.

of 'the Thessalonians' as discouraged and weak as a result of the false claim, lacking an experience of hope.

2 Thess. 3:1–5

Whether 2 Thess. 3:1–5 belongs more with the preceding or the succeeding section or is basically independent of both has been a matter of much altercation.

On the one hand, τὸ λοιπόν, ἀδελφοί and the striking shift in subject matter from 2:1–17 to 3:1–2 suggest that 3:1 does not introduce an inference from the preceding,[116] but rather a new section.[117] Verses 1–2 are a double-pronged prayer request: for the word of the Lord to enjoy easy, unhindered progress (τρέχῃ) and to be given due praise and honour, and for 'the missionaries' to experience deliverance (ῥυσθῶμεν [ἀπό], cf. 2 Cor. 1:8–11; Rom. 15:30–1) from 'perverse and evil men'[118] (cf. LXX Isa. 25:4; also Ps. 139:1), that is, from those who oppose the advance of the Gospel. This request is justified on the grounds that not all have faith (ἡ πίστις).

On the other hand, 2 Thess. 3:3–5 seem to be more closely related to 2:1–17 than are 3:1–2. In verse 3 'Paul' insists that the Lord is faithful and hence will strengthen (στηρίξει) 'the Thessalonians' and protect them from the evil one (verse 3). But to what specifically is 'Paul' alluding? A number of suggestions have been made, including the final tribulation,[119] ethical dangers,[120] and idleness;[121] however, evidence for such hypotheses is notably absent. Since στηρίξαι in 2:16–17 seems to allude to the impact of the eschatological claim (cf. 2:2's σαλευθῆναι ἀπὸ τοῦ νοός and 2:15's στήκετε καὶ κρατεῖτε), it is not unlikely that 3:3's στηρίξει

---

[116] Milligan, *Thessalonians*, 46 and Jewett, *Correspondence*, 80 are among those who have taken τὸ λοιπόν inferentially, as in later Greek (Milligan, *Thessalonians*, 46) and arguably in 1 Cor. 7:29; 2 Tim. 4:8 and 1 Thess. 4:1 (Krodel, *Deutero-Pauline Letters*, 51) (see BDAG, 603 on the inferential use of (τὸ) λοιπόν). It is, however, doubtful whether (τὸ) λοιπόν is ever used inferentially in the Pauline corpus. Λοιπόν in 1 Thess. 4:1 is accompanied by οὖν, which alone renders that verse inferential, and in both 1 Cor. 7:29 and 2 Tim. 4:8 it is probably best rendered 'for the future' or 'from now on' (cf. τοῦ λοιποῦ) (so BDAG, 602).

[117] In that the prayer request typically belongs to the epistolary conclusion (e.g. Rom. 15:30–2; 1 Thess. 5:25; Col. 4:3–4; Eph. 6:19), it is possible, though not necessary, that τὸ λοιπόν indicates that the conclusion is in view.

[118] The article is probably categorical.

[119] So *inter alios* Bruce, *Thessalonians*, 200; Best, *Thessalonians*, 328; Gundry-Volf, *Perseverance*, 70–1.

[120] So von Dobschütz, *Thessalonicher-Briefe*, 307.

[121] So *inter alios* Frame, *Thessalonians*, 293, who speculated that the idlers were claiming that the Enemy was too powerful for them.

does also. The reference to God's faithfulness certainly seems consistent with the emphasis on God's election and call of 'the Thessalonians' in 2:13–14 and 2:16's παράκλησιν αἰωνίαν καὶ ἐλπίδα ἀγαθήν (cf. 1 Thess. 5:24).

Moreover, the fact that 'Paul' castigates the eschatological claim as deceptive (2:3a) and even considers seriously the possibility of a forgery (2:2; 3:17) renders plausible the idea that he is interpreting the false idea as a Satanic assault on 'the Thessalonians'.

In verse 4 'Paul' asserts that he is confident in the Lord that 'the Thessalonians' are doing and will do what he commands. The future tense of ποιήσετε must refer to their reception of 2 Thessalonians. Many think that παραγγέλλω refers to 3:6ff., where the verb is employed three times (verses 6, 10 and 12). However, the intervening verse 5 does not support this reading. Moreover, it is more natural to understand παραγγέλλω in relation to what precedes than to what follows. And it is worth noting that the first two uses of παραγγέλλω in verses 6ff. (verses 6, 10) relate to the majority disciplining the idlers and only the third use in verse 12 relates to the idlers ceasing from their idleness; it is difficult to see how 'Paul' could be confident that the majority are already *disciplining* the idlers, unless he is assuming that the majority have deduced that from 1 Thess. 5:14's 'warn the ἄτακτοι'. If παραγγέλλω points back to earlier teaching, since it will be obeyed in the future (ποιήσετε) it must refer either to 2 Thess. 3:1–2 or, more likely, to the only strong admonition hitherto, 2:15, where 'the Thessalonians' are instructed to stand firm and hold on to the tradition so that they will no longer be shaken and scared by the false eschatological claim. In that case, the confidence of 'Paul' that 'the Thessalonians' are already heeding his instruction would presuppose the eschatological teaching of 1 Thess. 4:13–5:11. If we are correct, the relationship between 2 Thess. 3:3 and 4 is elucidated: since the Lord is faithful and can therefore be counted on to strengthen and protect them from the evil one, 'Paul' is confident that they are not being and will not be destroyed by the false eschatological idea.

In 3:5 we find another benedictory prayer (cf. 2:17): 'May the Lord direct your hearts εἰς τὴν ἀγάπην τοῦ θεοῦ καὶ εἰς τὴν ὑπομονὴν τοῦ Χριστοῦ.' While τὴν ἀγάπην τοῦ θεοῦ could be understood as an objective genitive, indicating human love for God, the subjective genitive seems preferable: (1) τὸ ἀγαπᾶν would have better expressed human love for God; (2) it seems more natural that the Lord would 'direct' them to God's love rather than to love for God. While 2 Thessalonians is silent with regard to love for God, 2:13 (cf. verse 16), which is an inextricable part of 'Paul's' treatment of the eschatological confusion, refers to the fact that 'the Thessalonians' are loved by the Lord. In that case the reference to divine love seems to reinforce the assurance that 'the Thessalonians' have been elected by God to parousia salvation (cf. 1 Thess. 1:4; Rom. 9:13, 15, 18, 21–4; Eph. 1:4–5). If so, it accords well with the reassuring thrust of 2 Thess. 3:3–4 (and 2:1–17).[122]

Some have argued that τὴν ὑπομονὴν τοῦ Χριστοῦ is an objective genitive, indicating 'patient waiting for Christ'.[123] However, (1) ὑπομονή never has this meaning in the Pauline corpus (note especially 2 Thess. 1:3–4 and 1 Thess. 1:3); (2) ἀναμένω in an infinitive construct would then have been expected; (3) if the first prepositional phrase is subjective, the second is more likely to be subjective also. Hence it is either the perseverance exemplified by Christ which is to be a model for 'the Thessalonians', or the perseverance imparted by Christ.

Why does 'Paul' link God's love, which is apparently related to the eschatological problem, and Christ's perseverance, which is seemingly related to the danger of not persevering? We suggest that the only satisfactory explanation is that 'Paul' perceives the false eschatology to represent a serious threat to the continued steadfastness of 'the Thessalonians' (particularly in view of their persecution, 1:4ff.). That he is concerned that the false claim is threatening to imperil their Christian endurance is supported by the choice of the verb στήκω in 2:15 and possibly also by στηρίξαι ἐν παντὶ ἔργῳ καὶ λόγῳ ἀγαθῷ in 2:17.

We propose, then, that 3:3–5 picks up on the eschatological problems of 2:1–17 and draws the treatment of it to a close. Verse 3 states that the Lord is faithful and will act to uphold the community. On this basis, in verse 4 'Paul' asserts his confidence in the Lord that 'the Thessalonians' will pull through their eschatological problem. Finally in verse 5 he commits the matter to the hands of the Lord, who is faithful and whom he trusts. Pastoral anxiety might explain the sudden shift from a prayer request in 3:1–2 back to the matter discussed in 2:1–17 in 3:3–5 (cf. 2 Cor. 11:28–9).[124] Possibly the mention of persecutions in 3:1–2 caused 'Paul'

---

[122] If 2 Thessalonians is an authentic letter of Paul, it will be significant that Pauline usage (Rom. 5:5; 8:35, 39; 2 Cor. 13:13) strongly favours the subjective genitive.

[123] Von Dobschütz, *Thessalonicher-Briefe*, 308–9; F. Hauck, 'Μένω, κτλ.', in *TDNT*, 4:586; O. Merk, *Handeln aus Glauben* (MTS; Marburg: Elwert, 1968), 64 n. 38; Friedrich, 'Zweite Brief', 271–2; Burkeen, 'Parousia', 369–70; Müller, *Anfänge*, 161; Krodel, *Deutero-Pauline Letters*, 52; Menken, *Thessalonians*, 129.

[124] This reading explains why scholars have been so divided regarding whether to interpret 3:1–5 as part of 2:1ff. or as part of a new section. For 3:1–2 do commence a new section (initially intended to be the concluding section), but 3:3–5 deal with the same issue as 2:1–17, especially verses 13–17. Hence there is no need to argue that τὸ λοιπόν is inferential in order to facilitate the continuity between 2:1–17 and 3:1–5, neither is there any need to downplay the fact that 3:6ff. is a new section.

to reflect on the persecutions of 'the Thessalonians', whose endurance must have been made more difficult by the false eschatological idea.[125]

Conclusion

We find precisely what we predicted in the light of our conclusion that the false claim was understood by 'the Thessalonians' at face value to mean that the Day of the Lord, and the parousia, had somehow come: it was apparently perceived to be bad news in view of the community's unchanged circumstances and particularly continued persecutions and so left 'the Thessalonians' fearful, confused and hopeless. Far from being joyfully excited by the false claim of 2:2c, they were afraid and shaken from adherence to what they had previously been taught (verses 2, 15). The explanation for this response emerges in verses 1 and 13–17, specifically in the stress on the sure participation of 'the Thessalonians' in the salvation of the parousia. The picture that emerges from 2:1–3:5 is one in which 'the Thessalonians', supposing that the Day and the parousia were co-referential, were deducing from the claim of 2:2c that salvation must somehow have bypassed them. This explains the emphatic identification of the Day of the Lord's victims as unbelievers (2:9–12) and its beneficiaries as 'the Thessalonians' (2:13–14). 'The Thessalonians' had therefore to be commanded to put their trust in the hope presented in the apostolic oral teaching and 1 Thessalonians rather than in the bizarre idea of 2:2c (verse 15); they had to be assured that the hope they had embraced at their conversion had been a good rather than a bad one (verse 16) and that God still loved them (verse 13; 3:5). There are even some indications that their continued perseverance in persecution may have been under threat (3:5; cf. 2:15).

Concluding summary

In this our first chapter considering the situation addressed in 2 Thessalonians, we have analysed 2:1–3:5. We have proposed that the false eschatological idea under the spell of which 'the Thessalonians' have come, ἐνέστηκεν ἡ ἡμέρα τοῦ κυρίου, should be rendered 'the Day of the Lord *has come*' and that 'Paul' is under the impression that 'the Thessalonians'

---

[125] On a formal level, there may be a word-play (πίστις/πιστός) and a parallel between πονηρῶν ἀνθρώπων and πονηροῦ, but these alone are inadequate to explain the actual development of thought and in particular the referential shift.

understand the Day and the parousia as co-referential.[126] Moreover, he seems to imply that the claim has been accepted on account of the status of the one who uttered it. And he intimates that 'the Thessalonians' have reacted to the false idea with despair, fear and trembling, probably wondering how the parousia could have come without their noticing, and realising that, in view of their unchanged circumstances, the claim left them without hope of salvation. It is difficult to avoid concluding that a confusion such as is envisioned in 2:1–3:5 could only have arisen in a young, insecure Gentile community still to come to terms with Jewish-Christian eschatological concepts. With this in view, we turn our attention to 1:1–12.

[126] Cf. Chrysostom, *Homily 1 on 2 Thessalonians* (PG 62); J. Lillie, *Lectures on the Epistles of Paul to the Thessalonians* (New York: R. Carter, 1860), 500; Bruce, *Thessalonians*, 166 and J. M. Bassler, 'The Enigmatic Sign: 2 Thessalonians 1:5', CBQ 46 (1984): 507–9.

6

PERSEVERANCE UNDER THREAT

Introduction

We turn now to 2 Thess. 1:1–12 to see whether it confirms and develops or contradicts our hypothesis concerning the eschatological problem underlying 2 Thess. 2:1–3:5.

The significance of the prescript (1:1–2)

The prescript of 2 Thess. 1:1–2 is notable in that it, like the one in 1 Thess. 1:1, lacks a reference to the sender's rank and has ἐν θεῷ πατρὶ ἡμῶν καὶ κυρίῳ Ἰησοῦ Χριστῷ. While some argue that these parallels reflect slavish dependence on 1 Thessalonians,[1] the ἡμῶν in verse 1 and ἀπὸ θεοῦ πατρὸς [ἡμῶν] καὶ κυρίου Ἰησοῦ Χριστοῦ in verse 2 suggest an alternative explanation. Although one must beware of building too much on the rather obscure clues of prescripts, it is worth noting that the two aforementioned striking features of this prescript do seem appropriate to the situation as we determined it from 2:1–3:5: 'Paul' does not seem convinced that there is a concerted opposition within 'the Thessalonian community', and 'the Thessalonians' do need to be reassured regarding their status before God (cf. 2:13–17) and concerning the fatherly love of God for them (2:16; 3:5).

Next we turn to the long and syntactically unwieldy sentence of 1:3–10.[2] First, we must answer two questions about 1:3.

---

[1] So, for example, Friedrich, 'Zweite Brief', 258 and Trilling, *Zweite Brief*, 35.

[2] While it cannot be doubted that this is an unpolished and grammatically awkward sentence, it is neither 'artificial' nor necessarily un-Pauline (*pace inter alios* Trilling, *Zweite Brief*, 39–40; Menken, *Thessalonians*, 32). Paul is perfectly capable of composing cumbersome sentences (see A. Q. Morton and J. McLeman, *Paul, the Man and the Myth* (London: Hodder & Stoughton, 1966), table 51), partly because he was apparently in the habit of dictating his epistolary thoughts to amanuenses.

Why have ὀφείλομεν and καθὼς ἄξιόν ἐστιν been included in the thanksgiving?

We might well ask why the usual Pauline introductory thanksgiving form has been modified. Some have postulated that the replacement of εὐχαριστοῦμεν with εὐχαριστεῖν ὀφείλομεν and the addition of καθὼς ἄξιόν ἐστιν disclose a cool and detached attitude on the part of 'Paul'.[3] However, the choice of the verbs ὑπεραυξάνει and πλεονάζει, the ἑνὸς ἑκάστου πάντων ὑμῶν εἰς ἀλλήλους, the unusually early presence of ἀδελφοί in verse 3 and the emphasis on boasting in verse 4 (note that it opens with ὥστε, indicating a close connection with verse 3) combine to refute that suggestion. We understand the tone here to be strikingly sincere and involved.

Aus has proposed that εὐχαριστεῖν ὀφείλομεν and καθὼς ἄξιόν ἐστιν are liturgical expressions and has pointed to 1 Clem. 38:4; Barn. 5:3; 7:1 and Herm. Sim. 9.28.5 and also some Jewish texts such as Philo, Spec. Leg. 1.224; 2.173 and 185 and Mut. 186 in support of the liturgical reading of εὐχαριστεῖν ὀφείλομεν, and to 1 Thess. 3:4; 5:11; 1 Cor. 1:6; 11:1 in support of a liturgical reading of καθὼς ἄξιόν ἐστιν.[4] However, the texts from the early church to which Aus has appealed in support of his liturgical reading of εὐχαριστεῖν ὀφείλομεν can be plausibly explained as indebted to 2 Thessalonians. Moreover, what is distinctive about 2 Thessalonians compared with the various 'parallels' produced by Aus is that it has *two* expressions of the obligation to give thanks. Hence we find the case for a liturgical reading of these phrases uncompelling and suggest that it is more likely that the language has been evoked by the situation.[5]

The most plausible explanation of these expressions is that they reassure 'the Thessalonians' in the face of real or potential doubts about

---

[3] Masson, *Thessaloniciens*, 83; M. Rist, 'Pseudepigraphy and the Early Christians', in *Studies in New Testament and Early Christian Literature* (ed. David Aune; NovTSup; Leiden: Brill, 1972), 82–3; Friedrich, 'Zweite Brief', 258; Bailey, 'Who?', 137; Trilling, *Zweite Brief*, 44; Müller, *Anfänge*, 54 and Menken, *Thessalonians*, 30–1 have argued that this reveals inauthenticity.

[4] R. D. Aus, 'The Liturgical Background of the Necessity and Propriety of Giving Thanks according to 2 Thess. 1:3', *JBL* 92 (1972–3): 432–8 and 'II Thessalonians', in *ACNT: 1–2 Timothy, Titus, 2 Thessalonians* (Minneapolis: Augsburg, 1984), 200.

[5] It should be noted that, although Aus does set his liturgical reading over against situational theories, he himself ('Liturgical', 438; cf. Richard, *Thessalonians*, 301) apparently understands the expressions to have some situational significance, judging that they are especially appropriate in contexts of suffering (he points to parallels in Herm. *Sim.* 9.28.5; *Pes.* 10:5; *Berakoth* 9:5; Rev. 3:4; 5:9 and 12).

the legitimacy of the thanksgiving for them before God.[6] This accords perfectly with our interpretation of 2:1–3:5: the false claim of 2:2c seems to imply that God is disapproving of and indeed has abandoned those to whom it is directed. It is not hard to imagine that those embracing the eschatological idea might have been perceived by 'Paul' as reluctant to accept the notion that they might be a worthy object of thanksgiving to God. This might also elucidate the striking appearance of ἀδελφοί unusually early in the letter, which indicates that 'Paul' plainly wishes to make especially explicit the close identification of 'the Thessalonians' with 'the missionaries'.

In verse 3 the legitimacy of the thanksgiving is grounded in the lavish love and abundant faith of 'the Thessalonians'. Notably, however, hope is omitted.

The absence of ἐλπίς from 1:3

This enigma of the missing ἐλπίς in verse 3 has been explained variously. Best speaks for several proponents of Pauline authorship when he suggests that it is insignificant, pointing to '1 Th. 3.6; Gal. 5.6; Phlm. 5; Col. 1.4; Eph. 1.15; 3.17; 6.23; cf. 1 Cor. 16.13f; 2 Cor. 8.7', where 'love' and 'faith' are found together without 'hope'.[7] However, given the subsequent preoccupation with hope in 2 Thess. 1:5–10, it is difficult to avoid the conclusion that the absence of hope here is significant. This is the case whether 2 Thessalonians is Pauline or not, for the triad was prominent in 1 Thessalonians (1:3; 5:8), which is either, together with 1 Corinthians (13:13), a demonstration that the triad is important for early Paul, or the text upon which a pseudonymous author is dependent. As Masson wrote, 'Il est étonnant . . . que l'espérance des Thessaloniciens ne soit plus mentionnée (cf. 1 Th. 1.3), car elle forme avec la foi et l'amour une triade, qui définit pour saint Paul la vie du chrétien par ses composantes essentielles, dont aucune ne saurait manquer sans qu'elle soit gravement altérée' ('It is surprising that the hope of the Thessalonians is no longer mentioned (cf. 1 Thess. 1:3), for it forms with faith and love a triad

---

[6] Cf. Frame, *Thessalonians*, 219–20, 221; Marshall, *Thessalonians*, 170. Marxsen, *Zweite Thessalonicherbrief*, 64, 74 judges that the thanksgiving is only illusory (cf. Holland, *Tradition*, 61), since the rest of the letter suggests that the faith of 'the Thessalonians' had not grown; he claims that the author of 2 Thessalonians really thought that his readers could not be sure of a place among all believers on that Day unless they persevered. However, although 1:11–12 and 2:13–3:5 may well suggest that their faith was under some degree of threat, they do not disallow the possibility that the faith of 'the Thessalonians' had grown.

[7] Best, *Thessalonians*, 251; cf. Whiteley, *Thessalonians*, 90.

which defines for Saint Paul the life of the Christian by its essential components, none of which may be lacking without its being gravely altered').[8]

Many argue that ὑπομονή in verse 4 is a substitute for ἐλπίς, on account of the parallel with 1 Thess. 1:3 and because 'the idea of patience and endurance without hope does not yield any sense'.[9] However, on the contrary, the concepts of endurance and hope are quite distinct and independently meaningful, and one does not imply the other, even in 1 Thess. 1:3. And, moreover, that ὑπομονή in verse 3 is not completing a triad is suggested by the facts that verse 4 opens with ὥστε and that ὑπομονή is itself linked with another πίστις, the meaning of which seems to have shifted from 'faith' in verse 3 to 'faithfulness' in verse 4.

Masson and Trilling concluded that the omission reflects a different authorial perspective from that evident in 1 Thessalonians,[10] but that judgment fails to take adequate account of the omission of hope from 1 Thess. 3:6. Furthermore, there is no need to attribute the omission to a different theology when a plausible alternative exists: that the exclusion of hope from the thanksgiving is due to a specific problem in relation to hope.

Rigaux proposed that hope was 'too alive' in Thessalonica and therefore suggested that ἐλπίς was left out here in order to avoid encouraging enthusiastic extremism.[11] However, not only is it questionable whether such a problem would have led to the omission of hope from the thanksgiving (in 1 Cor. 1:7 Paul thanks God for spiritual gifts which were in fact causing problems and which he would go on to correct), but there is elsewhere in 2 Thessalonians no evidence of eschatological excitement.

We suggest that it is much simpler to understand the omission as due to a *lack* of hope among 'the Thessalonians'. This is supported by the observation that 1:5–10 reassure 'the Thessalonians' concerning the justice of God at the eschaton. The absence of hope from the thanksgiving is precisely what we would expect if our analysis of 2:1–3:5 is correct:

[8] Masson, *Thessaloniciens*, 84.
[9] Müller, *Anfänge*, 54–5; cf. R. D. Aus, 'Comfort in Judgment: The Use of the Day of the Lord and Theophany Traditions in Second Thessalonians 1' (Ph.D. diss., Yale University, 1971), 52; Holland, *Tradition*, 61; Menken, *Thessalonians*, 83. Marshall, *Thessalonians*, 172 seems to see hope as implicit in πίστις and ὑπομονή (verse 4; cf. von Dobschütz, *Thessalonicher-Briefe*, 239; O'Brien, *Thanksgivings*, 175–6; Wanamaker, *Thessalonians*, 219).
[10] Masson, *Thessaloniciens*, 84; Trilling, *Zweite Brief*, 47.
[11] Rigaux, *Thessaloniciens*, 610, 614. Cf. Müller, 'Currents', 307–11.

the claim that the Day of the Lord had come eliminated the hope of those who embraced it.

Nevertheless, the thanksgiving stresses that the other two elements of the triad, faith and love, were present among 'the Thessalonians' in abundant measure and they constituted reliable grounds for thanksgiving before God and indeed the foundation for the rebuilding of hope.

The implication of αὐτοὺς ἡμᾶς in 1:4

In verse 4 'Paul' declares that 'the Thessalonians' are the object of the boasting of 'the missionaries'. Boasting in an object presupposes and conveys deep confidence and trust in that object and serves to elevate its status. Here the status of 'the Thessalonians' is being emphasised, just as the (God-owned and -approved) status of those among whom 'the missionaries' boast (ἐν ταῖς ἐκκλησίαις τοῦ θεοῦ) is highlighted.

Αὐτοὺς ἡμᾶς, here clearly intensive, has been understood variously. Some think that it implies that boasting was unexpected, indeed abnormal, for 'the missionaries'.[12] However, evidence is lacking that boasting in what God had accomplished was typically regarded as improper or abnormal among early Christians (see, for example, 1 Thess. 2:19; 1 Cor. 1:31; 2 Cor. 8:1–5; 9:2–4; 10:17). Others have suggested that 'Paul' is including 'the missionaries' with those mentioned in 1 Thess. 1:8–10.[13] But that text is too far removed to be in mind here.[14] It seems more probable that it implicitly contrasts the boasting of 'the missionaries' with the attitude of 'the Thessalonians',[15] which may also be suggested by the placement of ἡμᾶς close to ἐν ὑμῖν. And the very possibility that a forgery in Paul's name had caused their eschatological confusion would require that they be assured of his pastoral approval of and concern for them. Such an interpretation of αὐτοὺς ἡμᾶς fits well with our conclusion regarding verse 3's ὀφείλομεν and καθὼς ἄξιόν ἐστιν and, like them, seems to treat some of the symptoms of the false claim of 2:2c. 'Paul' is intent on affirming that 'the missionaries', and indeed God, approve of the faith of 'the Thessalonians'.

---

[12] Findlay, *Epistles of Paul*, 141; Rigaux, *Thessaloniciens*, 615; Callow, *Thessalonians*, 32 and Wanamaker, *Thessalonians*, 218, who have each maintained that an exception to the normal rule of 'Paul' is implied.

[13] H. Alford, *The Greek Testament* (5th edn; 4 vols.; London: Rivingtons, 1880), 3:284–5; Wrede, *Echtheit*, 85; R. C. H. Lenski, *The Interpretation of St. Paul's Epistles to the Colossians, to the Thessalonians, to Timothy, to Titus and to Philemon* (Minneapolis: Augsburg, 1961), 379.

[14] Wanamaker, *Thessalonians*, 218.   [15] Frame, *Thessalonians*, 223.

The content of the boasting is the 'endurance' and 'faithfulness' of 'the Thessalonians' in the midst of numerous and perhaps somewhat severe (πᾶσιν) afflictions (διωγμοῖς and θλίψεσιν).

In 1:5 what is an ἔνδειγμα of what?

An ἔνδειγμα is a 'sign', 'indication', 'guarantee', 'proof', or 'evidence' (data upon which to base a belief or claim).[16] Probably it is best to understand it as nominative, with ὅ ἐστιν having been omitted. The majority of scholars judge that it qualifies τῆς ὑπομονῆς ὑμῶν καὶ πίστεως (ἐν πᾶσιν τοῖς διωγμοῖς ὑμῶν καὶ ταῖς θλίψεσιν αἷς ἀνέχεσθε).[17] This proposal has in its favour the parallel in Phil. 1:28. However, that is far from decisive in the light of the focus on God's justice in 2 Thessalonians 1 and the fact that the 'sign' in Phil. 1:28 is to the unbelieving, whilst the one in 2 Thess. 1:5 is to the believing. A significant problem for this position is the subsequent context, in which the theme of perseverance is striking only by its absence. What is stressed is the fact and function of *persecution* (1:5b–7b): note especially ὑπὲρ ἧς καὶ πάσχετε (verse 5c) and τοῖς θλίβουσιν ὑμᾶς . . . τοῖς θλιβομένοις (verses 6–7a). We propose that the simplest and most natural reading of ἔνδειγμα is that it refers to ἐν πᾶσιν τοῖς διωγμοῖς ὑμῶν καὶ ταῖς θλίψεσιν, not least because the immediately preceding αἷς ἀνέχεσθε refers to this. But what does it mean to say that the persecutions which 'the Thessalonians' are experiencing are a sign of God's just judgment? First, the persecutions are a sign of God's *future* justice, as indicated by verses 5b–10 (esp. verses 7b–10), where 'Paul' is establishing the veracity of this anterior affirmation; these verses concern eschatological justice.[18] Second, the εἰς τό clause probably qualifies ἔνδειγμα and functions to spell out the meaning of τῆς δικαίας κρίσεως τοῦ θεοῦ: the persecutions are a proof that just judgment will yet come, that is, that 'the Thessalonians' will be counted worthy of God's kingdom.

But how can the persecutions be proof of God's future *just* judgment? Underlying the logic of verse 5 seems to be the principle that those destined to inherit the kingdom are characterised by afflictions, which function to purify them so that they will be counted worthy of the kingdom

---

[16] See *inter alios* J. P. Louw and E. A. Nida, *Greek–English Lexicon of the New Testament based on Semantic Domains* (2 vols.; New York: UBS, 1988), §28.52; Liddell and Scott, *Lexicon*, 558.

[17] *Inter alios* Hartman, 'Eschatology', 474; Bassin, *Thessaloniciens*, 190–1 including n. 3; Morris, *Epistles*, 197; Elias, *Thessalonians*, 256–7; Richard, *Thessalonians*, 304–5.

[18] *Contra*, for example, Alford, *Testament*, 3:285 and Marshall, *Thessalonians*, 173.

and so can inherit it (hence καταξιωθῆναι . . . τῆς βασιλείας τοῦ θεοῦ, ὑπὲρ ἧς καὶ πάσχετε) (cf. Dan. 11:35; 12:10; Rev. 7:14–17).[19] Therefore those who suffer for the kingdom can be certain that they will be counted worthy of that kingdom.

The function of 1:6–10

As we just noted, verses 6–10 constitute an attempt to justify the claim that the persecutions are a proof of God's future *just* judgment (τῆς δικαίας κρίσεως τοῦ θεοῦ).

First, in verses 6–7a 'Paul' assures 'the Thessalonians' that God's just judgment is just by anyone's standards, for it brings affliction to the persecutors and relief to the persecuted. Here we see the concept of a reversal of fortunes according to the *lex talionis* (ἀνταποδοῦναι; τοῖς θλίβουσιν . . . θλῖψιν; τοῖς θλιβομένοις ἄνεσιν). Second and more importantly, in verses 7b–10, he stresses when the just judgment comes. It is striking that verses 7b–10 have a distinctive chronological frame: ἐν τῇ ἀποκαλύψει τοῦ κυρίου Ἰησοῦ (verse 7b) and ὅταν ἔλθῃ[20] . . . ἐν τῇ ἡμέρᾳ ἐκείνῃ (verse 10). 'Revelation' (ἀποκαλύψει) reminds 'the Thessalonians' that Jesus the Judge is currently hidden from human sight, waiting to be revealed in splendour at the parousia (Sir. 22:21; 41:23; 4 Ezra 7:28; 13:32; cf. 2 Thess. 2:1, 8). The just judgment will be executed when Jesus appears to human eyes with fear-instilling brilliance (ἐν πυρὶ φλογός[21]), descending from heaven (ἀπ' οὐρανοῦ), and with angels of

[19] Bassler, 'Sign', 499ff. (cf. Aus, 'Comfort', 71–4 (but note his comments on pp. 358–9); Friedrich, 'Zweite Brief', 259; Wanamaker, *Thessalonians*, 222–3; B. B. Thurston, *Reading Colossians, Ephesians, and 2 Thessalonians: A Literary and Theological Commentary* (Reading the New Testament; New York: Crossroad, 1995), 171–2; B. R. Gaventa, *First and Second Thessalonians* (IBC; Louisville, Ky.: John Knox, 1998), 102–3), building on W. Wichmann, *Die Leidenstheologie* (BWANT; Stuttgart: Kohlhammer, 1930), esp. 27–9, supposes that the persecutions are being conceived of as God's present just punishment for sins (cf. 2 Macc. 6:12–16; 2 Bar. 13:3–10; 48:48–50; 52:5–7; 78:5; Ps. Sol. 13:9–10; Gen. R. 33:1) and that this prefigures the final judgment (cf. 2 Bar. 1:5–11; 13:3–10; 78:5). Menken, *Thessalonians*, 85 writes: 'the present sufferings of God's people are God's punishment for their sins, so that afterwards, at the final judgment, they will not have to be punished with the wicked but will participate in God's salvation'. However, Holland, *Tradition*, 37–8 is probably correct in claiming that the sufferings are disciplinary rather than punitive, as, for example, in Prov. 3:11–12; Job 40:1–2; Isa. 40:1–2; Ps. Sol. 13:9–10; 2 Macc. 6:12–16; 2 Bar. 13:3–10; 78:5; Wis. 11:9–10.

[20] Ὅταν plus the subjunctive here seems to indicate a particular event, the timing of which is inexact.

[21] This seems to be rooted in Old Testament judgment (esp. Isa. 66:15–16; Dan. 7:9–10; cf. 1QS 2:7–8; 4:13; 1QH 3:28ff.; 6:15–19; 1QpHab. 10:4–5, 12–13) and theophanic (e.g. Deut. 33:2; Ps. 18:8; Ezek. 1:13, 27; Hab. 3:4) imagery. It seems preferable to understand this phrase like the other two, as belonging closely to the preceding clause, although it also leads nicely into the succeeding clause. The preferred text here is ἐν πυρὶ φλογός, the more

his power (μετ' ἀγγέλων δυνάμεως αὐτοῦ) (2 Thess. 1:7b–8a). In verse 10 'Paul' stresses that the punishment of unbelievers will be dispensed at the time 'when [the Lord Jesus] comes to be glorified in his holy ones (cf. Zech. 14:5) and to be marvelled at by all (πᾶσιν) believers'. All this occurs 'on that day' (ἐν τῇ ἡμέρᾳ ἐκείνῃ), that is, on the Day of the Lord (cf. 2 Thess. 2:2c). Quite clearly, these verses build a *foundation* of eschatological hope. The question is, for what purpose? Some have hypothesised that 'Paul' is paving the way for a *demolition* of eschatological enthusiasm in 2:1ff.[22] However, our analysis of 2:1ff. suggests that there is no sound basis for judging that eschatological enthusiasm underlies 2:1ff. and so alleviates the need for such a paradoxical reading of 2 Thessalonians, permitting both 1:5ff. and 2:1ff. to be interpreted as establishing for the *hopeless* 'Thessalonians' a fresh foundation of future hope. The probability that 1:5ff. is a reinforcement of 2:1ff. is suggested not only by the emphasis on 'that day' in 1:10, but also by the theodicy of 1:6ff.

It is important to ask why 'Paul' engages in theodicy (ἔνδειγμα τῆς δικαίας κρίσεως τοῦ θεοῦ (verse 5) . . . εἴπερ δίκαιον παρὰ θεῷ . . . (verse 6); also ἐκδίκησιν in verse 8; δίκην in verse 9), defending the *justice* of God's *judgment* with respect to its nature (verses 6–7a) and its timing (verses 7b–10). We must look to the situation to explain this important aspect of these verses. It seems that 'the Thessalonians' (note the use of the second-person plural in verses 5–7a, 10b) are interpreting their persecutions as an indication of an unjust divine judgment. But why might they have jumped to that conclusion? While some have tried to explain it with reference to an exigency of persecution alone,[23] that seems implausible because ordinarily for a Christian, God's just judgment is not at stake merely on account of persecution, since just judgment is understood to be deferred until the eschaton. What could be different in this situation? We propose that the false claim of 2:2c as we have interpreted it above is essential for understanding 1:6ff.: if the Day had come, the natural questions for a Christian to ask are, 'why then have

difficult reading; probably it was changed to agree with LXX Isa. 66:15 (*contra* Richard, *Thessalonians*, 307, who does not explain how the ἐν πυρὶ φλογός reading came about, and R. D. Aus, 'The Relevance of Isa. 66:7 to Revelation 12 and 2 Thessalonians 1', *ZNW* 67 (1976): 266 including n. 58, who proposed rather unconvincingly that it derived from LXX Exod. 3:2 B).

[22] J. K. Fraser, 'A Theological Study of Second Thessalonians: A Comprehensive Study of the Thought of the Epistle and its Sources' (Ph.D. thesis, University of Durham, 1979), 334; Koester, 'Schemata', 456; cf. Munck, 'Missionary Preaching', 100; Aus, 'Comfort', 27 and 'Thessalonians', 200–1.

[23] *Pace inter alios* Rigaux, *Thessaloniciens*, 610–11 and Donfried, *Shorter*, 87–9.

our circumstances remained unchanged?' and 'what happened to God's just judgment?'.[24] The persecutions would naturally function as the focal point of confusion and distress; indeed, the afflictions might well have seemed to be an ἔνδειγμα that God's judgment was unjust.[25]

The response of 'Paul' seems ideally fashioned to deal with such sentiment, for, contrary to what 'the Thessalonians' might have thought, he insists that their persecutions are a sign of God's future just judgment, a guarantee that those persecuted would be counted worthy of the kingdom, since persecution functioned to purify God's people in preparation for the kingdom. 'Paul' makes the point that God's judgment will be truly just, involving a reversal of fortunes. Moreover, he stresses that it is sure, belonging to the still-future Day of the Lord (ἐν τῇ ἡμέρᾳ ἐκείνῃ), which would be recognisable because on that day Christ the Judge will be manifestly revealed, coming from heaven in glory and might, an unmistakably conspicuous and awe-inspiring sight. Until that happens, 'the Thessalonians' can be certain that the Day of the Lord has not come. On the grounds of the persecutions, 'the Thessalonians' can be confident that just judgment will come; the roles will yet be reversed (cf. Luke 16:25). Significantly, the emphatic (note its position at the culmination of the logic of 2 Thess. 1:5ff., esp. verses 7bff.) reference to the Day of the Lord here links 1:5–10 to 2:1–3:5.

In view of this, the emphasis on the identity of the victims of the Judge's just judgment – the Judge dispenses punishment on 'those who do not know God' and 'those who do not obey the Gospel of our Lord Jesus'[26] (verse 8b) – may well be intended to assure 'the Thessalonians' in the wake of the false claim that they are not in the number of those who are destined to be victims of the Day of the Lord.[27] This is apparently

[24] Cf. Bassler, 'Sign', 507–9.

[25] This would help to elucidate the function of 2:11–14: they seem to reinforce the point that *iustitia vindicativa et punitiva* is indeed in store for unbelievers and that salvation is due to believers.

[26] Although Richard, *Thessalonians*, 308 judges that τοῖς μὴ ὑπακούουσιν τῷ εὐαγγελίῳ τοῦ κυρίου ἡμῶν Ἰησοῦ refers to apostate believers, the context indicates that it does not refer to apostasy. The idea that implicit in this verse is a 'veiled threat to those within the community' (Wanamaker, *Thessalonians*, 228 (cf. W. A. Meeks, 'Social Function of Apocalyptic Language in Pauline Christianity', in *Apocalypticism in the Mediterranean World and the Near East* (ed. D. Hellholm; Tübingen: Mohr, 1983), 689)) also violates the context. The use of 'the Lord Jesus' here links disobedience of the Gospel with the revelation of the fearsome Judge in verse 7b, probably implying that the former leads to disadvantage at the latter.

[27] If 'Paul' had wished to feed the hunger of 'the Thessalonians' for vengeance on *persecutors* in verses 8b–9, the offence of persecution would presumably have been explicitly stated (as in verse 6). As it stands, the reference is generic, simply differentiating 'the Thessalonians' from all unbelievers.

confirmed by verse 10's ὅτι ἐπιστεύθη τὸ μαρτύριον ἡμῶν ἐφ' ὑμᾶς. Jesus is presented as coming to be glorified in (ἐν) his 'holy ones'[28] (cf. Zech. 14:5) and to be marvelled at by (ἐν) 'all (πᾶσιν) believers'. The ὅτι clause reveals that the focus is squarely on 'the Thessalonians'. It states the grounds (i.e. faith in the apostolic Gospel: cf. 2:14) for their participation in the glorification of Christ in his holy ones and the admiration of him by all believers, perhaps picking up especially on πᾶσιν τοῖς πιστεύσασιν,[29] and reinforces the impression that 'Paul' is assuring 'the Thessalonians' regarding their participation in the salvation of the parousia. Furthermore, it contrasts with 1:8's description of the victims of the parousia, who did not obey the Gospel.[30] In the light of the false claim, it is little wonder that the fate of the unbelievers – 'eternal destruction', eternal separation from the presence of the Lord and the glory of his might[31] (verse 9) – is categorically contrasted with the bright destiny of 'the Thessalonians' (verse 10). Further, in view of the suspicion that a forgery in Paul's name (2:2 and 3:17) might have given rise to the destructive false claim, it is especially understandable that 'Paul' seeks to reassure them by identifying himself with them in regard to suffering (καί, 1:5c; cf. ἀδελφοί, verse 3; ἡμῶν in verses 11 and 12) and eschatological destiny (μεθ' ἡμῶν, verse 7a).

Without the hope of justice and salvation, a primary motivation for perseverance disappeared (cf. 3:5, where eschatological reassurance and an encouragement to endure are apparently connected). This perhaps explains why 'Paul' moves so quickly from the perseverance and faith(fulness) of 'the Thessalonians' (1:4) to reassuring them that they have good reason to hope for justice (verses 5–10).

[28] 'Paul' has freely employed the language of LXX Ps. 88:8 to make his point, even though originally it referred to angels rather than believers. Lightfoot suggested that the sense of ἐνδοξασθῆναι ἐν is that the glory of the Lord will be seen in the saints (*Epistles*, 104). The reference would then be to the glorification of believers, the shining of the Lord's glory in them (cf. Rom. 8:18; Phil. 3:21; Col. 3:4). This seems plausible.
[29] Lightfoot, *Epistles*, 104–5 filled in the ellipsis between this clause and the preceding one with 'and therefore in you'.
[30] Cf. Trilling, *Zweite Brief*, 61. Τὸ μαρτύριον here is synonymous with τὸ εὐαγγέλιον, τὸ κήρυγμα and ἡ διδασκαλία; see von Dobschütz, *Thessalonicher-Briefe*, 252.
[31] The idea is derived from LXX Isa. 2:10, 19, 21, where God's terrifying judgment of the house of Jacob is described. The house of Jacob is advised to hide ἀπὸ προσώπου τοῦ φόβου κυρίου καὶ ἀπὸ τῆς δόξης τῆς ἰσχύος αὐτοῦ, a markedly positive and sensible action. Here in 2 Thess. 1:9, however, the language is used negatively of unbelievers; hence the omission of φόβος. Clearly 'Paul' is manipulating the phraseology of Isaiah flexibly in his articulation of the unbelievers' eschatological fate.

In conclusion, verses 5–10 beg to be understood in the light of 2:2c. It is worth noting that von Dobschütz argued that it was implausible that the false claim would have been interpreted at face value, for the persecutions of 'the Thessalonians' would have preserved them from thinking that the Day of judgment and redemption had actually come.[32] Strikingly, if we are correct, von Dobschütz came close to articulating the precise problem posed for 'the Thessalonians' by the eschatological idea: if the Day has indeed come and yet they are still suffering, they might wonder what is going on. Moreover, Peerbolte maintains that if the claim had been understood at face value, the emphasis in 2 Thess. 2:3ff. would have been on retribution and vindication.[33] It is enough to note that this is precisely the focus of 1:5–10 (cf. 2:9–14).

The situation that emerges is as follows: having been informed that the Day of the Lord had come, 'the Thessalonians' seem to have become greatly distressed, above all because they were still suffering persecution. 'Paul' assumes that the false claim has been understood as eliminating all hope of justice in the form of relief for them and affliction for their persecutors, and ultimately has threatened their continued perseverance. It makes good sense that he immediately begins confronting the false idea by tackling its most terrible and devastating perceived implication, that it rendered their eschatological hope null and void. We now turn to the prayer of verses 11–12.

Do 1:11–12 imply that the salvation of 'the Thessalonians' is contingent on prayer?

In view of (εἰς ὃ καί) the just judgment at the parousia (verses 5–10), specifically its positive dimension (verses 5, 7a and especially 10), 'Paul' continually prays that 'our'[34] God will make 'the Thessalonians' worthy (ἀξιώσῃ; cf. καταξιωθῆναι in verse 5) of his call (κλῆσις) of them (presumably to inherit salvation and/or his kingdom: cf. 1 Thess. 2:12) and that he will 'by his power' or 'powerfully' (ἐν δυνάμει, here adverbial in function) accomplish fully their every resolve to do good (πᾶσαν εὐδοκίαν

---

[32] Von Dobschütz, *Thessalonicher-Briefe*, 267 (cf. Friedrich, 'Zweite Brief', 253, 262).

[33] Peerbolte, *Antecedents*, 73.

[34] If ἡμῶν is important here, it does not reveal the author's wish 'to broaden the scope of the discussion beyond the audience's narrow perspective' (*pace* Richard, *Thessalonians*, 310), but rather 'Paul's' desire to unite 'the missionaries' with 'the Thessalonians' with respect to God.

ἀγαθωσύνης)³⁵ and their every work inspired by faith (πᾶσαν . . . ἔργον
πίστεως). The goal of the prayer is that 'the name of our Lord Jesus
Christ' may be glorified in 'the Thessalonians' and they in him.
That the glorification is present rather than future is indicated by κατὰ τὴν χάριν
τοῦ θεοῦ ἡμῶν καὶ κυρίου Ἰησοῦ Χριστοῦ: 'Paul' prays that the glorification that will certainly be theirs in the future will become part of their
present existence.

The destiny of 'the Thessalonians' is certain: they will be counted
worthy and be given relief from their afflictions and be numbered among
the blessed saints at the parousia (verses 5–10). But this necessitates that
God work in the present, and so it is for this that 'Paul' now prays.³⁶
It is not unlikely that this prayer reflects a worry about the threat to
continued perseverance posed by the persecution in the wake of the false
claim of 2:2c. Notably, 'Paul' himself moves to resolve the mild tension
between security and contingency of salvation with reference to God's
faithfulness in 3:3. Perhaps the prayer also functions to reassure 'the
Thessalonians' of 'Paul's' personal interest and belief in them, in case they
had received a forged letter attributed to Paul and accepted its devastating
implications.

Conclusion

Apparently, then, 2 Thess. 1:3–12 is aimed at overcoming a serious obstacle to continuing perseverance in the midst of persecutions: the idea
that the Day had come, together with the observation that justice had
not. For the persecutors seemed to have escaped punishment, while 'the
Thessalonians' themselves seemed to have missed relief from affliction. In the view of 'Paul', the eschatological idea of 2:2c had potentially devastating theological, christological and pastoral ramifications
for 'the Thessalonians'. In 1:3–10 'Paul', with a view to reinforcing endurance, reassures 'the Thessalonians' that they have good grounds for

---

³⁵ *Contra* von Dobschütz, *Thessalonicher-Briefe*, 253–7 and Calvin, *Thessalonians*,
393–4, the resolve is probably not God's. The parallelism ('work of faith') is almost certainly not used of God, and the usual meaning of ἀγαθωσύνη, as well as the absence of the
article before εὐδοκία, strongly suggests that the resolve is human and not divine.
³⁶ There is a slight paradox here, in that in the aftermath of a categorical assurance, 'Paul'
implies that the completion of their every resolve to do good and every work inspired by
faith is at least partly contingent upon prayer (and the perseverance of 'the Thessalonians').
Whether 2 Thessalonians is pseudonymous or authentic, it seems relevant that the apostle
Paul held to a form of what might be called 'compatibilism' (see D. A. Carson, *Divine
Sovereignty and Human Responsibility* (MTL; London: Marshall, Morgan & Scott, 1981)),
with strong emphases on both God's sovereign election and the responsibility of humanity.

hope.[37] He counters despair and rebuilds hope by stressing that they are approved by God and 'the missionaries', and show the fruits of genuine faith, and that persecutions demonstrate that God's just judgment will yet come and be seen to be just, on the manifestly spectacular Day of the Lord. Then he prays in verses 11–12 that in the meantime they will be enabled to persevere.

---

[37] Hughes, *2 Thessalonians*, 53–5 could hardly be further from the point when he claims that 2 Thessalonians 1 is a warning, consisting of two options for readers: either believe Paul's witness and so be among the elect, or be among those who do not know God/do not obey the Gospel, and so suffer eternal destruction. Verses 6 and 8–9, which refer to a negative fate at the parousia, relate to unbelievers alone, whilst verses 7a and 10, which refer to a positive destiny at the parousia, concern believers alone. There is a sustained *contrast* between the destiny of believers and that of unbelievers throughout the chapter. Also, the hearty thanksgiving for and boast in 'the Thessalonians' present a serious problem for Hughes's hypothesis.

7

THE PROBLEM OF EXPLOITING CHARITY AND THE CONCLUSION

Introduction

A formidable barrier to the acceptance of the reading of 2 Thessalonians' eschatological problem proposed in the preceding chapters is the assumption of most scholars in the nineteenth and twentieth centuries that the false eschatological claim of 2:2c underlies the problem of 'idleness' in 3:6–15.[1] Indeed, it has been argued that 2 Thess. 3:6ff. reveals why the eschatological problem of 'the Thessalonians' needed to be addressed.[2] Disagreement exists regarding whether 'Paul' is suggesting that the eschatology intensified the community members' perception of the parousia's imminence, with the consequence that they concluded there was no point in working,[3] perhaps feeling that proclamation of the nearness of the eschaton was more important and urgent;[4] or whether he is assuming

---

[1] For example, F. C. Baur, *Paul the Apostle of Jesus Christ* (ed. E. Zeller; trans. A. Menzies; TTFL; London: Williams and Norgate, 1875–6), 2:332; G. Lünemann, *Critical and Exegetical Handbook to the Epistles of St. Paul to the Thessalonians* (trans. P. J. Gloag; CECNT; Edinburgh: T. & T. Clark, 1880), 248; Lightfoot, *Epistles*, 60; Bornemann, *Thessalonicherbriefe*, 181, 393; Findlay, *Epistles of Paul*, xxxviii; Milligan, *Thessalonians*, xlvi–xlvii, 154; von Dobschütz, *Thessalonicher-Briefe*, 182, 309–11; Frame, *Thessalonians*, 307; H. E. Littleton, 'The Function of Apocalyptic in 2 Thessalonians as a Criterion for its Authorship' (Ph.D. diss., Vanderbilt University, 1973), 186–8, 196–7; Kümmel, *Introduction*, 268; Agrell, *Toil*, 122–3; Friedrich, 'Zweite Brief', 272–3, 274; Bailey, 'Who?', 137; Burkeen, 'Parousia', 370–1; Mearns, 'Development', 147; Müller, *Anfänge*, 162–7; Koester, 'Schemata', 456; Morris, *Epistles*, 253, 258; Schweizer, *Introduction*, 99; Barclay, 'Conflict', 528–9; K. Romaniuk, 'Les Thessaloniciens étaient-ils des paresseux?', *ETL* 69 (1993): 142–5; A. M. Okorie, 'The Pauline Work Ethic in 1 and 2 Thessalonians', *DBM* 14 (1995): 63, 64; Richard, *Thessalonians*, 390, 391; Murphy-O'Connor, *Critical Life*, 123; Gaventa, *Thessalonians*, 129; Légasse, *Thessaloniciens*, 434 including n. 4; Stacy, 'Introduction', 187. Schmithals, 'Historical Situation', 198–9 and Marxsen, *Introduction*, 39 contend that Gnosticism underlies the idleness of 3:6ff.

[2] So, for example, Hollmann, 'Unechtheit', 34–5.

[3] Aus, 'Thessalonians', 215–16; Morris, *Epistles*, 130 (who (p. 253), with Best, *Thessalonians*, 334, suggests that an especially strong sense of freedom in Christ may have led 'the Thessalonians' to abandon work); Brown, *Introduction*, 591; cf. C. K. Barrett, *Paul* (OCT; London: Geoffrey Chapman, 1994), 150.

[4] Bassin, *Thessaloniciens*, 264; cf. Lütgert, 'Enthusiasten', 628, 637–41.

that excited anticipation of the parousia so seized 'the Thessalonians' that they felt unable to carry out their tasks.[5] Some scholars question whether the false eschatology was the primary causative factor, preferring to see it as one contributing ingredient in a larger problem[6] or merely as a pretext.[7] Others view the ἄτακτοι as the originators of the erroneous eschatological claim referred to in 2:2c.[8]

Difficulties of reading 2 Thess. 3:6–15 as an eschatological problem

The most striking difficulty of reading the idleness of 2 Thess. 3:6–15 as an eschatological problem is the silence of 2, and indeed 1, Thessalonians regarding any explicit link between the idleness and eschatology. Not only is there no reference to eschatology in 2 Thess. 3:6–15 (or 1 Thess. 4:9–12), but there is also no suggestion that the eschatological problems in 2 Thess. 2:1ff. (or 1 Thess. 4:13–5:11) had direct ethical consequences.[9] It is necessary to examine the various proofs of a link which have been proposed over the last two centuries.

Hollmann saw in μετὰ ἡσυχίας (3:12) the 'sole quiet hint' in 2 Thess. 3:6ff. that the problem is essentially eschatological.[10] However, since μετὰ ἡσυχίας ἐργαζόμενοι appears to be a counter-concept to περιεργα-ζομένους,[11] the former can only reflect an eschatological background to the degree that the latter does.[12] Περιεργαζομένους itself (2 Thess. 3:11) has been viewed by many as an indication that the problem of the 'idlers'

[5] Neil, *Thessalonians*, 192 (cf. pp. 86–9, 194).

[6] For example, Frame, *Thessalonians*, 300; Marshall, *Thessalonians*, 219, 223 (cf. p. 117); Best, *Thessalonians*, 175, 334–5; Goulder, 'Silas', 88, 89 including n. 1, 97–8.

[7] So *inter alios* Rigaux, *Thessaloniciens*, 709, 712 (cf. pp. 519–21) and Evans, 'Eschatology', 78, 173–4.

[8] So *inter alios* Giblin, *Threat to Faith*, 147; Jewett, *Correspondence*, 177–8; Holland, *Tradition*, 55, 126, 151; Krodel, *Deutero-Pauline Letters*, 55 (cf. pp. 53–4).

[9] Kaye, 'Eschatology', 47–57; D. C. Aune, 'Trouble in Thessalonica: An Exegetical Study of I Thess 4.9–12, 5.12–14 and II Thess 6.6–15 in Light of First-Century Social Conditions' (Th.M. thesis, Regent College, 1989), 83–4, 93.

[10] Hollmann, 'Unechtheit', 35; see also von Dobschütz, *Thessalonicher-Briefe*, 179–80; Frame, *Thessalonians*, 307; Rigaux, *Thessaloniciens*, 712; Krodel, *Ephesians, Colossians, 2 Thessalonians*, 87; Best, *Thessalonians*, 341; Bassin, *Thessaloniciens*, 269 n. 2; Richard, *Thessalonians*, 390.

[11] *Contra* Frame, *Thessalonians*, 307 and Bicknell, *Thessalonians*, 94, although they at least acknowledge that they must choose between the eschatological interpretation of μετὰ ἡσυχίας ἐργαζόμενοι and viewing it as a counter-concept to περιεργαζομένους (unlike, for example, Findlay, *Epistles of Paul*, 210; von Dobschütz, *Thessalonicher-Briefe*, 314; Best, *Thessalonians*, 341).

[12] Μετὰ ἡσυχίας most naturally does not refer to the internal state of mind (*pace* Frame, *Thessalonians*, 307 and Morris, *Epistles*, 258), but the external manner in which the work

has an eschatological dimension.[13] However, such a conclusion can only be drawn by eisegesis. Περιεργαζομένους ('being a busybody', 'meddling in other people's affairs',[14] cf. 1 Thess. 4:11–12) seems highly appropriate as a concomitant of idleness (cf. περίεργος in 1 Tim. 5:13); understanding it to refer to apocalyptic missionising seems unnecessary and artificial.[15] Similarly, μετὰ ἡσυχίας makes good sense without reference to the eschatological reading.

Some have argued that τὴν ὑπομονὴν τοῦ Χριστοῦ in 2 Thess. 3:5 favours the eschatological reading of 3:6ff.[16] However, as we demonstrated in chapter 5 above, the genitive is probably subjective rather than objective. Nevertheless, our conclusion that 3:3–5 relates to the eschatological problem of 2:2c might be seen by some as evidence for 3:6ff. being rooted in the false eschatology. However, 3:6ff. is introduced as a new section, indeed an *addendum*, and 3:5 seems to serve as a benediction drawing to a close the section of which it is a part. These points also refute the contention of some that the general eschatological nature of 2 Thessalonians suggests that 3:6ff. should be interpreted in the light of the eschatological problems of 'the Thessalonians'.[17] Against this view one might also note that the *optimism* of 'Paul' in 3:4 concerning the conduct of 'the Thessalonians' in the present and in the future (upon receipt of 2 Thessalonians) in regard to their eschatological difficulties contrasts with the *pessimism* reflected in 3:6ff.

Neither are the similarities of 'Paul's' approach to the two issues – the emphasis on traditions (2:15; 3:6) and/or the reference to missionary teaching (2:5; 3:10) and the appeal to present knowledge (2:6; 3:7) – indicative of a link,[18] for such parallels seem best interpreted as reflecting distinct rather than correlated problems, as a brief summary of the material demonstrates. The παράδοσις in 3:6 probably refers to the

was carried out, as is verified by 1 Thess. 4:11–12 (ἡσυχάζειν), regardless of whether or not 2 Thessalonians is authentic, since if it is pseudonymous, it is dependent on 1 Thessalonians.

[13] So *inter alios* Agrell, 'Toil', 123; Krodel, *Ephesians, Colossians, 2 Thessalonians*, 87; O. Knoch, *1. und 2. Thessalonicherbrief* (SKKNT; Stuttgart: Katholisches Bibelwerk, 1987), 83–4; Bassin, *Thessaloniciens*, 268–9; Menken, *Thessalonians*, 137, 140 and 'Paradise', 287; Richard, *Thessalonians*, 390.

[14] See Louw and Nida, *Lexicon*, §88.243; *EDNT*, 3:73.

[15] *Pace* Richard, *Thessalonians*, 390. Cf. Barclay, 'Conflict', 528 and 529, although it is unclear upon what grounds Barclay bases his belief that the believers are engaged in 'full-time evangelism'.

[16] Agrell, *Toil*, 116; Krodel, *Deutero-Pauline Letters*, 54; Menken, *Thessalonians*, 129, 137.

[17] Von Dobschütz, *Thessalonicher-Briefe*, 182–3; Romanuik, 'Thessaloniciens', 143; Menken, *Thessalonians*, 137 and 'Paradise', 271.

[18] *Pace* Menken, *Thessalonians*, 137 and 'Paradise', 271–2.

example of 'the missionaries' (verses 7–9) and teaching (verse 10) during the mission with specific regard to work, whilst in 2:15 it refers to specifically eschatological (and perhaps soteriological) teachings communicated at the Thessalonian mission and in 1 Thessalonians. The reference to the missionary teaching in 3:10 concerns the command that charity is to be restricted to those willing to work, whilst in 2:5 it concerns the revelation of the rebel at the temple. Finally, the present knowledge in 3:7 relates to the example of 'the missionaries', whilst in 2:6 it relates to the restraint of the rebel's revelation. Such differences point to two different treatments of two distinct problems.

Krodel has seen anticipatory references to the problem of 3:6ff. in the 'catchwords' ἔργον πίστεως (1:11) and παντὶ ἔργῳ (2:17), which sandwich the eschatological material.[19] However, he fails to take adequate account of the fact that ἔργον πίστεως is paired with εὐδοκίαν ἀγαθωσύνης (1:11) and ἔργῳ with λόγῳ (2:17); besides, ἔργον is too common a term to bear the weight Krodel wishes to put on it.

There is in fact no convincing evidence of a link between the eschatological problem and the idleness in 2 Thessalonians. And, as we have demonstrated in chapter 4, evidence for a connection between the eschatological problems and idleness in 1 Thessalonians too is lacking. This lack of any explicit link is particularly conspicuous when we take into account that the problem underlying 2 Thess. 3:6ff., had it been as proponents of the eschatological position claim it was, would have virtually required some reference to the false eschatology.[20] For if the 'idlers' had been motivated by the false eschatology, one would have expected 'Paul' to stress that the work mandate taught at the founding mission *remained valid*. However, a reference to the apostles' example and teaching prior to the rise of the false eschatology is considered sufficient by 'Paul'. Hollmann attempted to explain the remarkable silence by claiming that the pseudepigrapher, opposed to imminentist expectation, could hardly have launched an explicit attack on such a prized tenet of early church teaching.[21] However, as we demonstrated in chapter 5, the problem reflected in 2 Thessalonians was probably not imminentism. Moreover, there are indications that 'Paul' adheres to belief in the parousia's imminence (1:5–10; 2:1, 13–14). We conclude that the silence

---

[19] Krodel, *Deutero-Pauline Letters*, 54.
[20] Hence when Menken, 'Paradise', 271 and Krodel, *Deutero-Pauline Letters*, 54 justify the silence by asserting that an explicit connection was hardly necessary when the addressees were already aware of the link, their explanation is inadequate.
[21] Hollmann, 'Unechtheit', 35.

is a formidable problem for the eschatological interpretation. A close examination of the text raises other problems for this position.

The fact that in 2 Thess. 3:6, 10 (cf. 1 Thess. 4:11) 'Paul' refers to the instruction delivered during the mission seems to favour the view that the 'idleness' and the erroneous eschatological notion (2 Thess. 2:2c) are viewed by him as unrelated. We can interpret the teaching at the mission either as stock catechetical instruction or as directed to a specific problem. With regard to the former option, it seems implausible that 'Paul' would have anticipated a problem of idleness motivated by misguided eschatological thinking;[22] after all, we have no other instance of an eschatologically inspired 'idleness' in the first century. Hence if the teaching was stock, it is unlikely to have had in view an off-shoot of eschatological confusion. With respect to the latter possibility[23] (which is arguably supported by the use of the verb παραγγέλλω in verse 10 and the choice of παρελάβοσαν rather than παρελάβετε in verse 6), in view of the fact that 'Paul' treats the eschatological problem underlying 2:2 (the idea that 'the Day of the Lord has come') as a new and surprising development, it seems that any earlier problem of idleness could not have been caused by the same eschatological confusion. That leaves as the sole possibility that a different type of eschatological problem (such as imminentism) gave rise to the earlier idleness. However, how plausible is it to suggest that the problem of idleness has remained constant, and perhaps even worsened, all the while its foundation, faulty eschatological thinking, has undergone such radical shifts – from imminentist excitement (at the mission) to fear that the Day was about to come (underlying 1 Thessalonians) to horror and discouragement that it had already come (underlying 2 Thessalonians)? But could we not conclude that a pseudonymous author had simply failed to create a realistic *Sitz im Leben*? Perhaps, but it must be acknowledged that by rejecting the eschatological reading of 2 Thess. 3:6–15 we avoid having to inculpate the author thus. It is surely more natural to assume a continuity between the motivation undergirding previous instruction about idleness and that undergirding 2 Thess. 3:6ff. than a discontinuity, and to conclude that the idleness was not therefore caused by eschatological thinking.

Furthermore, as Kaye has argued, the pragmatic nature of the argumentation in 3:6ff. seems distinctly unsuited to a problem which was rooted in

---

[22] *Pace* Burkeen, 'Parousia', 370–1.

[23] So Kaye, 'Eschatology', 53, 56–7; Aune, 'Trouble', 93; B. W. Winter, *Seek the Welfare of the City: Christians as Benefactors and Citizens* (FCCGRW; Grand Rapids: Eerdmans, 1994), 43.

errant theology.[24] Also, the problem underlying 2:1ff. seems to afflict the whole community, whilst the problem underlying 3:6ff. appears to be restricted to a minority grouping within the community. And with regard to tone, the reassurance of 2:1–17 contrasts sharply with 3:6–15's exasperation. In addition, the choice of περιπατεῖν with ἀτάκτως may suggest that the 'idleness' was a settled pattern of life, whilst the verbs in 2:2 appear to indicate that the eschatological problem was in its early stages.

Precisely why the coming of the Day of the Lord would have caused early Christians to abandon their work is not entirely clear: if they were too excited to be capable of work, then the emphasis on *unwillingness* to work in 3:10 seems peculiar and the discipline somewhat over-harsh. Certainly the idea that the parousia's coming would have rendered work null and void seems incompatible with the teaching of Genesis 2–3, where not work *per se*, but rather toil and sweat in work constituted part of the curse (cf. Gen. 3:17–19) which would be revoked when the eschaton came.[25] That man should work was a pre-Fall mandate (Gen. 2:5, 15). Hence it is difficult to see why the parousia's coming would have seemed to render work pointless. If the ἄτακτοι had abandoned their jobs to proclaim the Gospel, we might then wonder why the problem was apparently restricted to the manual labourers and why 3:6ff. does not confront directly the matter of the validity of the ἄτακτοι's ministry.

Other arguments have been used to defend the linking of the eschatology and the 'idleness', but none are compelling. Some appeal to examples of apocalyptic sects in church history,[26] but interpreting a text in the light of later parallels is a notoriously unreliable business. Furthermore, while many appeal to Hippolytus' story about the effects of a prophecy of eschatological judgment in Pontus,[27] they take insufficient account of the differences between events in Pontus and those in 'Thessalonica', especially in regard to the nature of the eschatological error.[28] The argument based on apparent parallels to 1 Cor. 4:8[29] presupposes too much about

---

[24] Kaye, 'Eschatology', 56.

[25] Cf. 2 Bar. 74:1, which envisions an eschatological age characterised by fruitful work without toil.

[26] Von Dobschütz, *Christian Life*, 93; Neil, *Thessalonians*, 87; Bruce, *Thessalonians*, 91; Müller, 'Currents', 308.

[27] So *inter alios* N. R. C. Cohn, *The Pursuit of the Millennium* (3rd edn; London: Paladin, 1970), 337–8; Agrell, *Toil*, 212 n. 15; Friedrich, 'Zweite Brief', 274; Aus, 'Thessalonians', 216; Müller, 'Currents', 308. See Hippolytus, *Commentary on Daniel* 4.19.

[28] Also, too few take account of the fact that in Hippolytus' story abandoning work follows the false claim, whereas in 2 Thessalonians idleness exists prior to the erroneous pronouncement.

[29] Best, *Thessalonians*, 334–5.

the situation there to be of any real value and is, notwithstanding, inconclusive. The idea that the eschatological implications of brotherly love and sharing possessions contributed to the problem of 3:6ff.[30] is rendered implausible by the emphasis on the *unwillingness* of the ἄτακτοι to work and yet their willingness to become a burden on other believers. According to two proponents of the eschatological interpretation who also accept the authenticity of 2 Thessalonians, the greater severity in tone in 2 Thess. 3:6ff. as compared with 1 Thess. 4:11–12 and 5:14 reflects a deterioration of the Thessalonian situation and is explicable only with reference to the new eschatological error in 2 Thess. 2:2c.[31] However, if we do assume authenticity, the greater severity can be plausibly explained in other ways, such as the amount of time the problem was taking to resolve or the exacerbation of the situation by more manual labourers joining the ranks of the ἄτακτοι or the reality of the problem having been impressed upon Paul in a new way.

Finally, it has been argued that there is no convincing alternative explanation of the situation in 2 Thess. 3:6ff.[32] Therefore our task is not complete until we have offered a reasonable alternative.

First, we shall overview non-eschatological proposals offered to elucidate the situation underlying 2 Thess. 3:6ff., then undertake an exegesis of the relevant section, 3:6–15, and finally, on the basis of that, construct a hypothesis to explain the problem of the ἄτακτοι.

Recent non-eschatological hypotheses

Over the past three decades, various hypotheses have been developed to explain the problem of the ἄτακτοι.

(1) Some have suggested that the section does not relate to a concrete situation, but constitutes a general reminder of catechetical instruction.[33] However, verse 11 clearly implies that the problem of 'the Thessalonians' is situationally specific.

(2) It has also been argued that, actually or potentially under the influence of Epicureanism/Cynicism, 'the Thessalonians' were tending to abandon their jobs, necessitating that 'Paul' distinguish Christian from

---

[30] *Contra* R. Jewett, 'Tenement Churches and Communal Meals in the Early Church: The Implications of a Form-Critical Analysis of 2 Thessalonians 3:10', *BR* 38 (1993): 41.

[31] Von Dobschütz, *Thessalonicher-Briefe*, 309; Aus, 'Thessalonians', 215.

[32] Romanuik, 'Thessaloniciens', 143–5.

[33] *Inter alios* Trilling, *Zweite Brief*, 144 and *Untersuchungen*, 98–101; Marxsen, *Zweite Thessalonicherbrief*, 98.

Epicurean/Cynic social attitudes.[34] However, this position relies exclusively on inconclusive comparisons.

(3) Russell contends that the problem relates to manual labourers and/or artisans, perhaps unemployed and/or dependent on patrons, who when brought into the 'circle of Christian love' might conceivably have 'appeared to outsiders to be idle beggars who exploited the generosity of the Christian community without any sense of reciprocal response to their new benefactors [*sic*]'.[35] Indeed, 'as the idle were caught up in new beliefs and practices, they rejected the idea of work to enjoy their understanding of brotherly love and to propagate their opinions and religious ideas. They became, consequently, a burden to those who were more responsible with work habits and who had financial means.'[36] However, while we concur that the issue probably did relate to manual labourers and artisans and that patronage may well have been a factor, it seems incongruous that an attempt to understand brotherly love could have resulted in such a violation of it. Further, there is no evidence that the 'idlers' were spreading religious ideas. Russell seems too willing to attribute the 'idleness' to a worthy cause. Rather than suggesting that 'Paul' was worried about unbelievers getting the wrong impression that idle beggars were exploiting the rich Christians in 'the Thessalonian community' when in fact the 'idlers' were motivated by worthy ambitions, it seems preferable to argue that what 'Paul' feared unbelievers might think and what was actually occurring did indeed correspond.

(4) Winter has proposed that the problem was caused by the unwillingness of Christians to abandon permanently the patron–client social structure. He suggests that this reluctance may have been initiated by difficult socio-economic circumstances induced by a famine between 1 and 2 Thessalonians, which had forced the poor back into dependence on patrons;[37] he postulates that post-mission converts may have refused to surrender their (Christian) patrons and/or that those converted at the mission may have reverted to dependent relationships, with new or existing (Christian) patrons after the missionaries left the city.[38]

However, not only is evidence lacking that the famine in AD 51 seriously affected Thessalonica, but it is far from clear that 2 Thessalonians

---

[34] A. J. Festugière, *Epicurus and his Gods* (trans. C. W. Chilton; Oxford: Blackwell, 1955), 57; A. J. Malherbe, *Social Aspects of Early Christianity* (2nd edn; Philadelphia: Fortress, 1983), 25–7 and *Paul and the Thessalonians*, 96–106 (cf. *Thessalonians*, 258–9, 454–7).

[35] R. Russell, 'The Idle in 2 Thess 3:6–12: An Eschatological or a Social Problem?', *NTS* 34 (1988): 110–13, esp. 113.

[36] Ibid., 113.   [37] Winter, *Welfare*, 42–60, esp. 53–7.   [38] Ibid., 57.

requires such a disaster. Furthermore, Winter's theory runs into problems in regard to the length of the hiatus between 1 and 2 Thessalonians, for in order to explain plausibly the phenomena of 2 Thessalonians, proponents of Pauline authorship must argue that the period between the letters was relatively brief. Yet Winter's theory necessitates that between the two letters there was time not only for a disaster, but also for the permanence of the dependence on patrons to become evident. This difficulty is propounded by the date he is forced to give 2 Thessalonians, late AD 51.

In addition, the scenario painted by Winter renders the rich Christian patrons as guilty as the poor clients, for they were accomplices in the error, gaining from clients 'prestige and power in the public place',[39] in particular benefiting from their clients' 'boisterous, political rabble-rousing behaviour' on their behalf at the *politeia*;[40] yet 'Paul' confronts only the poor, commanding them to live and work quietly (2 Thess. 3:12; cf. 1 Thess. 4:11). Also, one is left wondering why the patrons would have grown 'weary of doing good', if the situation was as Winter proposes.[41] Further, it remains to be proved that contemporary patrons would have been willing to underwrite their clients to such an extent that the latter would not have needed to work at all. Additionally, while Winter has provided an explanation of possible structures in which the problem of the ἄτακτοι might have manifested itself, he has not given a clear *motivation* for the refusal to work. And this hypothesis fails to explain adequately 2 Thess. 3:6 and 10 and 1 Thess. 4:9–12, which seem to demonstrate that precisely the same actual problem of idleness had been plaguing the Thessalonian church since its founding, well before the catalyst for the eschatological error of 2 Thess. 2:2 occurred.[42] Finally, we reject the idea that the ἄτακτοι might have been converted after the mission, since 'Paul' appeals to the teaching and example delivered at the mission.[43] And we find it difficult to believe that numerous sets of patrons and clients in Thessalonica converted to Christianity at the same time.

(5) The most helpful hypothesis yet developed is that of D. C. Aune, who argues that converted manual labourers, cut off from their *collegia*, looked to the church to meet their needs.[44] Motivated by greed, laziness and perhaps a sense that, because they were Christians, work was beneath

---

[39] Ibid., 57. [40] Ibid., 48.

[41] Winter (ibid., 58) seems to take 3:13 as directed to the ἄτακτοι, but later on the same page he appears to treat it as directed to the benefactors.

[42] Winter sees his famine hypothesis as '[explaining] the heightened eschatological expectation . . . in 2 Thessalonians' (ibid., 53–4, 57).

[43] Note that 3:10 seems to assume that the problem of 'idleness' existed during the mission; hence the structural context of the 'idleness' must already have been in place.

[44] Aune, 'Trouble', 87–90.

them, they began to take advantage of the charity of wealthier community members, which was extended to them in the name of love, and failed to show the expected appreciation to those supporting them.[45] As will become evident in the ensuing pages, while we would perhaps see the patron–client model as bearing more on the situation than *collegia*, and while we would be sceptical that lack of appreciation and self-importance constituted significant dimensions of the problem, we do concur with Aune in understanding the ἄτακτοι as manual labourers and viewing them as motivated by greed and laziness and as guilty of taking advantage of wealthy Christians' generous charity.

An exegesis of 2 Thess. 3:6–15

While some have interpreted 3:1's τὸ λοιπόν as covering verses 1–15,[46] with παραγγέλλομεν in verse 4 linking verses 1–5 and verses 6ff.,[47] the facts that verses 6ff. are introduced as a new section (with δέ . . . ἀδελφοί and παραγγέλλομεν) and are distinct in content and that verses 1–5 are concluded by a wish-prayer benediction (verse 5) suggest that verses 6ff. are an *addendum* rather than an anticipated part of the epistolary conclusion and hence verses 6ff. were probably not initially intended to be covered by τὸ λοιπόν.

The ὑμῖν, ἀδελφοί in verse 6 plainly refers to the majority of 'the Thessalonians', who are not characterised by 'idleness' or meddlesomeness. Some have perceived in παραγγέλλομεν an authoritarian, sharp tone;[48] in the light of the usage in verse 4 and the fact that those addressed are the 'innocent' section of the community (the non-ἄτακτοι), this assessment seems somewhat exaggerated; nevertheless, together with ἐν ὀνόματι τοῦ κυρίου [ἡμῶν] Ἰησοῦ Χριστοῦ, the verb certainly does underscore the authority of 'the missionaries'. The question naturally arises, why does the author feel the need to stress that disobedience to the command of 'the missionaries' is disobedience to the Lord? Findlay explains it with reference to the Thessalonians' disregard of 1 Thessalonians,[49] but then we might justifiably wonder why references to 1 Thessalonians are so

---

[45] Ibid., 90–2.

[46] Von Dobschütz, *Thessalonicher-Briefe*, 305; Frame, *Thessalonians*, 288, 289.

[47] So Wohlenberg, *Thessalonicherbrief*, 160; Krodel, *Deutero-Pauline Letters*, 51; Menken, *Thessalonians*, 128; Richard, *Thessalonians*, 371. Lünemann, *Thessalonians*, 248 and Bassin, *Thessaloniciens*, 265 claim that verses 6ff. represent the specific paraenesis and verses 1–5 the general.

[48] Trilling, *Untersuchungen*, 97 n. 94 and *Zweite Brief*, 143 n. 605; Collins, *Letters*, 233; Müller, *Anfänge*, 163 (including n. 145 and n. 146); Richard, *Thessalonians*, 371, 378.

[49] Findlay, *Epistles of Paul*, 204.

conspicuously absent from this section. Perhaps the answer is simply that 'Paul' is anticipating a reluctance on the part of 'the Thessalonian community' to discipline erring believers, especially where the majority may not have viewed the situation to be as grave as 'Paul' obviously did. The non-ἄτακτοι are instructed 'to disassociate from' or 'to withdraw from intimate contact with' (στέλλεσθαι) the ἄτακτοι. Exactly how this might have manifested itself in practice is difficult to determine in the light of verse 15's insistence that the disciplined member was to be 'warned as a brother'. One can resolve the tension by one of the following means: (1) by interpreting στέλλεσθαι in verse 6 as suggesting temporary excommunication and the warnings of verse 15 as administered outside the context of community meetings; or (2) by restricting the disassociation to a bar on fellowship at meals (and perhaps church meetings); or (3) by interpreting verse 15 as referring primarily to the conduct of the majority at the initiation of the disciplinary ostracism rather than during it; or (4) by viewing verses 14–15 as belonging to a distinct section from verses 6ff. *Contra* (3), it would then be difficult to understand why those to be warned are still regarded as 'brothers' (verses 6, 15). *Contra* (4), since there is no other matter requiring discipline in 2 Thessalonians, verses 14–15 probably refer to the same problem as verses 6ff. Deciding between (1) and (2) is difficult and for our purposes unnecessary.

The majority are to disassociate ἀπὸ παντὸς ἀδελφοῦ ἀτάκτως περιπατοῦντος. The precise nuance of ἀτάκτως here has been the source of much debate. In 2 Thessalonians, the adverb ἀτάκτως (verses 6, 12) and the verb ἀτακτέω (verse 7; cf. the adjective ἄτακτος, 1 Thess. 5:14) clearly describe an unwillingness to work for one's keep but a willingness to be a burden on others. Little wonder then that some have argued that ατακτ- should be rendered 'idle' or 'lazy' here.[50] Proponents of this view often appeal to P. Oxy. 2.275.24–5 and 4.725.39–40, which, they claim, lend credence to the possibility that in contemporary parlance ατακτ- could be used of idleness.[51] However, Spicq has demonstrated adequately that ατακτ- never means 'lazy' or 'idle', but can only mean 'disorderly', 'undisciplined', 'insubordinate' or 'disobedient';[52] even in the papyri cited above, the meaning 'undisciplined' seems preferable.[53]

[50] So Milligan, *Thessalonians*, 152–4; Dibelius, *Thessalonicher*, 53–4; cf. Frame, *Thessalonians*, 298, 299; BAGD, 119 (but see BDAG, 148).

[51] Milligan, *Thessalonians*, 153–4; Moulton and Milligan, *Vocabulary*, 89.

[52] C. Spicq, 'Les Thessaloniciens "inquiets" étaient-ils des paresseux?', *ST* 10 (1956): 1–13 and *Theological Lexicon of the New Testament* (trans. J. D. Ernest; 3 vols.; Peabody, Mass.: Hendrickson, 1994), 1:223–6.

[53] Spicq, '"Inquiets"', 6–8; cf. G. Forkman, *The Limits of Religious Community* (trans. P. Sjölander; ConBNT; Lund: Gleerup, 1972), 134.

If 'Paul' had wished to specify idleness or laziness *per se*, he could have used ἀργέω.

Some have argued that the meaning of ατακτ- here incorporates the sense of περιεργάζομαι in 2 Thess. 3:11 so that ατακτ- implies not just passive but also active indiscipline[54] or insubordination.[55] However, in the light of the facts that the example (verses 7–9) and teaching (verse 10) of 'the missionaries' relate to working rather than not working and that meddling seems most naturally understood as an outgrowth of not working, it seems wisest to avoid interpreting ατακτ- in the light of περιεργάζομαι. In addition, the view that 'Paul' is confronting active rebellion on the part of the ἄτακτοι is irreconcilable with the sentiment expressed in verse 15.

It seems that either ατακτ- 'does not in the first instance stress sloth, but the irresponsible attitude to the obligation to work'[56] or it refers to their refusal to work *qua* a failure to abide by the community rules and/or *qua* a violation of the creation order of Gen. 2:15. The 'idlers' are therefore designated as those who are shirking their responsibility or are undisciplined.

The nature of the offence is further defined as μὴ κατὰ τὴν παράδοσιν ἣν παρελάβοσαν[57] παρ' ἡμῶν. Those living ἀτάκτως are portrayed as not walking in accordance with the tradition passed on by 'the missionaries' during the founding mission. While παράδοσις here has been understood to refer generally to accepted catechetical apostolic ordinances on account of the definite article,[58] the subsequent context (2 Thess. 3:7–10, esp. verse 10) strongly favours the conclusion that tradition relating specifically to the necessity of working for one's keep is in mind here. This tradition had been communicated by example (verses 7–9) and oral instruction (verse 10); hence the ἄτακτοι were guilty of disobedience to the clear tradition of 'the missionaries'.

That γάρ in verse 7 primarily introduces the first reason for disassociating from the ἄτακτοι (and only indirectly confirms μὴ κατὰ τὴν παράδοσιν ἣν παρελάβοσαν παρ' ἡμῶν, which is essentially the other side of the coin from ἀτάκτως περιπατοῦντος) is indicated by the observation that οἴδατε is a second-person plural, agreeing with ὑμῖν and disagreeing with παρελάβοσαν. 'The Thessalonians' know that they ought (δεῖ) to live so as to imitate 'the missionaries'. There now follow two

---

[54] Rigaux, *Thessaloniciens*, 704–5; Bassin, *Thessaloniciens*, 265.

[55] Jewett, *Correspondence*, 104–5 (cf. 'Matrix', 69).   [56] Delling, 'Τάσσω', 48.

[57] For competent text-critical discussions which rightly judge the *lectio difficilior* παρελάβοσαν to represent the original text, see von Dobschütz, *Thessalonicher-Briefe*, 310–11 (esp. n. 5); Rigaux, *Thessaloniciens*, 703 and Metzger, *Textual Commentary*, 569.

[58] So Rigaux, *Thessaloniciens*, 705.

negative clauses and one positive clause defining the aspects of 'Paul's' example which relate to the problem at hand. First, in verse 7b it is stressed that 'the missionaries' had not been guilty of the same offence as the ἄτακτοι; then, second, in verse 8a, this claim is explicated: 'the missionaries' had not 'eaten bread', that is, 'received maintenance' (2 Sam. 9:7; cf. Did. 11:6) *gratis* from (i.e. had not been dependent on) any believer in Thessalonica. Third, 2 Thess. 3:8b presents positively the example of 'the missionaries' during the mission: they undertook toilsome and rigorous manual labour at all available moments day and night so that they could avoid being a burden to any believers. The implication is that the ἄτακτοι were refusing to work and were instead depending on other community members for their livelihood. The example of 'the missionaries' is particularly forceful because, unlike the ἄτακτοι, they had the right to such support, but chose to forfeit their right with a view to setting an example in regard to *willingness* to work, especially for manual labourers.[59] Hence verses 7–9 clearly indicate that the present behaviour of the ἄτακτοι was a breach of the standard clearly exhibited in the example of 'the missionaries'.

Verse 10's γάρ initiates the second ground for disassociating from the ἄτακτοι (and is a second indirect confirmation of μὴ κατὰ τὴν παράδοσιν ἣν παρελάβοσαν παρ' ἡμῶν). Not only had the ἄτακτοι been given the παράδοσις *qua* example, but they had also been given it *qua* oral instruction during the mission. While present 'the missionaries' had instructed or warned the believers that εἴ τις οὐ θέλει ἐργάζεσθαι μηδὲ ἐσθιέτω. This precise formulation of this command seems to be unique to this passage.[60] The stress is clearly on *unwillingness* to work; it refers not to those who cannot, but to those who will not work. Apparently the ἄτακτοι were unwilling to work and were receiving their living from the community.

Verse 11's γάρ introduces the explanation of why the ἄτακτοι are to be disciplined. A report has reached 'Paul' concerning 'the Thessalonians': some members of 'the Thessalonian community' are living ἀτάκτως.

---

[59] This suggests that the ἄτακτοι were not preachers, *contra*, for example, Lightfoot, *Epistles*, 60; Lütgert, 'Enthusiasten', 628, 641; Jewett, *Correspondence*, 177; Menken, *Thessalonians*, 140 and 'Paradise', 287; and Richard, *Thessalonians*, 384, 394, for then 'Paul' would surely have raised explicitly the matter of their ministry's invalidity.

[60] Cf. Did. 1:5; 12:3–5. Nevertheless, the rabbis had copious similar maxims (especially *Bereschith R.* 2:2; 14:12); see H. L. Strack and P. Billerbeck, *Kommentar zum Neuen Testament aus Talmud und Midrasch* (5 vols.; Munich: C. H. Beck, 1922–61), 2:10, 745; 3:338, 604, 641–2; Rigaux, *Thessaloniciens*, 707–8 and G. Bertram, '῎Εργον, κτλ.', in *TDNT*, 2:648–9 for many other parallel rabbinical sayings. And Hellenistic literature contains some parallels (e.g. Epictetus, *Diss.* 1.16.16–17; Pseudo-Phocylides 153–74). A. Resch, *Agrapha* (reprint: Darmstadt: Wissenschaftliche, 1974), 205–6 perceives an agraphon here, but evidence for that is completely lacking.

Μηδὲν ἐργαζομένους ἀλλὰ περιεργαζομένους is an example of *parono-masia*: they are not working but on the contrary are 'busybodies'. While the rhetorical device might perhaps caution us against taking περιεργα-ζομένους at face value, the μετὰ ἡσυχίας in verse 12 suggests that it may well reflect an aspect of the underlying situation. It seems that instead of spending their time in manual employment, the ἄτακτοι were occupying their time meddling in the affairs of others. The participle most naturally suggests not religious activity,[61] but rather irreligious prying into matters which do not concern them (cf. περίεργος in 1 Tim. 5:13, where it flows from idleness), here into the lives of others, probably of other community members (cf. 1 Thess. 4:9–12's περὶ δὲ τῆς φιλαδελφίας) but just possibly also of unbelievers.

In verse 12 the ἄτακτοι are addressed directly (τοῖς . . . τοιούτοις), the only time in the section. Concerning παραγγέλλομεν καὶ παρακαλοῦμεν, in this context it would seem that παρακαλοῦμεν injects a note of passionate pastoral pleading into the instruction. Ἐν κυρίῳ Ἰησοῦ Χριστῷ, which stresses the authority behind the command, probably goes with both verbs. The command is that the ἄτακτοι 'work with quietness, eating their own bread'. As we suggested above, μετὰ ἡσυχίας ἐργαζόμενοι seems to pick up on περιεργαζομένους and calls for the ἄτακτοι to become disciplined workers (cf. 1 Thess. 4:11) rather than useless busybodies. Such disciplined manual labour will enable them to maintain *themselves* (τὸν ἑαυτῶν ἄρτον ἐσθίωσιν; cf. verse 8's ἄρτον ἐφάγομεν παρά τινος); by means of hard work they will be financially independent and responsible, no longer depending on the charity of other community members.

Having addressed the ἄτακτοι in verse 12, the focus shifts back to the community as a whole in verse 13 with ὑμεῖς δέ, ἀδελφοί. Μὴ ἐγκακήσητε καλοποιοῦντες is conspicuously general in this context. It is hardly surprising then that some have concluded that we have a new section beginning in verse 13.[62] However, verses 14–15 clearly belong with verses 6–12, for there is no other issue in 2 Thessalonians which merits discipline. Hence it is most likely that verse 13 is an integral part of a larger unit, verses 6–15. The precise meaning of the encouragement 'not to grow weary in doing good' is unclear with regard to the nature and object of the 'doing good'. The options are: (a) the good which is earning one's living; (b) the general attitude of the community to the ἄτακτοι;

[61] *Pace* A. Roosen, *De Brieven van Paulus aan de Tessalonicenzen* (HNieT; Rome: Roermond, 1971), 167–8; Agrell, *Toil*, 122, 123; Best, *Thessalonians*, 340; Menken, 'Paradise', 287; Richard, *Thessalonians*, 390.

[62] Trilling, *Zweite Brief*, 153; Marxsen, *Zweite Thessalonicherbrief*, 102; Müller, *Anfänge*, 165–6; Krodel, *Deutero-Pauline Letters*, 54–5.

(c) doing good (1) generally or (2) to the ἄτακτοι; and/or (d) giving charity to (1) the ἄτακτοι, or (2) the non-ἄτακτοι who are deserving. We find option (a) improbable, since in verses 6–11 and 13–15 believers *qua* charity-givers are being addressed. Also, option (b) is questionable, because καλοποιοῦντες most naturally refers to deeds rather than an *attitude* of good or good in an abstract sense. *Contra* (c)(1), the context suggests that something more than general good deeds is in mind here. Verses 14–15 concern the community's treatment of the ἄτακτοι and this might suggest that 'Paul' has in mind general good deeds to the ἄτακτοι (option (c)(2)). However, the result of this reading of verses 13–15 seems forced and artificial: verse 13 calls on the community to do good to the ἄτακτοι, then verse 14 exhorts them to note the culprits and disassociate from them, before verse 15 qualifies this by stressing that the ἄτακτοι are to be treated as brothers and not enemies. *Contra* (d)(1), the meaning cannot be that the community are to give charity to the ἄτακτοι, for this is expressly forbidden in verses 6, 10 and 14. That verse 13 addresses the whole community, just as verse 12 specifically addresses the ἄτακτοι, favours the view that 'Paul' is here exhorting the community as a whole not to respond to the exploitation of the ἄτακτοι by growing weary of giving charity (perhaps more generally of doing good to others) to those non-ἄτακτοι who are needy ones deserving of charity (option (d)(2)). Tentatively, then, we conclude that (d)(2) is the most plausible reading.

Verses 14–15 return to the subject of how the ἄτακτοι are to be disciplined, anticipating that not all will heed the admonition. If any individuals (τις) disobey the instruction in 'this letter', that is, specifically verses 6–12, especially verse 12,[63] the rest of the community are to take note of (σημειοῦσθε) them and not associate with (μὴ συναναμίγνυσθαι) them. The purpose of the disassociation/ostracism is that the ἄτακτοι may be ashamed (ἐντραπῇ), that is, repent and be restored to the community, reformed and willing to fulfil their responsibilities. This disciplinary step could so easily degenerate into the community regarding the ἄτακτοι as enemies; so it is clarified that those under discipline are not to be regarded as enemies, but rather admonished as brothers.

A non-eschatological explanation of the problem of the ἄτακτοι

Only a defined segment of Greco-Roman society could have been in the position of the ἄτακτοι. That they were capable of choosing to cease from

---

[63] *Contra* Trilling, *Zweite Brief*, 154–5; Holland, *Tradition*, 52; Müller, *Anfänge*, 166–7; and Menken, *Thessalonians*, 141–2, who think that the entire content of the letter is in view.

their labours excludes the possibility that slaves were among their number. That they needed to work in order to be self-supporting eliminates the possibility that their number included the rich. These factors, together with the nature of the example of 'the missionaries' (cf. 1 Thess. 4:11's ταῖς [ἰδίαις] χερσὶν ὑμῶν), strongly suggest that the ἄτακτοι consisted of manual labourers.[64]

Determining whom the burden of maintaining the ἄτακτοι would have fallen upon depends largely on our assessment of the socio-economic constituency of the addressee community. Jewett judges that it was an inner-city *insula* 'tenement' church, in which there were no rich patron-figures sponsoring, and in which agapaic communalism was practised. In this case, the fault would have entailed the ἄτακτοι refusing to fulfil their obligations to the community by providing food for the love feast, with the result that the burden fell on the rest of the community.[65] According to this reading, the system of 'Christian communalism' was in danger of collapsing.[66] However, this 'tenement' model seems inappropriate to 1 and 2 Thessalonians: (1) Πρὸς τὸ μὴ ἐπιβαρῆσαί τινα ὑμῶν (2 Thess. 3:8) suggests not only that the burden of maintaining 'the missionaries' would have fallen on certain individuals within 'the Thessalonian community', presumably rich believers, but also that the burden of the ἄτακτοι's refusal to work in 2 Thess. 3:6ff. had fallen on these same individuals. (2) The example of 'the missionaries' relates to much more than contributions toward a love feast; it concerns depending on others for one's living (cf. 1 Thess. 4:12's μηδενὸς χρείαν ἔχητε); further, ἄρτον ἐφάγομεν (2 Thess. 3:8) and ἄρτον ἐσθίωσιν (verse 12) are but Hebraisms for receiving one's living (cf. 1 Cor. 9:4). Agapaic communalism practised in an inner-city *insula* 'tenement' church would hardly have been capable of supporting a number of manual labourers to the extent that they could afford to forsake their work. One would imagine that the situation would have become acute much earlier, were Jewett's hypothesis correct. So it seems that the

---

[64] There is no evidence to suggest that 2 Thess. 3:6ff. is confronting problems relating to the support or payment of local teachers (*pace* P. Day, 'The Practical Purpose of 2 Thessalonians', *AThR* 45 (1963): 203–6; E. E. Ellis, *Prophecy and Hermeneutic in Early Christianity* (WUNT; Tübingen: Mohr, 1978), 20–1; B. Holmberg, *Paul and Power* (Lund: Gleerup; Philadelphia: Fortress, 1978), 112, 159; W. Munro, *Authority in Peter and Paul* (SNTSMS; Cambridge: Cambridge University Press, 1983), 82–4; Collins, *Letters*, 235; Donfried, *Shorter*, 100). Indeed, περιεργαζομένους in verse 11 suggests that Christian work is not in view.

[65] Jewett, 'Communal Meals', 23–43, 'Tenement Churches and Pauline Love Feasts', *QR* 14 (1994): 43–58 and *Paul the Apostle to America* (Louisville, Ky.: Westminster/John Knox, 1994), 73–86; cf. Murphy-O'Connor, *Critical Life*, 117; De Vos, *Conflict*, 147–54.

[66] Cf. Neil, *Thessalonians*, 89.

burden of the ἄτακτοι's refusal to work would have fallen primarily on rich members of the community.[67] The alternative model for understanding the socio-economic make-up of Greco-Roman churches is 'love-patriarchalism'. According to this model as developed by Theissen, social differences are taken for granted, but ameliorated 'through an obligation of respect and love, an obligation imposed upon those who are socially stronger. From the weaker are required subordination, fidelity, and esteem.'[68] In this way 'a pattern of relationships between members of various strata' is sought, 'which would be characterised by respect, concern, and a sense of responsibility' and undergirded by 'a fundamental equality of status'.[69] Thus he defines 'love-patriarchalism'.[70] Recently Horrell has questioned the appropriateness of the label on the grounds that, while to an extent social differences are taken for granted (for example, owner–slave distinctions are accepted), subordination, fidelity and esteem from the weak are not required; indeed, in Horrell's opinion, the dominant social order is undermined and subverted by Paul.[71] Horrell insists that the ἐκκλησία is 'the "place" where the radical consequences of being "one in Christ" are already to be lived'.[72] In view of Horrell's study, it is perhaps better to speak of a 'transformative love-patriarchalism' in the Pauline and Paulinist churches, in which fundamental social structures are preserved but transformed from within by Christian love (cf. esp. Col. 3:22–4:1; Eph. 6:5–9), which points forward to the new social order to be ushered in at the eschaton (Gal. 3:28). With regard to the rich and poor, this meant that, while the rich were not expected to cast their wealth into a common pool from which any and every community member could draw, they were expected to be generous, providing their homes for community meetings and supporting the needy (Rom. 13:13; Gal. 2:10; cf. Eph. 4:28).

This 'transformative love-patriarchalist' model was subject to abuse at both ends. In 1 Cor. 11:17–34, for example, we see how the rich could

---

[67] Acts 17:4 claims that there were a number of wealthy converts to Christianity during Paul's Thessalonian mission.

[68] G. Theissen, *The Social Setting of Pauline Christianity* (trans. J. H. Schütz; Philadelphia: Fortress, 1982), 107–8.

[69] Ibid., 109.

[70] The model was derived from E. Troeltsch, *The Social Teaching of the Christian Churches* (trans. O. Wyon; London: Allen & Unwin, 1931), 1:69–89. Proponents of the paradigm include M. Hengel, *Property and Riches in the Early Church* (Philadelphia: Fortress, 1974), 36–9 and W. A. Meeks, *The First Urban Christians* (New Haven, Conn.: Yale University Press, 1983), 51–3.

[71] D. G. Horrell, *The Social Ethos of the Corinthian Correspondence* (SNTW; Edinburgh: T. & T. Clark, 1996), 196–7, cf. 155–6, 233, 282.

[72] Ibid., 196.

abuse their position.[73] Of course, the poor also could abuse their new situation: with remarkable access to wealthy 'patrons' who were willing to share generously their riches for the good of their brothers, the temptation of the poorer to exploit their wealthier brothers' loving charity must have been quite strong, especially for those who in their pagan pasts had mastered the art of leeching from wealthy patrons. In our judgment the problem which surfaces in 2 Thess. 3:6–15 (cf. 1 Thess. 4:11–12; 5:14) is most likely an example of the poor abusing the 'transformative love-patriarchalist' model. As ex-clients and perhaps former members of *collegia*, converted manual labourers would have naturally looked to richer Christians in *lieu* of their old patrons, especially when they encountered financial difficulties (which was not uncommon for manual labourers, since work was not always plentiful[74]) or perhaps lost employment because of social hostilities to the Gospel (cf. Eusebius, *Hist. Eccl.* 4.26.5; 7.15.2; see 2 Thess. 1:4ff.; cf. 1 Thess. 3:3–4). It is not difficult to imagine that some from the manual labouring class would have exploited the opportunity to be indolent rather than return to a life of hard manual work. In 2 Thess. 3:6–15 'Paul' calls on 'the Thessalonian community' to act to put an end to the sponging of the manual labourers, and he instructs the ἄτακτοι to work to support themselves, presumably in their former occupations or possibly doing jobs for those who provide for them. The new Christian society could not work if old pagan attitudes prevailed.[75]

To rich outsiders such a problem would have smacked of appalling exploitation; and, moreover, poor unbelievers might conceivably have contemplated joining the church simply to secure the same arrangement as the ἄτακτοι.

In conclusion, then, we suggest that *inertia vulgaris* manifesting itself in charitable abuse accounts for the problem of the ἄτακτοι. Instead of busying themselves working for a living, they were using their time to interfere in the business of others, making a nuisance of themselves.

[73] See especially Theissen, *Setting*, 145–74, esp. 151; G. D. Fee, *The First Epistle to the Corinthians* (NICNT; Grand Rapids: Eerdmans, 1987), 531–69.
[74] A. Burford, *Craftsmen in Greek and Roman Society* (AGRL; London: Thames and Hudson, 1972), 65; Russell, 'Idle', 112. For a helpful treatment of the social situation of manual labourers, see Aune, 'Trouble', 25–47.
[75] Our hypothesis applied to 1 Thess. 4:11–12 might explain why that text calls for the 'idlers' to live quietly, mind their own affairs and work with their hands *so that* they may behave decently in front of outsiders (περιπατῆτε εὐσχημόνως πρὸς τοὺς ἔξω (on πρός, see S. E. Porter, *Idioms of the Greek New Testament* (BLG; Sheffield: JSOT, 1992), 172–3: cf. Mark 4:1; Rom. 8:31; Acts 5:10)). Moreover, it might also shed light on why the instruction to the 'idlers' there is a part of a section relating to φιλαδελφία (1 Thess. 4:9–12).

This hypothesis facilitates all available evidence in a plausible and coherent manner, providing a credible alternative to the eschatological hypothesis, which, as we have seen, has few arguments for it and indeed some against it.

The situation underlying 2 Thess. 3:16–18

Recently Weima made the case that epistolary closings in the Pauline corpus typically 'echo major concerns and themes dealt with in their respective letter bodies'.[76] This renders the closing of 2 Thessalonians of particular significance for our study. That 3:16a belongs to the closing of the letter rather than the preceding section is suggested by: (1) the observation that Pauline letters regularly contain a peace benediction in their closings (e.g. Rom. 15:33; 2 Cor. 13:11; Phil. 4:9; 1 Thess. 5:23; cf. Eph. 6:23); (2) the fact that διὰ παντὸς ἐν παντὶ τρόπῳ is too general to refer to the problem of the ἄτακτοι alone; (3) the observation that 3:6–15 (even verse 15) do not concern peaceful relations, but rather the need for the community to discipline the ἄτακτοι.

We suggest, then, that δέ serves to introduce the epistolary closing. Αὐτός . . . ὁ κύριος is, as elsewhere in 2 Thessalonians (and in Paul's letters), Jesus rather than God.[77] The Lord is not the subject of the peace benediction or called ὁ κύριος τῆς εἰρήνης anywhere else in the Pauline corpus.[78] The unique formulation here is probably inspired by the fact that the main issue troubling 'the Thessalonians' relates to ἡ ἡμέρα τοῦ κυρίου (2:2; cf. 2:8b; 3:3–5), as is perhaps reinforced by the addition of αὐτός.

The Lord is the source and giver of εἰρήνη. Εἰρήνη, like the Hebrew שׁלום, 'embraces the panoply of blessings God makes available to his people in the age of fulfilment'.[79] As we observed in chapter 4 above, ὁ θεὸς τῆς εἰρήνης is not uncommon in Paul's letters. For Paul, 'peace' was almost synonymous with reconciliation, the healing of the breach and the inauguration of new relations between God and those who put their faith in Christ;[80] 'the God of peace' seems to have meant 'the God who initiated this peace and as a result of it is at peace with Christians'. For 'Paul' in

[76] J. A. D. Weima, *Neglected Endings* (JSNTSup; Sheffield: JSOT, 1994), 237.

[77] *Contra* Marxsen, *Zweite Thessalonicherbrief*, 103; Aus, 'Thessalonians', 218.

[78] However, it is worth noting that Christ is the source of peace in the introductory greeting of 2 Thess. 1:2 (cf. 1 Cor. 1:3; 2 Cor. 1:2; Gal. 1:3; Phil. 1:2; also Eph. 1:2; 1 Tim. 1:2; 2 Tim. 1:2; Tit. 1:4) and in Col. 3:15.

[79] D. J. Moo, *The Epistle to the Romans* (NICNT; Grand Rapids: Eerdmans, 1996), 911.

[80] See W. Foerster, 'Εἰρήνη, κτλ.', in *TDNT*, 2:411–17; H. Beck and C. Brown, 'Peace', in *NIDNTT*, 2:780–3; V. Hasler, 'Εἰρήνη', in *EDNT*, 1:396–7; Spicq, *Lexicon*, 1:432–3.

2 Thessalonians, since Christ reconciled to God those who put their faith in him and is himself also at peace with them, he can be designated ὁ κύριος τῆς εἰρήνης. The stress here seems to be on the fact that Christ, the eschatological saviour, regards and relates to 'the Thessalonians' as friends rather than enemies, a point which is particularly relevant if they had been shaken and scared by the implication of the claim that the Day of the Lord had come (2:2), namely that they had missed out on eschatological salvation.

'Paul' prays that the Lord of peace may grant (δῴη) 'the Thessalonians' τὴν εἰρήνην. The duplication of εἰρήνη in this verse is unique in the entire Pauline corpus and may plausibly be attributed to the particular appropriateness of the concept to the situation. Τὴν εἰρήνην διὰ παντός ('peace at all times') suggests that 'the Thessalonians' needed peace in the present and in the future: present peace is most naturally understood as the awareness of God's peace (cf. Rom. 8:6; Phil. 4:7), which issues from objective reconciliation and is indicative of eschatological destiny, rather than as peace *qua* absence of conflict, for which evidence in this letter is lacking. Since 'the Thessalonians' are perceived to be under a concerted attack from the evil one (3:3b), 'Paul' might also have in mind peace if and when further problems arose. With regard to the future, it would apply to the reception of eschatological salvation at the parousia. Τὴν εἰρήνην ἐν παντὶ τρόπῳ would seem to suggest not just *shalom* in a general sense, but also specifically peace rooted in a correct eschatology – instead of instability and fear rooted in a false eschatology (2:1ff.) – and peace in the midst of afflictions (1:5ff.), peace *qua* eschatological salvation (2:13–17) and perhaps even peace in the face of Satanic attacks (3:3b).

With regard to the wish-prayer ὁ κύριος μετὰ πάντων ὑμῶν, πάντων is particularly conspicuous; it probably reflects 'Paul' conscious inclusion of the whole community for pastoral reasons, perhaps especially because of the fact that some were distraught and felt abandoned by the Lord in the wake of the false eschatology.

In 3:17 'this greeting' is attributed to Paul's hand (τῇ ἐμῇ χειρί, cf. 1 Cor. 16:21; Gal. 6:11; Col. 4:18; Phlm. 19); this seems to assume the apparently common ancient Greco-Roman practice of an author dictating the bulk of a letter to an amanuensis before handwriting the conclusion himself, a practice apparently intended to demonstrate authenticity.[81] The statement presupposes that the new handwriting was 'somewhat distinctive' compared with the preceding. The greeting seems most naturally

---

[81] E. R. Richards, *The Secretary in the Letters of Paul* (WUNT; Tübingen: Mohr, 1991), 175.

understood as referring to verses 16–18, or possibly to verses 17–18, but almost certainly not verse 18 alone.[82]
The relative clause ὅ ἐστιν σημεῖον ἐν πάσῃ ἐπιστολῇ has been the source of much discussion. That 'Paul' so explicitly draws attention to the *handwritten* greeting as an authenticating sign (σημεῖον) in all of his letters[83] needs explanation. Perhaps 'Paul' is implying that the authenticity of 1 Thessalonians was being questioned by 'the Thessalonians', although 2 Thess. 2:1, 15 and 3:4 seem to assume that the teaching of 1 Thessalonians is not unacceptable to 'the Thessalonians'. Some proponents of Pauline authorship of 2 Thessalonians have proposed that the relative clause functions to defend 2 Thessalonians from the potential pretext of the 'idlers' for disobeying, that it was not truly written by the hand of Paul.[84] However, this seems unrealistic: why would Paul have considered such an obscure possibility, when in his other letters, even when dealing with more serious problems, he does not contemplate it? And if the author was merely authenticating the message of 2 Thessalonians, the relative clause would have been unnecessary, τῇ ἐμῇ χειρὶ Παύλου being sufficient.[85]

The clause probably has an exclusive rather than an inclusive function. By stressing explicitly that it was Paul's habit to include an authenticating mark consisting of a distinctive and obvious (to readers of the autograph) handwritten greeting, such as this one, in all his letters (σημεῖον ἐν πάσῃ ἐπιστολῇ· οὕτως γράφω), 'the missionaries' imply that it is possible that a letter falsely attributed to Paul may be in the possession of 'the Thessalonians'. By comparing all supposedly Pauline letters to 2 Thessalonians with respect to the handwriting of the final greeting, 'the Thessalonians' could discern what was forged from what was authentic.

It is unlikely that this is simply designed to counter the possibility of a future forgery in Paul's name:[86] would 'Paul' have so unquestioningly trusted the authenticating sign of 2 Thessalonians to expose forgeries if

[82] *Pace* Wohlenberg, *Thessalonicherbrief*, 168; Masson, *Thessaloniciens*, 116.

[83] The reference to 'all letters' assumes that Paul has written letters other than to the Thessalonians. Proponents of the pseudonymity of 2 Thessalonians often take this as evidence that the author had in his possession other Pauline letters in addition to 1 Thessalonians. For example, Giblin, 'Reread', 460–1 maintains that the pseudonymous author knew and accepted as authentic 1 Thessalonians and at least three other letters of Paul: 1 Corinthians, Galatians and Philemon. Of course, that raises the question why such an author would have elected to base his composition on 1 Thessalonians and make so little use of these other letters.

[84] Frame, *Thessalonians*, 311; Weima, *Endings*, 126–7.

[85] Note that this objection holds against those who claim that the relative clause is evidence of 2 Thessalonians' pseudonymity.

[86] Aus, 'Thessalonians', 218; cf. Lünemann, *Thessalonians*, 254.

forgeries could conceivably have imitated it? 3:17 is precisely what we would expect if 'the missionaries' thought that a forgery in Paul's name might possibly exist.[87] We conclude that the most obvious interpretation of 3:17 is correct: it is countering a suspected forgery in Paul's name (cf. 2:2). Verse 18's grace benediction is similar to that in 1 Thess. 5:28, except for the addition of πάντων, which seems to serve the same function as in 2 Thess. 3:16b.

In conclusion, we return to the question of what this epistolary closing reveals about the emphases of the letter. Weima has pointed out the distinctive features of the epistolary closing of 2 Thessalonians as compared with other letters in the Pauline corpus: (1) αὐτός; (2) 'the Lord' rather than 'God' as the source of peace; (3) δῴη . . . τὴν εἰρήνην; (4) διὰ παντὸς ἐν παντὶ τρόπῳ, all in verse 16a; (5) ὁ κύριος μετὰ πάντων ὑμῶν in verse 16b; (6) the explanation of the autograph in 3:17; and (7) πάντων in verse 18.[88] We suggest that each of these features points primarily, if not exclusively, to the treatment of the eschatological confusion rooted in the false claim of 2:2c,[89] which seems to be the primary exigency of the letter.

Conclusion to Part 3

In Part 3 we have been exploring the situation reflected in 2 Thessalonians. We proposed in chapter 5 that the false claim of 2:2c, that the Day of the Lord had come, seems to have caused 'the Thessalonians' to become fearful, probably because they understandably inferred that they had no hope of salvation, not having experienced any significant change in their circumstances. In chapter 6 we suggested that this erroneous claim had

---

[87] *Contra* Wrede, *Echtheit*, 57, who claims that we would have expected more than this. Trilling, *Zweite Brief*, 159 (cf. Marxsen, *Zweite Thessalonicherbrief*, 104–5) has suggested that the remark ἐν πάσῃ ἐπιστολῇ was the pseudepigrapher's crucial mistake, letting slip that he was writing later than AD 50. However, it seems perfectly plausible that Paul wrote letters prior to 1 Thessalonians (*contra* Marxsen, *Zweite Thessalonicherbrief*, 104–5), perhaps even including Galatians. Concerning the date of Galatians, most proponents of the South Galatian theory (e.g. W. M. Ramsey, *St. Paul the Traveller and the Roman Citizen* (reprint: Grand Rapids: Baker, 1962), 91–193; F. F. Bruce, *The Epistle to the Galatians* (NIGTC; Grand Rapids: Eerdmans, 1982), 3–18; C. J. Hemer, *The Book of Acts in the Setting of Hellenistic History* (ed. C. H. Gempf; WUNT; Tübingen: Mohr, 1989), 227–307; R. N. Longenecker, *Galatians* (WBC; Dallas: Word, 1990), lxi–lxxxviii) and at least one proponent of the North Galatian theory (H. D. Betz, *Galatians* (Hermeneia; Philadelphia: Fortress, 1979), 5, 12 (AD 50–5)) give Galatians an early date.

[88] Weima, *Endings*, 188.

[89] Weima (ibid., 189–90) argues, unconvincingly, that the closing strongly alludes to the 'idlers' also.

apparently raised a critical question about the justice of God's judgment, especially in view of the ongoing persecutions. In this chapter we have proposed that the 'idleness' of 3:6–15 was almost certainly not related to the false eschatology. Rather, the 'idleness' probably consisted simply of *inertia vulgaris*, Christian manual labourers exploiting the charity of richer believers. Moreover, we highlighted that the conclusion, 3:16–18, reflects the broader eschatological focus of 2 Thessalonians and reveals the suspicion of 'the missionaries' that a forgery in Paul's name may have been circulating.

We propose therefore that the situation underlying 2 Thessalonians consisted not of eschatological joyful excitement or enthusiasm, but rather of Gentile Christians' shakenness, fear and despair on account of succumbing to the erroneous claim that the Day of the Lord had come.

Having now completed our analysis of the situations reflected in 1 and 2 Thessalonians, we are finally in a position to consider whether the situation reflected in 2 Thessalonians is compatible with that underlying 1 Thessalonians and whether situational considerations tend to support the authenticity or pseudonymity of 2 Thessalonians.

PART FOUR

8

SYNTHESIS AND CONCLUSION

Summary of the situation underlying 1 Thessalonians

In our analysis of the situation underlying 1 Thessalonians in Part 2, we concluded that the Thessalonian community had been deeply perturbed by the deaths of fellow-community members on account of their failure to think in terms of a resurrection of saints, probably because of ignorance concerning it (4:13–18). Without such a hope for their dead, they seem to have inferred that the deceased would not be able to participate in the salvation of the parousia.

With regard to 5:1–11, we proposed that the unexpected deaths may have raised doubts about the status and destiny of the whole community before God, for if some of their number had by their deaths proved to be non-elect, the foundation of the others' hope became suspect. Indeed, we suggested that the deaths may ultimately have been perceived to be a *prodigium*, causing the Thessalonians to wonder whether the Day of the Lord *qua* judgment was about to come upon them.

The rest of 1 Thessalonians confirmed and developed our hypothesis about the eschatological aspect of the situation underlying 4:13–5:11. The readers needed to be reassured regarding their destiny (1:10c; 2:12; 5:24), were without hope (3:6), were lacking in some fundamentals of their faith (3:10) and could be described as 'faint-hearted' and 'weak' (5:14). Moreover, we judged that the entire argument of 1:2–3:13 seemed to be designed primarily to reassure the converts of the authenticity of their conversion before God and ultimately to demonstrate the certainty of their election (1:4), both with respect to the missionaries' ministry of the Gospel during the mission (1:5, 9a; 2:1–12, 13–16) and afterwards (2:17–3:13), and with respect to the Thessalonians' reception of the Gospel (1:6–8, 9b–10). We found it striking that Paul's defence of the community's status and destiny in these regards corresponds with the explanations of the unexpected deaths, and the divine wrath seemingly announced by them, which would most naturally have occurred to the

Thessalonian believers. Significantly, we proposed that the reassurance regarding election in 1:4ff. was ultimately an attempt to reinforce 5:1–11, in which election apparently functioned to reconfirm those insecure as a result of the deaths (5:9). The extended absence of the missionaries (especially of Paul) might well have raised serious questions about their (especially Paul's) pastoral care of and commitment to the converts, and Paul was apparently concerned that this might have fuelled Thessalonian doubts regarding whether the missionaries were genuinely approved by God.

Some Gentile community members were apparently having difficulties conforming to the Christian sexual ethic (4:1–8), and some were failing to fulfil their responsibilities with regard to work and providing for themselves (4:9–12). It seems that the leaders had yet to establish themselves and to command fully the community's esteem (5:12–13a) and that community members might have been undervaluing prophecies (5:19–22) and possibly also Timothy (hence the need for Paul's endorsement in 3:2), thereby cutting themselves off from potential sources of divine help and encouragement.

According to our study, the opinion of many that the community was characterised by eschatological enthusiastic excitement is quite unfounded; indeed, the letter was essentially a reassurance or reconfirmation of believers whose hope had been vanquished. Moreover, we judged that claims that the disobedience to the sexual ethic (4:3–8), the problem of 'idleness' (4:10b–12) and the rejection of prophecy (5:19–22) were rooted in the community's eschatological problems could not be substantiated. Neither did we find evidence of any concerted opposition within the community. However, we determined that the community certainly had suffered persecution during and in the aftermath of the mission (1:6–7; 2:14; 3:3a) and that this probably continued to afflict and shake the community at the time of Timothy's visit (3:3b–4), although there is no evidence that the persecution exacerbated the eschatological confusion of the community.[1]

In conclusion, then, we have proposed that the situation underlying 1 Thessalonians was essentially one of distress, fear and insecurity in the wake of the unexpected deaths of fellow-community members; most strikingly, lacking a resurrection hope for their deceased, the community members seem to have despaired for them and for themselves, apparently interpreting the deaths as a sign that the Day of the Lord was about to come. The community's problems reflect an immature and

---

[1] *Pace inter alios* Still, *Conflict*, 268, 284–5.

Gentile Christian faith, not fully conversant with Jewish eschatological ideas.

Summary of the situation underlying 2 Thessalonians

In our study of the situation underlying 2 Thessalonians in Part 3, we determined that 'the Thessalonians' were characterised by hopelessness rather than enthusiastic excitement. In chapter 5 we concluded that the section 2:1–3:5 suggests that they believed that they had been reliably informed (whether by an intra-communal prophecy or instruction or a forged Pauline letter) that 'the Day of the Lord had come', which probably meant to them that the parousia had passed them by. 'Paul' implies that they had forgotten what they had previously been taught: the supreme eschatological rebel's revelation and the final rebellion of humanity must occur prior to the Day. He also intimates that the false claim was greeted with horror, confusion and disillusionment, presumably because it meant that God had abandoned 'the Thessalonians' and that they had missed salvation. It had shaken 'the Thessalonians' from the apostolic tradition and necessitated that they be assured of their election to eschatological salvation, of God's love and of the soundness of Christian hope.

In chapters 5 and 6 we posited that, although 'the Thessalonians' were persevering, the false claim seems to have threatened their continued endurance. With regard to 2 Thessalonians 1, we judged that the persecutions might well have been perceived by them as a sign of the injustice of God's judgment, quite possibly as a result of the eschatological idea of 2:2c. 'Paul' must therefore assure them that God's judgment will indeed be just, consisting of a reversal of fortunes for them and their persecutors, and he must make it clear when that just judgment will come, who will be its victims and what it will look like. We judged that there was a lack of hope and insecurity among 'the Thessalonians' regarding their status before God and 'Paul'.

In chapter 7, as well as seeing in the conclusion (3:16–18) support for our reading of the eschatological aspect of the situation, we noted that the claim that the problem of 'idleness' underlying 3:6–15 was spurred on by eschatological excitement was unsubstantiable and indeed seemed to go against the evidence. We proposed that the problem was adequately explained with reference to manual labourers exploiting the charity of rich Christians and 'transformative love-patriarchalism' by depending on wealthier community members for their maintenance rather than earning their own living (*inertia vulgaris*). We saw no connection between the 'idleness' problem and the community's eschatological quandary.

We concluded that 'Paul' was unaware of the manner of entry of the idea into the 'Thessalonian community' (2:2). Although he took seriously the possibility of a forged letter in Paul's name (3:17), the evidence suggests that he did not seem to think that there was a concerted intra-communal opposition (1:1). And while there were indications of impatience with the 'idlers', the tone in regard to the treatment of the eschatological problem was not harsh or cold, but reassuring and comforting. All the evidence points once again to an immature and probably young and predominantly Gentile community having difficulties processing Jewish eschatological notions.

In summary, the situation underlying 2 Thessalonians seems to have been one of fear, consternation and despair in the aftermath of the false claim that the Day of the Lord had come; in view of the continued persecution of 'the Thessalonians', the erroneous declaration may have seemed to indicate that God had abandoned them and that his judgment was unjust.

Points of continuity and discontinuity

The situations underlying 1 and 2 Thessalonians are strikingly similar in numerous respects. Most importantly, in both, the timing of the Day of the Lord is central to the concrete eschatological problems. Moreover, in each the import of the phrase 'the Day of the Lord' is akin, referring to the parousia/eschaton, especially in its negative dimension. In both letters the eschatological problems are soteriological: it is the participation of 'the Thessalonians' in the parousia's salvation which seems to be at stake. And in both, their emotional state is one of fear and insecurity. In both, the community are regarded as displaying faith and love in the present and are characterised as distinctly lacking hope and needing to be reassured of their status and destiny before God (each letter can be viewed as a *reconfirmatio* or *promittatio*). Evidence for eschatological enthusiasm or joyful excitement in either is distinctly lacking.[2] Nor is the case for an eschatological reading of the 'idleness' problem convincing in either; in both, the problem seems to consist simply of *inertia vulgaris*. Moreover, in both letters the community was suffering persecution and was apparently shaken by it.[3] Finally, in each the nature of the problems seems to portray

[2] *Contra inter alios* Lütgert, 'Enthusiasten', 618ff.; Graafen, *Echtheit*, 50–1; Reicke, *Diakonie*, 244–6; F. F. Bruce, 'St. Paul in Macedonia: 2. The Thessalonian Correspondence', *BJRL* 62 (1980): 333; Mearns, 'Development', 141, 157; E. W. Saunders, *1 Thessalonians, 2 Thessalonians, Philippians, Philemon* (Atlanta: John Knox, 1981), 2–3, 41; Marshall, *Thessalonians*, 40; Jewett, *Correspondence*, 176–8.
[3] *Contra* Manson, 'Thessalonians', 438–41 and Lindemann, 'Abfassungszweck', 43, the persecutions of 1 Thessalonians should not be regarded as entirely past: 1 Thess. 3:3a

Thessalonian Christian recipients who are young, immature and mainly Gentile.

The situations underlying these letters, however, are also notably dissimilar in numerous ways. Most significantly, while in 1 Thessalonians the addressees seem to think that the Day will come imminently, in 2 Thessalonians 'the Thessalonians' think that it has come. Moreover, the addressees of 1 Thessalonians lack hope, probably because they are filled with anxiety and fear that the Day might bring ill to them, while 'the Thessalonians' of 2 Thessalonians lack hope and feel despair because the false claim of 2:2c has been understood to render Christian hope null and void and so has shaken and terrified them. Accordingly, in the situation underlying the second letter the problem caused by persecution is particularly acute for the community, possibly because it seems anomalous in the light of the false claim. And there appears to have been a significant risk that the persecution would undermine the commitment of 'the Thessalonians' to persevere. By contrast, in the first letter, evidence is lacking that the persecution was related to the eschatological problems of the Thessalonians. Knowing about the resurrection of the saints would have preserved the Thessalonian community from the error underlying 1 Thessalonians; remembering prior eschatological teaching about the rebel and apostasy would have kept 'the Thessalonians' from the error underlying 2 Thessalonians.

While the idea that the Day of the Lord was imminent (1 Thessalonians) may have been understood in the wake of, if not founded on, the unexpected deaths, there is no explicit statement concerning the grounds for the idea that the Day of the Lord had come (2 Thessalonians). Furthermore, we do not know if any particular person was responsible for the eschatological confusion underlying 1 Thessalonians, but it does seem that the most likely source of the trouble underlying 2 Thessalonians was a prophecy, a word of instruction, or a forged Pauline letter.

The plausibility of development between the two situations, assuming the Pauline authorship of 2 Thessalonians

We must now address the matter of whether and how the situations underlying 1 and 2 Thessalonians can be synthesised. In the light of our study we propose that it is quite plausible that the question of the Thessalonians concerning the 'when' of the Day of the Lord has been answered

and b (cf. verse 8) demonstrate that the persecutions are perceived to be present. Hence the alleged contrast between past persecutions in 1 Thessalonians and present persecutions in 2 Thessalonians would seem to be fallacious.

by someone suggesting that 'the Day of the Lord has come'. That is, the person responsible for the erroneous pronouncement underlying 2 Thess. 2:2c might well have been participating in the same discussion as Paul himself is in 1 Thess. 5:1–11, answering the question 'Is the Day of the Lord about to come?' by claiming that it *has already come*.

Therefore the two situations may simply reflect two stages of the *same single* crisis. It is easy to imagine how a presently fearful, insecure and immature Macedonian Gentile Christian community, recently shaken from their neophyte hope, anxiously asking when the Day of the Lord (*qua* wrath) would come and waiting for an answer from Paul, might be vulnerable to the suggestion that the Day of the Lord had actually come.[4] All that would be required for such a change in the situation from nervous dread to perturbed despair is precisely what 2 Thess. 2:2 says, a prophetic word, a teaching, or a forged letter attributed to Paul, stating that the Day had come.

As Barclay has noted with regard to 2 Thessalonians, 'divine wrath can explain many types of calamity' and 'almost any unusual event' can be interpreted as 'an eschatological moment'.[5] We proposed in chapter 2 that the Thessalonians were having significant difficulties processing the deaths among them in view of what they believed (and did not believe) about the eschaton, and in chapter 3 that the deaths were construed as 'an eschatological moment', functioning as the catalyst for the question relating to the timing of the Day of the Lord underlying 1 Thess. 5:1–11. In the light of this, it is very tempting to think that the false claim underlying 2 Thess. 2:2c, which also relates to the timing of the Day of the Lord, might have been understood by the Thessalonians as an attempt to answer the question raised by the deaths. Certainly, the false claim appears to have been perceived as reinforcing the insecurity and hopelessness communicated by those deaths. However, since 2 Thessalonians assumes that its readers had access to 1 Thessalonians (note especially 2 Thess. 2:15), we might well ask why Paul's reply to their question in 1 Thess. 5:1–11 did not preserve them from succumbing to the false idea.

Before addressing that matter, we must deal with the suggestion of some that the author of 2 Thessalonians considered that 1 Thessalonians may

---

[4] *Contra* Bailey, 'Who?', 137, it is wrong to suggest that the epistolary situation indicates a community which has been established for a number of years.

[5] Barclay, 'Conflict', 528. Note that Barclay ('Social Contrasts', 72 and 'Conflict', 527–8) thinks that the Thessalonians, with their 'fevered apocalyptic imagination', understood the claim positively, meaning that judgment had begun to fall on unbelievers. He admits ('Conflict', 528) that a link with earthquakes and famines in 51–2 (mentioned by Tacitus, *Ann.* 12.43) is 'precarious', although he seems to give the suggestion some credence (cf. Winter, *Welfare*, 53–4, 57; Still, 'Eschatology', 200).

have been the source of the problem underlying 2 Thess. 2:2c.[6] We insist that 1 Thessalonians could not realistically have caused the new problem. For none of the candidates in 1 Thessalonians which have been suggested as possible catalysts for the eschatological claim underlying 2 Thess. 2:2c – 1 Thess. 2:16, 18a, 18b; 3:11–13; 5:1–5, 6–10 – lends itself to the idea that the Day had come or even that it was so imminent that it might occur immediately.[7] Moreover, as we observed above, in his reference to 1 Thessalonians in 2 Thess. 2:15, the author assumes that its message is not subject to misunderstanding. Further, in 2 Thess. 2:2 and 3:17 he does not even consider the possibility of a misunderstanding of the first letter (cf. 1 Cor. 5:9–10!), but only that of a forged letter in his name.

Many scholars have rooted their belief that 1 Thessalonians may have caused the problem underlying 2 Thessalonians in 2 Thess. 2:2, which they believe indicates that the false pronouncement may have derived from a misunderstanding of 1 Thessalonians. The issue largely revolves around whether and how ὡς δι' ἡμῶν modifies ἐπιστολῆς. Ὡς δι' ἡμῶν may modify only 'letter',[8] or 'word' and 'letter',[9] or 'spirit', 'word' and 'letter',[10] or the verbs σαλευθῆναι and θροεῖσθαι,[11] or the following clause ὡς ὅτι ἐνέστηκεν ἡ ἡμέρα τοῦ κυρίου (simply signifying the author's

---

[6] So, e.g., von Dobschütz, *Thessalonicher-Briefe*, 266–7; Frame, *Thessalonians*, 247; Dibelius, *Thessalonicher*, 44; Bruce, *Thessalonians*, 164, 166; Jewett, *Correspondence*, 184–91; Donfried, *Shorter*, 88; Barrett, *Paul*, 150.

[7] Even Jewett, who contends that a misunderstanding of 1 Thessalonians led to the problem underlying 2 Thess. 2:2c, concludes his study of possible candidates in 1 Thessalonians (*Correspondence*, 186–91) by determining that 'None of them, in my opinion, is sufficiently plausible that a theory of misunderstanding could be based on evidence within 1 Thessalonians alone' (p. 191).

[8] So *inter alios* Tertullian; Findlay, *Epistles to the Thessalonians*, 141; Moffatt, 'Thessalonians', 4:47; Rigaux, *Thessaloniciens*, 651–2; Moore, *Thessalonians*, 99–100; Trilling, *Zweite Brief*, 77–8; Bruce, *Thessalonians*, 164; Holland, *Tradition*, 44–5; Barrett, *Paul*, 150; Elias, *Thessalonians*, 275–6; Richard, *Thessalonians*, 325; RSV; NLT; BDAG; BDF.

[9] Theodoret; Alford, *Testament*, 288–9; Ellicott, *Thessalonians*, 107; Lünemann, *Thessalonians*, 205–7; P. W. Schmiedel, *Thessalonicher, Korinther* (HKNT; Freiburg: Mohr, 1892), 37; Wrede, *Echtheit*, 54; cf. W. Hendriksen, *New Testament Commentary: Exposition of 1 and 2 Thessalonians* (Grand Rapids: Baker, 1955), 168 n. 119.

[10] Lightfoot, *Epistles*, 109–10; Milligan, *Thessalonians*, 96–7; von Dobschütz, *Thessalonicher-Briefe*, 265–7; von Harnack, 'Problem', 560–78; Frame, *Thessalonians*, 246–8; Lenski, *Thessalonians*, 402–3; Ward, *Thessalonians*, 154; Callow, *Thessalonians*, 58; Marshall, *Thessalonians*, 186–7; Best, *Thessalonians*, 278; Wanamaker, *Thessalonians*, 239; Morris, *Epistles*, 215 n. 11; D. E. Hiebert, *1 and 2 Thessalonians* (rev. edn; Chicago: Moody, 1992), 327.

[11] E. H. Askwith, *An Introduction to the Thessalonian Epistles* (London: Macmillan, 1902), 92–100, esp. 98 ('That ye be not quickly shaken from your mind, nor yet be troubled, either through prophesying, or through oral teaching or through a letter, as if such disturbance came through us . . .'); Wohlenberg, *Thessalonicherbrief*, 138–9.

denial that he is responsible for the false idea).[12] We begin by observing not only that ὡς δι' ἡμῶν is more naturally adjectival than adverbial, but also that the verbs are too far from ὡς δι' ἡμῶν to be modified by it. Moreover, immediately following δι' ἐπιστολῆς, ὡς δι' ἡμῶν most naturally belongs with that phrase, not with the following clause.

Concerning the contention based on 2 Thess. 2:15 that ὡς δι' ἡμῶν belongs with the last two of the prepositional phrases, we note that contextual factors (*one* ὡς δι' ἡμῶν after *three* occurrences of μήτε διά with the genitive) suggest that it refers either to all three or to the last alone. Moreover, granted that the 'word' and 'letter' in verse 15 are viewed positively whereas those in verse 2 are viewed negatively, the *true* word and letter of verse 15 clearly contrast with the *false* word and letter of verse 2. With regard to the view that it belongs with all three prepositional phrases, we might then wonder how the idea could have been attributed to Paul since he was absent. Certainly it seems implausible that a prophecy or word uttered by one of the missionaries in Corinth could have caused the problem in Thessalonica. Moreover, Timothy's report (which underlay 1 Thessalonians) would have assured Paul that the community had not misinterpreted the missionaries' instruction given at the mission. And a past saying of his would hardly have provoked the kind of reaction evident in verse 2. Further, if Paul were simply denying that he said or wrote that the Day had come, he would surely have done so more clearly.

We conclude that it modifies the last prepositional phrase, 'by letter', alone, which is the simplest reading. This allows ὡς in ὡς δι' ἡμῶν to keep its natural sense 'as if', implying denial. This interpretation seems to be confirmed by 3:17: there was a serious possibility that a forgery in Paul's name existed which gave rise to the mistaken notion that the Day had come. Taking ὡς δι' ἡμῶν with 'letter' alone would of course mean that the 'spirit' and 'word' were conceived of as having been communicated to the community not by Paul, but by someone else (either a member of the community or a visitor). As we stated in chapter 5 above, the common denominator of these three suggestions is that each of them might have wielded sufficient authority to win the Thessalonians over to the new eschatological idea of 2:2c.

Fee objects to such an interpretation of ὡς δι' ἡμῶν by claiming that διά always indicates secondary agency and that had Paul wished to express 'from', he would have employed παρά or ἀπό.[13] However, aside from the fact that it seems unwise to base so much on an unprovable supposition that the 'early Paul' was unbendingly strict in his syntax, it is worth noting

---

[12] Fee, *Empowering*, 71–5.   [13] Ibid., 73–4, esp. 73 n. 132.

that Gal. 1:1 provides evidence that διά could be used by Paul of primary agency and that 1 Cor. 3:15 and Rom. 5:16 and 18 demonstrate that ὡς διά can have a sense barely distinguishable from ἐκ. Therefore we propose that 2 Thess. 2:2 gives no support to the idea that the false claim had arisen on account of a misunderstanding of 1 Thessalonians[14] and that 2:2 is notable for its omission of 1 Thessalonians as a possible source of the eschatological error. Indeed, we maintain that the problem underlying 2 Thessalonians could not plausibly have arisen if 1 Thessalonians had already been in the possession of the addressees of 2 Thessalonians, for its blatant futurity and the reassuring nature of 1 Thess. 1:10; 2:12; 3:13; 4:13–18, and particularly 5:1–11, which is presented as the express answer to the Thessalonians' question, would have been a prophylaxis against the false claim of 2 Thess. 2:2c.[15] And for similar reasons we find it difficult to accept that 1 Thessalonians could have been perceived even to *endorse* the idea that the Day of the Lord had come.

Having demonstrated that 1 Thessalonians probably did not cause, or contribute to, the problem underlying 2 Thessalonians, we return to our question, why did Paul's answer in 1 Thessalonians not preserve the Thessalonians from succumbing to the erroneous notion? We suggest that the solution to this most perplexing of issues is to be found in reconsidering the matter of when 1 Thessalonians arrived in Thessalonica. Our starting-point must be our earlier conclusions that 1 Thessalonians probably preceded 2 Thessalonians and that both letters seem to have been addressed to the same community. Any authenticity hypothesis must acknowledge that the period between the letters must have been short, as can be inferred from the observation that the Thessalonians were apparently still suffering persecution and the fact that Timothy and Silas were still with Paul in Corinth. Most proponents of authenticity generally concur with this,[16] but critically they also presuppose that 1 Thessalonians was

---

[14] Concerning ὡς ὅτι, we suggest that the force of the ὅτι is probably retained, with ὡς simply implying the falsity of the content of the ὅτι clause.

[15] *Pace inter alios* Fee, 'Pneuma', 200 and *Empowering*, 71–2. Wrede, *Echtheit*, 46–7 acknowledged that the problem of 2 Thess. 2:2c could not have directly derived from 1 Thessalonians itself, although he judged that some readers might have thought that it was *confirmed* by 1 Thessalonians and other Pauline letters. However, this view depends on Wrede's belief that 2 Thess. 2:2c's pronouncement reflects an immediate imminentism, and it also takes inadequate account of the reassuring dimension of the eschatological instruction of 1 Thessalonians.

[16] Von Harnack, 'Problem', 574–5 proposed that 2 Thessalonians was written in the immediate aftermath of 1 Thessalonians; Graafen, *Echtheit*, 49–51 believed that only a few days separated them; von Dobschütz, *Thessalonicher-Briefe*, 22; Frame, *Thessalonians*, 19–20 and Jewett, *Correspondence*, 60 proposed that second followed the first within five to seven weeks; Neil, *Thessalonians*, xix–xx judged that the gap 'cannot be more than a

already in the possession of the Thessalonians when the problem underlying 2 Thessalonians developed. We question whether this is a secure
assumption, for, while we do know that the author is sure that 1 Thessalonians is available to those reading 2 Thessalonians (2 Thess. 2:15), we
lack evidence that it arrived before the new eschatological problem arose.

A number of scholars have mentioned in passing the possibility that
the report underlying 2 Thessalonians might have been gathered by the
person who delivered 1 Thessalonians.[17] If true, this would explain why
2 Thessalonians does not mention as a possible source of the false idea
of 2:2c a misunderstanding of 1 Thessalonians: it could not possibly
have been responsible because it was not even present at the time. It
is profitable to examine this proposal more closely, for the delivery of 1
Thessalonians is the only contact between the community in Thessalonica
and the missionaries in Corinth since Timothy's visit for which we have
evidence.

Concerning the courier of 1 Thessalonians, we confidently propose
that it can hardly have been one of the missionaries: the silence of 1
Thessalonians concerning the courier and the fact that Timothy and Silas
are referred to as co-authors make that clear. In a helpful survey of how
first-century letters might have been delivered, Murphy-O'Connor suggests credibly that travellers, traders or businessmen based in the locality
from where a given letter was being sent and who were passing through
or visiting the city to which the letter was addressed were ideal bearers of
Paul's letters.[18] Although he is open to the possibility that a non-Christian
might have borne early Pauline letters, that seems improbable in the light
of Paul's view of humanity outside Christ. It is very tempting to imagine that a Christian from Corinth, possibly on a business trip, acting as

few weeks' (cf. Kümmel, *Introduction*, 268; Barclay, 'Conflict', 528); Best, *Thessalonians*,
59 and Morris, *Epistles*, 19 were less specific, the former contending that the second was
written 'shortly' afterwards, and the latter estimating that the second letter was sent 'within
the matter of weeks or even months' of the first; Stepien, 'Tessaloniczan', 171–4 postulated
a three-month interim; and Elias, *Thessalonians*, 29–30 suggested that 'less than a year'
stood between them.

[17] For example, Milligan, *Thessalonians*, 115; Bicknell, *Thessalonians*, xxi; Neil,
Thessalonians, xix–xx; Rigaux, *Thessaloniciens*, 710; Morris, *Epistles*, 11 (but note that
elsewhere on the same page Morris deduces from 2 Thessalonians that 'The first letter was
evidently successful in doing some of the things Paul set out to do' (*sic*)); Still, *Conflict*,
59 (but see 283, esp. n. 59 and 284–5, where he presupposes that 1 Thessalonians was in
the possession of the Thessalonians prior to the commencement of the problem underlying
2 Thessalonians); cf. A. Plummer, *A Commentary on St. Paul's Second Epistle to the
Thessalonians* (London: Robert Scott, 1918), xv. Remarkably, no one has ever developed
our suggestion.

[18] J. Murphy-O'Connor, *Paul the Letter-Writer* (GNS; Collegeville: Liturgical, 1995),
39–40.

courier of 1 Thessalonians, also gathered the report which underlies 2 Thessalonians. That would explain why Paul trusted the report but did not know some details such as the avenue by which the false idea of 2 Thess. 2:2c had entered the community.[19] Ἀκούομεν in 2 Thess. 3:11, the sole mention of contact between the missionaries and the community since the first letter was written, most naturally suggests that an oral report has inspired the second letter. In addition, it seems to indicate that the news concerning the 'idlers' was somehow unexpected,[20] which seems peculiar since in 1 Thessalonians Paul makes reference to a problem of idleness in the community. It appears that the person reporting to Paul must have impressed upon him afresh the acuteness of the problem. It is therefore not inconceivable that 3:11 ultimately reflects something of the mind of the person who gathered the report underlying 2 Thessalonians, specifically an unfamiliarity with the history of the Thessalonian community and perhaps an antipathy to the idleness which characterised some of its members. These tentative gleanings from 3:11 seem in accord with the profile of a typical letter courier in the first century AD.

Of course, it is also conceivable that the report underlying 2 Thessalonians was delivered to Paul by someone else, after 1 Thessalonians had been sent but before it had arrived at its destination.

Each of these two hypotheses would suggest that the gap between the writing of the two letters, and between the two reports underlying them, was short, perhaps as little as a few weeks.

Credence may be lent by 2 Thess. 3:4 to our proposal that the report underlying 2 Thessalonians was gathered at the same time as or before 1 Thessalonians was delivered, since it seems to imply that Paul does not *know* how the Thessalonians have responded to 1 Thessalonians. Πεποίθαμεν δὲ ἐν κυρίῳ seems to build on πιστός . . . ὁ κύριος of verse 3: because the Lord is faithful, Paul is confident in the Lord. This, together with the present tense ποιεῖτε, which indicates present doing of what he instructs, strongly suggests that πεποίθαμεν is genuine confidence grounded in the Lord rather than an indirect admonition.[21] Significantly, the statement is a matter of faith rather than knowledge (cf. οἶδα). The confidence in the Lord which Paul has relates to the

---

[19] J. Wrzól, *Die Echtheit des zweiten Thessalonicherbriefes* (BibS(F); Freiburg: Herder, 1916), 72 explained the vagueness and the suggestion that a forgery may possibly exist as due to Paul's having received a sketchy report from a visitor to the community.

[20] As was noted by Manson, 'Thessalonians', 441–2; Rigaux, *Thessaloniciens*, 710; Weiss, *Earliest Christianity*, 1:291 n. 17.

[21] *Contra inter alios* Krodel, *Ephesians, Colossians, 2 Thessalonians*, 79.

Thessalonians' conformity with his past teachings (which they were in a position to obey currently, ποιεῖτε) and his present teachings (to which they would in the future conform, ποιήσετε). If, as seems likely, ἃ παραγγέλλομεν . . . ποιήσετε refers back to earlier teaching in this letter which the readers will in the *future* obey, it would seem to pick up on 2:15, since that is the only strong admonition hitherto. There the readers are instructed to stand firm and hold on to the tradition so that they will no longer be shaken and scared by the false eschatology. The (past) instruction which Paul is confident is being heeded in the *present* (ποιεῖτε) could then only be 1 Thess. 4:13–5:11 (note 4:18 and 5:11), where the converts are instructed to encourage each other with assuring words concerning their and their dead community members' eschatological destiny. Therefore, we conclude that 2 Thess. 3:4 may indicate that the author of 2 Thessalonians did not *know* how the community had responded to 1 Thessalonians, but was *confident* that its content would help turn the situation around, especially when reinforced by 2 Thessalonians.

Furthermore, 2 Thess. 3:17 may provide additional evidence that 1 Thessalonians arrived in Thessalonica after the false idea had entered the community. For, assuming that 1 Thessalonians did contain the trademark handwritten closing, the appeal to the handwritten concluding greeting as a criterion to unmask a possible forgery makes most sense if the apostle could assume that any forger could not have seen 1 Thessalonians and so could not have copied the authenticating handwriting. If the Thessalonians had been in possession of 1 Thessalonians prior to the commencement of the eschatological problem underlying 2 Thessalonians and hence the possible forgery, Paul would surely have assumed that a forger who was capable of passing off to the Thessalonian community his forged letter as an authentic letter might have had access to 1 Thessalonians and so could have copied its autographed conclusion. Therefore we judge that the assumption in 3:17 that the authenticating handwriting would expose a forgery may support the view that 1 Thessalonians came into the possession of the Thessalonian community only after the erroneous pronouncement had been made.

Finally, it is striking that in 3:6–15 the author does not refer to the teaching of 1 Thess. 4:11–12 or 5:14. Proponents of a reversal of the canonical order of 1 and 2 Thessalonians see this as a significant proof of their hypothesis.[22] However, if the report behind 2 Thessalonians was gathered at the same time as or before the arrival of 1 Thessalonians, the omission is explicable, since in that case the ἄτακτοι's

---

[22] For example, Wanamaker, *Thessalonians*, 285.

disobedience would have related to the missionary teaching but not yet
1 Thessalonians.

Our proposal, then, is that 1 Thessalonians arrived at Thessalonica
after the eschatological problem underlying 2 Thessalonians had arisen
and that 2 Thessalonians was written, perhaps as soon as one or two weeks
later, primarily to reinforce 1 Thessalonians in the face of the problem
caused by the false claim, which essentially represented the second stage
of a single eschatological crisis. That would make 2 Thessalonians an
addendum to 1 Thessalonians. Significantly, three texts in 2 Thessalonians suggest that it functions in precisely that capacity: 2:1, 15 and 3:4.
To victims of the false eschatological claim underlying 2 Thess. 2:2c, 1
Thessalonians would have offered some valuable help (especially its assurance of hope for the deceased in Christ and for the whole community,
and its description of the parousia in 4:13–5:11), but without an explicit
treatment of the new error it was independently inadequate.

All of this raises the question, what might the originator of the false
claim have meant by it? It must be acknowledged that this historical
question is impossible to answer with any degree of certainty. We are
limited to the author's 'historical' viewpoint, which is quite a restriction
given that he seems to have been unsure as to the source of the erroneous
pronouncement (note μήτε . . . μήτε . . . μήτε in 2:2 and κατὰ μηδένα
τρόπον in 2:3) and presumably also lacked clarity regarding the intended
meaning, motive and manner of diffusion of the originator of the false
claim. It is therefore unwise for us to presuppose that even he had given
careful consideration to the who, why and how questions relating to the
eschatological claim; he is much more concerned to dispute the authority
of the pronouncement and to refute its inferred meaning. Only if we
assume that his information was accurate and that his assessment of the
situation was perceptive can we hope to deduce even vaguely what gave
rise to the new development. Quite possibly, the actual situation was so
utterly bizarre that we could never guess what precisely happened.

First, let us make some relatively confident assertions based on our earlier exegetical analysis which can provide guideposts within which we
can consider the possibilities. (1) As we suggested above, the three hypothetical sources suggested by the author in 2 Thess. 2:2 were probably
a prophecy/teaching delivered by someone within the community or by
a visitor, and a letter wrongly attributed to Paul. (2) From the mention of
these three sources it appears that the author considered that the source of
the erroneous pronouncement must have had revelatory or authoritative
status in the view of the addressees, in order to explain why they had succumbed to such an implausible idea. (3) Perhaps because it was difficult

to imagine that a prophet or teacher would have been perceived to have sufficient authority to convince 'the Thessalonians' of something which conflicted with the tradition, the author seems to give the forgery hypothesis surprising credence (3:17). (4) The false claim probably sought to address the same question regarding the timing of the Day of the Lord as that which underlay 1 Thess. 5:1–11. (5) The claim raised more questions than it answered, casting doubt even on the addressees' Christian hope, and caused more problems than it solved, filling them with despair. As a result of it, they were disturbed and frightened.

It has been suggested that the originator of the erroneous claim meant his pronouncement to be positively exhilarating (perhaps as a proto-Gnostic or realised eschatological (cf. 1 Thess. 4:13ff.) declaration or as a proclamation that Christ had returned to earth already (cf. Mark 13:6, 21–3)) but that the Thessalonians perceived it negatively to be disturbing. In that case we would have the peculiar situation of the inference not matching the implication. That would seem to require that, of the author's three hypothetical sources, the most historically plausible would be an intra- or extra-community prophet or an extra-community teacher (but not an intra-communal teacher, for then we would have expected him to clarify his meaning). While it is just possible that a forger might have been well-intentioned (perhaps seeking to counter the community's negative eschatological reading of their circumstances with an over-positive one), that seems rather unlikely, given that the author gives serious consideration to the possibility that a forger might have gone to considerable lengths to deceive his readers into thinking that his was an authentic letter (3:17). As to the possible association with a beneficially intended false claim to the deaths, a direct relationship would seem unlikely; that is, if intended positively, the statement about the Day of the Lord, while answering the same question as underlies 1 Thessalonians 5, would probably not represent a commentary on the deaths *per se* (whether or not the listeners understood it in that context). If it was intended positively, perhaps the originator had fallen victim to a rumour that Jesus had returned to earth or considered some phenomenon to have eschatological significance. There are many possible explanations of the data which do not require us to attribute to the originator any kind of 'eschatological enthusiasm'.[23]

If the meaning and significance of the originator cohered with the inference drawn by the Thessalonians (for example, if the claim was a comment on the deaths), his intentions must have been malicious. It is

[23] *Pace* Wrede, *Echtheit*, 67; cf. Lüdemann, *Heretics*, 118.

possible that ἐξαπατήσῃ in verse 3 supports this reading (although it may refer to the effect of the claim rather than the motivation for its creation) (cf. 3:3). The author's suggestion of a forgery (2:2; 3:17) would seem to indicate that he is considering the possibility that the originator had intentionally deceived the community by trickery in a malicious attempt to derail their neophyte faith. That would point to a charlatan insider or visitor, or an outright opponent of the Christian church being responsible for the prophecy, word or forgery which led the community astray. Quite simply, like the author we do not have a clear idea what transpired; there are many possible permutations of events which could explain the data.

It remains for us to look briefly at the *inertia vulgaris* and the persecution underlying 2 Thessalonians to see whether they accord with our Pauline hypothesis. Concerning the idleness, it makes excellent sense that the nature of the report brought to Paul which caused him to write 2 Thessalonians, together with the persistence (and even exacerbation) of the problem since Timothy's visit, caused Paul to become slightly more intolerant than he was in 1 Thess. 4:10b–12 and to expand upon 1 Thess. 5:14's νουθετεῖτε τοὺς ἀτάκτους. Moreover, the longer the problem of 'idleness' persisted, the more evident it would have become that the ἄτακτοι were guilty of nothing less than exploitation of their richer brothers. With regard to the persecution, it seems perfectly plausible that the fact of persecution in both situations (and perhaps at the founding mission?) might be explained with reference to a single outbreak. And in view of the false claim mentioned in 2 Thess. 2:2c and the serious dilemma it would have posed for those currently being persecuted, the greater focus on afflictions in 2 Thessalonians (1:4ff.) is perfectly understandable.

In conclusion, we propose that the situations underlying 1 and 2 Thessalonians can be synthesised under the assumption that 2 Thessalonians is authentic. There is good reason to think that the report underlying 2 Thessalonians may have been gathered at the time of the delivery of 1 Thessalonians or before. And it seems plausible that the epistolary situations underlying the two letters represent two stages of a single, rapidly developing eschatological crisis ultimately rooted in an unfortunate interpretation of the unexpected deaths. We suggest, then, that at the mission the Thessalonians had embraced hope focused on the parousia as an essential part of their faith (1:3, 10a). However, their hope appears to have lacked a belief in the final resurrection of dead saints. Some time later, when some community members died, the community were deeply shaken, grieving hopelessly for the dead and seemingly concluding that the deaths might be a prodigy, indicating that the divine realm was displeased with them and that imminent disaster *qua* the Day of the Lord was in store for them. We proposed that the Thessalonians communicated via Timothy to Paul an anxious and fearful question regarding whether the Day of the Lord was about to come. However, while awaiting an answer to their question from Paul, it seems that a prophet, a teacher or a letter falsely attributed to Paul informed the community that the Day of the Lord had already come. The believers were apparently shaken, horrified and filled with despair as they considered the implication that God had abandoned them and that there was now no hope remaining for them. For people who had known the joys of Christian hope just a short time before, their speedy, spiralling descent from hope into despair would probably have been an especially bitter experience. And naturally, *Hoffnungslosigkeit* would have threatened the Thessalonians' perseverance in the faith. Although written with a knowledge of the problem only as it existed at the time of Timothy's report, Paul's first letter would have arrived into this changed situation. When the new development was reported to Paul, he judged a second letter necessary, although he was confident that the first letter would help to ease the problem with its reassurances about the status and destiny of the readers. In view of all this, it would make good sense that when 2 Thessalonians was written, Paul would have perceived the community to be under attack from the evil one (2 Thess. 3:3).

The case for pseudonymity evaluated in the light of our study

In chapter 1 we stressed the importance of determining the situations underlying the two letters for deducing whether 2 Thessalonians is authentic or pseudonymous. It is important now to re-examine each of the difficulties concerning the relationship between the two Thessalonian letters to draw out more fully the ramifications of our study for that debate.

The literary parallels

The literary affinities between 1 and 2 Thessalonians have been the backbone of the case against the authenticity of 2 Thessalonians since Wrede's 1903 study. According to proponents of pseudonymity, the parallels are such that 2 Thessalonians must be read as the work of a different author. Space constraints prevent an exhaustive examination of this problem of literary affinities. However, our thesis does offer a foundation for an alternative reading of the parallels. If we are correct in proposing that 2 Thessalonians is highly situational and that it can and should be read as directed to a persecuted community reeling under the impact of a false claim that the Day of the Lord has come and experiencing problems related to some poorer Christians exploiting the charity of richer community members so as to avoid manual labour, then it is worth asking to what extent the literary parallels between 1 and 2 Thessalonians might be explained with reference to the continuities and discontinuities of the situations underlying the letters. Moreover, we must consider the possibility that some other features of the text of 2 Thessalonians which parallel 1 Thessalonians may themselves have been called for by the situation underlying the second letter. And we must ponder the usefulness of our hypothesis regarding the relationship of the letters, namely that the first letter may have arrived on the scene at Thessalonica at the same time as or after the report behind 2 Thessalonians was gathered, for elucidating the problem of the literary parallels.

As to the matter of the extent to which the affinities can be explained with reference to the similarities of the situations, it is worth first observing how striking it is that 2 Thess. 2:1–12, the part of 2 Thessalonians which most lacks affinities with 1 Thessalonians, is also the part which situationally is most dissimilar to 1 Thessalonians. One of the few affinities between that section and 1 Thessalonians, the focus on the parousia (τῆς παρουσίας τοῦ κυρίου) and specifically the Thessalonians' participation in it (ἡμῶν ἐπισυναγωγῆς ἐπ' αὐτόν) in 2 Thess. 2:1 – cf. 1 Thess. 4:14–17 – is explicable with reference to our judgment that in both epistolary situations the community's hope in the parousia and, more particularly, hope for participation in its salvation was at stake. That 2 Thess. 2:1 alludes back to the eschatological instruction of 1 Thessalonians makes excellent sense if, as we have proposed, 2 Thessalonians is essentially an appendix of 1 Thessalonians, reinforcing its message in the face of the false claim.

In addition, concerning the presence of two thanksgivings in each letter, the fact that all four of these relate to the divinely elect and beloved status of the Thessalonian believers (2 Thess. 1:3; 2:13–14/1 Thess. 1:2–4; 2:13–14) can be plausibly explained with regard to a need in both situations, stemming from the eschatological confusion, for encouragement and reassurance regarding the believers' standing and destiny before God and Christ. Similarly, the striking prepositional phrase ἐν θεῷ πατρὶ καὶ κυρίῳ Ἰησοῦ Χριστῷ (2 Thess. 1:1–2/1 Thess. 1:1), the boasting of the missionaries in the Thessalonians (2 Thess. 1:4/1 Thess. 2:19–20) and the references to 'the churches of God' (2 Thess. 1:4/1 Thess. 2:14) in both letters may be justified with reference to readers' need for reassurance regarding their status before God and Christ in the face of doubts provoked by eschatological confusion. Moreover, the emphasis in both letters on

God's election and call of the believers to the receiving (περιποίησις) of eschatological salvation/glory through the Lord Jesus Christ and the remarkably unqualified reassurances (2 Thess. 2:13–14/1 Thess. 5:9; cf. 2:12), as well as the stress on God's fatherhood of the Thessalonians and their bond with the Lord Jesus Christ in both (2 Thess. 1:1–2; 2:16/1 Thess. 1:1; 3:11), are all explicable as authorial attempts to offset eschatological insecurity. And immaturity and instability on the part of the addressees (together with the missionaries' concern for their converts) would elucidate the preponderance of στήκω and στηρίζω in both letters (2 Thess. 2:15, 17; 3:3/1 Thess. 3:2, 8, 13) and the apparent concern that the persecutions might ultimately cause them to fall away (2 Thess. 1:4/1 Thess. 3:2–5). Furthermore, a lack of concerted opposition within the community addressed in each letter would explain the omission of any reference to the senders' rank in them (2 Thess. 1:1–2/1 Thess. 1:1). The ἡμεῖς before εὐχαριστέω in the second thanksgiving of both letters (2 Thess. 2:13/1 Thess. 2:13) can be plausibly accounted for with respect to the addressees' self-doubts and the author's attempts to put the weight of the missionaries' status behind the assurances given to the community.

Moreover, the presence of actual problems relating to some poor community members exploiting the charity of richer members and so evading the divine mandate to work might well elucidate the deployment of a particular conceptualisation of these people as shirkers in both (ατακτ-, 2 Thess. 3:6, 7, 11/1 Thess. 5:14), the appeals to previous teaching (2 Thess. 3:6, 10/1 Thess. 4:11) and the calls for 'idlers' to work for themselves (2 Thess. 3:12/1 Thess. 4:11–12).[24] And they might explain the use of παραγγέλλω in regard to the 'idlers' in each letter (2 Thess. 3:12 (cf. verses 6, 10)/1 Thess. 4:11–12; cf. νουθετέω in 1 Thess. 5:14), especially the second, where the persistence of the problem might conceivably have worn down Paul's patience.

It is important also to note that many other features of 2 Thessalonians which are regarded by proponents of pseudonymity as evidence of dependence on 1 Thessalonians may be explained with respect to the situation underlying the letter. Notably, the description in the Thessalonian letters (2 Thess. 1:7b–8a; cf. 1 Thess. 4:16–17a) of the parousia as consisting of the revelation of Christ descending from heaven with attendant angels is plausibly elucidated with reference to the need to highlight the *evident* nature of the Day of the Lord (note ἐν τῇ ἡμέρᾳ ἐκείνῃ in 2 Thess. 1:10)

---

[24] Note that the concept of imitation in 2 Thess. 3:7 is more typical of Pauline usage than that in 1 Thess. 1:6 and 2:14, since in 2 Thessalonians it is exhortatory and in 1 Thessalonians it is reaffirming, while the related idea of τύπος in 2 Thess. 3:9 and 1 Thess. 1:7 is employed in a manner consistent with Pauline usage.

in the wake of the false claim that it has already come, just as in 1 Thess. 4:16–17a it is explicable with regard to the need to remove the addressees' ignorance of the resurrection of the saints. Also, the appeals to the Thessalonians' memory of teaching at the mission may be justified in 2 Thess. 2:5, since their acceptance of the false idea of verse 2c would have indicated to Paul that they must have 'forgotten' earlier eschatological teaching (namely verses 3–4, 6ff.), just as it can be explained in 1 Thessalonians, where it disarms the community's potential or actual resentment that they had not been adequately prepared for the persecutions they had endured (3:3b–4).

The assurance that the Thessalonians would be counted worthy of God's kingdom in 2 Thess. 1:5b is explicable with reference to the eschatological confusion issuing from the false claim of 2:2c, in the same way that Paul's appeal to the fact that his message consisted of exhortations to live in a way that was worthy of God (who calls the Thessalonians into his kingdom) in 1 Thess. 2:12 seems intended to underline the authenticity and integrity of the missionaries' ministry and so disarm the Thessalonians' doubts and fears about the deaths of their fellow-believers and the absence of the missionaries. Furthermore, the emphasis on the Lord as an avenger is understandable in 2 Thess. 1:7b–8a, where the Thessalonians are being assured that just judgment will come to the persecuted, apparently in the face of what the false claim asserted, just as it is understandable in 1 Thess. 4:6b, where it underlines the need for former Greek pagans to resist the pull of their old sexual habits. That the Thessalonians need comfort in 2 Thess. 2:16–17 and 3:5 probably reflects how much the false claim has disallowed joy and hope, and that they need comfort in 1 Thess. 3:2 is explicable with regard to the addressees being distraught concerning the persecution that had come on them.

Divine peace (2 Thess. 3:16/1 Thess. 5:23), as well as being a familiar Pauline concept (Rom. 15:33; 16:20; 2 Cor. 13:11; Phil. 4:9; cf. Eph. 6:23),[25] is also an emphasis especially appropriate for the situation underlying 2 Thessalonians, as demonstrated by διὰ παντὸς ἐν παντὶ τρόπῳ. Also, the phrase πᾶσιν τοῖς πιστεύσασιν in 2 Thess. 1:10 (cf. 1 Thess. 1:7) is especially appropriate in its context, since the author is seeking to highlight that the Thessalonian community members by virtue of having *believed* the missionaries' Gospel will be among the number of those saved when Jesus returns on the Day of the Lord (note

---

[25] Trilling, *Untersuchungen*, 110ff. argued that Pauline concepts such as 'Gospel', 'truth', 'tradition' and imitation are invested with un-Pauline nuances. But see the refutations by Jewett, *Correspondence*, 13 and Wanamaker, *Thessalonians*, 26.

ὅτι ἐπιστεύθη τὸ μαρτύριον ἡμῶν ἐφ᾽ ὑμᾶς). And the concern with the strengthening/encouragement of the Thessalonians' hearts (τὰς καρδίας) (2 Thess. 2:17 and 3:5/1 Thess. 3:13) is perfectly understandable if our reconstruction of the eschatological problem underlying 2 (and 1) Thessalonians is valid. Finally, ἐν ἁγιασμῷ in 2 Thess. 2:13 (cf. 1 Thess. 4:4) is explicable with reference to the contrast between the community members in verses 13–14 and unbelievers in verses 9–12, who exist in a realm of Satanic deception and divine delusion.[26]

Our hypothesis regarding the relationship of 1 and 2 Thessalonians suggests that the interval between the two letters was shorter than most have hitherto thought, and that renders plausible the explanation that some of the parallels may be accounted for with regard to the apostle's ways of thinking and expressing himself having remained constant between 1 and 2 Thessalonians. Indeed, this may account for the bulk of the remaining parallels. First, it seems credible that judging a community in terms of the triad of virtues (2 Thess. 1:3/1 Thess. 1:3; 3:6; 5:8) might remain constant over the short period between the letters, especially in view of the prominence of faith and love as characteristics of the community and the problems regarding hope. And if Paul really did pray, as he claims he did, that the Thessalonians would abound in love for one another (1 Thess. 3:12), it would hardly be surprising that just a brief time afterwards he thanks God that they are indeed all abounding in love for one another (2 Thess. 1:3), using some of the same words (ἀγάπη with πλεονάζω and εἰς ἀλλήλους). Second, it seems plausible that Paul's belief that the community's suffering was ultimately a proof of their status and destiny before God (1 Thess. 2:14; cf. 1:6–7a) might have remained a few weeks later (2 Thess. 1:4–5). Third, the conceptualisation of unbelievers and believers in terms of LXX Jer. 10:25 (τοῖς μὴ εἰδόσιν θεόν in 2 Thess. 1:8/τά μὴ εἰδότα τὸν θεόν in 1 Thess. 4:5; cf. Gal. 4:8) and LXX Zech. 14:5b (2 Thess. 1:10/1 Thess. 3:13; 4:14b) respectively might credibly have remained constant over a very short period. Fourth, the conceptualisation of believers' persecutions in terms of θλῖψις (2 Thess. 1:6–7a/1 Thess. 1:6), reflecting dependence on LXX Dan. 12:1b, in two letters separated by perhaps only a week or two is hardly surprising, especially when

---

[26] With a view to the christology of 2 Thessalonians, Trilling, *Untersuchungen*, 128–32 maintained that the portrayal of Christ belongs to the post-Pauline period. He pointed out that Old Testament attributes of *Yahweh* are ascribed to Christ: most strikingly, he is conceived of as Judge and is consistently referred to as κύριος (cf. Friedrich, 'Zweite Brief', 255). However, the christology of 2 Thessalonians is no more developed than that of 1 Thessalonians (1:10; 3:13; 4:14–17; 5:9–10). Such high conceptualisations of Christ are particularly apt in eschatological contexts, where Christ is viewed as the agent of Yahweh.

we consider that both letters allude to LXX Dan. 11:36–12:2 (2 Thess. 2:4–7/1 Thess. 3:3b–4; 4:13ff.). Fifth, it would hardly be surprising if the same author within a short period were to look to divine faithfulness as the basis for hope that the Thessalonians would persevere (2 Thess. 3:3/1 Thess. 5:24; note the similar structure in 1 Cor. 10:13: πιστός . . . ὁ θεός, ὅς . . .) or were to conceive of the Christian's inheritance of his eschatological reward as a περιποίησις (2 Thess. 2:14/1 Thess. 5:9) or were to use particular uncommon (for him generally, at least as represented by his extant letters) words or phrases such as κατευθύνω (in the optative mood) in his prayers (2 Thess. 3:5/1 Thess. 3:11), ἐρωτάω (2 Thess. 2:1/1 Thess. 5:12) and ἔργον πίστεως (2 Thess. 1:11/1 Thess. 1:3).

Even the more impressive parallel of 2 Thess. 3:8/1 Thess. 2:9 is explicable if we allow that Paul may have employed stock language at a particular stage of his missionary travels to express his personal philosophy regarding payment for ministry, probably primarily with a view to differentiating himself from charlatan itinerants (cf. 1 Thess. 2:1ff.),[27] although it is also perfectly appropriate as an example for Greek manual labourers who converted to Christianity (cf. 2 Thess. 3:6ff.).

Our hypothesis would also mean that we should not be surprised to find extremely similar concluding grace wishes in both letters (2 Thess. 3:18/1 Thess. 5:28; cf. Rom. 16:20; 1 Cor. 16:20), more similar versions of the standard opening greeting than in the rest of the Pauline corpus (2 Thess. 1:1–2/1 Thess. 1:1), similar requests for prayer (2 Thess. 3:1–2/1 Thess. 5:25) and a particular way of opening prayers, αὐτός with the divine subject (2 Thess. 2:16; 3:16/1 Thess. 3:11; 5:23). It is an empirical fact that authors addressing on more than one occasion the same group with largely similar problems over a short period are likely to express themselves in similar words, phrases and concepts, such as we see in 1 and 2 Thessalonians.[28]

[27] See especially A. E. Harvey, '"The Workman is Worthy of his Hire": Fortunes of a Proverb in the Early Church', *NovT* 24 (1982): 212–16. This resemblance is so conspicuous that it has been a principal reason for many scholars deducing literary dependence and hence pseudonymity (P. Ahsmann, '"Wie niet wil werken moet ook maar niet eten." 2 Thessalonicenzen 3,10', *Schrift* 64 (1979): 146–52; Marxsen, *Zweite Thessalonicherbrief*, 100–1; Müller, *Anfänge*, 164; F. Laub, 'Paulinische Autorität in nachpaulinischer Zeit (2 Thes)', in *TC*, 417; Richard, *Thessalonians*, 381). However, Trilling, *Zweite Brief*, 147 acknowledges that the problem is significantly reduced if 2 Thessalonians followed close on the heels of 1 Thessalonians. With regard to Harvey's hypothesis, certainly Paul's decision to work rather than depend on others did cause some controversy (cf. 1 Cor. 9:1ff.; 2 Cor. 11:10ff.) and might conceivably have led to his adoption of standard formulae to explain his unusual practice (cf. 2 Cor. 11:27's κόπῳ καὶ μόχθῳ and 11:9's ἀβαρῆ and 12:16's κατεβάρησα).

[28] Parallels such as 2 Thess. 3:15's ἡγεῖσθε/1 Thess. 5:13's ἡγεῖσθαι are of little weight in the case for pseudonymity, since ἡγέομαι in these two instances has different nuances:

We suggest, then, that our thesis undermines the argument for pseudonymity based on literary affinities, for it explains the striking number of
parallels quite successfully without resorting to literary dependence. Of
course, we have no other two letters of Paul written to the same community within a couple of weeks of each other in which the situations
being addressed are apparently so similar – but it is important to note that
proponents of pseudonymity have not demonstrated that the parallels
and dissimilarities are precisely what we would expect of a pseudonymous work. We cannot definitively verify our explanation of the literary
parallels, but certainly the evidence of 1 and 2 Thessalonians seems to
accord with what one might have expected if Paul had written two letters to the same community struggling with similar problems within a
short period.[29] What seems to prevent most proponents of pseudonymity
from considering the situational explanation of the affinities is the presupposition that eschatological enthusiasm/excitement[30] or Gnosticism[31]
underlies the letters.[32]

in the former it means 'regard', and in the latter, 'esteem'. The predominant use of the
first-person plural in 1 and 2 Thessalonians may be due to Paul's attempt to present a united
front to offset any under-appreciation of Timothy (note 1 Thess. 3:2 and the use of the
first-person plural; cf. 2 Cor. 1:1 and the portrayal of Timothy in 2 Tim. 1:6–8; 2:1–3 and
1 Tim. 4:12, 14, 16; 5:23; 6:20).

[29] Several scholars have pointed out that the cross and resurrection and justification are
not present in 2 Thessalonians; such omissions have often been viewed as evidence of
2 Thessalonians' theological poverty (so *inter alios* Friedrich, 'Zweite Brief', 255; R. F.
Collins, ' "The Gospel of our Lord Jesus" (2 Thes 1,8): A Symbolic Shift of Paradigm',
in *TC*, 439 and Légasse, *Thessaloniciens*, 349–50). However, these absences are readily
explicable with regard to the letter's exigency and purpose, as proponents of pseudonymity such as Lindemann, 'Abfassungszweck', 45–6 and Hartman, 'Eschatology', 479 have
acknowledged.

[30] For example, Kern, '2 Thess 2,1–12', 214; Wrede, *Echtheit*, 47–50, 66–70; Hollmann,
'Unechtheit', 34–5; Trilling, *Untersuchungen*, 86, 91, 124–5; Beker, *Heirs*, 73, 82; Menken,
Thessalonians, 62–4, 140.

[31] *Inter alios* Marxsen, *Introduction*, 38–40, 44; Bailey, 'Who?', 142–3; Donfried,
Shorter, 88–9.

[32] Our hypothesis also promises to explain why the differences between 2 and 1 Thessalonians are concentrated in 2 Thess. 2:1–12 and why 1 Thess. 2:1–3:10 need not be repeated
in 2 Thessalonians (*contra* Wrede, *Echtheit*, 17–19). Wrede's argument from structural
similarities (*Echtheit*, 17–18) depends on artificial epistolary divisions (1 Thess. 1/2 Thess.
1; 1 Thess. 3:11–4:8/2 Thess. 2:15–3:5; 1 Thess. 4:10–12/2 Thess. 3:6ff.; and 1 Thess.
4:15–5:5/2 Thess. 2:1ff.) and fails to take adequate account, not only of the observation
that one need not appeal to dependence to explain the structure of 2 Thessalonians (since
the various sections of 2 Thessalonians fit well their respective contexts), but also of the
fact that the eschatological sections (2 Thess. 2:1ff./1 Thess. 4:15–5:5) are out of place,
of 2 Thessalonians' lack of correspondences to 1 Thess. 2:1–3:10 and 5:6–28, and of how
unremarkable it is to find both letters commencing with a thanksgiving. Accordingly, the
argument from parallels in corresponding sections (*Echtheit*, 18–20) also lacks weight. One

The irreconcilability of the eschatologies

In the light of our study, we can make several pertinent points of criticism of the suggestion that the two eschatologies are incompatible.

First, our exegesis suggests that the purported contradiction seems to be a lot less pointed than many proponents of pseudonymity have postulated. In our analysis of 1 Thess. 5:1ff. we attempted to demonstrate that the thief motif does not relate to suddenness or imminence *per se*, but rather to sudden destruction for those 'in the night' (verse 2). The explication of the motif in verse 3 and its application in verses 4–5 indicate that the thief aspect of the Day of the Lord's coming is relevant for unbelievers (those who blindly claim peace and security and who are 'in the darkness'), but not for believers such as the members of the Thessalonian community. The repetition of the same fundamental point in verse 9, that the Thessalonian believers are not destined for wrath but for salvation, seems to confirm our interpretation. With regard to 2 Thess. 2:1ff., it is clear that the 'signs' of the rebel's revelation and the associated apostasy are signs only to believers, for the unbelievers will be deceived by Satan's miracles and deception and deluded by God (verses 9–12), whereas believers will not be deceived or deluded (verses 13–14). Moreover, we note that 2 Thess. 1:5–10 (esp. 5, 6–7a and 10); 2:1 and 13–14 imply that Paul expects the Thessalonians themselves and their contemporaries to live to witness the parousia. Hence as a result of our analysis of the text of 1 and 2 Thessalonians we judge that the tension between 1 and 2 Thessalonians with regard to the eschatologies is not nearly so pronounced as is commonly claimed.

Second, to the degree that there remains a tension between the eschatologies of the two letters, our situational hypotheses go a long

---

expects correspondences between paraenetic sections and between introductory thanksgivings (e.g. εὐχαριστεῖν, τῷ θεῷ, πάντοτε and περὶ ὑμῶν) written by the same author to the same addressees within a short period. And, in view of situational continuities, it is hardly notable that idleness is a prominent feature of the paraenetic sections or that the community's response to suffering is mentioned in the introductory thanksgivings. Moreover, none of the words and phrases in 2 Thessalonians which Wrede claimed are proofs that specific sections are dependent on corresponding sections of 1 Thessalonians show signs of having been artificially included in a particular section. Wrede's argument from parallels (*Echtheit*, 24–7) throughout the letters is uncompelling also – one expects to find prescripts at the commencement of letters and thanksgivings soon afterwards, and benedictory greetings toward the conclusion as well as postscripts at the conclusion; and one does not wonder that benedictory prayers close the first major section of each letter, or that λοιπόν (2 Thess. 3:1/1 Thess. 4:1) commences a new section. The development of 2 Thessalonians is explicable on its own terms, independently of the parallels in 1 Thessalonians.

way to resolving it. We made the point in chapter 1 that the argument against authenticity based on signs in 2 Thessalonians versus suddenness/ imminence in 1 Thessalonians ultimately boils down to a situational question, specifically whether the same author could have written 1 and 2 Thessalonians to the same community within a relatively short period of time. Our study has definitively answered that question: we demonstrated earlier in the chapter that the situations underlying 1 and 2 Thessalonians can be plausibly synthesised if we allow that 1 Thess. 5:1ff. responds to a question motivated by the fear that the Day of the Lord *qua* wrath may be about to fall upon the community and that 2 Thess. 2:1ff. addresses those who are fearful and shaken in the wake of an erroneous claim that the Day of the Lord has come. The two epistolary situations may well reflect two stages of a single crisis, with each stage calling for the particular emphasis which emerges in each letter.

It is important to recognise that the emphasis on sudden destruction in 1 Thess. 5:1ff. is intended to address an explicit question of the Thessalonian community concerning the timing of the Day of the Lord, a question which reflects the fundamental insecurity and fear of that community, probably in the wake of the unexpected deaths. We proposed that their query should perhaps be formulated as 'Is the Day of the Lord about to come?', with the deaths functioning as the catalyst for the concern. Such a situation would of course have *necessitated* that Paul focus on *sudden* destruction if he was to relieve his converts' concerns.

The emphasis on signs in 2 Thessalonians is provoked by the erroneous pronouncement that the Day of the Lord has come (2:2). In response to such an idea, the author could only describe the Day so that the readers would know that it has not occurred, which the author does in 1:5–10 and which he knows has already been done in 1 Thess. 1:10; 3:13 and 4:14–17, and/or highlight the events which must precede it and define its character and which have clearly not come to pass, which is precisely what our author does in 2 Thess. 2:1ff. The latter is particularly important if the Thessalonians are perceived by the author to be vulnerable to further confusion regarding the eschatological timetable, as 3:3 may imply, and if the mistake really did fly in the face of previous eschatological instruction, as 2:5 and 15 suggest.

The difference in the situations underlying these two letters is explicable with reference to our suggestion that the Thessalonians, waiting for Paul's response to the question 'Is the Day of the Lord about to come upon us?' (1 Thess. 5:1ff.), fell victim to the erroneous claim that the Day had in fact come, because it issued from what they regarded as a trusted source.

We propose therefore that the situations underlying 1 and 2 Thessalonians may have been such as virtually to require the somewhat different eschatological emphases which characterise these letters, and that the new developments in 2 Thessalonians are explicable with reference to what 2 Thessalonians explicitly states. Hence there is no argument of substance to be had from the diverse eschatological emphases of signs and suddenness in the two letters.

Crown,[33] building on Whiteley,[34] has propounded what he claims is an improved version of the argument for pseudonymity based on eschatological contradiction. He believes that the contradiction relates to the context in which the parousia occurs: it is described as being peaceful and secure in 1 Thess. 5:3 and as a period of turmoil and disturbance in 2 Thess. 2:3ff. Moreover, he thinks that this contradiction is reinforced by the fact that both of these teachings were supposed to have been communicated during the Thessalonian mission (1 Thess. 5:2; 2 Thess. 2:5).[35]

However, in our study of 1 Thess. 5:1–11 we saw that those living in peace and security are probably those in the darkness, as indicated by the context and the Jeremiah background.[36] Further, 1 Thess. 5:3 refers to the *perception* of those unbelievers. Moreover, the suggestion that 2 Thessalonians 2 portrays the pre-parousia era as one of turmoil and disturbance is not strictly correct. It is rather depicted *objectively* as a time when the

---

[33] Crown, 'Eschatological Language', 222–6.

[34] Whiteley, *Thessalonians*, 13–14, 100–1.

[35] Ibid., 100–1; Crown, 'Eschatological Language', 224–5.

[36] In the light of the allusion to Jer. 6:14 (cf. 8:11) in 1 Thess. 5:3, it is worth noting that Jer. 6:9–15 bears resemblances to the view of the world at the end as expressed in 2 Thess. 2:1–12: (1) the Day of the Lord (*qua* punishment) is imminent, because the wrath of God has reached its fullness (Jer. 6:9–11; cf. 2 Thess. 2:3, 8; 1:6–10). (2) Corruption and depravity are total (Jer. 6:13; cf. 2 Thess. 2:11–12). (3) False prophecy claims peace on the brink of judgment (Jer. 6:14; cf. 2 Thess. 2:4, 9–10; Rev. 13; Matt. 24:15–24 and parallels). (4) An 'abomination' or 'disgrace' (cf. Dan. 9:27) has been perpetrated, which should have evoked shame but did not, and which causes God to pour out his wrath (Jer. 6:15; cf. 2 Thess. 2:4, 12; Dan. 9:27; 11:45–12:1; Matt. 24:15ff. As W. L. Holladay, *Jeremiah 1* (Hermeneia; Philadelphia: Fortress, 1986), 217 notes, תועבה ('abomination') is a very strong term in Hebrew. In the context of Jeremiah the 'abomination' is the worship in Topheth which consisted of the sacrificing of sons and daughters: Jer. 2:7; 4:1; 7:31; 19:1–15). (5) False religion with specific reference to the Jerusalem temple is the focus of the wrath of God (Jer. 6:13; 7:1ff.; cf. 2 Thess. 2:4; Dan. 9:27; 12:11). Jer. 6:13–15 and 8:10b–12 seem to frame the intervening section, which is an indictment of false religion centred on the temple cult. We conclude that the parallels between Jeremiah 6 and 8 and 1 Thess. 5:3/2 Thess. 2:1–12 (cf. 1:3–10) are indeed remarkable. Given that Paul alludes to the Jeremiah passages to describe the state of the world at the eschaton and that those texts bear such a striking resemblance to 2 Thess. 2:1–12, which also describes the state of the world at the end, it is tempting to conclude that Paul intended the reference in 1 Thess. 5:3a to summarise a view of the state of the unbelieving world on the verge of the Day of the Lord which is developed in 2 Thess. 2:1–12.

rebel sets himself up in the temple proclaiming himself to be God and when unbelieving humanity are deluded by God and seduced by Satanic power in the form of miracles and deception, leading them to believe the lie that the rebel is worthy of worship. There is no indication that unbelievers will perceive that period to be disturbing. Perhaps the depiction of the pre-parousia context as an era of turmoil and disturbance may reflect a misinterpretation of what is meant by ἀνομία. The only possible hint that the rebel's revelation and the apostasy might be characterised by upheaval and chaos is the reference in 2:6–7 to the 'mystery of rebellion' already at work, which could allude to present persecutions of Christians and perhaps indirectly to the tribulations due to be experienced by God's people in the final era. But even if that is the case, there is no contradiction with 1 Thess. 5:3, which relates to the experience of *unbelievers*. We suggest that these two teachings are readily synthesised and that both could easily have been held by the same person and indeed that the situations underlying the letters called forth such different emphases.

Hence the reformulation of the eschatological argument against authenticity ultimately fails. And the appeal to the references in 1 and 2 Thessalonians to the eschatological content of the missionary instruction does little to strengthen the case, for (1) 1 Thess. 5:2's reference to the readers' existing knowledge refers to the rest of verse 2, not necessarily verse 3 – hence we cannot be sure that the Thessalonians would have been familiar with the content of verse 3; (2) if the teachings of 1 and 2 Thessalonians regarding the pre-parousia state can be synthesised and if indeed both reflect dependence on Old Testament (especially Danielic) and contemporary Jewish ideas, their inclusion together in the instruction passed on during the mission does not constitute a problem.[37]

In summary, then, we judge the problem posed by the different eschatologies of 1 and 2 Thessalonians to be no real problem at all. Indeed, rather than constituting evidence against authenticity, we would suggest that the eschatological aspects of the situations underlying the letters are so readily reconciled that they speak in favour of authenticity.

2 Thess. 2:2, 15; 3:4 and 17

As we observed in chapter 1 above, proponents of pseudonymity point to 2 Thess. 2:2 and 3:17 as reasons to question the authenticity of 2

[37] One could argue that his assumption of the readers' knowledge of the content of Dan. 12:1 in 2 Thess. 2:4–7 (assuming that the removal of the restrainer is indeed rooted in Dan. 12:1) might suggest that they were also familiar with the content of Dan. 12:2 (the foundational text for the development of the idea of a resurrection of the saints). Nevertheless, the evidence from 2 Thess. 2:3ff. is that some of Paul's eschatological ideas were ultimately rooted in Daniel 10–12, not that he actually taught them Daniel 10–12.

Thessalonians, and many variants of the authenticity position also root their hypotheses in these verses. We have proposed earlier in this chapter a fresh hypothesis which we believe better facilitates what 2:2 and 3:17, and also 2:15 and 3:4, indicate about the relationship between the letters. First, 2:15 demonstrates that Paul has written a letter to the Thessalonian community prior to 2 Thessalonians and indeed that he believes that they already have this letter at the time of writing 2 Thessalonians, or at least will have it by the time 2 Thessalonians arrives. Second, 3:4 suggests that Paul did not *know* how the first letter had been received by the Thessalonians,[38] but that he was *confident* that its impact would be positive. Moreover, 2:2 seems to show that he did not consider 1 Thessalonians to have been a possible source of the false claim, but only a prophecy or word delivered in Thessalonica or a forged letter in the name of the missionaries. Finally, 3:17 demonstrates that a forged letter attributed to the missionaries was viewed by him as a serious possibility and that 1 Thessalonians could be easily differentiated from such a letter. Our hypothesis that 1 Thessalonians arrived after the problem underlying 2 Thessalonians had developed, specifically that the courier of 1 Thessalonians may have gathered the report underlying the second letter, or perhaps that the report underlying 2 Thessalonians was gathered before 1 Thessalonians was delivered, synthesises nicely all of the available evidence.

Wrede objected to the proposal that 2 Thess. 2:2 and 3:17 referred merely to the *possibility* of a forgery on the grounds that if Paul's information about the details of the situation had been deficient, we would then have expected more than simply 3:17, specifically questions regarding why they thought that he had written the letter.[39] However, as we have suggested, the three possible sources of the false idea in 2:2 may stem from Paul's conviction that only an authoritative source could have persuaded the believers of such an implausible and bizarre notion, and that left only three realistic options. Granted that Timothy had earlier reported that the Thessalonians had previously shown a reluctance to embrace prophetic utterances (1 Thess. 5:19–22) and perhaps that they may have been reluctant to respect the teaching of their 'pastors' (5:12–13a), the initially rather implausible possibility of a forged letter in the missionaries' name might have become more credible in Paul's mind. Moreover, he would have known that the Thessalonians had been awaiting a response to the question communicated *via* Timothy and hence that any forged

---

[38] But it is just possible that ὀφείλομεν in 2 Thess. 1:3 and 2:13 indicates that the Thessalonians' very initial response to 1 Thessalonians was known to Paul, although assuming that is unnecessary, since it may well simply be the author's attempt to pre-empt a predictable response of the Thessalonians in view of the false idea.
[39] Wrede, *Echtheit*, 57–8. Cf. Friedrich, 'Zweite Brief', 256.

letter purporting to state his opinion on the matter would potentially have had an open reception among the Thessalonians. Nevertheless, he was still only guessing and was therefore hardly going to push his speculation any further.[40] Besides, knowing the precise source of the false idea was much less important than refuting it, except to the extent that the idea may have been accepted on account of the authority of the person who first presented it (hence his appeal to reject the idea regardless of its origin, 2:2–3a). This latter fact, however, meant that it was conceivable that if a forgery was by any chance responsible for the false claim, all that he had hitherto written might be insufficient to dispel the problem entirely, for the question of whether the missionaries had penned the forgery or 1 and 2 Thessalonians might possibly lead to further problems. Hence he goes out out of his way to eliminate that eventuality in 3:17. Therefore we insist that Wrede's refutation fails to undo our hypothesis that 2:2 and 3:17 present a forged letter as one of the *possible* sources of the false claim referred to in 2:2c.

We might well ask how realistic the possibility of a forgery really was. We propose that, if a forgery existed, it must have arrived in the community after Timothy's visit, but before the courier of 1 Thessalonians delivered that letter and before the report underlying 2 Thessalonians had been gathered. Precisely how long that period of time would have been is impossible to say. Depending on his route, Timothy, as Paul's co-worker, may yet have had to visit other Christian communities such as those in Berea and/or Philippi before returning to Paul in Corinth. The period separating Timothy's departure and the arrival of 1 Thessalonians may have been a few weeks long. In view of the probability that the false claim was an answer to the question the Thessalonians had asked Paul *via* Timothy regarding the timing of the Day of the Lord, it is not unlikely that Paul would have considered that any forgery must have exploited the time lapse between Timothy's departure and the arrival of his reply in 1 Thessalonians (5:1–11), although, given that he would have known that the Thessalonians had (presumably) been seeking for an answer to their eschatological question before Timothy's visit, he may have reckoned with the possibility that a forgery might have been *composed* before that visit. Moreover, it should be noted that the false claim may not have entered the community until shortly before the report behind 2 Thessalonians was gathered, for the situation underlying 2 Thessalonians appears

---

[40] The objection that 'if Paul had thought they had been deceived in this way he would have made his denunciation of the forgery much clearer' (Best, *Thessalonians*, 278) assumes that the author would have known for a fact that a forgery existed. It does not refute our hypothesis that the author merely suspected that a forgery might possibly exist.

to be in its early stages – the author seems to be concerned about their continued perseverance in the light of the false claim, but his report still gives him reason to give thanks for their endurance and faith (1:4–12), and the verbs in 2:2 seem to indicate that the problem was not far advanced. Consequently, we suggest that there would probably have been enough time for the forgery hypothesis to seem plausible in Paul's mind. Awaiting from Paul a definitive answer to their eschatological question, the immature Thessalonian community would have been vulnerable, desperate and unaware what a Pauline letter looked like, and therefore more prone to embracing a forgery attributed to the missionaries.

As regards the motive Paul might have attributed to a forger, since he seems to have perceived Satan behind the Thessalonians' problems (3:3) and since he regarded Satan as a great deceiver (2:9–10a; 2 Cor. 11:14), it seems plausible that he would have considered seriously the possibility that Satan might have been using an opponent of the community to undermine subtly the faith of the neophyte Christians (cf. 2 Thess. 3:1–2). The view of humanity in Adam set forth in Rom. 1:18–32 and 2 Thess. 2:3–12 and the picture of Jews presented in 1 Thess. 2:14–16; Rom. 11:28a and Galatians suggests that Paul would not have been surprised if an unbeliever, Gentile or Jew, would have sought to destroy the Thessalonian church by means of a forgery in his name. Therefore we conclude that the idea that a forgery could have caused the problem mentioned in 2:2 might have seemed plausible to Paul.

In conclusion, we suggest that 2 Thess. 2:2 and 3:17 do not constitute solid grounds for judging 2 Thessalonians to be a pseudonymous letter. They, and 2:15 and 3:4, can be adequately explained with reference to Pauline authorship.

The difference in tone between 1 and 2 Thessalonians

In the light of our study, we are in a better position to criticise the argument against authenticity based on a supposed difference in tones between the letters. First, it must be highlighted that the tone of 2 Thessalonians, especially as regards the eschatological problems of the community, is certainly not cold and official; rather it is warm and reconfirming (see especially 1:3, 4, 5–10, 11–12; 2:13–14, 15, 16–17; 3:3–5, 16). We argued that the addition of ὀφείλομεν to the two thanksgivings in 2 Thessalonians did not reflect a lack of emotion, but was probably a reassurance in the face of self-deprecatory sentiment inspired by the false idea of 2:2. Moreover, if, as we have suggested, 2 Thessalonians is essentially an appendix of 1 Thessalonians, following soon after it, the absence of personal remarks in 2 Thessalonians becomes explicable. This point is reinforced when we consider that the personal remarks of 1 Thess. 2:1–3:10 were motivated by the community's insecurity regarding its status before God and by questions raised by the extended absence of the missionaries, especially Paul. Further, while the author does show signs of intolerance with regard to the problem of 'idleness' in 2 Thess. 3:6–15, so also does Paul in 1 Thess. 5:14. And 1 Thess. 4:6b–8 is as threatening and authoritative as anything in 2 Thessalonians – note that 2 Thess. 3:15 greatly softens the tone of verses 6ff. and that παραγγέλλω (verses 4, 6, 10 and 12) is not necessarily indicative of an un-Pauline authoritarian attitude (1 Thess. 4:6b; cf. 1 Cor. 7:10; 11:17). Therefore, we suggest that the claim that 1 Thessalonians' warm and personal tone contrasts with 2 Thessalonians' cold and officious tone is an over-simplification and reflects a serious misconstrual of the letters, especially in respect to their rhetoric, the situations they presuppose and the relationship between them.[41]

Moreover, we propose that the tone of 2 Thessalonians is entirely appropriate to the situation as we have reconstructed it and that one need not therefore resort to pseudonymity to explain it. With regard to the eschatological problems, 2 Thessalonians is every bit as consistently reassuring as 1 Thessalonians. With regard to the apparently greater seriousness with which 2 Thessalonians treats the 'idleness' problem, we need only suppose that the situation slightly worsened between Timothy's visit and the gathering of the report behind 2 Thessalonians, and/or that the reporter impressed upon Paul in a new way the seriousness of the problem, and/or that the report indicated that the 'idlers' had ignored the warnings of Timothy (not 1 Thessalonians, which is strikingly absent from 2 Thess. 3:6ff.). Any of these might plausibly have provoked the slightly more impatient tone of the second letter.

Therefore we judge that the attempt to argue for pseudonymity based on a supposed difference in tone between 1 and 2 Thessalonians is unsuccessful.[42]

---

[41] As Marshall, *Thessalonians*, 34 has written, 'it is surely time that the myth of the cold tone of the letter was exploded'. *Contra* von Dobschütz, *Thessalonicher-Briefe*, 43–4; Rigaux, *Thessaloniciens*, 150; Jewett, *Correspondence*, 11 (including n. 48); Stacy, 'Introduction', 183–4; Still, *Conflict*, 53.

[42] In his important work on authenticity, Trilling, *Untersuchungen*, 46–66 argued that unusual stylistic considerations, such as the number of compound verbs, uncommon expressions and preferred words and phrases (together with the official tone) suggest inauthenticity, although not conclusively so. He also pointed to the lack of typically Pauline features in the letter, such as brief sentences, rhetorical questions and diatribe, as suggestive of inauthenticity. Although such matters are outside the scope of this book, it should be noted that Trilling's failure to conduct a detailed study of the style of the indisputably authentic Pauline

Concluding evaluation of the four arguments for pseudonymity

In conclusion, there can be little doubt that the case for reading 2 Thessalonians as a pseudonymous document based on literary affinities with 1 Thessalonians, contradictory eschatologies, 2 Thess. 2:2 and 3:17 and the irreconcilable tones of 1 and 2 Thessalonians becomes much less compelling in the light of our thesis. The situational compatibility of 1 and 2 Thessalonians, together with the plausibility of the hypothesis that 2 Thessalonians is essentially an appendix of 1 Thessalonians, written perhaps as little as one or two weeks afterwards to offset an unexpected twist in the situation, offers to explain each of the difficulties adequately without resort to pseudonymity.

Trilling expressed misgivings about attempts to explain the problems of 2 Thessalonians with reference to situational hypotheses. He regarded the situational approach as being in danger of succumbing to a methodological circle by reading the solution into the foundation and he claimed that situational descriptions must always reckon with too many unknown factors.[43] Of course, Trilling has a point: determining the situation underlying a given letter is a notoriously tricky and circular business. Nevertheless, it is also a *sine qua non* of the exegetical task, for letters are contingent communications. Moreover, there are principles which can be applied (and, in the case of this monograph, have been applied) to make situational analysis a less subjective enterprise.[44] In the case of 2 Thessalonians,

---

letters undermines his argument (as Jewett, *Correspondence*, 11 notes). Moreover, given the uniqueness of the problems facing the Thessalonians and the peculiarity of the epistolary purpose, together with the apparent urgency of the letter's composition, any distinctive vocabulary is understandable. Finally, Trilling failed to give due acknowledgement to the fact that the bulk of the stylistic and lexicographical evidence speaks strongly in favour of Pauline authorship. The linguistic cases for authenticity presented by von Dobschütz, *Thessalonicher-Briefe*, 37ff.; Frame, *Thessalonians*, 28–37, 45ff. and Rigaux, *Thessaloniciens*, 76–111 are still worth consulting.

[43] Trilling, *Untersuchungen*, 27.

[44] One must, of course, avoid assuming that the supposed readers are the real readers; note that in Part 3 we consistently referred to the apparent author as 'Paul' and the supposed recipients as 'the Thessalonians'. Determining whether a specific part of a letter is situationally specific or general necessitates that certain principles are brought to bear on the text in question. As an example, we shall consider what to do with exhortations in 1 Thessalonians. One important rule is that the more unexpected, especially the more unfamiliar in Paul's other letters (and elsewhere in the New Testament), a particular exhortation is, the more likely it is that that exhortation is specific; likewise, the more expected or common a given exhortation is, the more probable it is that it is general (unless every other instance of the exhortation is situationally specific). However, we must bear in mind that we have only a limited sample of Paul's letters and that even general paraenesis is issued because the author perceives it as relevant for the addressees. Moreover, it is perfectly possible that familiar problems are being confronted and indeed that common paraenesis is being issued for *specific*

the author helps us by giving explicit clues to some of the specifics of the situation, most importantly 1:4; 2:2 and 3:11. Such explicit clues provided a solid foundation for our study of the argumentation of the letter's parts with a view to determining more about the situation. Credibility is added to our situational hypothesis regarding 2 Thessalonians in that our reading is plausible and in that it harmonises well with our reading of the situation underlying 1 Thessalonians.

Proponents of pseudonymity frequently present their case against authenticity as a cumulative one.[45] However, we rejoin with Jewett that several pieces of uncompelling evidence do not combine to make a strong case, for cumulative doubt must also be taken into account: 'there is a serious logical misconception in this idea of the cumulative weight of evidence, because the degree of plausibility with which the general conclusion can be advanced decreases with each new piece of marginal evidence'.[46]

Is 2 Thessalonians an epistolary pseudepigraph?

We noted in chapter 1 that proponents of pseudonymity must identify 2 Thessalonians either as a general paraenetic and didactic tract or a 'typological pseudepigraph'. We shall examine each of these alternatives in turn.

situations – as J. M. G. Barclay, 'Mirror Reading a Polemical Letter: Galatians as a Test Case', *JSNT* 31 (1987): 84 has pointed out, a prohibition implies at least that there is some possibility that what is prohibited is being done, at most that some are flagrantly disobeying what is prohibited, and a command implies at least that some are in danger of neglecting what is commanded, at most that some are deliberately flouting it – and indeed that the inclusion of similar paraenesis in Paul's other letters may have been influenced by his experience of the *Thessalonian* problem. The more informed the author is of a particular community's situation, the more correspondence we would expect between his paraenesis and the situation (we must assume that his information is correct). If the exhortation is inextricably linked to what is known to be situationally specific, the likelihood of that exhortation being motivated by specific needs is strong; if the context, especially the immediate context, of the paraenesis is determined to be situationally specific, this strengthens the case for interpreting the paraenesis in question similarly. Further, repetition, sanctions and urgency suggest especial pastoral concern, the catalyst often being the specifics of the situation. Finally, the resultant situational hypothesis should be historically and rhetorically plausible and cohere with what is otherwise known about the epistolary occasion. This method should be applied in the case of 2 Thessalonians (concerning which we cannot assume authenticity), precisely because it purports to be a Pauline letter and we are primarily concerned with the *supposed* situation.

[45] So *inter alios* Hilgenfeld, 'Thessalonicher'; Holtzmann, 'Thessalonicherbrief', 97–108; Trilling, *Untersuchungen*, 45 and *Zweite Brief*, 23–4; Krodel, *Ephesians, Colossians, 2 Thessalonians*, 77; Menken, *Thessalonians*, 27–43.

[46] Jewett, *Correspondence*, 14; also 11.

Is 2 Thessalonians a general paraenetic and didactic
pseudepigraph?

In the chapter of his *Untersuchungen zum zweiten Thessalonicherbrief*,
Trilling built a form-critical argument for inauthenticity.[47] He contended
that 2 Thessalonians is not a letter to a particular community, but a general
didactic and paraenetic tract claiming apostolic authority.[48] However, we
judge his reading of 2 Thessalonians to be artificial and skewed. First, let
us consider 2:2. With a cavalier dismissal, Trilling discounted the value
of this verse for determining the occasion and purpose of the letter and
claimed that verses 1ff. are not really a denial of the false idea concerning
the Day of the Lord.[49] He represented the erroneous claim as one of
enthusiastic imminentism, which allowed him to argue that the problem
addressed was a general one and that 2 Thessalonians was written to
tackle the resurgence of apocalypticism in the post-70 era.[50] However,
in chapter 5 we demonstrated that the verb ἐνέστηκεν must be translated
'has come', meaning that the Day has arrived, not that it is about to occur.
Moreover, we found that the response which 'Paul' combats is one of
shakenness and fear rather than positive excitement and joy. Furthermore,
we found that the whole of verses 1–17 was a unit which tackled the very
specific problem implied by the false claim. Trilling's attempt to locate
the purpose of 2 Thessalonians 2 not in verses 3–4 and 8–10a (which
he claimed are traditional apocalyptic material), but rather in verses 5–7
and 10b–12 (which he claimed represent the author's interpretation of
that material),[51] is unsuccessful, especially when we recognise that the
background for the idea of the restrainer (verses 6–7) seems to be Daniel
10–12 and that the removal of Michael from the scene, based on Dan.
12:1a, appears to have been understood as God's giving Satan permission
to act in the fullness of his power through his agent who is camped at the
Jerusalem temple. For that paradigm knits verses 5–7 closely with verses
3–4 and 8–10a. Also, verses 10b–12 are not simply a general treatment
of the causes and consequences of unbelief,[52] but rather finish off the
thought begun in verse 3's ἀποστασία and shift the focus to the identity
of those who will be victims of the Day of the Lord, in preparation for
verses 13–14, which deal explicitly with an implication of the erroneous
idea.

[47] Trilling, *Untersuchungen*, 67–108.   [48] Ibid., 108.   [49] Ibid., 90.
[50] Trilling, *Zweite Brief*, 26–8, 79–80 (see also *Untersuchungen*, 91, 124–5); cf. Laub,
Verkündigung, 140, 156–7.
[51] Trilling, *Untersuchungen*, 75–93.   [52] Ibid., 87–8.

Second, as we argued in chapter 6, 2 Thessalonians 1 seems most naturally understood as a situationally specific reassurance in the face of the false claim of 2:2 (note especially 1:10's ἐν τῇ ἡμέρᾳ ἐκείνῃ). The prescript is understandable with regard to the community's problems. The omission of hope from the thanksgiving in 1:3 accords with our understanding of the problem underlying 2:1ff. and reinforces the impression that chapter 1 is not nearly as general as Trilling contended. It seems best to interpret the apparent concern with theodicy in the face of persecutions and the focus on the nature and timing of the coming of the Day of the Lord in 1:5ff. as reflecting a particular problem stemming from the erroneous claim of 2:2.

In chapter 5, we also argued that 3:3–5 are not formal and general, but must be interpreted as assuming a specific complex of problems, particularly the persecution and the eschatological insecurity of the Thessalonians.

In chapter 7, we examined 3:6–15. We argued that verses 13–15 are best interpreted as belonging to verses 6–12 rather than as an independent unit.[53] This, together with 3:11's ἀκούομεν and the apparently specific nature of the situation underlying verses 6ff., suggests that this section is not general.[54] Trilling claimed that 3:6ff. relate to more than a mere aversion to work; he proposed that they concern a more serious and general (post-Pauline) problem of Christian profession no longer tallying with lifestyle.[55] However, this is to go beyond the evidence; as we argued in chapter 7, nothing in the text points to anything other than *inertia vulgaris* (some manual labourers were seemingly sponging off wealthier members of the Christian community, as in 1 Thess. 4:10b–12), which seems perfectly at home in an urban neophyte community in the middle of the first century.[56]

Finally, Trilling sought to avoid the situational specificity of 3:16–17.[57] Nevertheless, the suspicion of a forged letter in 3:17 suggests a specific situation, and the concern with 'peace in all times and in all ways' seems to reflect various facets of the situation underlying the letter, as we suggested in chapter 7.

---

[53] *Pace* ibid., 98–9.   [54] Ibid., 96–101.   [55] Ibid., 101.

[56] Although Trilling (ibid.) argued against reading 2 Thess. 3:6ff. as directed at a mere aversion to work in Thessalonica at the time of Paul, by pointing to the ατακτ- language, the length of the text, the supposed sharpness of the tone and the content of the injunction in verse 6, we insist that all of these features can be adequately explained with reference to *inertia vulgaris* having persisted from the inception of the community, in spite of the missionaries' warnings during the mission.

[57] Ibid., 101–8.

In conclusion, then, in the light of our study we find Trilling's form-critical argument for inauthenticity uncompelling. Rather than being a general paraenetic and didactic tract, 2 Thessalonians is most naturally read as a letter to a particular community, addressing issues specific to it. When we consider how readily the situation apparently supposed by 2 Thessalonians seems to harmonise with that underlying 1 Thessalonians, Trilling's argument is further undermined. That raises the question of whether 2 Thessalonians is a 'typological pseudepigraph', the only other category of pseudepigraphy under which 2 Thessalonians could conceivably be subsumed.

Is 2 Thessalonians a typological pseudepigraph?

Does 2 Thessalonians meet the criteria to qualify as a 'typological pseude-pigraph'? According to this reading, 2 Thess. 2:2 would be the most important link between the supposed and real situation. Many interpret 2:2 as linking a supposed and real situation of enthusiastic imminentist eschatological expectation.[58] In this reading the real readership has fallen foul of a renewal of apocalyptic enthusiasm in the post-70 era.[59] Others understand the link to relate to Gnostic Christian ideas about the resurrection, but rather similarly judge the real situation to be a product of the last few decades of the first century.[60] Our study casts serious doubt on these proposed connections, for in neither 1 nor 2 Thessalonians are there any signs that the addressees were enthusiastic (we may also question whether there really was a resurgence of apocalypticism in the final few decades of the first century AD). Further, in 2 Thessalonians the false claim of 2:2c reads 'the Day of the Lord has come' and therefore can hardly refer to imminentist expectation on either a supposed or a real level. And the recipients' response of fear and perturbation combated in 2 Thess. 2:1ff. is hardly what we would expect if enthusiastic imminentism or Gnosticism were the central problem. In our study we have proposed that the situation addressed in 2 Thessalonians was something rather less common than enthusiasm or (proto-) Gnosticism; rather it was the more peculiar problem of believers falling victim to a somewhat ridiculous and implausible notion to the effect that the Day of the Lord has come. Quite why a

---

[58] For example, Wrede, *Echtheit*, 69; Hollmann, 'Unechtheit', 34–5, 37; Friedrich, 'Zweite Brief', 256–7, 262–3; Koester, *Introduction*, 2:242–4; Beker, *Heirs*, 82; Richard, *Thessalonians*, 28–9.
[59] See especially Trilling, *Zweite Brief*, 80; also Menken, *Thessalonians*, 65–6.
[60] Marxsen, *Introduction*, 38–40, 44 and *Zweite Thessalonicherbrief*, 76ff.; Bailey, 'Who?', 142–3.

second- or third-generation Christian would need to resort to pseudonymity to refute such an idea is difficult to explain; and it is hard to imagine such a confusion outside a rather immature first-generation Gentile Christian community, not conversant with the Old Testament and Jewish eschatological ideas.

The real readers must also have been suffering persecution and asking questions about the implications of that persecution for the justice of God's judgment, quite possibly in view of the erroneous eschatological pronouncement (2 Thess. 1:4ff.). And they must have had a further problem with regard to manual labourers exploiting rich believers and so avoiding work (2 Thess. 3:6–15, especially verse 11).[61] The problem with three different points of correspondence (two of which may be interrelated) between the supposed and real situations is that the more there are, the less credible it becomes that a given letter is pseudonymous, for it requires increased boldness and sophistication on the part of the real author and increased gullibility on the part of the real readers (note that the author presupposes in 3:17 that his readers would judge any letter falsely attributed to Paul unacceptable). Finding a *Sitz im Leben* for a pseudepigraphal 2 Thessalonians is therefore even more challenging than has hitherto been thought. No convincing historical setting for a pseudonymous 2 Thessalonians has yet been put forward.

Moreover, the fact that the situation underlying 2 Thessalonians fits so well with that underlying 1 Thessalonians as we have reconstructed it – an immature, persecuted Gentile community having difficulties with manual labourers exploiting richer community members and having problems processing Jewish eschatological ideas, awaiting word from Paul concerning the timing of the Day of the Lord, and shaken by the deaths into thinking that God was angry with them – means that 2 Thessalonians is either authentic or a remarkably skilful work of pseudepigraphy. This is reinforced by the observation that there is less historical scene-setting than we would have expected if 2 Thessalonians were pseudonymous. The more skilful a pseudonymous author we are forced to postulate in order to explain the evidence, the more attractive the authenticity hypothesis becomes.

In conclusion, we suggest that 2 Thessalonians does not readily meet the criteria to be either a 'general tract' or a 'typological' pseudepigraph.

[61] Most proponents of pseudonymity conclude that the 'idleness' stemmed from the eschatological problem both in the supposed and in the real situation (so *inter alios* Hollmann, 'Unechtheit', 34–5; Agrell, *Toil*, 122–3; Holland, *Tradition*, passim, esp. 91–2; Giblin, '2 Thessalonians', 872, 875; Menken, *Thessalonians*, 137–41). But Wrede, *Echtheit*, 51–3 is sceptical of such a link.

Conclusion

In this chapter we have suggested that the points of continuity and discontinuity between the situations reflected in 1 and 2 Thessalonians are such that a course of development can be charted between them. The false claim in 2 Thess. 2:2c may well be an answer to the question concerning the timing of the Day of the Lord underlying 1 Thess. 5:1ff., which was originally inspired by the unexpected deaths (4:13–18). We postulated that the eschatological problem underlying 2 Thessalonians might simply constitute the second stage of a single crisis, with 2 Thessalonians functioning as something of an *addendum* to 1 Thessalonians. That the situations are closely related seems to be confirmed when we observe that a plausible case can be made for viewing the problems of both *inertia vulgaris* and persecution as having continued between the time of Timothy's visit and the gathering of the report underlying 2 Thessalonians. We proposed that the problem underlying 2 Thess. 2:2 probably arose completely independently of 1 Thessalonians and indeed that the report underlying 2 Thessalonians was gathered at the same time as, or possibly prior to, the arrival of 1 Thessalonians in Thessalonica. We concluded that we have evidence in 1 and 2 Thessalonians of a rapidly deteriorating eschatological problem in Thessalonica, with hope, which characterised the community at the mission, giving way to despair.

Then we evaluated the four main 'problems' of 2 Thessalonians which have become the major grounds for scholars concluding in favour of pseudonymity. The literary affinities are explicable with reference to similarities in the situations underlying the letters, our situational analysis of 2 Thessalonians and our hypothesis concerning the historical relationship between the two letters, especially the very short gap separating them, rather than with reference to different authorship of 2 Thessalonians. We suggested that the tension between the eschatologies of the letters was greatly relieved by the observation that 1 Thess. 5:1ff. indicates that the Day will be suddenly destructive to those in the night and by the observation that the signs of 2 Thess. 2:1ff. are only for believers. Also, we postulated that our situational studies of 1 and 2 Thessalonians went a long way toward resolving what tension remained between the eschatologies of 1 and 2 Thessalonians. With regard to 2 Thess. 2:2 and 3:17 (and 2:15 and 3:4), we noted that our hypothesis concerning the relationship of 1 and 2 Thessalonians established the basis for synthesising these verses satisfactorily and refuted Wrede's objection to our proposal. And with respect to the apparent difference in tone, we argued that the tone of 2 Thessalonians was not nearly so cold and official as proponents of

pseudonymity have contended, especially not in regard to the eschatological confusion, and we proposed that the tones of the letters seem to
be entirely appropriate to the underlying situations. Therefore our thesis
poses a serious challenge to the pseudonymous hypothesis.

Finally, we examined 2 Thessalonians to see whether it fulfilled the
necessary criterion to be a pseudepigraph: could it be a general paraenetic
and didactic tract? Or could its supposed situation really be a type of a
subsequent real situation? Concerning the former suggestion, we pointed
out that the whole of 2 Thessalonians begs to be understood as directed
to a specific situation. With regard to the latter proposal, given that 2
Thess. 2:2 seems to indicate that the community is terrified by the bizarre
claim that the Day has come and given that such a correspondence would
have to exist also in regard to persecution (1:4) and 'idleness' (3:11),
we judged that 2 Thessalonians' 'supposed' situation was too peculiar
and complicated to qualify as the *type* of a 'real' situation. Hence we
concluded that the pseudonymous hypothesis was not as plausible as
many have claimed.

We therefore propose that our situational synthesis and related Pauline
hypothesis regarding the relationship between the letters offer a more
promising way ahead for Thessalonians scholarship. Scholars have frequently acknowledged that no wholly satisfactory solution to the problems of 2 Thessalonians has yet been proposed.[62] Our solution seems to
incorporate many of the strengths of previous hypotheses, while avoiding many of their weaknesses. For example, it explains satisfactorily the
extensive literary parallels between 1 and 2 Thessalonians, the eschatological differences between them, 2 Thess. 2:2 and 3:17 and the tones of the
letters without recourse to the slippery theory of pseudonymity, thereby
avoiding the problem of 2:4's temple reference and the difficulties of date
and destination which plague that hypothesis. In particular, it respects
the totality of the case for pseudonymity.[63] Along with proponents of

---

[62] Bornemann, *Thessalonicherbriefe*, 478; Neil, *Thessalonians*, xxi; Rigaux, *Thessaloniciens*, 149. Cf. Trilling, *Untersuchungen*, 35.

[63] Note that Trilling (*Untersuchungen*, 17 and 19) criticised critics of pseudonymity for
tackling individual points in Wrede's case, but not the whole. Our hypothesis offers a macro-
explanation of the literary parallels and indeed the apparent eschatological contradiction as
well as the seeming difference in tone, and 2:2 and 3:17. Wrede, *Echtheit*, 29–30, followed
by Trilling, *Untersuchungen*, 18, formulated the literary argument as a whole in the form of
a series of 'coincidences' which together constitute a coincidence too great to be explicable
with reference to authenticity. However, it is notable that Wrede's argument is based on the
assumption that Pauline authorship would entail a period of months between the two letters
and a very different view of the situation presupposed in the letter. Our hypothesis postulates
that as little as one or two weeks may separate the letters and that the predominant feature
of the situation is fear and despair. Accordingly, the implausibility of the concurrence of
the 'coincidences' seems to dissipate.

the replacement hypothesis, it acknowledges that 2:2 and 3:17 do most naturally suggest that a forgery is in view, but it does not play down the significance of 2:15 and so avoids concluding that 1 Thessalonians is being represented as a forgery. Similarly, it avoids having to conclude that Paul kept a copy of 1 Thessalonians and referred extensively to it in the writing of 2 Thessalonians. Moreover, our thesis makes a strong case for the temporal proximity of 2 Thessalonians to 1 Thessalonians.[64] It gives due attention to the observation of several scholars, such as von Harnack and Graafen, who insisted that for Paul to be the author of 2 Thessalonians, he must have written it a short time after 1 Thessalonians.[65] At the same time, it avoids postulating that two different audiences are addressed or concluding that no fresh news regarding the Thessalonians has reached Paul since 1 Thessalonians was written. It recognises the importance of situational analysis for the authenticity debate, but avoids the problems of reading the Thessalonian correspondence as directed against enthusiastic excitement or Gnosticism, offering instead a hypothesis which is more sensitive to the argumentation of each letter.

In conclusion, we believe that this thesis offers a fresh way forward for scholarship of the Thessalonian correspondence. It is hoped that this contribution can move Thessalonians scholarship, particularly with respect to the authenticity debate, beyond the present deadlock.

[64] Thus it seems to evade a criticism of Bornemann's work by Wrede, which was applied to Wrzól and Graafen by Trilling, *Untersuchungen*, 28.

[65] Von Harnack, 'Problem', 574–5; Graafen, *Echtheit*, 12, 50–1; also Trilling, *Untersuchungen*, 43–4; Laub, *Verkündigung*, 148; Friedrich, 'Zweite Brief', 257.

APPENDIX

MICHAEL, THE RESTRAINER REMOVED
(2 THESS. 2:6–7)*

Introduction: 2 Thess. 2:6–7 and the restrainer

One of the most enduring exegetical enigmas of the Pauline corpus is the identification of ὁ κατέχων/τὸ κατέχον in 2 Thess. 2:6–7. Discussion of the issue has reached something of an impasse, with some recent contributions expressing pessimism regarding the whole enterprise and a few even postulating that the author himself had no particular referent in mind.[1] Certainly one could be forgiven for concluding that the key to unlocking the secrets of 2 Thess. 2:6–7 has yet to be, and perhaps never will be, discovered.[2] Nevertheless, the quest for the elusive key continues. The goal of this appendix is to question the most common interpretations and to suggest where the key to this most controversial conundrum may be found.

First, we shall undertake a brief exegesis of 2 Thess. 2:6–7. Οἴδατε[3] and the enigmatic nature of these two verses indicate that the readers already know about the κατέχων (-ον) and suggest that the author is seeking to jog his readers' memories in order that they might apply their existing knowledge to their new situation. If they do so, it will help them recover from the erroneous eschatological claim concerning the Day of the Lord to which they have apparently succumbed (verse 2b). The flow of thought in verses 6–7 (and arguably the νῦν in verse 6) makes it clear that the present activity of the κατέχων (-ον) is being contrasted with

---

* An earlier version of this Appendix was published in the *Journal of Theological Studies* 51 (2000): 27–53.

[1] So *inter alios* Trilling, *Untersuchungen*, 87–8, 93 and *Zweite Brief*, 89–90, 102; L. J. L. Peerbolte, 'The κατέχον/κατέχων of 2 Thess. 2:6–7', *NovT* 39 (1997): 138–50; Légasse, *Thessaloniciens*, 392, 397–8.

[2] Note the claim of J. Schmid, 'Der Antichrist und die hemmende Macht (2 Thess 2, 1–12)', *TQ* 129 (1949): 330: 'Der Schlüssel zur Lösung dieses Rätsels ist unauffindbar verloren und alle Versuche, es zu lösen, beweisen nur, daß dem so ist' ('The key to solving this riddle is lost without trace and every quest to solve it merely demonstrates that this is so').

[3] In view of verse 5, οἴδατε probably refers to conceptual knowledge gained at the time of the mission rather than experiential knowledge (*contra* Giblin, *Threat*, 159–66; Stephens, 'Themes', 340).

future inactivity. Since the purpose clause εἰς τὸ ἀποκαλυφθῆναι αὐτὸν ἐν τῷ ἑαυτοῦ καιρῷ depends not on οἴδατε[4] but rather on τὸ κατέχον,[5] it seems that τὸ κατέχον operates so that the rebel (αὐτόν) might be revealed (cf. verses 3, 8) in 'his own' (ἑαυτοῦ) time, the time appointed by God.

The emphatically positioned τὸ μυστήριον in verse 7 stands in contrast to ἀποκαλυφθῆναι, indicating that this verse functions to explain (γάρ) the preceding clause. Until the ἄνομος is revealed at a definite time in the future, ἀνομία is at work (ἐνεργεῖται) as a 'mystery', that is, in an 'unrevealed' state.[6] Ἀνομία in its 'mystery' form may well refer to anti-God sentiment (cf. 1 Cor. 7:26, 28ff.; 1 Thess. 3:3–4) prior to the outbreak of the eschatological tribulations at the revelation of the rebel (see Dan. 9:27; Eph. 6:13; Mk. 13:14ff. par. Matt. 24:15ff.; Rev. 13:2ff.);[7] the readers were victims of such present rebellious antipathy toward God (2 Thess. 1:3–10). The κατέχων performs his function in the present (ἄρτι) to keep rebellion in its unrevealed state, but he will do

---

[4] Pace Giblin, Threat, 204–10; Stephens, 'Themes', 341; P. S. Dixon, 'The Evil Restraint in 2 Thess 2:6', JETS 33 (1990): 447.

[5] Since οἴδα denotes not an action but rather a cognitive process, it cannot govern εἰς τὸ ἀποκαλυφθῆναι αὐτὸν ἐν τῷ ἑαυτοῦ καιρῷ (cf. M. Barnouin, 'Les Problèmes de traduction concernant II Thess. II.6–7', NTS 23 (1977): 484). Indeed, not only is οἴδατε never followed by a dependent εἰς τό clause in the Pauline corpus, but here it already has a direct object (Best, Thessalonians, 291). The peculiar word order is not entirely surprising in this context of syntactical irregularities, and may be partially explained by the author's bringing forward τὸ κατέχον from its expected position between οἴδατε and the final prepositional clause, for emphasis.

[6] Τῆς ἀνομίας is either an attributive or descriptive genitive or a genitive of product. It is not that the ἄνομος himself is currently masked until his unveiling (pace Baur, Paul, 2:326–7; Hollmann, 'Unechtheit', 36; C. C. Caragounis, The Ephesian Mysterion: Meaning and Content (ConBNT; Lund: Gleerup, 1977), 27; J. T. Townsend, 'II Thessalonians 2:3–12', SBLSP 1980, 238; Richard, Thessalonians, 330–1); rather, the ἀνομία exists as mystery until it is revealed in the ἄνομος. Μυστήριον here probably does not denote 'beyond human knowledge', referring to the 'mysterious disposition of divine providence whereby evil is allowed to exist and work in the world' (pace R. E. Brown, The Semitic Background of the Term 'Mystery' in the New Testament (FBBS; Philadelphia: Fortress, 1968), 39). The focus in this context is rather on the existence of anti-God rebellion as a preliminary, veiled force (perhaps also as an uncombined and unorganised force, as Ellicott, Thessalonians, 113 thinks), not yet seen in its fullness (since the κατέχων/κατέχον keeps rebellion in this state until the time comes for it to be disclosed in its fullness). Anti-God hostility will only be expressed in its unadulterated form when the κατέχων/κατέχον is removed. Evidence for a link with the mystery religions (Holland, Tradition, 114; cf. Donfried, 'Cults', 353; Giblin, Threat, 192–204, 246) and/or the imperial cult (cf. Elias, Thessalonians, 285) is lacking.

[7] So also Holland, Tradition, 70, 113; D. Farrow, 'Showdown: The Message of Second Thessalonians 2:1–12 and the Riddle of the "Restrainer"', Crux 25.1 (1989): 24; Müller, 'Currents', 309; Richard, Thessalonians, 330; contra von Dobschütz, Thessalonicher-Briefe, 280–1, who takes it as referring to societal moral decline.

so only (μόνον) until (ἕως) he disappears (ἐκ μέσου γένηται),[8] at which point lawlessness *qua* mystery will become lawlessness *qua* personified revelation. In the New Testament κατέχω can mean 'hold fast' (Luke 8:15; Rom. 7:6; 1 Cor. 11:2; 1 Thess. 5:21; Heb. 3:6, 14; 10:23; cf. Acts 27:40), 'hold back'/'delay'/'restrain' (Luke 4:42; Rom. 1:18; Phlm. 13), 'hold in possession' (1 Cor. 7:30; 2 Cor. 6:10) and 'take hold or possession of [a place]' (Luke 14:9).[9] In this context where the operation of the κατέχον causes rebellion to stay in its unrevealed state until the point when the κατέχων is removed from the scene, it is little wonder that most scholars have interpreted κατέχω in its common (especially in classical literature) sense of 'hold back' or 'restrain'.[10]

After stressing that the rebel is revealed only after the restrainer has been removed (verses 7–8a) and that the rebel's revelation is followed by the parousia (verse 8b), the author states that the rebel's parousia is κατ' ('by', indicating means/agency) ἐνέργειαν τοῦ σατανᾶ ἐν πάσῃ δυνάμει . . . καὶ ἐν πάσῃ ἀπάτῃ ἀδικίας. Since δυνάμει and ἀπάτῃ are singular, πάσῃ should be rendered 'all' or 'full' (cf. Phil. 1:20) rather than 'every kind of';[11] hence, 'whose parousia is (enabled) by the working of Satan in full power . . . and in full deception of wickedness'. The choice of πάσῃ is particularly important in the light of verses 6–8a's reference to the restrainer, for only after the restrainer's disappearance is Satan free to operate in his *full* power and *full* deception on behalf of his henchman. The full power is manifest in καὶ σημείοις καὶ τέρασιν ψεύδους, 'signs' and 'wonders' leading to 'deception' (cf. v. 11; cf. Rev. 13:13–14a). That

---

[8] This phrase is not found in Biblical Greek, but only in secular Greek (e.g. Plutarch, *Timoleon* 5.3, *Comparatio Niciae et Crassi* 2.6.4 and *Quaestiones conviviales* 618 D1; Achilles Tatius, *Leucippe and Clitophon* 2.27.2; Ps.-Aeschines, *Ep.* 12:6), where it means 'be removed', 'disappear' (cf. 1 Cor. 5:2; Col. 2:14). Barnouin's rendering of ἐκ μέσου γένηται, 'come out of a state of restriction' ('Problèmes', 494–6), lacks substantiation and is dependent on his rather implausible reconstruction of verses 6–7's syntax.

[9] Cf. Milligan, *Thessalonians*, 101 and Additional Note H; H. Hanse, 'κατέχω', *TDNT*, 2:829–30; Stephens, 'Themes', 351, 355, 327–38.

[10] See Liddell and Scott, *Lexicon*, 926. The context usually indicates the relevant nuance of κατέχω; for example, where the subject and object of κατέχω are two opponents, 'restrain' is the most likely option. For examples of κατέχω being used of restraining, or holding in captivity, see *Papyri Graecae Magicae. Die Griechischen Zauberpapyri* (ed. K. Preisendanz; Stuttgart: Teubner, vol. 1: 1928; vol. 2: 1941; vol. 3: Leipzig and Berlin: Teubner, 1941), 13.804–5; P15a; P. Giess. 70.3; cf. P. Flor. 61, 60; *BGU* 372 1.16; P. Oxy. 101.3644.30; 105.3807.38, 42; 106.3859.8; 108.3932.11; 109.3979.13; 109.4000.12; Appian, *Bell. Civ.* 2.149 §622; Themistocles, *Ep.* 13.4; Philo, *Leg. All.* 3.21; LXX Gen. 24:56; 42:19; Judg. 13:15, 16; 19:4; Ruth 1:13; Job 34:14.

[11] *Pace* Lünemann, *Thessalonians*, 220; Rigaux, *Thessaloniciens*, 674–5; Bassin, *Thessaloniciens*, 248; Richard, *Thessalonians*, 334; NIV.

Satan's full power and full deception are utilised to seduce this group means that the perishing will inevitably succumb (cf. Rev. 13:14b, and 3–4, 8) and the eschatological rebellion (2 Thess. 2:3) certainly occur. Clearly, then, the restrainer's present activity functions both to hold back the rebel's revelation until the appointed time and to prevent the premature unleashing of Satan's full power and full deception.

The restrainer: the options

The κατέχων/κατέχον ('restrainer') has been variously identified as: (1) (a) the Roman emperor/empire[12] or (b) a particular human ruler/the principle of law and order;[13] (2) Paul/the proclamation of the Gospel;[14] (3) Satan/rebellion;[15] (4) God/God's will and/or plan;[16] and (5) the Holy Spirit.[17] Each of these suggestions has considerable problems. Concerning option (1), given that the ἀνομία is rebellion not against human authority, but rather against God's revelation, it is difficult to understand exactly how or why human government or rulers would restrain the ἀνομία and

[12] Proponents of this view have included Tertullian, *De Carnis Resurrectione* 24; Hippolytus, *Commentary on Daniel* 4.21; Bornemann, *Thessalonicherbriefe*, 325; W. Bousset, *The Antichrist Legend* (trans. A. H. Keane; London: Hutchinson, 1896), 123ff.; R. H. Charles, *A Critical History of the Doctrine of a Future Life* (2nd edn; JL; London: A. & C. Black, 1913), 440; cf. Wanamaker, *Thessalonians*, 256–7.

[13] This has been suggested by, among others, Lightfoot, *Notes*, 114; Milligan, *Thessalonians*, 101; Morris, *Thessalonians*, 227; Richard, *Thessalonians*, 338–40.

[14] See, for example, O. Cullmann, 'Le Caractère eschatologique du devoir missionaire et de la conscience apostolique de saint Paul. Etude sur le κατέχον (-ων) de 2 Thess. 2:6–7', *RHPR* 16 (1936), 210–45; J. Munck, *Paul and the Salvation of Mankind* (trans. F. Clarke; London: SCM, 1959), 36–42; cf. A. L. Moore, *The Parousia in the New Testament* (NovTSup; Leiden: Brill, 1966), 112–14, who contends that it is probably a reference to 'Paul himself, or more probably ... "the preacher" who gives actual form to the restraining force, τὸ κατέχον, namely the gospel itself'.

[15] See, for example, Frame, *Thessalonians*, 261–2 (although he concludes on a rather agnostic note); Dixon, 'Restraint', 446–9; cf. Best, *Thessalonians*, 299–302.

[16] See, for example, A. Strobel, *Untersuchungen zum eschatologischen Verzögerungsproblem auf Grund der spätjüdisch-urchristlichen Geschichte von Habakuk 2.2ff.* (NovTSup; Leiden: Brill, 1961), 98–116; J. Ernst, *Die Eschatologischen Gegenspieler in den Schriften des Neuen Testamentes* (BU; Regensburg: Friedrich Pustet, 1967), 55ff.; Stephens, 'Themes', 304–62; Burkeen, 'Parousia', 348–50.

[17] See, for example, Thomas, 'Thessalonians', 324–5. Ford, *Abomination*, 218–25 sees the restrainer as the Holy Spirit through human government, whilst A. J. McNicol, *Jesus' Directions for the Future* (NGS; Macon, Ga: Mercer, 1996), 59–60 argues for the Spirit through the preaching of the Gospel and church growth, and C. E. Powell, 'The Identity of the "Restrainer" in 2 Thessalonians 2:6–7', *BSac* 154 (1997): 328–32 for the Spirit as the κατέχων and the preaching of the Gospel as the κατέχον. D. W. MacDougall, 'The Authenticity of II Thessalonians with special reference to its Use of Traditional Material' (Ph.D. thesis, University of Aberdeen, 1993), chapter 5 has suggested that the restrainer is the church.

why the removal of such a restrainer would permit the rebel's revelation.[18] And that Caligula came so close to blasphemous desecration not dissimilar to that of the eschatological rebel of 2 Thess. 2:3b–4 surely renders dubious the idea that this author viewed the imperial government as serving such a positive eschatological role. Moreover, *contra* (1a), if the Roman empire and/or its emperor had to fall, that would constitute a further sign in addition to the ἀποστασία and the rebel's revelation; yet the author explicitly states that only these latter two are the signs (2:3b). Indeed, to have such a specific and definite contemporary historical reference seems out of place in a passage which otherwise keeps to veiled and allusive language.[19] Finally, the lack of substantial parallels to the concept of the Roman government as a *restrainer* also speaks against this view.[20]

Regarding option (2), even when we allow the presupposition that Paul wrote 2 Thessalonians, at the time of writing 1 Thessalonians Paul clearly expected to survive until the parousia (1 Thess. 4:15, 17). Furthermore, it is unclear why Paul would have referred to himself and his death in such a cryptic way and why his death would result in the revelation of the rebel.

We now turn to supernatural options,[21] which seem to be more suitable candidates for the task of restraining the eschatological rebel. Concerning option (3), the fact that the rebel's parousia is 'by (κατά) the working of Satan' (2 Thess. 2:9–10a) renders Satan a highly implausible restrainer. Moreover, it is unclear why his removal would bring about the rebel's revelation. Options (4) and (5) are eliminated since neither God nor his Spirit can be spoken of as being 'removed from the scene'. With regard to the former, in 2 Thess. 2:11–12, subsequent to the restrainer's removal, God is portrayed as actively deluding the perishing, causing them to believe the rebel's lie. With regard to the latter, in Pauline (and presumably Paulinist) thought the Holy Spirit abides with believers until the

---

[18] As Ford, *Abomination*, 218 writes, 'There needs to be some logical connection demonstrated between the work of hindering and the nature of the object hindered.'

[19] Cf. Frame, *Thessalonians*, 260; Masson, *Thessaloniciens*, 99; Best, *Thessalonians*, 296. Indeed, in the light of the author's imminentism (1:6–7a, 10) and Daniel's prophecy that the eschatological anti-God rebel would head an earthly kingdom which would have Israel within its jurisdiction (Dan. 7:24–5), it is arguable that the rebel would have been conceived of as a future Roman emperor.

[20] Indeed, as Peerbolte, '2 Thess. 2:6–7', 142 (cf. Friedrich, 'Zweite Brief', 265) notes, contemporary Jewish and Christian eschatology tended to portray Rome in a bad light (e.g. Revelation 17–18; Sib. Or. 7.108–13; 8.37–193).

[21] It should be noted that the earthly and supernatural options are not necessarily mutually exclusive. See n. 17 above for examples of eclectic proposals.

parousia.[22] Further, why would the author have referred to God or his Spirit in such exceptionally enigmatic terms?[23] The question is, who or what could the supernatural figure be if not Satan, God or the Holy Spirit? It seems that we are forced to the view put forward by a number of interpreters that the restrainer is an angel.[24] Only an angel could restrain the eschatological rebel's revelation, execute God's will and be removed. Further, an interpretation along these lines seems to accord best with the apocalyptic nature of the passage. Nevertheless, the failure of proponents to posit a precise background for the concept of the restrainer and for the restrainer's removal in contemporary Judaism or Christianity represents the biggest obstacle to acceptance of this angelic hypothesis. It is at this point that we propose to make a contribution.

Without doubt the most plausible angelic candidate for the restrainer is the archangel Michael.[25] In Jewish and Christian thought Michael was

[22] Attempts to change the subject of ἐκ μέσου γένηται from the κατέχων to the rebel and render it 'emerges out of the midst' (Farrow, 'Showdown', 25) are illegitimate grammatically and lexically. Further, the attempt of Powell, 'Identity', 331 to limit the removal of the Spirit to the removal of his restraining ministry through the church (cf. R. H. Gundry, *The Church and the Tribulation* (Grand Rapids: Zondervan, 1973), 126–7, who argues that it is the removal of the restraining ministry, although not through the church) seems invalid since the subject of the removal is referred to with respect to his person (note the masculine κατέχων).

[23] Strobel, *Untersuchungen*, 98–116 (cf. Ernst, *Gegenspieler*, 55ff.) based his case that God was the κατέχων on Hab. 2:3, but the influence of this text on 2 Thess. 2:6–7 cannot be substantiated: note that κατέχω occurs here but χρονίζω in Hab. 2:3 and that κατέχω does not normally mean 'delay'. For more criticism of Strobel, see Fraser, 'Study', 238–9.

[24] See Marshall, *Thessalonians*, 199–200 and Menken, *Thessalonians*, 113.

[25] We have traced the following proponents of this view: J. B. Orchard, 'Thessalonians and the Synoptic Gospels', *Bib* 19 (1938): 40–1; F. Prat, *The Theology of Saint Paul* (trans. J. L. Stoddard; 4th edn; 2 vols.; Washington: Burns, Oates and Washbourne, 1942), 1:82–3; J. M. G. Ruiz, 'La incredulidad de Israel y los impedimentos del Anticristo segun 2 Tes 2.6f.', *EstBib* 10 (1951): 189–203; P. G. Rinaldi, *Le Lettere ai Tessalonicesi* (Milan: G. Daverio, 1951), 157–8 and *La Sacra Bibbia: Daniele* (Turin and Rome: Marietti, 1962), 150–1; L. Turrado, *Biblia commentada VI – Hechos de los Apostoles y Epistolas paulinas* (BAC; Madrid, 1965), 671–2; G. Vos, *The Pauline Eschatology* (reprint: Grand Rapids: Eerdmans, 1972), 131–2; H. Ridderbos, *Paul: An Outline of his Theology* (trans. J. R. DeWitt; Grand Rapids: Eerdmans, 1975), 525; E. M. Rusten, 'A Critical Evaluation of the Dispensationalist Interpretation of the Book of Revelation' (Ph.D. diss., New York University, 1975), 449–57; Fraser, 'Study', 289–301; Goulder, 'Silas', 99; C. M. Pate, *The Glory of Adam and the Afflictions of the Righteous: Pauline Suffering in Context* (New York: Edwin Mellen, 1993), 307–9; D. D. Hannah, *Michael and Christ: Michael Traditions and Angel Christology in Early Christianity* (WUNT; Tübingen: Mohr, 1999), 132–4 (cf. his 'The Angelic Restrainer', in *Calling Time* (ed. M. Percy; Sheffield: Sheffield Academic Press, 2000), 29–45); cf. H. Gunkel, *Schöpfung und Chaos* (1st edn; Göttingen: Vandenhoeck & Ruprecht, 1895), 224–5. Note the claim of Prat, *Theology*, 82–3: 'Until the baffled exegetes have found a better solution it is here that we shall seek for the mysterious "obstacle" that retards the appearance of the Antichrist.'

a major figure: one of the archangels (e.g. 1 Enoch 9:1; 20:1–7; 71:3; 4 Bar. 9:5; T. Abr. A 1:4; *Num. R.* 2:10), usually the most important one (e.g. 1 Enoch 24:6; T. Isaac 2:1; Asc. Isa. 3:15–16; 1QM 17:7; 3 Enoch 17:3; *b.Ber.* 4b; *b.Yoma* 37a; cf. Dan. 7:13–14?;[26] Jub. 1:27–2:1?; *Pirqe R. El.* 4),[27] charged with the task of defending Israel (e.g. 1 Enoch 20:5; T. Mos. 10:2?; *Pirqe R. El.* 26, 33, 36, 38, 42, 50; *Tg. Ps.-J. Gen.* 38:25–6; *Exod. R.* 18:5; *Esth. R.* 7:12; 10:9; cf. Dan. 7:13–14?; CD 5:17b–19?; 1QM 9:15–16; 13:10; 17:6–8a; 11QMelch 2:5ff.[28]) and of interceding for it (e.g. T. Abr. A 14:5–6, 12ff.; T. Dan. 6:2; T. Levi 5:5–6; *Ruth R. proem* 1; *b.Yoma* 77a; *Pesiq. R.* 44; cf. 3 Bar. 11:4–9; 14:2; *Pirqe R. El.* 37; *Tg. Ps.-J. Gen.* 32:25). He was often regarded as a military angel (e.g. 1QM 9:15–16; 17:6–8; *Exod. R.* 18:5), indeed the *archistrategos* (e.g. 1 Enoch 90:14; 2 Enoch 22:6–7; 33:10–11; 72:5 (J); T. Abr. A 1:4; 2:1ff.; 19:5; T. Abr. B 14:7; 1QM 17:6–8a; 3 Bar. 11:4ff. (Grk); Gr. Apoc. Ezra 4:24; cf. Origen, PG 12:821), and as having a significant eschatological role (e.g. T. Levi 5:5–6; 1QM 9:14–16; *Exod. R.* 18:5; cf. Dan. 12:1; 1 Enoch 68:2–5; Rev. 12:7–9; 4Q285:10; 3 Bar. 11:2; Apoc. Paul 14),[29] as exemplified in his blowing the trumpet at the final judgment (e.g. Apoc. Mos. 22:1; cf. especially 1 Thess. 4:16).[30] Michael was the primary opponent of Satan/Belial (e.g. 1 Enoch 69; Adam and Eve 13–14; 1QM 17:5–6; *Exod. R.* 18:5; cf. 1 Enoch 88:3; Jude 9; Rev. 12:7–9; *Pirqe R. El.* 27, 42; *Ques. Barth.* 4:52–5; Origen, *Princ.* 3.2.1; Gelasius Cyzicenus, *Eccles. Hist.* 2.21.7),[31] whom he defeats at the end (e.g. T. Mos. 10:1–2?; cf. 1QM

---

[26] N. Schmidt, 'The Son of Man in the Book of Daniel', *JBL* 19 (1900): 22–8; C. Rowland, *The Open Heaven: A Study of Apocalyptic in Judaism and Early Christianity* (New York: Crossroad, 1982), 178–82 and J. J. Collins, *Daniel* (Hermeneia; Minneapolis: Fortress, 1993), 304–10, 318–19 identify the Son of Man in Dan. 7:13–14 as Michael.

[27] Notably Theodoret linked the Colossian 'worship of angels' with a cult of the archangel Michael in Pisidia and Phrygia (PG 82:613). In Hekhalot literature Metatron, probably originally Michael, has been elevated to divine status; see Hannah, *Michael*, 116–21.

[28] It is likely that Melchizedek in the Dead Sea Scrolls is Michael (11QMelch 2:5ff.; 4Q'Amram 2:3ff.; 3:2; cf. 1QM 13:10; 17:7); see especially Hannah, *Michael*, 70–4. The sectarians in Qumran viewed Michael as leading them into battle. While Michael was a prominent and significant figure in the sectarians' thought, he is mentioned directly and explicitly in their sectarian literature rarely (1QM 9:15–16; 17:6–7; 4Q470:2, 5 and 4Q529:1).

[29] He was also widely thought of as the guide of the souls of the righteous into paradise (T. Abr. A 20:1–12; Jude 9; Apoc. Mos. 37; *Deut. R.* 11:10; cf. T. Isaac 2:1ff.; 6:24ff.; T. Jac. 1:5–6; T. Abr. B 14:7; also Adam and Eve 47; Apoc. Paul 22, 25–7).

[30] R. H. Charles, 'Michael', in *A Dictionary of the Bible* (ed. J. Hastings; 5 vols.; Edinburgh: T. & T. Clark, 1900–4), 3:362–3 wrote, 'As the end draws nigh the strife grows fiercer, and Michael, Israel's angelic guardian, becomes the great hero of the last days.'

[31] It seems that Michael was commonly invoked by those seeking to overpower demons (T. Sol. 1:6–7; 6:8; 18:1–42; 22:20; cf. *PGM* 1.300–1; 43.1–27; 79.1–7; 80.1–5).

13:10) and, as one of the archangels, he was going to punish the fallen angels (e.g. 1 Enoch 10:11ff.; 54:6).[32]

This pre-eminence of Michael in contemporary Jewish thought, especially as *archistrategos*, opponent of Satan and protector of God's people, renders him an especially plausible candidate for the role of 'restrainer'.[33] However, could the author of 2 Thessalonians have conceived of Michael as a *restrainer* who would be *removed* before the revelation of the rebel in 2 Thess. 2:6–7? We propose that Michael could reasonably have been, and indeed was, viewed as a restrainer and that there is good reason to think that the author of 2 Thessalonians thought of Michael as one who would be removed immediately before the onset of the final unequalled distress, at the point when the final temple desecration was about to occur.

Michael as a restrainer

Given that Daniel was the primary source of the concept of an eschatological antagonist in early Christianity, any investigation into the identity of the restrainer of the antagonist's 'revelation' or 'parousia' should begin there. That the author of 2 Thessalonians is dependent on Daniel in his portrayal of the man of lawlessness is indicated by his allusion to Dan. 11:36–7 in 2 Thess. 2:4a and by his reference to a final, literal desecration of the Jerusalem temple[34] in 2 Thess. 2:4b, which is rooted in Daniel's

---

[32] See W. Lueken, *Michael. Eine Darstellung und Vergleichung der jüdischen und der morgenländisch-christlichen Tradition vom Erzengel Michael* (Göttingen: Vandenhoeck & Ruprecht, 1898), esp. 24ff., 106ff. and, more recently, J. P. Rohland, *Der Erzengel Michael: Arzt und Feldherr, zwei Aspekte des vor- und frühbyzantinischen Michaelskultes* (BZRGG; Leiden: Brill, 1977); Hannah, *Michael*, 25–162. It is also likely that in Qumran Michael was the Angel of Light (1QM 17:6–8a), the Prince of Light (1QM 13:10; 1QS 3:20) and the Angel of His Truth (1QS 3:24), who fought for the sons of light against the sons of darkness, who are led by the Angel of Darkness (1QS 3:20–2).

[33] Evidence like this leads Prat, *Theology*, 82–3 (cf. Rinaldi, *Daniele*, 150–1 and *Tessalonicesi*, 157–8) and Fraser, 'Study', 291–300 to the conclusion that Michael is the restrainer. Ruiz, 'Incredulidad', 195–203 argues from Michael's role as Israel's protector in Dan. 10:12–14; 12:1; 1 Enoch 20:5; T. Levi 5:6 and T. Dan 6:2. Pate, *Glory*, 307–9 bases his case primarily on the references to Michael in Daniel 7, 11, 12 and Revelation 12 and 13. Hannah, *Michael*, 132–4 argues from Michael's activity in Dan. 10:13 and 21, from the coincidence of Michael's 'coming' and the career of the 'Antichrist' in Dan. 12:1, from the author of 2 Thessalonians' use of Dan. 11:36–7 in 2 Thess. 2:3–4, from Michael's opposition to Satan in Jude and Rev. 12:7 and from *PGM* 4.2770. Up to this point, however, no one has explained the most important point of 2:6–7: the origin of the concept of Michael's removal. Moreover, the Danielic background for the idea that Michael is a restrainer has never been fully explored; neither has a proponent of the Michael hypothesis offered a satisfactory explanation for the author's employment of the masculine and the neuter in reference to Michael.

[34] Τὸν ναὸν τοῦ θεοῦ is the Jerusalem temple: (1) since the author is contradicting the false eschatological claim of 2:2c, we would expect a concrete, observable and conspicuous

prophecies (Dan. 9:27; 12:11; cf. 8:13; 11:31). Therefore our suggestion that the background for the idea of the restrainer in 2 Thess. 2:6–7 is the vision of a great צבא (Dan. 10:1 MT) found in Dan. 10:1–12:3, in which Michael functions to restrain the forces of evil, is quite natural and plausible. צבא literally means 'army';[35] in the light of the use of the term in Dan. 8:10–12 and in view of the references to Michael, the commander of the heavenly army, in 10:13, 20–1 and 12:1, this may indicate that the angelic revelation of Daniel 10:10–12:3 relates primarily to what Michael and his army are doing. Alternatively, we might render צבא 'war'[36] (10:1), and interpret it as covering two dimensions: first and foremost, a celestial one in which Michael combats the princes of the Persian and Greek kingdoms (10:20–1; cf. verse 13) and, second, an earthly one centred on kings of the North and kings of the South (11:2–45), followed by a further glimpse of the celestial war (12:1a) and then of the earthly situation (12:1b–3).

This, together with the fact that the celestial scene relates to the Princes of Persia and then Greece (10:20) and the earthly one to Persian and then Greek rulers (11:2ff.), suggests that there is interplay between the two realms,[37] with what happens in heaven determining what happens on earth.[38] We may wonder why Michael is fighting the princes of Persia

event; (2) the use of καθίσαι seems more naturally to suggest a literal, physical temple; (3) the definite articles clearly allude to a particular temple of the true God, which can only refer to the Jerusalem temple; (4) the immediately preceding reference to σέβασμα favours a material temple.

[35] Aquila translates it with στρατεία and Theodotion with δύναμις (cf. Vulgate). The LXX's πλῆθος is peculiar.

[36] So J. E. Goldingay, *Daniel* (WBC; Dallas: Word, 1988), 275 n. 1d; NIV; NASB; S. R. Miller, *Daniel* (NAC; Nashville, Tenn.: Broadman & Holman, 1994), 277; cf. L. F. Hartman and A. A. DiLella, *The Book of Daniel* (AB; Garden City, N.Y.: Doubleday, 1978), 262.

[37] As J. B. Doukhan, *Daniel: The Vision of the End* (Berrien Springs, Mich.: Andrews University Press, 1987), 75 writes, 'The battle will take place on both fronts, heaven and earth, implying . . . a special connection between the two.' Goldingay, *Daniel*, 292–3: it is 'the heavenly correspondents of these earthly powers' who are 'restrained' by Michael and the revelatory angel.

[38] P. David, 'Daniel 11,1: A Late Gloss?', in *The Book of Daniel in the light of New Findings* (ed. A. S. van der Woude; BETL; Louvain: Leuven University Press, 1993), 509–10 also contends that the celestial, supra-historical battle lies behind the historical situation. Cf. G. L. Archer, 'Daniel', in *EBC*, 7:127–8. S. R. Driver, *The Book of Daniel* (CBSC; Cambridge: Cambridge University Press, 1905), 157: 'The idea of the passage is that the fortunes of nations are determined by the angels representing them in heaven: the success or failure of these angels regulating the success or failure of the nations themselves.' Goldingay, *Daniel*, 291–2: 'there are heavenly armies that oppose Yahweh, so that earthly battles reflect battles in heaven; whichever side wins in heaven, its equivalent wins on earth.' Note that in 1QM 17:7 when Michael is exalted among the angels, Israel is exalted among humans. In Dan. 11:1 the revelatory angel 'strengthened and defended' (MT) Darius in the first year of his reign, when the decree to rebuild Jerusalem and specifically the temple went forth, presumably because the prince over Persia would have disapproved of such favour being extended to God's people.

and Greece.[39] One clue is located in 10:21, where he bears the title 'your prince' according to the MT.[40] Another clue is found in 12:1, where he is called 'the great prince who stands over your people' (MT) or 'the great angel who stands over the sons of your people' (LXX). Michael combats the princes of Persia and Greece, who presumably were attempting to work evil against God's people, in his capacity as the protector of Daniel's people. We see a glimpse of Michael's role in 10:13, where the revelatory angel, on a mission to respond to Daniel's prayers (10:12) by revealing to Daniel the destiny of his people in the end of days (10:14), encounters opposition from the prince of Persia which retains him for twenty-one days. In this instance Michael intervenes to help the revelatory angel and restrain the prince of Persia, thereby allowing the angel to show Daniel God's sovereign plan for history (10:13). It would seem therefore that Michael's overarching task is to ensure the proclamation (to Daniel) and actual accomplishment of God's sovereign will with particular regard to God's people in the face of the schemes of the princes of Persia and Greece.

In the light of this, the purpose of Dan. 11:2–45's terrestrial revelation emerges. The focus is on those nations which directly affect Daniel's people. The main, recurring theme of 11:2ff. is the failure to prevail (especially 11:4, 5, 6b, 7a, 9, 11, 12–13a, 14, 15b, 17b, 18b–19, 20b, 24b, 25b–26, 27b, 30a, 41b, 44). One notes that, as far as God's people are concerned, matters could be worse: even during the period when a desolator abominates and brutally persecutes the people of God (verses 30b–35), they will receive 'a little help' (verse 34). It seems undeniable that this sketch of the rise and fall of numerous human rulers is intended to reveal the impact of Michael's resistance to the princes of Persia and subsequent kingdoms. While the princes of the kingdoms attempt to concentrate power in the hands of individuals hostile to divine purposes, and to stop God's purpose for human history coming to fulfilment, especially as it relates to God's people, Michael restrains[41] these

[39] Dan. 10:20b is perhaps best interpreted as referring to the revelatory angel's leaving the battle against the prince of Persia (Driver, *Daniel*, 161; R. H. Charles, *A Critical and Exegetical Commentary on the Book of Daniel* (Oxford: Clarendon, 1929), 266; Collins, *Daniel*, 376) rather than his departure from Daniel; hence the Greek prince arises to fight after the Persian one has finished fighting.

[40] The LXXp-967 has 'the angel'. Moreover, LXXp-967 adds 'the powerful commander who stands over the sons of your people' (*Der Septuaginta-Text des Buches Daniel Kap. 5–12, zusammen mit Susanna, Bel et Draco* (ed. A. Geissen; PTA; Bonn: Rudolf Habelt, 1968), 240–1); but this LXXp-967 reading is probably a gloss introduced from 12:1 (so also David, 'Daniel 11, 1', 511).

[41] Note Theodotion's use of ἀντεχόμενος in Dan. 10:21: καὶ οὐκ ἔστιν εἷς ἀντεχόμενος μετʼ ἐμοῦ περὶ τούτων ἀλλʼ ἢ Μιχαηλ ὁ ἄρχων ὑμῶν (cf. Hannah, *Michael*, 133).

princes and helps God's people, thwarting the advances of earthly kingdoms and thus causing kings to fail in their attempts to secure ever more
power.[42] He acts in his capacity as celestial ally and guardian of God's
people and as primary opponent of the celestial princes of Persia and
Greece.

In Daniel 10–12, then, Michael has been cast as a restrainer.[43] The
major question which we must yet address is, was he regarded as such
subsequent to the writing of Daniel?

That Michael was thought of specifically as a restrainer within Judaism
appears to be demonstrated in one of the *Zauberpapyri* (*Papyri Graecae
Magicae*), the great Paris magical papyrus, where κατέχων is employed
with the sense of 'restraining' to describe the archangel Michael's activity
with regard to the great dragon (the devil): ὁ ἐπάνω καθήμενος Μιχαήλ·
ἑπτὰ ὑδάτων κρατεῖς καὶ γῆς, κατέχων, ὃν καλέουσι δράκοντα μέγαν.[44]
This striking reference to Michael apparently testifies to the existence of
a Jewish adaptation of the ancient chaos myth, almost certainly based
on Daniel 10–12.[45] In 1937 Dibelius proposed that the ancient chaos
myth constituted the narrative framework for the concept of the κατέχων
(-ον) in 2 Thess. 2:6–7.[46] This hypothesis works best if we suppose that
the author would have transposed the cosmological myth into a strictly
Jewish/Christian theological framework.[47] While Gunkel suggested that

---

[42] In the Testament of Solomon demons have thwarting angels assigned to them (e.g.
T. Sol. 2:4 mentions that the demon Ornias has the thwarting angel Ouriel and 5:9 states
that Asmodeus is thwarted by Raphael). The origin of this concept may well be Daniel
10–12, where the princes of Persia and Greece are thwarted by Michael and the anonymous
revelatory angel. Cf. 4Q270 10:2:18.

[43] Angels were often conceived of as executing a binding function in apocalyptic literature (e.g. 1 Enoch 10:4ff.; 18:12ff.; 21:1ff.; T. Levi 18:12; Rev. 20:1ff.).

[44] *PGM* 4.2768–72. O'Neil as cited by H. D. Betz, ed., *The Greek Magical Papyri in
Translation* (Chicago: University of Chicago Press, 1986), 90 renders κατέχων here 'keeping in check'. In *PGM* 1.300–1 we find καὶ σὲ τὸν οὐράνιον κόσμον κατέχοντα, Μιχαήλ
(cf. 3.211–12, where the same is used of Raphael), but there κατέχω means 'possess'. For
more on angels in the Greek magical papyri, see L. T. Stuckenbruck, *Angel Veneration and
Christology* (WUNT; Tübingen: Mohr, 1995), 194–200.

[45] While this papyrus dates from the third or fourth century, it is commonly agreed that
many of its concepts, doctrines and formulae reflect traditions which are much earlier, from
the first century BC to the second century AD. On this issue, see especially A. D. Nock,
'Greek Magical Papyri', in *Essays on Religion and the Ancient World* (ed. Z. Stewart; 2 vols.;
Oxford: Clarendon, 1972), 1:176–94; G. Luck, *Arcana Mundi: Magic and the Occult in
the Greek and Roman Worlds* (Baltimore: Johns Hopkins, 1985), 14, 16–17; Betz, *Magical*,
xlv. A case for the relevance of the Greek magical papyri for the first-century AD Greco-
Roman world has been made by C. E. Arnold, *Ephesians: Power and Magic* (SNTSMS;
Cambridge: Cambridge University Press, 1989).

[46] Dibelius, *Thessalonicher*, 47–51.

[47] Cf. Masson, *Thessaloniciens*, 99. Note the criticism of irrelevance in Giblin,
Threat, 20.

Elijah replaced the mythical divine warrior in its transposed form,[48] Daniel 10–12 and the *Zauberpapyrus* (and Rev. 12:7–9) make Michael a much more plausible candidate.[49] The Danielic traditions concerning Michael's celestial functions were taken up and expanded in apocalyptic, Qumranic and rabbinic literature. Michael became especially prominent as the heavenly protector and ally of God's people and the primary opponent of Belial, and, moreover, as the *archistrategos*, the highest archangel, the eschatological hero and the heavenly intercessor on behalf of Israel, as we demonstrated above.[50] Indeed, we even find the Danielic idea that Michael's heavenly activities vis-à-vis Belial determine the fate of the earthly people of God (vis-à-vis the sons of darkness) in 1QM 17:5–8a.[51] Hence Danielic Michael traditions which were constituent parts of the idea that Michael was a restrainer of eschatological evil were apparently quite well known in Second Temple Judaism and would almost certainly have been familiar to the author of 2 Thessalonians.

We propose then that Michael could legitimately have been viewed as a celestial restrainer, on the basis of Daniel 10–12, and indeed that there is good reason to conclude that he was thought of by at least some contemporaries of the author of 2 Thessalonians in precisely this way. We turn next to examine whether Michael could have been thought of as 'disappearing' or 'being removed'.

The removal of Michael

The fact that the author of 2 Thessalonians bases his expectation of a final, supremely arrogant and blasphemous antagonist in 2 Thess. 2:4a on Dan. 11:36–7 suggests that he is interpreting Dan. 11:36ff. as referring not to Antiochus IV Epiphanes, but rather to a still-future figure (much as did

---

[48] Gunkel, *Schöpfung*, 223ff. Dibelius, *Thessalonicher*, 47–51 suggested that the author may not have had a clear idea of precisely who or what the κατέχων (-ον) was.

[49] Note that in 1 Enoch 20:6 (Grk), Michael is said to be 'set over the best part of humanity and *chaos*' (italics mine).

[50] Also, in 4Q552–3 we find a reference to the prince of Persia and apparently to princes of Greece and Rome, which is almost certainly derived from Dan. 10:13–21. In 1 Thess. 2:17–18 Paul attributes to Satan's working the failure of the missionaries to return to Thessalonica; it seems plausible that this is an example of celestial Satanic opposition being perceived behind earthly obstacles.

[51] See A. J. Tomasino, 'Daniel and the Revolutionaries: The Use of Daniel Tradition by Jewish Resistance Movements of Late Second-Temple Palestine' (Ph.D. diss., University of Chicago, 1995), 141–4. More generally, the idea that events in the celestial realm have a direct bearing on terrestrial events is found elsewhere in the War Scroll (e.g. 1QM 11:16–17; 12:4–5; 16:11).

Hippolytus and Jerome[52] after him). It also demonstrates that the author's portrait of the eschatological opponent of God is significantly dependent on Dan. 11:36ff. In the light of this, an appeal to Dan. 11:45–12:1 as the background of the reference to the *removal* of the restrainer of 2 Thess. 2:6–7 has some credibility.

We commence with the reference in Dan. 11:45a to the eschatological opponent's activity vis-à-vis the 'glorious, holy hill', the hill of Zion, the *locus* of the Jerusalem temple.

MT: ויטע אהלי אפדנו בין ימים להר־צבי־קדש

LXX: καὶ στήσει αὐτοῦ τὴν σκηνὴν τότε ἀνὰ μέσον τῶν θαλασσῶν καὶ τοῦ ὄρους τῆς θελήσεως τοῦ ἁγίου.

Theodotion: καὶ πήξει τὴν σκηνὴν αὐτοῦ εφαδανω ἀνὰ μέσον τῶν θαλασσῶν εἰς ὄρος σαβι [= Rahlfs; σαβαιν = Ziegler] ἅγιον.

The MT, LXX and Theodotion are agreed that the eschatological opponent is establishing his tents, but not in regard to the precise place

---

52 Hippolytus, *Commentary on Daniel* 4.48–50; Jerome, *Commentary on Daniel*, in loc. (Patrologiae Cursus Completus: Series Latina 25:570ff.). While the consensus of modern scholarship is that Daniel is a Maccabean pseudepigraph and that Dan. 11:36ff./11:40ff. represent the author's mistaken predictions regarding Antiochus Epiphanes, one cannot assume that the author of 2 Thessalonians shared this view. The claim in Dan. 11:40 is that verses 40ff. refer to the time of the end, and we have every reason to think that readers after Antiochus' death would have assumed that they applied to a still-future opponent of God. Tomasino ('Daniel') has argued plausibly that 1QM 1 (cf. 10–19) is based primarily on Dan. 11:40–12:3, and more generally on Daniel 7–12 (pp. 118–50; cf. F. F. Bruce, *Biblical Exegesis in the Qumran Texts* (Exegetica; Grand Rapids: Eerdmans, 1959), 62–5), and that 1QM interprets Dan. 11:40ff. as referring to the still-future downfall of the Romans (Kittim) at the point when they invade Egypt, and to the simultaneous incoming of God's Kingdom (pp. 126–40; interestingly, the Qumran identification of the king of the North as the king of the Kittim indicates that the close of Daniel 11 (11:36ff./11:40ff.) was being interpreted in isolation from the first part of the chapter, where the Kittim oppose the king of the North (11:30)). He also suggests that 4Q285 (pp. 150–8) reflects a similar understanding of Dan. 11:40ff. and that 4Q246 (pp. 180–93, esp. 188–93) paints a picture of an eschatological God-opposing ruler of the world, which is probably derived from Dan. 11:36ff. Josephus provides some evidence that Dan. 9:27, and perhaps 11:36ff., was understood by some in the late first century as referring to Rome as the last eschatological kingdom before God's intervention (esp. *Ant.* 10.276; cf. 10.195–211; see R. Marcus, *Josephus: Jewish Antiquities* (LCL; Cambridge, Mass.: Harvard University Press, 1987), 8:310–11 n. c; Tomasino, 'Daniel', 252 n. 55, 260–72, 276–306). It is difficult to know to what degree Rome was identified specifically as the fourth kingdom of Daniel 7 before the Jewish War (see Tomasino, 'Daniel', chapter 7); 4Q552–3 seems to suggest that Rome is the third kingdom, with God's kingdom being the fourth and final one. Certainly the identification of the fourth kingdom as Rome was common in later literature, for example 4 Ezra 11–12; 2 Baruch 36–40 and *Bahodesh* 9 (see Tomasino, 'Daniel', 265–9).

where the opponent does so. The Hebrew בֵּין followed by לְ is subject to two readings reflected in the Greek translations: it is an example either of 'between . . . and' (cf. LXX)[53] or of 'between . . . at/toward' (cf. Theodotion; Aquila; Symmachus).[54] According to the first reading, the opponent establishes his tents between the sea[55] and the temple mount; according to the second, he establishes them between the seas at or facing the temple mount.[56] It is difficult to avoid the conclusion that the latter reading reflects a tradition of interpretation which understands Dan. 11:45a as alluding to the final abomination of desolation, which elsewhere in Daniel is apparently an immediate harbinger of the coming of God's kingdom (esp. 9:27; 12:11; cf. 7:24b–27). Understanding Dan. 11:45a as alluding to the abomination of desolation is comprehensible in the period after Antiochus' death, when those who accepted Daniel's prophecies as authentic would naturally have looked for a further, more complete fulfilment of his prophecies relating to the abomination of desolation.

Certainly there is some indication that Dan. 11:45a was understood by at least some in the first century AD as alluding to the future time immediately preceding the abomination of desolation. Matthew (24:15–26) and Mark (13:14–22) both attribute to Jesus the view that Daniel's prophecy concerning unequalled tribulation (Dan. 12:1b) was inextricably bound

---

[53] Cf. Syriac; Apollinarius; Porphyry. Also J. A. Montgomery, *A Critical and Exegetical Commentary on the Book of Daniel* (ICC; Edinburgh: T. & T. Clark, 1927), 467; Charles, *Daniel*, 322; J. Barr, 'Some Notes on Ben "Between" in Classical Hebrew', *JSS* 23 (1978): 5; Hartman and DiLella, *Daniel*, 260; A. Lacocque, *The Book of Daniel* (trans. D. Pellauer; London: SPCK, 1979), 220; Collins, *Daniel*, 389. See B. K. Waltke and M. O'Connor, *An Introduction to Biblical Hebrew Syntax* (Winona Lake, Ind.: Eisenbrauns, 1990), §11.2.6 and especially Barr, 'Notes', 1–22.

[54] Also Jerome, *Commentary on Daniel*, in loc. (Patrologiae Cursus Completus: Series Latina 25:574–5); Vulgate; cf. J. Calvin, *Commentaries on the Book of the Prophet Daniel* (trans. T. Myers; 2 vols.; Edinburgh: Calvin Translation Society, 1853), 2:364–6; D. Ford, *Daniel* (Nashville, Tenn.: Southern Publishing Association, 1978), 274–5; Miller, *Daniel*, 312–13, esp. n. 115; GV; AV; NIV.

[55] This reading requires that the יַמִּים is poetical plural, as in Judg. 5:17; Deut. 33:19 and Gen. 49:13, referring to the Mediterranean Sea (Driver, *Daniel*, 200; Charles, *Daniel*, 322; Hartman and DiLella, *Daniel*, 273; Collins, *Daniel*, 389; BDB, 410; cf. Montgomery, *Daniel*, 467). The Syriac renders it as a singular.

[56] Jerome, *Commentary on Daniel*, in loc. (Patrologiae Cursus Completus: Series Latina 25:574); Ford, *Daniel*, 275; Archer, 'Daniel', 148; Miller, *Daniel*, 312; cf. Lacocque, *Daniel*, 223. While בֵּין followed by לְ occurs up to thirty times (Barr, 'Notes', 4–5, 12) meaning 'between X and Y', the plural יַמִּים in Dan. 11:45 may well be an example of a one-member בֵּין phrase (cf. Barr, 'Notes', 2–3) followed by an independent preposition לְ indicating more definitely the place where the king establishes his royal tents. In favour of this understanding is that (1) usually בֵּין plus לְ 'between . . . and' constructions are non-specific; (2) usually in 'between . . . and' constructions the total phrase is short with the 'Y'-element frequently just one word. If לְ is an independent preposition, the plural will be genuine.

up with the abomination of desolation temple desecration (when the opponent would stand where he ought not (Mark 13:14), in the holy place (Matt. 24:15)[57]), the latter heralding the commencement of the former. This could only have been derived from Dan. 11:45–12:1. That Dan. 11:45a was interpreted in this way is of particular interest to us in view of the remark in 2 Thess. 2:4b concerning the eschatological rebel's temple desecration.

In Dan. 12:1a we find a reference to Michael, the guardian of God's people, at what is clearly the climactic point of world history. The question is, what is Michael doing? It is helpful to compare the various renderings of Dan. 12:1a.

MT: ובעת ההיא יעמד מיכאל השר הגדול העמד על־בני עמך

LXX: καὶ κατὰ τὴν ὥραν ἐκείνην παρελεύσεται
           Μιχαηλ ὁ ἄγγελος ὁ μέγας ὁ ἐστηκὼς ἐπὶ τοὺς
           υἱοὺς τοῦ λαοῦ σου.

Theodotion: καὶ ἐν τῷ καιρῷ ἐκείνῳ ἀναστήσεται Μιχαηλ
           ὁ ἄρχων ὁ μέγας ὁ ἐστηκὼς ἐπὶ τοὺς υἱοὺς τοῦ
           λαοῦ σου.

It is clear that the Theodotionic ἀναστήσεται ('he will arise') is a literal translation of the Hebrew text represented in the MT, יעמד ('he will stand').[58] In contrast to this, it is not immediately obvious how the LXX translator arrived at the translation παρελεύσεται here, or indeed what he meant by it. Schneider maintains that παρέρχομαι here is 'a technical term for the appearance of an angel'.[59] However, not only is his claim of a *terminus technicus* on the basis of but one usage illegitimate, but it seems that this Greek verb never means 'appear'. Jeansonne claims that it means 'come forward' and asserts that it results from a confusion

---

[57] Cf. 1 Enoch 91–105; 2 Bar. 25–9; 32; 48:31–41; 70–2; 4 Ezra 5:1–12; 6:21–3; 9:3ff.; T. Dan 6:6; T. Levi 4:1; Sib. Or. 3; 4Q174:3–4; 4Q177:12–13; 4Q246:1–2; 4Q554 3:20–1. It is also worth noting that the Matthean and Marcan eschatological discourses warn about false Christs and false prophets performing signs and wonders (Matt. 24:23–6; Mark 13:21–3); cf. 2 Thess. 2:9–10a.

[58] While S. P. Jeansonne, *The Old Greek Translation of Daniel 7–12* (CBQMS; Washington, D.C.: Catholic Biblical Association of America, 1988), 21–2 and E. Tov, 'Die griechischen Bibelübersetzungen', *ANRW* 2:20.1 (1986): 177–8 have claimed that Theodotion is a revision of the LXX, T. McLay, 'The Theodotion and Old Greek Texts of Daniel', in *Origen's Hexapla and Fragments* (ed. A. Salvesen; TSAJ; Tübingen: Mohr, 1998), 231–54 (cf. Hartman and DiLella, *Daniel*, 82) concludes that it seems more like an independent translation.

[59] J. Schneider, 'Παρέρχομαι', *TDNT*, 2:681–2. Most modern scholars assume that יעמד in Dan. 12:1a indicates that Michael stands to assume his responsibility to fight for and protect God's people or that he stands as champion and prosecutor.

of יעמד and יעבר ('shall pass over/through/on/beyond/along/away'[60]).[61]
However, Jeansonne provides no evidence that παρέρχομαι ever meant
'come forward'. Moreover, it seems that she has not exercised sufficient
methodological caution in drawing her conclusion that the LXX reading
reflects an unintentional transcriptional error. Jeansonne's proposal requires that half of the word has been misread (here Jeansonne claims not
only that a ד was mistakenly read as a ר, but also that the מ was thought to
be a כ). We suggest that such a conclusion should be drawn only after all
the alternative explanations have been examined and found wanting.[62] In
this instance, even when one presupposes that the LXX reading reflects
a variant Hebrew *Vorlage*, יעבר, one must consider first the possibility
that יעבר resulted from an intentional change and indeed the possibility
that it represents the original text of Daniel.

However, we suggest that there is no need to conclude that the LXX
translation reflects an otherwise unattested variant Hebrew text.[63] For עמד
is quite a slippery Hebrew verb,[64] and while it usually means 'stand', it can
also mean 'stand still', 'stop' or 'cease moving' (Josh. 10:13; Hab. 3:11; 1
Sam. 9:27; 2 Sam. 2:28; Nah. 2:9 and 2 Kgs. 4:6), refer to inactivity (2 Chr.
20:17), describe the cessation of an action (2 Kgs. 13:18; cf. Gen. 29:35;
30:9; Josh. 1:15) or mean 'stand silent' (Job 32:16).[65] It is not difficult to
see why one of these latter meanings would have been regarded as more
appropriate in the case of Dan. 12:1a, since this reference to what Michael
does is immediately followed by a reference to the unequalled distress
undergone by the people whom Michael protects (verse 1b). Rashi, using

---

[60] BDB, 716–18.
[61] Jeansonne, *Daniel 7–12*, 77; cf. Montgomery, *Daniel*, 473; J. Lust, E. Eynikel and
K. Hauspie, *A Greek–English Lexicon of the Septuagint* (2 vols.; Stuttgart: Deutsche
Bibelgesellschaft, 1992, 1996), 2:358. This view can be traced back to Charles,
Daniel, 325.
[62] We do not maintain that this was impossible, only that one should not too readily jump
to this conclusion. Jeansonne, *Daniel 7–12*, 77 n. 21 suggests that this precise confusion
occurs in 2 Sam. 19:40 (Lucian's LXX, Codex Coislinianus and Codex Basiliano-Vaticanus
reading עמד and the MT having עבר. However, if the MT preserves the original text (it is the
more difficult reading), the variant may represent an intentional scribal change, designed to
overcome an apparent problem in the logic of the MT reading (see S. R. Driver, *Notes on
the Hebrew Text and the Topography of the Books of Samuel* (2nd edn, Oxford: Clarendon,
1913), 338, who, on the question of which text is original, sits on the fence.)
[63] In terms of method it is preferable to examine the possibility that a given LXX reading
'reflects types of exegesis which introduced elements that deviate from a literal representation of the Hebrew text' before presuming to reconstruct a variant Hebrew text (E. Tov, *The
Text-Critical Use of the Septuagint in Biblical Research* (2nd edn; JBS; Jerusalem: Simor,
1997), 39).
[64] Charles, *Daniel*, 324 calls this verb as used in Daniel 'a maid-of-all-work'.
[65] BDB, 764.

the MT text, claimed that יעמד should be rendered 'he shall stand still'.[66] Strikingly, παρέρχομαι is frequently used in a figurative sense, meaning 'to disappear' or 'to pass away'. This is the only conceivable sense of παρέρχομαι which works in Dan. 12:1a; we posit that the LXX translator is attempting to capture accurately the connotation of the Hebrew in this context,[67] interpreting יעמד in the light of Dan. 12:1b. The logic seems to be that the eschatological tribulation could only come upon God's people if Michael, the guardian of God's people, ceased from protecting them.[68] The fact that *Ruth Rabbah's proem* 1 interprets יעמד in Dan. 12:1a in a similar way, as we point out below, suggests that the Hebrew text behind the LXX's παρελεύσεται was that of the MT. It remains possible, however, that παρελεύσεται is a translation of יעבר. In this case, where the text refers to a celestial prince who protects God's people, the only plausible meaning of עבר is 'pass away', which would seem to assume an exegetical rationale similar to that which we attributed to the LXX translator above. If so, that would explain why a scribe might have intentionally changed the obscure, or apparently inappropriate, יעמד, to the clearer, or more contextually appropriate, יעבר. Alternatively, it is just possible that יעבר represents the original Hebrew text,[69] with the MT's *Vorlage* reflecting an intentional change grounded in a different exegesis of Dan. 12:1a and b (perhaps a refusal on the part of the translator or a scribe to contemplate the possibility that Michael might ever abandon God's people) or, less likely, an unintentional error, יעמד being read instead

[66] Rashi on Dan. 12:1. See *The Judaica Press Complete Tanach with Rashi* (CD-ROM; Davka Corporation and Judaica Press, 1999).

[67] That the LXX translator of Daniel was generally attempting to render accurately the Hebrew text into 'well-constructed Greek prose' is demonstrated by Jeansonne, *Daniel 7–12, passim*, esp. 131–3. She concludes that the translator felt free to paraphrase or stress a particular connotation of a term, but only in a way which seemed to draw out in a readable and interesting Greek style the meaning of the Hebrew text before him.

[68] According to this reading, Dan. 12:1a refers back to 11:45a rather than 11:45b, rendering 11:45b something of a parenthetical comment, which interrupts the chronological development of 11:36–12:3 and which is intended to emphasise that even this ultimate and supremely blasphemous opponent of God will come to an end (cf. 11:27b). This reading has some legitimacy, for if 12:1a had been intended to refer back to 11:45b, the reference to the unequalled tribulations in 12:1b would be difficult to understand: one would hardly expect the worst tribulation hitherto experienced by the people of God to come to pass only after the demise of the final and ultimate opponent (at which point God will apparently hand the kingdom over to the saints: 7:19–22, 24–7; 9:27; 12:7–12); rather one would most naturally expect it to occur during his career (cf. 7:21, 25; 12:11–12).

[69] It is perhaps worth noting with Charles, *Daniel*, lix that 'The Masoretic text of our author may on the whole be regarded as representing the substance of the original, but in scores or rather hundreds of passages it is wholly untrustworthy as to the form of the original and occasionally as to its subject-matter.' He regards the LXX to be 'of great value for the reconstruction of the Text' (*Daniel*, l).

of יעבר. Nevertheless, for the reasons that we have adduced above, we regard it as preferable to understand the LXX's παρελεύσεται as a translation of יעמד rather than יעבר.

Significantly, according to Manuscript 233, one of the revisers of the LXX, either Aquila or Symmachus, rendered the Hebrew by ἀναχωρήσει[70] ('go away', 'withdraw', 'retire'[71]). Not only does this reinforce the suggestion that contemporary interpreters did understand Dan. 12:1a as referring to Michael's withdrawal, but it also strengthens the case that this is what the LXX's παρελεύσεται meant. Ἀναχωρήσει probably reflects an interpretation of the Hebrew יעמד similar to that of the LXX (and indeed it may represent an attempt to improve the LXX reading), although it might possibly indicate the use of a common variant Hebrew text (יעבר).

Ruth Rabbah's proem 1 (c. AD 500[72]) approvingly cites two rabbis who conclude that Michael in Dan. 12:1a is not defending God's people. First, the author of *Ruth Rabbah* attributes to R. Yohanan (fl. c. 240–79) the following: 'At that moment the angelic defender of Israel [Michael] remains silent. That is the meaning of the verse, "At that time shall Michael stand up (יעמד)" (Dan. 12:1).'[73] After raising the question of whether angels as a rule sit in heaven,[74] the author dismisses the idea with reference to R. Hanina (fl. c. late second century–250), to whom he then attributes the following: 'And yet the verse at hand says, "And at that time Michael shall stand up" (Dan. 12:1)! What is the meaning of "And at that time shall Michael stand up" (Dan. 12:1)? He is silenced, as in this usage: "And shall I wait because they speak not, because they stand still (עמדו) and do not answer any more(?)" (Job 32:16).'[75] At this point *Ruth Rabbah* apparently returns to the teaching of R. Yohanan: 'Said to him the Holy One, blessed be he, "Do you stand silent (נשתתקת) and not defend my children (ואין אתה מלמד סניגוריא על בני)?"'[76] This serves as a witness to the fact that the Hebrew verb עמד in Dan. 12:1a was being interpreted in

---

[70] So *Septuaginta. Vetus Testamentum Graecum. Vol. 16.2. Susanna, Daniel, Bel et Draco* (ed. J. Ziegler; SVTG; Göttingen: Vandenhoeck & Ruprecht, 1954), 210. According to Montgomery, *Daniel*, 473, Manuscript 233 reads ἀναχωρήσεται.

[71] BAGD, 63.

[72] So H. L. Strack and G. Stemberger, *Introduction to the Talmud and Midrash* (ed. and trans. M. Bockmuehl; Edinburgh: T. & T. Clark, 1996), 344.

[73] Translation by J. Neusner, *The Components of the Rabbinic Documents: From the Whole to the Parts. III. Ruth Rabbah* (SFAC; Atlanta, Ga.: Scholars Press, 1997), 4.

[74] As rendered by L. Rabinowitz, *Midrash Rabbah: Ruth, Ecclesiastes* (trans. H. Freedman and M. Simon; London: Socino, 1939), 2.

[75] Translation by Neusner, *Ruth Rabbah*, 4.

[76] Ibid., 4. Note the parallel in Yalqut, Exod. §241, where Michael, when called upon by Uzza, the tutelar angel of Egypt, to plead to God on Israel's behalf, 'remained silent'; as a result God himself defended Israel.

a manner similar to that which we have observed in the LXX and in the Greek translation of either Aquila or Symmachus.

In summary, then, we suggest the following: at the time of LXX Daniel (late second century BC[77]) Dan. 12:1a was understood to speak of Michael's 'passing aside'. This interpretation probably seemed more appropriate than the 'standing up' interpretation, in view of the reference to the tribulation in Dan. 12:1b. Although this reading of Dan. 12:1a was not apparently taken up by Theodotion, it seems to have been approved and adapted as 'withdrawing' or 'retreating' by the reviser quoted in Manuscript 233, either Aquila or Symmachus in the second century AD. *Ruth Rabbah* testifies to the existence in third-century (Galilean) rabbinic interpretation of an understanding of the Hebrew text of Dan. 12:1a which was close to the 'passing aside'/'retreating' interpretation: Michael will 'be silent' and not speak on Israel's behalf. It can therefore be taken as likely that an interpretation of Dan. 12:1a which understood Michael as 'passing aside' was current when 2 Thessalonians was being composed. We propose that the author of 2 Thessalonians shared this view of Dan. 12:1a, perhaps even influenced by the rendering of the LXX, the Greek Bible of the early Christians. The author of 2 Thessalonians, having described the eschatological antagonist's arrogance and blasphemy with reference to Dan. 11:36–7, may well have proceeded to think of Dan. 11:45–12:1, which he seems to have understood to indicate that Michael's removal is a prerequisite for the perpetration of the ultimate temple desecration by the eschatological opponent of God and indeed for the outbreak of the eschatological tribulation upon God's people.

That the cessation of Michael's activities vis-à-vis Satan was indeed viewed in the first century as a *sine qua non* for the commencement of the eschatological opponent's blasphemous activities and the unequalled persecution of God's people is confirmed by Rev. 12:7–9.[78] There we find a Christian adaptation of the ancient chaos myth similar to that which we observed above in the magical papyrus, apparently shaped by Daniel 10–12, in which Michael battles with the red dragon in heaven in his role as protector of God's people and commander of the heavenly army and chief opponent of Satan. Michael's war with the dragon culminates in the

[77] LXX Daniel is probably to be dated to the second half of the second century BC (Montgomery, *Daniel*, 38; Charles, *Daniel*, li; Hartman and DiLella, *Daniel*, 78): note the dependence of 1 Maccabees (e.g. 1:54) and possibly of Theodotionic Daniel (which may have been utilised by some New Testament authors (so Collins, *Daniel*, 8–9)) on LXX Daniel.

[78] Although Revelation is possibly to be dated to the early 90s, individual parts such as 12:7–9 may reflect earlier traditions (so, for example, A. Y. Collins, *The Combat Myth in the Book of Revelation* (HDR; Missoula: Scholars, 1976), 101–19, esp. 114).

latter being cast down to the realm of the earth, using the eschatological beast to deceive the entire world and persecuting the woman's offspring through him (12:7ff.).[79] Although in Revelation Michael is not regarded as a *restrainer per se*, and the cessation of his activity is regarded as a victory for him and a defeat for the dragon, whereas in 2 Thess. 2:6–7 he is regarded as a restrainer and the cessation of his activity is viewed as a removal for him and a release from restraint for Satan, this celestial scenario attests to the contemporaneity of a tradition which linked the cessation of Michael's war against Satan to the onset of the eschatological antagonist's blasphemous activities and the outbreak of unequalled tribulation upon God's people, which was undoubtedly rooted in Dan. 11:45–12:1.[80] This strongly reinforces the plausibility of the interpretation of 2 Thess. 2:7 which we are proposing.[81]

The chronological schema to which the author of 2 Thessalonians seems to have adhered was as follows: (1) the antagonist is ready to commit the abomination of desolation (Dan. 11:45a); (2) Michael is removed from the scene (12:1a); (3) God's people pass through a period of unequalled distress (12:1b); and (4) the eschaton comes (12:1c–3).[82] There is, of course, an apparent absence of any explicit reference to unequalled tribulation in 2 Thessalonians 2. However, this constitutes no real problem for our hypothesis, for the idea is almost certainly implicit in the term ἀνομία. In 2 Thess. 2:3b–8a the author stresses the shift from rebellion (ἀνομία) as a mystery to rebellion as revealed through a person (ἄνομος), which occurs when the restrainer is removed. Such ἀνομία in its mystery form (cf. 1:4ff.) included hostility directed against God's people. Hence it is probably safe to assume that the author of 2 Thessalonians would have believed that when the ἄνομος/ἀνομία is revealed (ἀποκαλυφθῇ)

---

[79] It is worth noting that here, as in Rev. 12:7–9, Michael's role is less significant than that of Christ (only Christ destroys the rebel (2 Thess. 2:8)), although it is still important. This observation sheds some light on angel/angelic/angelomorphic christology in early Christianity. Important recent discussions in this area include L. Hurtado, *One God, One Lord: Early Christian Devotion and Ancient Jewish Monotheism* (London: SCM, 1988); M. Mach, *Entwicklungsstadien des jüdischen Engelglaubens in vorrabbinischer Zeit* (TSAJ; Tübingen: Mohr, 1992); Stuckenbruck, *Angel*; Hannah, *Michael*; P. R. Carrell, *Jesus and the Angels* (SNTSMS; Cambridge: Cambridge University Press, 1997).

[80] Cf. *Ques. Barth.* 4:12ff., which views Michael as sounding his trumpet so that the 'Antichrist' figure arises.

[81] It is conceivable that the connection between Michael's activity, on the one hand, and the rise of the beast and outbreak of the final tribulation, on the other hand, in Revelation 12–13 may be rooted in an alternative interpretation of Dan. 12:1, in which Michael's 'standing' is understood in a military sense (i.e. 'standing to fight').

[82] Matthew 24 and Mark 13 testify to the fact that (1), (3) and (4) were understood as chronologically sequential; the absence of (2) may possibly have been due to the fact that the focus there is on terrestrial events (cf. Matt. 24:3; Mark 13:4).

and the eschatological outbreak of evil occurs, persecution of God's people would be one of its primary features. While the author does not develop this explicitly on account of the fact that he is highlighting those elements of his eschatology which are discontinuous with the present in order to correct the false claim of 2 Thess. 2:2, it seems very likely that he would have been united with other early Christians in conceiving of the rebel as the supreme persecutor of God's people. It is worth noting that in the Pauline corpus there is some evidence of belief in the concept of an eschatological tribulation which is still in store for the people of God (1 Cor. 7:26, 29–31; Eph. 6:13; cf. 1 Thess. 3:3–4; Col. 1:24; Rom. 8:17–18, 23).[83] We conclude therefore that the chronology of 2 Thess. 2:3–8 does indeed seem to be largely dependent on Dan. 11:36–12:3.

It is important to note that only the Michael hypothesis can explain the fact that the restrainer *is removed* and, moreover, *must be removed*, since the outbreak of the eschatological rebellion against God requires that Michael first suspend his normal activities.[84] Michael's restraint in Daniel ensures the protection of God's people *qua* Jews from their enemies (Dan. 10:13, 20–1; cf. 12:1b). The author of 2 Thessalonians seems to have understood Michael as the guardian of God's people *qua* Christians.[85] According to the reading of Daniel 10–12 which the author of 2 Thessalonians appears to have adopted, the cessation of Michael's restraint results in unequalled distress for God's people, which is intended to refine and purify them (Dan. 12:10; cf. 9:24; 11:35; 4Q174:4; 4Q177:7, 9–13, 20, 26) so that they are ready to inherit the kingdom (2 Thess. 1:4ff.; cf. Dan. 7:8–14, 21–2, 26–7; 4Q174:4). Michael's withdrawal permits the fulfilment of this key prerequisite of the eschaton (cf. 1 Thess. 3:13; 5:23; 1 Cor. 1:8; Phil. 1:10; Eph. 5:27; 2 Cor. 11:2).[86] It seems that Michael's celestial restraint of the princely forces of evil keeps terrestrial opposition to God and his people in check until the time God has appointed for the forces of evil to be given 'free rein', consisting of unprecedented authority over God's people to persecute them (cf. Dan. 7:25; also Rev. 13:5, 7) and unequalled supremacy over the earth (cf. Dan. 7:23). Only when

---

[83] Note the use of the term θλῖψις (LXX Dan. 12:1b) in 2 Thess. 1:4, 6 and in Col. 1:24; 1 Thess. 1:6; 3:3 and elsewhere in the New Testament (e.g. Mark 13:19, 24; Rev. 7:14).

[84] This line of argumentation was suggested to me by Professor M. D. Hooker.

[85] In his *Commentary on Matthew* 14, Origen interprets Michael as protector of Christians, although in PG 12:821 he understands Michael as Israel's guardian. Hippolytus, *Commentary on Daniel* 4.36ff. adopts the latter view.

[86] It appears that the Qumran sectarians reconciled belief in the celestial protection of Michael with belief in the earthly afflictions of God's people by appealing to the mysteries of God (e.g. 1QM 16:11). According to T. Levi 5:5–7, the people of God will be in especial need of Michael's help to ensure that they are not defeated in 'the day of tribulation'.

Michael ceases from thwarting the plans of the heavenly princes can this happen and the eschatological opponent of God commit the supreme act of blasphemy, and evil be consummated; only then can the pattern of failure to succeed in Dan. 11:2ff. be broken.[87]

In conclusion, we suggest that Michael could plausibly have been viewed as a restrainer-figure, on the basis of Daniel 10–12, and that there is evidence that he was viewed in precisely this way in subsequent Jewish thought. Moreover, significantly, the LXX, Manuscript 233 and *Ruth Rabbah* testify to the fact that Dan. 12:1a was interpreted by contemporaries of the author of 2 Thessalonians as indicating that Michael will 'pass aside' or 'withdraw' before unequalled tribulation breaks out upon God's people (12:1b). The author of 2 Thessalonians appears to have understood Dan. 12:1a similarly. In the light of 2 Thess. 2:4b, it is difficult to avoid the conclusion that he understood Dan. 11:45a as referring ominously to the events immediately preceding the abomination of desolation. This would naturally have led him to conclude that Michael would be removed just prior to the temple desecration and the outbreak of the final tribulation. Such an interpretation of Dan. 11:45–12:1 would explain eminently well the logic of 2 Thess. 2:6–8a.[88]

The use of the neuter τὸ κατέχον

Perhaps the single greatest objection to our suggestion that Michael is the restrainer is the use of the neuter gender τὸ κατέχον in verse 6.[89] Many

[87] Michael's disappearance from the scene, in allowing the rebel to be revealed, also facilitates God's delusion of all unbelievers so that they are condemned when the parousia occurs (2 Thess. 2:10b–12). Presumably Michael will not be removed until the Gentile mission has been completed (Rom. 15:19–24; cf. 2 Thess. 2:10b–12; Luke 10:18–20) and until the fullness of the Gentiles has come to pass (Rom. 11:25), and possibly until 'all Israel' has accepted the Gospel of Christ (Rom. 11:11–15, 25–6a, 28, 31). On Rom. 11:25–6a, see J. Munck, *Christ and Israel: An Interpretation of Romans 9–11* (trans. I. Nixon; Philadelphia: Fortress, 1967), 131–8; Moo, *Romans*, 713–26; *contra* N. T. Wright, *The Climax of the Covenant: Christ and the Law in Pauline Theology* (COQG; Edinburgh: T. & T. Clark, 1991), 249–51. However, we note, with E. P. Sanders, *Paul, the Law, and the Jewish People* (Minneapolis: Fortress, 1983), 192–4, the tension between the idea that the Gentile mission would provoke the Jews to jealousy before the parousia (Rom. 11:11–16, 28, 31) and the quotation of Isa. 59:20 (Rom. 11:26b–27) which seems to suggest that the Redeemer himself would be the catalyst for the salvation of Israel. Finally, it is worth noting that Satan's full power and deception, together with God's delusion (2 Thess. 2:9–12), mean that no unbeliever will not worship the rebel; hence all those destined to believe in the Gospel will presumably do so prior to the disappearance of the restrainer.

[88] It is worth noting that this interpretation of Dan. 12:1a and b presupposes that prior to his removal Michael is fulfilling the function of a restrainer, holding back the onset of the eschatological tribulation.

[89] Giblin, *Threat*, 19–20.

have sought to solve the enigma of the two genders by seeking a subject which is both a non-person (i.e. a thing, principle or power) (neuter) and a person (masculine).[90] It is possible that we should understand the masculine as referring to Michael, and τὸ κατέχον as a reference to τὸ θέλημα τοῦ θεοῦ,[91] or to τὸ στράτευμα τοῦ θεοῦ/τῶν οὐρανῶν, or to the force[92] alongside whom Michael fights, or perhaps to the destruction of Jerusalem[93] or the conversion of Israel.[94] However, pairing Michael with such as these seems too unnatural to be plausible; indeed, the whole presupposition that the neuter designates a non-person seems arbitrary and unhelpful. The masculine and neuter here, used of the same subject in close proximity, are most readily understood as referring to a single entity, not two different entities which are closely associated.[95]

Pate has suggested that the ambiguity regarding the gender of angels which is evident in Matt. 22:30 and Mark 12:25 may have led to a *constructio ad sensum*.[96] However, we cannot be confident that this ambiguity regarding the gender of angels was widespread in the first century and we certainly cannot presume that the author of 2 Thessalonians would have been familiar with the particular tradition represented in Matt. 22:30 and Mark 12:25. Moreover, it is questionable whether a belief in angels' asexuality might have led to the employment of the neuter (we are aware of no other example of this), and indeed, if it might have, whether in that case the masculine would also have been used.

The solution to the enigma of the neuter is probably to be found in the observation that Greek could employ the neuter gender referring to a person, 'provided that the emphasis is less on the individual than on some outstanding general quality' (e.g. 1 Cor. 11:5; 1 Cor. 1:27–8; Gal. 3:22 (cf. Rom. 11:32); John 3:6; 17:24; 1 John 5:1–4; Matt. 12:6),[97] in the case of 2 Thess. 2:6–7, the restraining of ὁ κατέχων.[98] We suggest then that by

---

[90] Perhaps the majority have opted for *government/the Roman empire* and a particular ruler, *God's will/plan* and God, or *the proclamation of the Gospel* and Paul. As we saw above, each of these suggestions (and each of the many others which have been proposed) has significant problems.

[91] Hannah, *Michael*, 133 interprets the neuter as God's plan as it finds expression in Michael's restraint (cf. Menken, *Thessalonians*, 112–13).

[92] Prat, *Theology*, 82–3.   [93] Orchard, 'Thessalonians', 40–1.

[94] Ruiz, 'Incredulidad', 189–203.

[95] Some have suggested that the restrainer is the Holy Spirit on the grounds that πνεῦμα is neuter (e.g. Thomas, 'Thessalonians', 324–5 and most dispensationalist evangelicals), while the Spirit is typically conceived of as masculine; however, there is no example of the Spirit being referred to in the neuter except where dependent on πνεῦμα.

[96] Pate, *Glory*, 308–9.   [97] Turner, *Syntax*, 21; cf. BDF, §138 (1).

[98] Turner, *Syntax*, 21 actually mentions 2 Thess. 2:6–7 as an example of this phenomenon, although this seems to have gone unnoticed by subsequent scholars.

the neuter the author is referring to Michael with his focus on Michael's restraining activity and by the masculine he is referring to Michael as a person. Hence the use of the neuter constitutes no real obstacle to the proposal that Michael is the restrainer.

Conclusion

The matter of the restrainer's identity has plagued scholarship for between one-and-a-half and two millennia, resulting in copious hypotheses and widespread cynicism about the feasibility of the task. This appendix has sought to suggest that Michael could reasonably have been regarded as a restrainer, on the basis of Daniel 10–12 (esp. 10:13, 20–1), and indeed that there is evidence that his activity was understood in precisely those terms. Moreover, we have proposed that the key to unlocking the enigmatic language of 2 Thess. 2:6–7 is found in a previously unnoticed contemporary interpretation of Dan. 12:1a. In that interpretation Michael is removed just prior to the outbreak of the eschatological tribulation.[99]

Only one final question remains to be addressed: could the readers of 2 Thessalonians have reasonably been expected to understand such a specific Jewish eschatological *topos* as this? We maintain that there is good reason to think that they could. For the author presupposes that his readers are familiar with the Old Testament prophetic concept of the 'Day of the Lord' (2 Thess. 2:2) and the Danielic concept of an eschatological opponent of God who desecrates the temple (2:3ff.). Moreover, the author of 2 Thessalonians assumes that his readers will know 1 Thessalonians (2 Thess. 2:15), and in that letter we see Jewish language such as 'sons of light' and 'of darkness' (1 Thess. 5:5), a belief in God's eschatological wrath (1:10c; 5:9) and in archangels (4:16–17a[100]), and, most importantly, the concept of the so-called 'messianic woes' (1 Thess. 3:3–4), which is rooted in Dan. 12:1b. It would seem safe therefore to conclude that the readers of 2 Thessalonians might very well have been familiar with specific Jewish eschatological *topoi* such as we find in Daniel 10–12.

In conclusion, then, there is a good case for supposing the restrainer removed in 2 Thess. 2:6–7 to be Michael. For Michael could legitimately be, and indeed was, viewed as a celestial restrainer, on the basis of Daniel 10–12, and, significantly, he was also understood by contemporary

[99] Perhaps the identity of the restrainer was lost partly because of the post-New Testament church's preference for the Theodotionic version of Daniel. See Montgomery, *Daniel*, 46; Hartman and DiLella, *Daniel*, 78–9.

[100] Note the claim of Dibelius, *Thessalonicher*, 26 regarding 1 Thess. 4:16: 'Der Rufende ist wahrscheinlich Michael.' Cf. Findlay, *Epistles of Paul*, 101.

interpreters as 'passing aside' or 'withdrawing' (Dan. 12:1a) just after a reference to the eschatological antagonist's setting up of his royal tents near or at the temple mount (11:45a) and immediately before a reference to the breaking out of the final, unequalled tribulation upon God's people (12:1b).[101]

[101] I am grateful to Professor M. D. Hooker, Professor W. Horbury and Dr M. Bockmuehl for their helpful critiques of earlier drafts of this appendix.

BIBLIOGRAPHY

Primary sources

References to Aeschylus; Appian; Aristotle; Cicero; Dio Chrysostom; Diogenes Laertius; Horace; Josephus; Livy; Lucian; Philo; Pliny; Plutarch; Polybius; Sophocles; Tacitus and Xenophon are, unless otherwise stated, from the Loeb Classical Library. Cambridge, Mass.: Harvard University Press. References to Augustine; Chrysostom; Epiphanius; Eusebius; Gelasius; Irenaeus; Jerome; John of Damascus; Oikoumenios; Origen; Philo of Carpasia and Theodoret are, unless otherwise stated, from J. P. Migne, ed., *Patrologiae Cursus Completus* (Paris: Gaume, 1857–1912).

acCordance Bible Software 5.5. Gramcord Institute, 2002.

Ägyptische Urkunden aus den Königlichen Museen zu Berlin. Griechische Urkunden. Vols. 1–4. Berlin: Weidmann, 1895–1912.

Ägyptische Urkunden aus den Staatlichen Museen zu Berlin. Griechische Urkunden. Vols. 5– . Berlin: Weidmann, 1919– .

Aland, Kurt, ed. *Synopsis Quattuor Evangeliorum: Locis Parallelis Evangeliorum Apocryphorum et Patrum Adhibitis.* 14th edn. Stuttgart: Württembergische Bibelanstalt, 1995.

Amidon, P. R., ed. and trans. *The Panarion of St. Epiphanius, Bishop of Salamis: Selected Passages.* Oxford: Oxford University Press, 1990.

Apuleius, Lucius. *Apologie; Florides.* Ed. P. Vallette. CUF. Paris: Les Belles Lettres, 1924.

Behrind, B., ed. *Jerusalem Talmud with Commentary from the Cracow Edition of 1609.* Krotoschin, 1866.

Berkowitz, L. and K. A. Squitier. *Thesaurus Linguae Graecae Canon of Greek Authors and Works.* New York: Oxford University Press, 1990.

Betz, Hans Dieter, ed. *The Greek Magical Papyri in Translation Including the Demotic Spells.* London: University of Chicago Press, 1986.

Bible Companion XML Software, 5.0.

Biblia Sacra: Iuxta Latinam Vulgatam Versionem. LSal. Rome: Typis Polyglottis Vaticanis, 1957.

Bihlmeyer, K., ed. *Die apostolischen Väter.* Tübingen: Mohr, 1970.

Black, Matthew, trans. *The Book of Enoch or 1 Enoch: A New English Edition with Commentary and Textual Notes.* SVTP. Leiden: Brill, 1985.

Blackman, P., ed. *Midrash. Mishnayoth with an English Translation.* 7 vols. 2nd edn. New York: Judaica Press, 1963–4.

Blass, F., ed. *Aeschines: Speeches.* Teubner. Leipzig: Teubner, 1896.

Bonwetsch, G. N. and H. Achelis, eds. *Hippolytus Werke: Exegetische und Homiletische Schriften.* Leipzig: Hinrichs, 1897.

Burnett, Andrew, M. Amandry and P. P. Ripolles. *Roman Provincial Coinage.* Vol. 1: *From the Death of Caesar to the Death of Vitellius (44 BC–AD 69).* London: British Museum, 1992.

Burnett, Andrew, U. Wartenberg and R. Witschonke, eds. *Coins of Macedonia and Rome.* FS C. Hersch. London: British Museum, 1998.

Butcher, S. H. and W. Rennie, eds. *Demosthenes: Orationes.* 3 vols. in 4. SCBO. Oxford: Clarendon, 1903–31.

Caryophilus, Joannes Matthaeus, ed. *Themistoclis epistolae ex vetusto codice Bibliothecae Vaticanae nunc primum erutae, & Latinitate donatae.* Rome: Grignanus, 1626.

Charles, R. H., trans. *The Book of Enoch, or 1 Enoch.* TED. London: SPCK, 1929.

Charles, R. H., ed. *The Apocrypha and Pseudepigrapha of the Old Testament in English.* 2 vols. Oxford: Clarendon, 1913.

Charlesworth, J. H., ed. *The Old Testament Pseudepigrapha.* 2 vols. Garden City, N.Y.: Doubleday, 1983–5.

The Dead Sea Scrolls: Hebrew, Aramaic, and Greek Texts with English Translations. 5 vols. to date. Tübingen: Mohr, 1994– .

Chrysostom, John. *Homilies on Galatians, Ephesians, Philippians, Colossians, Thessalonians, Timothy, Titus, and Philemon.* Trans. G. Alexander, J. A. Broadus and P. Schaff. NPNF. Grand Rapids: Eerdmans, 1988.

Comparetto, D. and G. Vitelli, eds. *Papiri greco-egizii: Papiri fiorentini.* 3 vols. Milan: U. Hoepli, 1905–15.

Crusius, Otto Carl Friedrich Hermann, ed. *Babrii Fabulae Aesopeae recognovit prolegomenis et indicibus instruxit Otto Crusius; accedunt fabularum dactylicarum et iambicarum reliquiae. Ignatii et aliorum tetrasticha iambica recensita a Carolo Fredrico Müller.* Teubner. Leipzig: Teubner, 1897.

Danby, H., ed. and trans. *The Mishnah Translated from the Hebrew with Introduction and Brief Explanatory Notes.* London: Oxford University Press, 1933.

Dindorf, Ludwig, ed. *Ioannis Malalae Chronographia.* CSRB. Bonn: Weber, 1831.

Dionis Chrysostomi Orationes. 2 vols. Teubner. Leipzig: Teubner, 1857.

Dindorf, Ludwig and T. Buttner-Wobst, eds. *Polybii Historiae.* 5 vols. Teubner. Leipzig: Teubner, 1882–1904.

Dindorf, W., ed. *Scholia Graeca in Euripidis Tragoedias ex Codicibus Aucta et Emendata.* 4 vols. Oxford: Academico, 1863.

Dion Chrysostomos: Sämtliche Reden. Trans. W. Elliger. Zurich: Artemis, 1967.

Eger, O., E. Kornemann and P. M. Meyer, eds. *Griechische Papyri im Museum des Oberhessischen Geschichtsvereins zu Giessen.* Leipzig, 1910–12.

Eliger, K. and W. Rudolph, eds. *Biblia Hebraica Stuttgartensia.* 13th edn. Stuttgart: Deutsche Bibelgesellschaft, 1987.

Elliott, J. K., ed. *The Apocryphal New Testament.* Oxford: Clarendon, 1993.

Epiphanius. *Ancoratus und Panarion.* 3 vols. Ed. K. Holl. GCS. Leipzig: Hinrichs, 1915–33.

Euripides. *Hecuba.* Ed. S. G. Daitz. Teubner. Leipzig: Teubner, 1973.

Evans, Ernest, trans. *Tertullian's Treatise on the Resurrection.* London: SPCK, 1960.

Field, F., ed. *Sancti Patris Nostri Joannis Chrysostomi . . . Interpretatio Omnium Epistolarum Paulinarum per Homilias Facta.* 7 vols. Oxford: Parker, 1849–62.

Origenis Hexaplorum quae Supersunt. 2 vols. Oxford: Clarendon, 1875.

Francis, Fred. O. and J. Paul Sampley. *Pauline Parallels.* FF. Philadelphia: Fortress; Missoula: Scholars, 1975.

Freedman, H. and M. Simon, eds. *Midrash Rabbah.* 10 vols. London: Socino, 1939.

Friedlander, Gerald, ed. and trans. *Pirke de Rabbi Eliezer.* New York: Bloch, 1916.

Gebhardt, O. de, ed. *Novum Testamentum Graece.* 2 vols. Leipzig, 1888.

Geissen, A., ed. *Der Septuaginta-Text des Buches Daniel Kap. 5–12, zusammen mit Susanna, Bel et Draco.* PTA. Bonn: Rudolf Habelt, 1968.

Goldschmidt, L., ed. *Der babylonische Talmud.* 2nd edn. 8 vols. Leipzig: Harrassowitz, 1906–9.

Grenfell, B. P. and A. S. Hunt, eds. *The Hibeh Papyri: Part 1.* London: Egypt Exploration Fund, 1906.

Grenfell, B. P. and A. S. Hunt *et al.*, eds. and trans. *The Oxyrhynchus Papyri.* 87 vols. to the present. London: Egypt Exploration Fund, 1898–.

Harvey, W. W., ed. *Sancti Irenaei Episcopi Lugdunensis . . . Contra Omnes Haereses Libri Quinque.* 2 vols. Sancti Irenaei Episcopi Lugdunensis Quae Supersunt Omnia. Leipzig: Weigel, 1848–53.

Head, B. V. A. *A Catalogue of the Greek Coins in the British Museum.* London: British Museum, 1879.

Hennecke, E. and W. Schneemelcher, eds. *New Testament Apocrypha.* 2 vols. Trans. R. McL. Wilson. Rev. edn. Cambridge: James Clark, 1991–2.

Holtzmann, O., trans. *Das Neue Testament nach dem Stuttgarter Griechischen Text übersetzt und erklärt.* 2 vols. Giessen: Töpelmann, 1926.

Holy Bible, New Living Translation. Wheaton: Tyndale House Publishers, 1996.

Horst, P. W. van der, ed. *The Sentences of Pseudo-Phocylides (with Introduction and Commentary).* SVTP. Leiden: Brill, 1978.

James, M. R., trans. *The Biblical Antiquities of Philo.* TED. London: SPCK, 1917.

John of Damascus. *Opera omnia quae exstant, et ejus nomine circumferuntur.* 2 vols. Venice: Gaspar Ghirardus, 1748.

Jones, H. S., ed. *Historiae, Thucydides.* 2nd edn. 2 vols. SCBO. Oxford: Clarendon, 1942–76.

Jong, M. de, ed. *The Testaments of the Twelve Patriarchs: A Critical Edition of the Greek Text.* PVTG. Leiden: Brill, 1978.

Justinus, Marcus Junianus. *Epitome of the Philippic History of Pompeius Trogus.* Trans. J. C. Yardley. Ed. R. Develin. CRS. Atlanta: Scholars Press, 1994.

Kenyon, F. G. and H. I. Bell, eds. *Greek Papyri in the British Museum.* 5 vols. London: British Museum, 1893–1917.

Knibb, Michael A., ed. and trans. *The Ethiopic Book of Enoch: Introduction, Translation, and Commentary.* 2 vols. Oxford: Clarendon, 1978.

Lake, K., ed. *The Apostolic Fathers, with an English Translation.* 2 vols. LCL. Cambridge, Mass.: Harvard University Press, 1976–7.

Lauterbach, J. Z., ed. and trans. *Mekilta de-Rabbi Ishmael with an English Translation.* 3 vols. JPS Library of Jewish Classics. Philadelphia: Jewish Publication Society, 1976.

Malherbe, Abraham J. *Moral Exhortation: A Greco-Roman Sourcebook*. LEC. Philadelphia: Westminster, 1986.

Ancient Epistolary Theorists. SBibS. Atlanta: Scholars, 1988.

Marcus, R., ed. *Josephus: Jewish Antiquities* LCL. Cambridge, Mass.: Harvard University Press, 1987.

Martinez, Florentino Garcia, eds. *The Dead Sea Scrolls Translated*. Trans. W. G. E. Watson. Leiden: Brill, 1994.

Martinez, Florentino Garcia and E. J. C. Tigelaar, eds. and trans. *The Dead Sea Scrolls Study Edition*. 2 vols. Leiden: Brill, 1997–8.

Migne, J. P., ed. *Patrologiae Cursus Completus*. Paris: Gaume, 1857–1912.

Milligan, George, ed. *Selections from the Greek Papyri*. Cambridge: Cambridge University Press, 1912.

Neusner, J., trans. *The Tosefta*. 6 vols. New York: Ktav, 1977–86.

The Talmud of Babylonia. BJS. Atlanta: Scholars, 1984– .

The Talmud of the Land of Israel: A Preliminary Translation and Explanation. 35 vols. CSJH. Chicago: University of Chicago Press, 1982–94.

The Mishnah: A New Translation. New Haven: Yale University Press, 1988.

The Components of the Rabbinic Documents: From the Whole to the Parts. 31 vols. SFAC. Atlanta, Ga.: Scholars Press, 1997– .

New American Standard Bible. N.p.: Creation World, 1973.

New English Bible with the Apocrypha. Oxford: Oxford University Press, 1970.

New Jerusalem Bible. London: Darton, Longman & Todd, 1985.

Novum Testamentum Graece. Ed. B. Aland, K. Aland, J. Karavidopoulos, C. Martini and B. M. Metzger. 27th edn. Stuttgart: Deutsche Bibelgesellschaft, 1984.

Oudendorpio, Francisco, ed. *Julii Obsequentis quae supersunt ex libro de Prodigiis: cum animadversionibus Joannis Schefferi, et supplementis Conradi Lycosthenis*. Lugduni Batavorum: Samuel Luchtmans, 1720.

Parkard Humanities Institute. *PHI Greek Documentary Texts CD-ROM #5.3: Latin Texts and Bible*. N.p.: Packard Humanities Institute, 1991.

PHI Greek Documentary Texts CD-Rom #7: Inscriptions. N.p.: Packard Humanities Institute, 1991–6.

Preisendanz, K., ed. *Papyri Graecae Magicae. Die Griechischen Zauberpapyri*. Stuttgart: Teubner, vol. 1: 1928; vol. 2, 1941; vol. 3: Leipzig and Berlin: Teubner, 1941.

Rabinowitz, L. *Midrash Rabbah: Ruth, Ecclesiastes*. Trans. H. Freedman and M. Simon. London: Socino, 1939.

Rahlfs, A., ed. *Septuaginta, id est Vetus Testamentum Graece iuxta LXX Interpretes*. 2 vols. Stuttgart: Deutsche Bibelgesellschaft, 1979.

Rashi. *The Torah, with Rashi's Commentary Translated, Annotated and Elucidated: The Saperstein Edition*. New York: Mesorah, 1995.

Rengstorf, Karl Heinrich. *A Complete Concordance to Flavius Josephus*. 4 vols. Leiden: Brill, 1973–83.

Reuter, Rainer. *Synopse zu den Briefen des Neuen Testaments*. ARGU. Frankfurt: Peter Lang, 1997.

Schaff, Philip, ed. *A Select Library of the Nicene and Post-Nicene Fathers of the Christian Church*. 2nd edn. Reprint: Grand Rapids: Eerdmans, 1975.

Schenkl, Henricus and Johann Schweighauser, eds. *Epicteti Dissertationes ab Arriano Digestae*. Teubner. Leipzig: Teubner, 1916.

Schwartz, Eduard, ed. *Scholia in Euripidem*. 2 vols in 1. Berlin: Reimer, 1887–91.
Souter, A., ed. *Pelagius' Expositions of Thirteen Epistles of St. Paul*. 2 vols. TS. Cambridge: Cambridge University Press, 1922–6.
Swete, H. B., ed. *Theodori Episcopi Mopsuesteni in Epistolas B. Pauli Commentarii. The Latin Version with the Greek Fragments, with an Introduction, Notes and Indices*. 2 vols. Cambridge: Cambridge University Press, 1880–2.
The Ante-Nicene Christian Library: Translations of the Writings of the Fathers Down to AD 325. Ed. A. Roberts and J. Donaldson. 10 vols. Grand Rapids: Eerdmans, 1951–3.
The Apocrypha of the Old Testament: Revised Standard Version. The Oxford Annotated Apocrypha. Ed. B. M. Metzger. New York: Oxford University Press, 1977.
The Apostolic Fathers. 2nd edn. Trans. J. B. Lightfoot and J. R. Harmer. Ed. Michael Holmes. Grand Rapids: Baker, 1990.
The Authorised Version: The Holy Bible containing the Old and New Testaments. London: British and Foreign Bible Society, 1930.
The Early Christian Fathers. Ed. H. Bettenson. Oxford: Oxford University Press, 1956.
The Holy Bible containing the Old and New Testaments with the Apocryphal / Deuterocanonical Books. New Revised Standard Version. New York: Oxford University Press, 1989.
The Holy Bible: New International Version. London: Hodder & Stoughton, 1979.
The Holy Bible with the Books Called Apocrypha: The Revised Version. Cambridge: Cambridge University Press, 1909.
The Judaica Press Complete Tanach with Rashi: The Complete Tanach on CD-ROM Featuring the Judaica Press English Translation of Tanach and Rashi together with the Hebrew text of Tanach with Rashi. Chicago: Davka Corporation and Judaica Press, 1998.
The New American Bible. Paterson, N.J.: St Antony Guild Press, 1970.
The Revised English Bible with the Apocrypha. Oxford: Oxford University Press, 1989.
The Soncino Hebrew–English Edition of the Bablylonian Talmud. 30 vols. Ed. I. Epstein. London: Soncino, 1967–87.
Thesaurus Linguae Graecae Workplace 8.0. Cedarville, Tex.: Silver Mountain Software, 2000.
Tischendorf, C., ed. *Novum Testamentum Graece*. Leipzig: Giesecke & Devrient, 1872.
Tragelles, S. P., ed. *The Greek New Testament*. London: Samuel Bagster, 1857–79.
Treat, Jay Curry. 'Lost Keys: Text and Interpretation in the Old Greek "Song of Songs" and its Earliest Manuscript Witnesses'. Unpublished Ph.D. diss., University of Pennsylvania, 1996.
United Bible Societies' Greek New Testament. 4th rev. edn. Stuttgart: Deutsche Bibelgesellschaft, 1994.
VanderKam, James C., ed. and trans. *The Book of Jubilees*. CSCO. Louvain: Peeters, 1989.
Vermes, Geza, trans. *The Dead Sea Scrolls in English*. 4th edn. Sheffield: Sheffield Academic Press, 1995.
Vogels, H. J., ed. *Ambrosiastri qui dicitur Commentarius in Epistulas Paulinas*. 3 vols. CSEL. Vienna: Hoelder-Pichler-Tempsky, 1966–9.

Weber, R., ed. *Biblia Sacra: Iuxta Vulgatam Versionem*. Stuttgart: Württemberg-
    ische Bibelanstalt, 1969.
Westcott, Brooke Foss and Fenton John Anthony Hort, eds. *The New Testament
    in the Original Greek*. Cambridge: Macmillan, 1890.
The New Testament in the Original Greek. Vol. 1: Text; vol. 2: Introduction
    and Appendix. 2nd edn. London: Macmillan, 1896.
The New Testament in the Original Greek. London: Macmillan, 1909.
Whiston, William, ed. and trans. *The Works of Josephus: Complete and
    Unabridged*. Rev. edn. Peabody, Mass.: Hendrickson, 1987.
Williams, F., trans. *The Panarion of Epiphanius of Salamis*. 2 vols. NHS. Leiden:
    Brill, 1987–94.
Wise, Michael, Martin Abegg and Edward Cook, trans. *The Dead Sea Scrolls: A
    New Translation*. London: HarperCollins, 1996.
Yadin, Y., ed. *The Scroll of the War of the Sons of Light against the Sons of
    Darkness*. Trans. B. and C. Rabin. London: Oxford University Press, 1962.
Yonge, C. D., trans. *The Works of Philo: Complete and Unabridged*. Rev. edn.
    Peabody, Mass.: Hendrickson, 1993.
Ziegler, Joseph, ed. *Septuaginta. Vetus Testamentum Graecum. Vol. 16.2.
    Susanna, Daniel, Bel et Draco*. SVTG. Göttingen: Vandenhoeck & Ruprecht,
    1954.

Secondary sources

Aarde, A. van. 'The Second Letter to the Thessalonians Reread as Pseudepigraph'.
    JHC 3 (1996): 237–66.
Adinolfi, Marco. *La prima lettera ai Tessalonicesi nel mondo greco-romano*.
    BPAA. Rome: Pontificium Athenaeum Antonianum, 1990.
Agrell, G. *Work, Toil and Sustenance: An Examination of the View of Work in the
    New Testament, Taking into Consideration Views Found in Old Testament,
    Intertestamental and Early Rabbinic Writings*. Trans. S. Westerholm and
    G. Agrell. Lund: Ohlssons, 1976.
Ahn, Joseph Yong-Sik. 'The Parousia in Paul's Letters to the Thessalonians,
    the Corinthians, and the Romans, in relation to its Old Testament-Judaic
    Background'. Ph.D. thesis, Fuller Theological Seminary, 1989.
Ahsmann, Piet. ' "Wie niet wil werken moet ook maar niet eten." 2 Thessaloni-
    cenzen 3,10'. *Schrift* 64 (1979): 146–52.
Aland, Kurt. 'The Problem of Anonymity and Pseudonymity in the Christian
    Literature of the First and Second Centuries'. In *Authorship and Integrity
    of the New Testament: Some Recent Studies by K. Aland and others*, ed.
    K. Aland, 1–13. TC. London: SPCK, 1965.
Alföldy, Géza. *The Social History of Rome*. Trans. D. Braund and F. Pollock.
    London: Croom Helm, 1985.
Alford, Henry. *The Greek Testament*. 5th edn. 4 vols. London: Rivingtons, 1880.
Allo, E. Bernard. *Saint Paul: Première épître aux Corinthiens*. EBib. 2nd edn.
    Paris: Gabalda, 1956.
Anderson, A. A. *2 Samuel*. WBC. Dallas: Word, 1989.
Archer, G. L. *Jerome's Commentary on Daniel*. Grand Rapids: Baker, 1958.
'Daniel'. In *EBC*, ed. F. E. Gaebelein, 7:1–157. 12 vols. Grand Rapids:
    Zondervan, 1985.

Arnold, Clinton E. *Ephesians: Power and Magic. The Concept of Power in Eph-esians in Light of its Historical Setting.* SNTSMS. Cambridge: Cambridge University Press, 1989.

Ascough, Richard S. 'The Thessalonian Christian Community as a Professional Voluntary Association'. *JBL* 119 (2000): 311–28.

Askwith, Edward Harrison. *An Introduction to the Thessalonian Epistles: Containing a Vindication of the Pauline Authorship of both Epistles and an Interpretation of the Eschatological Section of 2 Thess. ii.* London: Macmillan, 1902.

Aune, D. C. 'Trouble in Thessalonica: An Exegetical Study of I Thess 4.9–12, 5.12–14 and II Thess 6.6–15 in Light of First-Century Social Conditions'. Th.M. thesis, Regent College, 1989.

Aus, Roger David. 'Comfort in Judgment: The Use of the Day of the Lord and Theophany Traditions in Second Thesalonians 1'. Ph.D. diss., Yale University, 1971.

'The Liturgical Background of the Necessity and Propriety of Giving Thanks according to 2 Thess. 1:3'. *JBL* 92 (1972–3): 432–8.

'The Relevance of Isa. 66:7 to Revelation 12 and 2 Thessalonians 1'. *ZNW* 67 (1976): 252–68.

'God's Plan and God's Power: Isaiah 66 and the Restraining Factors of 2 Thess. 2:6–7'. *JBL* 96 (1977): 537–53.

'II Thessalonians'. In *ACNT: 1–2 Timothy, Titus, 2 Thessalonians.* Minneapolis: Augsburg, 1984.

Bailey, J. A. 'Who Wrote II Thessalonians?' *NTS* 25 (1978–9): 131–45.

Bailey, John W. '1 Thessalonians', '2 Thessalonians'. In *IB*, ed. G. A. Buttrick, 11:243–339. 12 vols. Nashville: Abingdon, 1955.

Balz, Horst and Gerhard Schneider. *EDNT.* Trans. J. W. Medendorp and Douglas W. Scott. 3 vols. Grand Rapids: Eerdmans, 1990–3.

Bammel, Ernst. 'Judenverfolgung und Naherwartung: Zur Eschatologie des ersten Thessalonicherbriefes'. *ZTK* 56 (1959): 294–315.

'Ein Beitrag zur paulinischen Staatsanschauung'. *TLZ* 85 (1960): 837–40.

'Preparation for the Perils of the Last Days: I Thessalonians 3:3'. In *Suffering and Martyrdom in the New Testament*, ed. W. Horbury and B. McNeil, 91–100. FS G. M. Styler. Cambridge: Cambridge University Press, 1981.

Barclay, John M. G. 'Mirror Reading a Polemical Letter: Galatians as a Test Case'. *JSNT* 31 (1987): 73–93.

'Thessalonica and Corinth: Social Contrasts in Pauline Christianity'. *JSNT* 47 (1992): 49–74.

'Conflict in Thessalonica'. *CBQ* 55 (1993): 512–30.

Barnes, O. L. *The Song of Songs.* Newcastle: Progressive Printers Ltd, 1961.

Barnouin, M. 'Les Problèmes de traduction concernant II Thess. II. 6–7'. *NTS* 23 (1977): 482–98.

'Un "lieu intermédiaire" mythique en 2 Thess. 2.7'. *NTS* 40 (1994): 471.

Barr, James. 'Some Notes on *Ben* "Between" in Classical Hebrew'. *JSS* 23 (1978): 1–22.

Barrett, Charles Kingsley. *Paul: An Introduction to his Thought.* OCT. London: Geoffrey Chapman, 1994.

Bassin, François. *Les Epîtres de Paul aux Thessaloniciens.* CEB. Vaux-Sur-Seine: Edifac, 1991.

Bassler, Jouette M. 'The Enigmatic Sign: 2 Thessalonians 1:5'. *CBQ* 46 (1984): 496–510.

Bauckham, Richard J. 'Pseudo-Apostolic Letters'. *JBL* 107 (1988): 469–94.

Bauer, W., F. Danker, W. F. Arndt and F. W. Gingrich. *A Greek–English Lexicon of the New Testament and Other Early Christian Literature*. 3rd edn. Chicago: University of Chicago Press, 2000.

Baumann, A. 'המה'. In *TDOT*, ed. G. J. Botterweck and H. Ringgren, 3:414–18. 13 vols. to date. Grand Rapids: Eerdmans, 1974– .

Baumgarten, Jörg. *Paulus und die Apokalyptik. Die Auslegung apokalyptischer Überlieferungen in den echten Paulusbriefen*. WMANT. Neukirchen-Vluyn: Neukirchener, 1975.

Baur, F. C. *Paul the Apostle of Jesus Christ: His Life and Works, his Epistles and Teachings. A Contribution to a Critical History of Primitive Christianity*. 2 vols. Ed. E. Zeller. Trans. A. Menzies. TTFL. London: Williams and Norgate, 1875–6.

Beard, Mary, John North and Simon Price. *Religions of Rome. Volume 2: A Sourcebook*. Cambridge: Cambridge University Press, 1998.

Beck, H. and C. Brown. 'Peace'. In *NIDNTT*, ed. C. Brown, 2:776–83. 3 vols. Grand Rapids: Zondervan, 1975–8.

Becker, Jürgen. *Auferstehung der Toten im Urchristentum*. SBS. Stuttgart: Katholisches Bibelwerk, 1976.

'Die Frage nach den entschlafenen Christen in 1 Thess 4, 13–18'. *Im Lichte der Reformation. Jahrbuch des Evangelischen Bundes* 23 (1980): 45–60.

Behm, J. 'Νοῦς'. In *TDNT*, ed. G. Kittel and G. Friedrich, 4:951–60. 10 vols. Trans. G. W. Bromiley. Grand Rapids: Eerdmans, 1964–76.

Beker, J. Christiaan. *The Heirs of Paul: Paul's Legacy in the New Testament and in the Church Today*. Minneapolis: Augsburg Fortress, 1991.

Bertram, Georg. 'Ἔργον, κτλ.'. In *TDNT*, ed. G. Kittel and G. Friedrich, 2:635–55. 10 vols. Trans. G. W. Bromiley. Grand Rapids: Eerdmans, 1964–76.

'Σαλεύω, σάλος'. In *TDNT*, ed. G. Kittel and G. Friedrich, 7:65–71. 10 vols. Trans. G. W. Bromiley. Grand Rapids: Eerdmans, 1964–76.

Best, Ernest. *The First and Second Epistles to the Thessalonians*. 2nd edn. BNTC. London: A. & C. Black, 1986.

A Critical and Exegetical Commentary on Ephesians. ICC. Edinburgh: T. & T. Clark, 1998.

Betz, Hans Dieter. *Galatians: A Commentary on Paul's Letter to the Churches in Galatia*. Hermeneia. Philadelphia: Fortress, 1979.

Betz, Otto. 'Der Katechon'. *NTS* 9 (1962–3): 276–91.

Bicknell, E. J. *The First and Second Epistles to the Thessalonians*. WC. London: Methuen, 1932.

Bitzer, Lloyd F. 'The Rhetorical Situation'. *Philosophy and Rhetoric* 1 (1968): 1–14.

Black, David Alan. 'The Weak in Thessalonica: A Study in Pauline Lexicography'. *JETS* 25 (1982): 307–22.

Blass, F. and A. Debrunner. *A Greek Grammar of the New Testament and Other Early Christian Literature*. Trans. R. W. Funk. Chicago: University of Chicago Press, 1961.

Bloch, Raymond. *Les Prodiges dans l'antiquité classique (Grèce, Etrurie et Rome)*. Paris: Presses Universitaires de France, 1963.

Bock, Darrell L. *Luke.* 2 vols. BECGNT. Grand Rapids: Baker, 1994.
Boer, Willis Peter de. *The Imitation of Paul: An Exegetical Study.* Kampen: Kok, 1962.
Boor, Werner de. *Die Briefe des Paulus an die Thessalonicher erklärt.* 3rd edn. WSB. Wuppertal: Brockhaus, 1973.
Bornemann, Wilhelm. *Die Thessalonicherbriefe, völlig neu bearbeitet.* KEK. Göttingen: Vandenhoeck & Ruprecht, 1894.
Bousset, W. *The Antichrist Legend: A Chapter in Christian and Jewish Folklore.* Trans. A. H. Keane. London: Hutchinson, 1896.
Bover, J. M. 'El principio de autoridad, obstaculo à la parición del Anticristo. Un texto mysterioso de S Pablo (II Thess., II, 3–8)'. *Razon e Fe* 118 (1939): 94–103.
Braun, Herbert. 'Zur nachpaulinischen Herkunft des zweiten Thessalonicherbriefes'. *ZNW* 44 (1952–3): 152–6.
Brown, F., S. R. Driver and C. A. Briggs. *The New Brown, Driver, Briggs, Gesenius Hebrew and English Lexicon: With an Appendix containing the Biblical Aramaic.* Peabody, Mass.: Hendrickson, 1979.
Brown, Raymond E. *The Semitic Background of the Term 'Mystery' in the New Testament.* FBBS. Philadelphia: Fortress, 1968.
An Introduction to the New Testament. ABRL. Garden City, N.Y.: Doubleday, 1997.
Brown, Stephen G. 'The Intertextuality of Isaiah 66:17 and 2 Thessalonians 2:7: A Solution to the "Restrainer" Problem'. In *Paul and the Scriptures of Israel,* ed. C. Evans and J. Sanders, 254–77. JSNTSup. Sheffield: JSOT, 1993.
Brox, N. *Falsche Verfasserangaben: Zur Erklärung der heidnischen und jüdischchristlichen Antike.* Darmstadt: Wissenschaftliche Buchgesellschaft, 1977.
Bruce, F. F. *Biblical Exegesis in the Qumran Texts.* Exegetica. Grand Rapids: Eerdmans, 1959.
'Christianity under Claudius'. *BJRL* 44 (1961–2): 309–26.
'St. Paul in Macedonia: 2. The Thessalonian Correspondence'. *BJRL* 62 (1980): 328–45.
1 and 2 Thessalonians. WBC. Waco: Word, 1982.
The Epistle to the Galatians. NIGTC. Grand Rapids: Eerdmans, 1982.
The Book of Acts. Rev. edn. NICNT. Grand Rapids: Eerdmans, 1988.
The Acts of the Apostles: The Greek Text with Introduction and Commentary. Rev. edn. Grand Rapids: Eerdmans, 1990.
Brunec, M. 'De "homine peccati" in 2 Thess. 2.1–12'. *VD* 35 (1957): 3–33.
Bruyne, D. De. 'Les Anciennes Versions latines du Cantique des cantiques'. *Revue Bénédictine* 38 (1926): 97–122.
Buck, Charles and Greer Taylor. *Saint Paul: A Study of the Development of his Thought.* New York: Scribner's, 1969.
Burford, A. *Craftsmen in Greek and Roman Society.* AGRL. London: Thames and Hudson, 1972.
Burkeen, W. H. 'The Parousia of Christ in the Thessalonian Correspondence'. Ph.D. thesis, University of Aberdeen, 1979.
Burton, Ernest De Witt. 'The Politarchs'. *AJT* 2 (1898): 598–632.
A Critical and Exegetical Commentary on the Epistle to the Galatians. ICC. Edinburgh: T. & T. Clark, 1921.
Byrne, Brendan. *Romans.* SP. Collegeville: Liturgical Press, 1996.

Callow, J. *A Semantic Structural Analysis of Second Thessalonians*. Dallas: Summer Institute of Linguistics, 1982.

Calvin, John. *Commentaries on the Book of the Prophet Daniel*. Trans. T. Myers. 2 vols. Edinburgh: Calvin Translation Society, 1853.

The Epistles of Paul the Apostle to the Romans and to the Thessalonians. Ed. D. W. and T. F. Torrance. Trans. R. MacKenzie. CC. Edinburgh: Oliver and Boyd, 1961.

Caragounis, C. C. *The Ephesian Mysterion: Meaning and Content*. ConBNT. Lund: Gleerup, 1977.

Carrell, P. R. *Jesus and the Angels*. SNTSMS. Cambridge: Cambridge University Press, 1997.

Carroll, Robert P. *Jeremiah*. OTL. London: SCM, 1986.

Carson, Donald A. *Divine Sovereignty and Human Responsibility: Biblical Themes in Tension*. MTL. London: Marshall, Morgan & Scott, 1981.

Chapa, J. 'Consolatory Patterns? 1 Thes 4, 13.18; 5, 11'. In *TC*, ed. R. F. Collins, 220–8. BETL. Louvain: Leuven University Press, 1990.

'Is First Thessalonians a Letter of Consolation?' *NTS* 40 (1994): 150–60.

Charles, R. H. 'Michael'. In *A Dictionary of the Bible*, ed. J. Hastings, 3:362–3. 5 vols. Edinburgh: T. & T. Clark, 1900–4.

A Critical History of the Doctrine of a Future Life in Israel, in Judaism and in Christianity: or Hebrew, Jewish and Christian Eschatology from Pre-Prophetic Times till the Close of the New Testament Canon. 2nd edn. JL. London: A. & C. Black, 1913.

A Critical and Exegetical Commentary on the Book of Daniel. Oxford: Clarendon, 1929.

Cohn, Norman Rufus Colin. *The Pursuit of the Millennium: Revolutionary Millenarians and Mystical Anarchists of the Middle Ages*. 3rd edn. London: Paladin, 1970.

Collins, Adela Yarbro. *The Combat Myth in the Book of Revelation*. HDR. Missoula: Scholars, 1976.

Collins, John J. *Daniel*. Hermeneia. Minneapolis: Fortress, 1993.

Collins, Raymond F. *Introduction to the New Testament*. Garden City, N.Y.: Doubleday, 1983.

Studies on the First Letter to the Thessalonians. BETL. Louvain: Leuven University Press, 1984.

Letters that Paul did not Write: The Epistle to the Hebrews and the Pauline Pseudepigrapha. GNS. Wilmington: Michael Glazier, 1988.

'"The Gospel of our Lord Jesus" (2 Thes 1, 8): A Symbolic Shift of Paradigm'. In *TC*, ed. R. F. Collins, 426–40. BETL. Louvain: Leuven University Press, 1990.

'The Function of Paraenesis in 1 Thess 4, 1–12; 5, 12–22'. *ETL* 74 (1998): 398–414.

Conzelmann, Hans. *1 Corinthians: A Commentary on the First Epistle to the Corinthians*. Trans. James W. Leitch. Hermeneia. Philadelphia: Fortress, 1975.

Coppens, Joseph. 'Les Deux Obstacles au retour glorieux du Sauveur'. *ETL* 46 (1970): 383–9.

'Une diatribe antijuive dans I Thess. II.13–16'. *ETL* 51 (1975): 90–5.

'Le Katechon et le Katechôn: derniers obstacles à la parousie du Seigneur Jésus'. In *L'Apocalypse Johannique et l'Apocalyptique dans le Nouveau*

Testament, ed. J. Lambrecht, 345–7. BETL. Gembloux: Duculot; Louvain: Leuven University Press, 1980.

Cosby, Michael R. 'Hellenistic Formal Receptions and Paul's Use of ΑΠΑΝΤΗΣΙΣ in 1 Thessalonians 4:17'. *BBR* 4 (1994): 15–34.

Cothenet, E. 'Le Deuxième Epître aux Thessaloniciens et l'apocalypse synoptique'. *RSR* 42 (1954): 5–39.

Craigie, Peter C., Page H. Kelley and Joel F. Drinkard. *Jeremiah 1–25*. WBC. Dallas: Word, 1991.

Cranfield, C. E. B. *A Critical and Exegetical Commentary on the Epistle to the Romans*. ICC. 2 vols. Edinburgh: T. & T. Clark, 1975–9.

'A Study of 1 Thessalonians 2.' *IBS* 1 (1979): 215–26.

The Bible and Christian Life: A Collection of Essays. Edinburgh: T. & T. Clark, 1985.

Crown, R. W. 'The Non-Literal Use of Eschatological Language in Jewish Apocalyptic and the New Testament'. D.Phil. thesis, Oxford University, 1986.

Croy, N. Clayton. *A Primer of Biblical Greek*. Grand Rapids: Eerdmans, 1999.

Cullmann, Oscar. 'Le Caractère eschatologique du devoir missionaire et de la conscience apostolique de saint Paul. Etude sur le κατέχον (-ων) de 2 Thess. 2:6–7'. *RHPR* 16 (1936): 210–45.

Cumont, F. J. *Lux Perpetua*. Paris: P. Geuther, 1949.

David, P. 'Daniel 11, 1: A Late Gloss?' In *The Book of Daniel in the light of New Findings*, ed. A. S. van der Woude, 505–14. BETL. Louvain: Leuven University Press, 1993.

Davies, W. D. 'Paul and the People of Israel'. *NTS* 24 (1978): 4–39.

Paul and Rabbinic Judaism: Some Rabbinic Elements in Pauline Theology. 4th edn. Philadelphia: Fortress, 1980.

Day, Peter. 'The Practical Purpose of 2 Thessalonians'. *AThR* 45 (1963): 203–6.

Dehandschutter, B. 'Polycarp's Epistle to the Philippians: An Early Example of "Reception"'. In *The New Testament in Early Christianity*, ed. J.-M. Sevrin, 275–91. BETL. Louvain: Leuven University Press, 1989.

Deissmann, A. *Light from the Ancient East: The New Testament Illustrated by Recently Discovered Texts of the Graeco-Roman World*. Trans. R. M. Strachan. London: Hodder & Stoughton, 1927.

Delling, Gerhard. 'Πληροφορέω, πληροφορία'. In *TDNT*, ed. G. Kittel and G. Friedrich, 6:309–11. 10 vols. Trans. G. W. Bromiley. Grand Rapids: Eerdmans, 1964–76.

'Τάσσω, κτλ.'. In *TDNT*, ed. G. Kittel and G. Friedrich, 8:27–48. 10 vols. Trans. G. W. Bromiley. Grand Rapids: Eerdmans, 1964–76.

Delobel, Joël. 'The Fate of the Dead according to 1 Thessalonians 4 and 1 Corinthians 15'. In *TC*, ed. R. F. Collins, 340–7. BETL. Louvain: Leuven University Press, 1990.

'One Letter Too Many in Paul's First Letter? A Study of (ν)ηπιοι in 1 Thess. 2:7'. *LS* 20 (1995): 126–33.

Demke, C. 'Theologie und Literarkritik im 1. Thessalonicherbrief. Ein Diskussionsbeitrag.' In *Festschrift für Ernst Fuchs*, ed. G. Ebeling, E. Jungel and G. Schunack, 103–24. Tübingen: Mohr, 1973.

Denis, Albert-Marie. 'L'Apôtre Paul, prophète "messianique" des Gentils. Etude thématique de 1. Thess II, 1–6'. *ETL* 33 (1957): 245–318.

Dewailly, Louis-Marie. *La Jeune Eglise de Thessalonique: Les Deux Premières Epîtres de Saint Paul.* LD. Paris: Cerf, 1963.

'Course et gloire de la parole (II Thess. III,1)'. *RB* 71 (1964): 25–41.

Dibelius, Martin. *From Tradition to Gospel.* Trans. B. L. Wolf. London: Ivor Nicholson and Watson, 1934.

An die Thessalonicher I, II. HNT. Tübingen: Mohr, 1937.

Dixon, Paul S. 'The Evil Restraint in 2 Thess 2:6'. *JETS* 33 (1990): 445–9.

Dobschütz, Ernst von. *Christian Life in the Primitive Church.* Ed. W. D. Morrison. Trans. G. Bremmer. TTFL. London: Williams and Norgate, 1904.

Die Thessalonicher-Briefe. KEK. Göttingen: Vandenhoeck & Ruprecht, 1909.

Donelson, L. R. *Pseudepigraphy and the Ethical Argument in the Pastoral Epistles.* HUT. Tübingen: Mohr, 1986.

Donfried, Karl P. 'Paul and Judaism: I Thessalonians 2:13–16 as a Test Case'. *Int* 38 (1984): 242–53.

'The Cults of Thessalonica and the Thessalonian Correspondence'. *NTS* 31 (1985): 336–56.

'The Theology of 1 Thessalonians as a Reflection of its Purpose'. In *To Touch the Text*, ed. M. P. Morgan and P. J. Kobelski, 243–60. FS J. Fitzmyer. New York: Crossroad, 1989.

'1 Thessalonians, Acts and the Early Paul'. In *TC*, ed. R. F. Collins, 3–26. BETL. Louvain: Leuven University Press, 1990.

'War Timotheus in Athen? Exegetische Überlegungen zu 1 Thess 3, 1–3'. In *Die Freude an Gott – unsere Kraft*, ed. J. J. Degenhardt, 189–96. FS B. Knoch. Stuttgart: Katholisches Bibelwerk, 1991.

The Theology of the Shorter Pauline Letters. NTT. Cambridge: Cambridge University Press, 1993.

'2 Thessalonians and the Church of Thessalonica'. In *Origins and Method: Towards a New Understanding of Judaism and Christianity*, ed. B. H. McLean, 128–44. FS John C. Hurd. JSNTSup. Sheffield: JSOT, 1993.

Donfried, Karl P. and J. Beutler, eds. *The Thessalonians Debate: Methodological Discord or Methodological Synthesis?* Grand Rapids: Eerdmans, 2000.

Doukhan, J. B. *Daniel: The Vision of the End.* Berrien Springs, Mich.: Andrews University Press, 1987.

Driver, S. R. *The Book of Daniel.* CBSC. Cambridge: Cambridge University Press, 1905.

Notes on the Hebrew Text and the Topography of the Books of Samuel. 2nd edn. Oxford: Clarendon, 1913.

Duff, A. M. *Freedmen in the Early Roman Empire.* Cambridge: Heffer, 1958.

Duff, Jeremy N. 'A Reconstruction of Pseudepigraphy in Early Christianity'. D.Phil. thesis, Oxford University, 1998.

Dunham, Duane A. '2 Thessalonians 1:3–10: A Study in Sentence Structure'. *JETS* 24 (1981): 39–46.

Dunn, James D. G. *Jesus and the Spirit: A Study of the Religious and Charismatic Experience of Jesus and the First Christians as Reflected in the New Testament.* NTL. London: SCM, 1975.

Romans 1–8, Romans 9–16. WBC. Waco: Word, 1988.

Unity and Diversity in the New Testament: An Inquiry into the Character of Earliest Christianity. 2nd edn. London: SCM, 1990.

The Partings of the Ways Between Christianity and Judaism and their Significance for the Character of Christianity. London: SCM, 1991.

The Theology of Paul the Apostle. Edinburgh: T. & T. Clark; Grand Rapids: Eerdmans, 1998.

Dupont, Jacques. *ΣΥΝ ΧΡΙΣΤΩΙ. L'Union avec le Christ suivant Saint Paul.* Paris: Desclée de Brouwer, 1952.

Eckart, Karl-Gottfried. 'Der zweite Brief des Apostels Paulus an die Thessalonicher'. *ZTK* 58 (1961): 30–44.

Edgar, Thomas R. 'The Meaning of "Sleep" in I Thessalonians 5:10'. *JETS* 22 (1979): 344–9.

Edson, Charles. 'Cults of Thessalonica'. *HTR* 41 (1948): 153–204.

Egelkraut, Helmuth. 'Die Bedeutung von 1 Thess 4,13ff für eine Umschreibung christlicher Zukunftserwartung'. *Zukunftserwartung in biblischer Sicht: Beiträge zur Eschatologie,* ed. G. Maier, 86–97. MSB. Wuppertal: Brockhaus; Giessen: Brunnen, 1984.

Elias, Jacob W. 'Jesus who Delivers us from the Wrath to Come (1 Thess 1:10): Apocalyptic and Peace in the Thessalonian Correspondence'. In *SBLSP 1992,* 121–32.

1 and 2 Thessalonians. BCBC. Scottsdale, Penn.: Herald, 1995.

Ellicott, Charles J. *St. Paul's Epistles to the Thessalonians with a Critical and Grammatical Commentary, and a Revised Translation.* London: Longman, Green, Longman, Roberts & Green, 1880.

Ellingworth, Paul. 'Which Way are we Going? A Verb of Movement, especially in 1 Thess 4:14b'. *BT* 25 (1974): 426–31.

Ellingworth, Paul and Eugene Nida. *A Translator's Handbook on Paul's Letters to the Thessalonians.* HFT. Stuttgart: UBS, 1976.

Ellis, E. Earle. 'Paul and his Co-Workers'. *NTS* 17 (1971): 437–52.

Prophecy and Hermeneutic in Early Christianity. WUNT. Tübingen: Mohr, 1978.

'Pseudonymity and Canonicity of NT Documents'. In *Worship, Theology and Ministry in the Early Church,* ed. M. J. Wilkins and T. Paige, 212–24. JSNTSup. Sheffield: JSOT, 1992.

'Coworkers, Paul and his'. In *DPL,* ed. G. F. Hawthorne and R. P. Martin, 183–9. Downers Grove: IVP, 1993.

Ernst, J. *Die Eschatologischen Gegenspieler in den Schriften des Neuen Testaments.* BU. Regensburg: Friedrich Pustet, 1967.

Evans, C. F. *Saint Luke.* TPINTC. London: SCM, 1990.

Evans, Craig A. 'Ascending and Descending with a Shout: Psalm 47:6 and 1 Thessalonians 4:16'. In *Paul and the Scriptures of Israel,* ed. C. A. Evans and J. A. Saunders, 238–53. JSNTSup; SEJC. Sheffield: JSOT, 1993.

Evans, Owen E., *Saints in Christ Jesus: A Study of the Christian Life in the New Testament.* D. J. James lectures. Swansea: Penry, 1975.

Evans, R. M. 'Eschatology and Ethics: A Study of Thessalonica and Paul's Letters to the Thessalonians'. D.Theol. diss., Basel University, 1967. Princeton: McMahon, 1968.

Farrow, D. 'Showdown: The Message of Second Thessalonians 2:1–12 and the Riddle of the "Restrainer"'. *Crux* 25.1 (1989): 23–6.

Faw, Charles E. 'On the Writing of First Thessalonians'. *JBL* 71 (1952): 217–32.

Fee, Gordon D. *The First Epistle to the Corinthians*. NICNT. Grand Rapids: Eerdmans, 1987.
'On Text and Commentary on 1 and 2 Thessalonians'. In *SBLSP 1992*, 165–83.
God's Empowering Presence: The Holy Spirit in the Letters of Paul. Peabody, Mass.: Hendrickson, 1994.
'Pneuma and Eschatology in 2 Thessalonians 2.1–2: A Proposal about "Testing the Prophets" and the Purpose of 2 Thessalonians'. In *To Tell the Mystery*, ed. T. E. Schmidt and M. Silva, 196–215. JSNTSup. Sheffield: JSOT, 1994.
Festugière, A. J. *Epicurus and his Gods*. Trans. C. W. Chilton. Oxford: Blackwell, 1955.
Findlay, George G. *The Epistles to the Thessalonians*. CBSC. Cambridge: Cambridge University Press, 1894.
'Recent Criticism of the Epistles to the Thessalonians'. *The Expositor*, 6th series 2 (1900): 251–61.
The Epistles of Paul the Apostle to the Thessalonians. CGTSC. Cambridge: Cambridge University Press, 1904.
Finley, M. I. *The Ancient Economy*. 2nd edn. London: Hogarth, 1985.
Fitzer, Gottfried. 'Φθάνω, προφθάνω'. In *TDNT*, ed. G. Kittel and G. Friedrich, 9:88–92. 10 vols. Trans. G. W. Bromiley. Grand Rapids: Eerdmans, 1964–76.
Fitzmyer, Joseph. *The Gospel According to Luke*. 2 vols. AB. Garden City, N.Y.: Doubleday, 1981–5.
Foerster, Werner. 'Ἀήρ'. In *TDNT*, ed. G. Kittel and G. Friedrich, 1:165–6. 10 vols. Trans. G. W. Bromiley. Grand Rapids: Eerdmans, 1964–76.
'Ἁρπάζω, ἁρπαγμός'. In *TDNT*, ed. G. Kittel and G. Friedrich, 1:472–74. 10 vols. Trans. G. W. Bromiley. Grand Rapids: Eerdmans, 1964–76.
'Εἰρήνη, κτλ.'. In *TDNT*, ed. G. Kittel and G. Friedrich, 2:400–20. 10 vols. Trans. G. W. Bromiley. Grand Rapids: Eerdmans, 1964–76.
'Κύριος, κτλ.'. In *TDNT*, ed. G. Kittel and G. Friedrich, 3:1039–58, 1081–98. 10 vols. Trans. G. W. Bromiley. Grand Rapids: Eerdmans, 1964–76.
Ford, Desmond. *Daniel*. ABS. Nashville, Tenn.: Southern Publishing Association, 1978.
The Abomination of Desolation in Biblical Eschatology. Washington, D.C.: University Press of America, 1979.
Forkman, Göran. *The Limits of Religious Community*. Trans. P. Sjölander. ConBNT. Lund: Gleerup, 1972.
Fox, Robin Lane. *Pagans and Christians in the Mediterranean World from the Second Century A.D. to the Conversion of Constantine*. Harmondsworth: Viking, 1986.
Frame, James Everett. 'Οἱ Ἄτακτοι (1 Thess. 5.14)'. In *Essays in Modern Theology and Related Subjects*, 191–206. FS C. A. Briggs. New York: Scribner's, 1911.
A Critical and Exegetical Commentary on Paul's Letters to the Thessalonians. ICC. Edinburgh: T. & T. Clark, 1912.
Frank, T. *Economic History of Rome*. 2nd edn. London: Jonathan Cape, 1927.
Fraser, Janice Kay. 'A Theological Study of Second Thessalonians: A Comprehensive Study of the Thought of the Epistle and its Sources'. Ph.D. thesis, University of Durham, 1979.
Freese, N. F. 'Τὸ κατέχον und ὁ κατέχων (2 Thess 2.6f.)'. *TSK* 93 (1920–1): 73–7.

Friedrich, Gerhard. 'Εὐαγγελίζομαι κτλ.'. In *TDNT*, ed. G. Kittel and G. Friedrich, 2:707–37. 10 vols. Trans. G. W. Bromiley. Grand Rapids: Eerdmans, 1964–76.

'1 Thessalonicher 5, 1–11, der apologische Einschub eines Späteren'. *ZTK* 70 (1973): 288–315.

'Der erste Brief an die Thessalonicher', 'Der zweite Brief an die Thessalonicher'. In *Die Briefe an die Galater, Epheser, Philipper, Kolosser, Thessalonicher und Philemon*, ed. J. Becker, H. Conzelmann and G. Friedrich, 201–76. NTD. Göttingen: Vandenhoeck & Ruprecht, 1976.

Fuchs, Ernst. *Glaube und Erfahrung. Zum christologische Problem im Neuen Testament*. Tübingen: Mohr, 1965.

Garnsey, Peter, ed. *Non-Slave Labour in the Greco-Roman World*. PCPSSup. Cambridge: Cambridge Philological Society, 1980.

Garrett, Duane A. *Proverbs, Ecclesiastes, Song of Songs*. NAC. Nashville: Broadman, 1993.

Gaventa, Beverly Roberts. 'Apostles as Babes and Nurses in 1 Thessalonians 2:7'. In *Faith and History*, ed. J. T. Carroll, C. H. Cosgrove and E. E. Johnson, 193–207. FS P. W. Meyer. Atlanta: Scholars, 1990.

First and Second Thessalonians. IBC. Louisville, Ky.: John Knox, 1998.

Geoghagen, Arthur T. *The Attitude towards Labor in Early Christianity and Ancient Culture*. Washington, D.C.: Catholic University Press, 1970.

Gesenius, F. H. W. *Gesenius' Hebrew Grammar*. Ed. E. Kautsch and A. E. Cowley. 2nd edn. Oxford: Clarendon, 1910.

Giblin, C. H. *The Threat to Faith: An Exegetical and Theological Re-examination of 2 Thessalonians 2*. AnBib. Rome: Pontifical Biblical Institute, 1967.

'2 Thessalonians'. In *NJBC*, ed. R. E. Brown, J. A. Fitzmyer and R. E. Murphy, 871–5. London: Geoffrey Chapman, 1990.

'2 Thessalonians 2 Reread as Pseudepigraphal: A Revised Reaffirmation of *The Threat to Faith*'. In *TC*, ed. R. F. Collins, 459–69. BETL. Louvain: Leuven University Press, 1990.

Giesen, Heinz. *Studien zum Neuen Testament und seiner Umwelt*. Linz, Austria: Fuchs, 1985.

Gill, D. W. J. 'Macedonia'. In *The Book of Acts in its Graeco-Roman Setting*, ed. D. Gill and C. H. Gempf, 397–417. BAFCS. Grand Rapids: Eerdmans, 1994.

Gilliard, Frank D. 'The Problem of the Anti-Semitic Comma between 1 Thessalonians 2.14 and 15'. *NTS* 35 (1989): 481–502.

'Paul and the Killing of the Prophets in 1 Thess. 2:15'. *NovT* 36 (1994): 259–70.

Gillman, John. 'Transformation and 1 Thessalonians 4:13–18'. *CBQ* 47 (1985): 263–81.

'Paul's Εἴσοδος: The Proclaimed and the Proclaimer (1 Thess. 2, 8)'. In *TC*, ed. R. F. Collins, 62–70. BETL. Louvain: Leuven University Press, 1990.

Gnilka, Joachim. *Der Philipperbrief*. HTKNT. Freiburg: Herder, 1968.

Paulus von Tarsus: Apostel und Zeuge. HTKNTSup. Freiburg: Herder, 1997.

Goguel, Maurice. 'L'Enigme de la seconde épître aux Thessaloniciens'. *RHR* 71 (1915): 248–72.

Goldingay, John E. *Daniel*. WBC. Dallas: Word, 1988.

Goodwin, W. W. *A Greek Grammar*. New York: St Martin's, 1894.

Gordis, Robert. *The Song of Songs: A Study, Modern Translation and Commentary.* TSJTSA. New York: Jewish Theological Seminary of America, 1954.

Goulder, M. D. 'Silas in Thessalonica'. *JSNT* 48 (1992): 87–106.

Graafen, J. *Die Echtheit des zweiten Thessalonicherbriefs.* NTAbh. Münster: Aschendorff, 1930.

Gräßer, Erich. '1 Thess 4,13–18'. In *Bibelarbeiten, gehälten auf der rheinischen Landessynode 1967 in Bad-Godesberg*, 10–20. Mühlheim, 1967.

Green, E. M. B. 'A Note on 1 Thessalonians iv.15, 17'. *ExpTim* 69 (1957–8): 285–6.

Green, Gene L. *The Letters to the Thessalonians.* Pillar New Testament Commentary. Grand Rapids: Eerdmans, 2002.

Gregson, R. 'A Solution to the Problem of the Thessalonian Epistles'. *EvQ* 38 (1966): 76–80.

Grimm, C. L. W. 'Die Echtheit der Briefe an die Thessalonicher'. *TSK* 23 (1850): 753–813.

Gundry, Robert H. *The Church and the Tribulation.* Grand Rapids: Zondervan, 1973.

'The Hellenization of Dominical Tradition and the Christianization of Jewish Tradition in the Eschatology of 1–2 Thessalonians'. *NTS* 33 (1987): 161–78.

'A Brief Note on "Hellenistic Formal Receptions and Paul's Use of ΑΠΑΝΤΗΣΙΣ in 1 Thessalonians 4:17"'. *BBR* 6 (1996): 39–41.

Gundry-Volf, Judith M. *Paul and Perseverance: Staying in and Falling Away.* Louisville, Ky.: Westminster/John Knox, 1990.

Gunkel, H. *Schöpfung und Chaos in Urzeit und Endzeit: Eine religionsgeschichtliche Untersuchung über Gen 1 und Ap Joh 12.* Göttingen: Vandenhoeck & Ruprecht, 1895 (1st edn), 1921 (2nd edn).

Guntermann, Friedrich. *Die Eschatologie des Hl. Paulus.* NTAbh. Münster: Aschendorff, 1932.

Guthrie, D. and R. P. Martin. 'God'. In *DPL*, ed. G. F. Hawthorne and R. P. Martin, 354–69. Downers Grove: IVP, 1993.

Haack, Ernst. 'Eine exegetisch-dogmatische Studie zur Eschatologie über 1 Thessalonicher 4:13–18'. *ZST* 15 (1938): 544–69.

Hadorn, W. *Die Abfassung der Thessalonicherbriefe in der Zeit der dritten Missionsreise des Paulus.* BFCT. Gütersloh: Bertelsmann, 1919.

'Die Abfassung der Thessalonicherbriefe auf der dritten Missionsreise und der Kanon des Marcion'. *ZNW* 19 (1919–20): 67–72.

Händel, P. 'Prodigium'. In *Realencyclopädie der classischen Altertumswissenschaft*, ed. A. F. von Pauly and G. Wissowa, 23.2:2283–96. Stuttgart: Druckenmüller, 1959.

Hands, A. R. *Charities and Social Aid in Greece and Rome.* AGRL. London: Thames and Hudson, 1968.

Hannah, Darrell D. *Michael and Christ: Michael Traditions and Angel Christology in Early Christianity.* WUNT. Tübingen: Mohr, 1999.

'The Angelic Restrainer'. In *Calling Time*, ed. M. Percy, 29–45. Sheffield: Sheffield Academic Press, 2000.

Hanse, Hermann. 'Κατέχω'. In *TDNT*, ed. G. Kittel and G. Friedrich, 2:829–30. 10 vols. Trans. G. W. Bromiley. Grand Rapids: Eerdmans, 1964–76.

Harnack, A. von. 'Das Problem des 2. Thessalonicherbriefes'. *SPAW* 31 (1910): 560–78.

Harnisch, Wolfgang. *Eschatologische Existenz: Ein Exegetischer Beitrag zum Sachanliegen von 1. Thessalonicher 4, 13–5, 11*. FRLANT. Göttingen: Vandenhoeck & Ruprecht, 1973.
Harrison, P. N. *Polycarp's Two Epistles to the Philippians*. Cambridge: Cambridge University Press, 1936.
Hartman, Lars. *Prophecy Interpreted: The Formation of Some Jewish Apocalyptic Texts and of the Eschatological Discourse, Mark 13 Par.* ConBNT. Lund: Gleerup, 1966.
'The Eschatology of 2 Thessalonians as Included in a Communication'. In *TC*, ed. R. F. Collins, 470–85. BETL. Louvain: Leuven University Press, 1990.
Hartman, Louis F. and Alexander A. DiLella. *The Book of Daniel*. AB. Garden City, N.Y.: Doubleday, 1978.
Harvey, A. E. '"The Workman is Worthy of his Hire": Fortunes of a Proverb in the Early Church'. *NovT* 24 (1982): 209–21.
Hasler, V. 'Εἰρήνη'. In *EDNT*, ed. H. Balz and G. Schneider, 1:394–7. 3 vols. Trans. J. W. Thompson and J. W. Medendorp. Grand Rapids: Eerdmans, 1990–3.
Hauck, Friedrich. 'Μένω, κτλ.'. In *TDNT*, ed. G. Kittel and G. Friedrich, 4:574–88. 10 vols. Trans. G. W. Bromiley. Grand Rapids: Eerdmans, 1964–76.
Head, B. V. A. *A Catalogue of the Greek Coins in the British Museum*. London: British Museum, 1879.
Hemberg, Bengt. *Die Kabiren*. Uppsala: Almquist & Wiksell, 1950.
Hemer, Colin J. *The Book of Acts in the Setting of Hellenistic History*. Ed. C. H. Gempf. WUNT. Tübingen: Mohr, 1989.
Hendriksen, William. *New Testament Commentary: Exposition of 1 and 2 Thessalonians*. Grand Rapids: Baker, 1955.
Hendrix, Holland Lee. 'Thessalonicans Honor Romans'. Ph.D. thesis, Harvard University, 1984.
'Archaeology and Eschatology at Thessalonica'. In *The Future of Early Christianity*, ed. B. A. Pearson, 107–18. Minneapolis: Augsburg, 1991.
'Benefactor/Patron Networks in the Urban Environment: Evidence from Thessalonica'. *Semeia* 56 (1992): 39–58.
Hengel, Martin. 'Anonymität, Pseudepigraphie und "Literarische Fälschung" in der jüdisch-hellenistischen Literatur'. In *Pseudepigrapha*, ed. K. Fritz, 229–308. Entretiens sur l'antiquité classique. Geneva: Fondation Hardt, 1972.
Property and Riches in the Early Church. Philadelphia: Fortress, 1974.
Acts and the History of Earliest Christianity. Trans. J. Bowden. London: SCM, 1979.
'Entstehungszeit und Situation des Markusevangelium'. In *Markus-Philologie*, ed. H. Cancik, 1–45. WUNT. Tübingen: Mohr, 1984.
Studies in the Gospel of Mark. London: SCM, 1985.
Earliest Christianity: Containing Acts and the History of Earliest Christianity and Property and Riches in the Early Church. Trans. J. Bowden. London: SCM, 1986.
Henneken, B. *Verkündigung und Prophetie im ersten Thessalonicherbrief*. SBS. Stuttgart: Katholisches Bibelwerk, 1969.
Herman, Zvonimir Izidor. 'Il significato della morte e della risurrezione di Gesú nel contesto escatologico di 1 Ts 4, 13–5, 11'. *Anton* 55 (1980): 327–51.

Hester, James D. 'The Invention of 1 Thessalonians: A Proposal'. In *Rhetoric, Scripture and Theology: Essays from the 1994 Pretoria Conference*, ed. S. E. Porter and T. H. Olbricht, 251–79. JSNTSup. Sheffield: Sheffield Academic Press, 1996.

Hiebert, D. Edmond. *1 and 2 Thessalonians*. Rev. edn. Chicago: Moody, 1992.

Hilgenfeld, A. 'Die beiden Briefe an die Thessalonicher nach Inhalt und Ursprung'. *ZWT* 5 (1862): 225–64.

Hill, Judith Lynn. 'Establishing the Church in Thessalonica'. Ph.D. diss., Duke University, 1990.

Hock, Ronald F. *The Social Context of Paul's Ministry, Tentmaking and Apostleship*. Philadelphia: Fortress, 1980.

Hoffmann, Paul. *Die Toten in Christus. Eine religionsgeschichtliche und exegetische Untersuchung zur paulinischen Eschatologie*. 2nd edn. NTAbh. Münster: Aschendorff, 1966.

Holladay, William L. *Jeremiah 1: A Commentary on the Book of the Prophet Jeremiah 1–25*. Hermeneia. Philadelphia: Fortress, 1986.

Holland, Glenn S. 'Let No one Deceive you in Any Way: 2 Thessalonians as a Reformulation of the Apocalyptic Tradition'. In *SBLSP 1985*, 327–41.

The Tradition that You Received from Us: 2 Thessalonians in the Pauline Tradition. HUT. Tübingen: Mohr, 1988.

'"A Letter Supposedly from Us": A Contribution to the Discussion about the Authorship of 2 Thessalonians'. In *TC*, ed. R. F. Collins, 394–402. BETL. Louvain: Leuven University Press, 1990.

Hollander, H. W. and M. De Jonge. *The Testaments of the Twelve Patriarchs: A Commentary*. SVTP. Leiden: Brill, 1985.

Hollmann, G. 'Die Unechtheit des zweiten Thessalonicherbriefes'. *ZNW* 5 (1904): 28–38.

Holmberg, B. *Paul and Power: The Structure of Authority in the Primitive Church as Reflected in the Pauline Epistles*. Lund: Gleerup; Philadelphia: Fortress, 1978.

Holmes, Michael W. 'Polycarp of Smyrna'. In *DLNT*, ed. R. P. Martin and P. H. Davids, 934–8. Downers Grove: IVP, 1997.

1 & 2 Thessalonians. NIVAC. Grand Rapids: Zondervan, 1998.

Holmstrand, Jonas. *Markers and Meaning in Paul: An Analysis of 1 Thessalonians, Philippians and Galatians*. ConBNT. Stockholm: Almquist & Wiksell, 1997.

Holsten, C. 'Zur Unechtheit des ersten Briefes an die Thessalonicher'. *JProtT* 36 (1877): 731–2.

Holtz, Traugott. '"Euer Glaube an Gott": Zu Form und Inhalt von I Thess 1, 9f.'. In *Die Kirche des Anfangs*, ed. R. Schnackenburg, J. Ernst and J. Wanke, 459–88. Freiburg: Herder, 1978.

'Der Apostel des Christus: Die paulinische "Apologie" 1. Thess. 2, 1–12'. In *Als Boten des gekreuzigten Herrn*, ed. H. Falcke, M. Omnasch and H. Schultze, 101–16. FS W. Krusche. Berlin: Evangelische Verlagsanstalt, 1982.

'Traditionen im 1. Thessalonicherbrief'. In *Die Mitte des Neuen Testaments: Einheit und Vielfalt neutestamentlicher Theologie*, ed. U. Luz and H. Weder, 55–78. FS E. Schweizer. Göttingen: Vandenhoeck & Ruprecht, 1983.

Der erste Brief an die Thessalonicher. EKKNT. Zurich: Benziger, 1986.

'The Judgement on the Jews and the Salvation of All Israel: 1 Thes 2, 15–16 and Rom 11, 25–26'. In *TC*, ed. R. F. Collins, 284–94. BETL. Louvain: Leuven University Press, 1990.

Holtzmann, Heinrich Julius. *Einleitung in das Neue Testament*. 2nd edn. Freiburg: Mohr, 1886.

'Zum zweiten Thessalonicherbrief'. *ZNW* 2 (1901): 97–108.

Hooker, Morna D. 'Adam in Romans 1'. *NTS* 6 (1959–60): 297–306.

'Trial and Tribulation in Mark XIII'. *BJRL* 65 (1982–3): 78–99.

'1 Thessalonians 1.9–10: A Nutshell – but What Kind of Nut?'. In *Geschichte – Tradition – Reflexion*, ed. H. Cancik, H. Lichtenberger and P. Schäfer, 3:435–48. 3 vols. Tübingen: Mohr, 1996.

Hoppe, R. 'Der erste Thessalonicherbrief und die antike Rhetorik – Eine Problemskizze'. *BZ* 41 (1997): 229–37.

Horbury, William. 'I Thessalonians ii.3 as Rebutting the Charge of False Prophecy'. *JTS* 33 (1982): 492–508. Reprinted in *Jews and Christians in Contact and Controversy*, 111–26. Edinburgh: T. & T. Clark, 1998.

Horrell, David G. *The Social Ethos of the Corinthian Correspondence: Interests and Ideology from 1 Corinthians to 1 Clement*. SNTW. Edinburgh: T. & T. Clark, 1996.

Howard, Tracy L. 'The Meaning of "Sleep" in 1 Thessalonians 5:10 – A Reappraisal'. *GTJ* 6 (1985): 337–48.

'The Literary Unity of 1 Thessalonians 4:13–5:11'. *GTJ* 9 (1988): 163–90.

Huey, F. B. *Jeremiah, Lamentations*. NAC. Nashville: Broadman, 1993.

Hughes, Frank Witt. *Early Christian Rhetoric and 2 Thessalonians*. JSNTSup. Sheffield: JSOT, 1989.

'The Rhetoric of 1 Thessalonians'. In *TC*, ed. R. F. Collins, 94–116. BETL. Louvain: Leuven University Press, 1990.

Hunzinger, Claus H. 'Die Hoffnung angesichts des Todes im Wandel der paulinischen Aussagen'. In *Leben angesichts des Todes. Beiträge zum theologischen Problem des Todes*, 69–88. FS H. Thielicke. Tübingen: Mohr, 1968.

Hurtado, Larry W. *One God, One Lord: Early Christian Devotion and Ancient Jewish Monotheism*. London: SCM, 1988.

Hyldahl, Niels. 'Auferstehung Christi – Auferstehung der Toten'. In *Die Paulinische Literatur und Theologie*, ed. S. Pedersen, 119–35. Teologiske Studier. Århus: Forlaget Aros; Göttingen: Vandenhoeck & Ruprecht, 1980.

Jackson, Paul Norman. *An Investigation of κοιμάομαι in the New Testament: The Concept of Eschatological Sleep*. Lewiston, N.Y.: Edwin Mellen, 1996.

Jeansonne, S. P. *The Old Greek Translation of Daniel 7–12*. CBQMS. Washington, D.C.: Catholic Biblical Association of America, 1988.

Jenks, G. C. *The Origins and Early Development of the Antichrist Myth*. BZNW. Berlin: de Gruyter, 1991.

Jeremias, Joachim. *Unbekannte Jesusworte*. 1st edn. ATANT. Zurich: Zwingli, 1948. 3rd edn. Gütersloh: Mohn, 1963.

Unknown Sayings of Jesus. Trans. R. H. Fuller. London: SPCK, 1957.

Jervell, Jacob. *Imago Dei: Gen. 1, 26f. im Spätjudentum, in der Gnosis und in den paulinischen Briefen*. FRLANT. Göttingen: Vandenhoeck & Ruprecht, 1960.

Jewett, Robert. 'Enthusiastic Radicalism and the Thessalonian Correspondence'. In *SBLSP 1972*, 1:181–245.

The Thessalonian Correspondence: Pauline Rhetoric and Millenarian Piety. FF. Philadelphia: Fortress, 1986.

'A Matrix of Grace: The Theology of 2 Thessalonians as a Pauline Letter'. In *Pauline Theology I: Thessalonians, Philippians, Galatians, Philemon,* ed. J. M. Bassler, 63–70. Minneapolis: Fortress, 1991.

'Tenement Churches and Communal Meals in the Early Church: The Implications of a Form-Critical Analysis of 2 Thessalonians 3:10'. *BR* 38 (1993): 23–43.

Paul the Apostle to America: Cultural Trends and Pauline Scholarship. Louisville, Ky.: Westminster/John Knox, 1994.

'Tenement Churches and Pauline Love Feasts'. *QR* 14 (1994): 43–58.

Johanson, Bruce. *To All the Brethren: A Text-Linguistic and Rhetorical Approach to 1 Thessalonians.* ConBNT. Stockholm: Almquist & Wiksell, 1987.

Johnson, Luke Timothy. *The Gospel of Luke.* SP. Collegeville: Liturgical, 1991.

Jones, A. H. M. *The Greek City from Alexander to Justinian.* Oxford: Clarendon, 1940.

The Roman Economy: Studies in Ancient Economic and Administrative History. Ed. P. Brunt. Oxford: Blackwell, 1974.

Jones, Douglas Rawlinson. *Jeremiah.* NCBC. Grand Rapids: Eerdmans, 1992.

Jouon, Paul. *A Grammar of Biblical Hebrew.* Trans. and ed. T. Muraoka. SubBi. Rome: Pontifical Biblical Institute, 1991.

Judge, Edwin A. *The Social Pattern of Christian Groups in the First Century.* CCC. London: Tyndale, 1960.

Juel, Donald H. '1 Thessalonians'. In *ACNT: Galatians, Philippians, Philemon and 1 Thessalonians,* 211–54. Minneapolis: Augsburg, 1985.

Jülicher, Adolf. *An Introduction to the New Testament.* Trans. J. P. Ward. London: Smith, Elder & Co., 1904.

Jülicher, Adolf and E. Fascher. *Einleitung in das Neue Testament.* 7th edn. GTW. Tübingen: Mohr, 1931.

Jurgensen, Hubert. 'Saint Paul et la parousie: 1 Thessaloniens 4.13–5.11 dans l'exégèse moderne contemporaine'. D.Th. diss., Université des Sciences Humaines de Strasbourg, 1992.

'Awaiting the Return of Christ: A Re-Examination of 1 Thessalonians 4:13–5:11 from a Pentecostal Perspective'. *JPentT* 4 (1994): 81–113.

Kabisch, Richard. *Die Eschatologie des Paulus in ihren Zusammenhängen mit dem Gesamtbegriff des Paulinismus dargestellt.* Göttingen: Vandenhoeck & Ruprecht, 1893.

Kaye, Bruce N. 'Eschatology and Ethics in 1 and 2 Thessalonians'. *NovT* 17 (1975): 47–57.

Kennedy, George A. *New Testament Interpretation through Rhetorical Criticism.* SR. Chapel Hill: University of North Carolina Press, 1984.

Kennedy, H. A. A. *St. Paul's Conceptions of the Last Things.* The Cunningham Lectures. London: Hodder & Stoughton, 1904.

Kern, F. H. 'Über 2 Thess 2, 1–12. Nebst Andeutungen über den Ursprung des 2. Briefs an die Thessalonicher'. *TZT* 2 (1839): 145–214.

Kieffer, R. 'L'Eschatologie en 1 Thessaloniciens dans une perspective rhétorique'. In *TC,* ed. R. F. Collins, 206–19. BETL. Louvain: Leuven University Press, 1990.

Kiley, Mark. *Colossians as Pseudepigraphy.* BS. Sheffield: JSOT, 1986.

Kittel, Gerhard. 'λέγω, λόγος'. In *TDNT*, ed. G. Kittel and G. Friedrich, 4:100–43. 10 vols. Trans. G. W. Bromiley. Grand Rapids: Eerdmans, 1964–76.

Klein, G. 'Apokalyptische Naherwartung bei Paulus'. In *Neues Testament und christliche Existenz*, ed. H. D. Betz and L. Schottroff, 241–62. FS H. Braun. Tübingen: Mohr, 1973.

Klijn, A. F. J. '1 Thessalonians 4:13–18 and its Background in Apocalyptic Literature'. In *Paul and Paulinism*, ed. M. D. Hooker and S. G. Wilson, 67–73. FS C. K. Barrett. London: SPCK, 1982.

Knoch, Otto. *1. und 2. Thessalonicherbrief*. SKKNT. Stuttgart: Katholisches Bibelwerk, 1987.

Knox, A. D. 'Τὸ μηδένα σαίνεσθαι ἐν ταῖς θλίψεσιν ταύταις (I Thess. iii, 3)'. *JTS* 25 (1924): 290–1.

Koester, Helmut. '1 Thessalonians: Experiment in Christian Writing'. In *Continuity and Discontinuity in Church History*, ed. F. F. Church and T. George, 33–44. FS G. H. Williams. SHCT. Leiden: Brill, 1979.

———. 'Apostel und Gemeinde in den Briefen an die Thessalonicher'. In *Kirche*, ed. D. Lührmann and G. Strecker, 287–98. FS G. Bornkamm. Tübingen: Mohr, 1980.

———. *Introduction to the New Testament: Vol. 1: History, Culture, and Religion of the Hellenistic Age. Vol. 2: History and Literature of Early Christianity*. FF. Philadelphia: Fortress, 1982.

———. 'From Paul's Eschatology to the Apocalyptic Schemata of 2 Thessalonians'. In *TC*, ed. R. F. Collins, 441–58. BETL. Louvain: Leuven University Press, 1990.

Kreitzer, Larry Joseph. *Jesus and God in Paul's Eschatology*. JSNTSup. Sheffield: JSOT, 1987.

Krentz, Edgar M. 'Through a Lens: Theology and Fidelity in 2 Thessalonians'. In *Pauline Theology I: Thessalonians, Philippians, Galatians, Philemon*, ed. J. Bassler, 52–62. Minneapolis: Fortress, 1991.

———. 'Thessalonians, First and Second Epistles to the'. In *ABD*, ed. D. N. Freedman, 6:515–23. 6 vols. Garden City, N.Y.: Doubleday, 1992.

Krodel, Gerhard. '2 Thessalonians'. In *Ephesians, Colossians, 2 Thessalonians, the Pastoral Epistles*, ed. G. Krodel, 73–96. PC. Philadelphia: Fortress, 1978.

———. 'The "Religious Power of Lawlessness" (*Katechon*) as Precursor of the "Lawless One" (*Anomos*): 2 Thess 2:6–7'. *CurTM* 17 (1990): 440–6.

———. '2 Thessalonians'. In *The Deutero-Pauline Letters: Ephesians, Colossians, 2 Thessalonians, 1–2 Timothy, Titus*, ed. G. Krodel, 39–58. PC. Minneapolis: Fortress, 1993.

Kümmel, Werner. 'Das literarische und geschichtliche Problem des ersten Thessalonicherbriefes'. In *Neotestamentica et Patristica*, ed. W. C. Van Unnik, 213–27. FS O. Cullmann. NovTSup. Leiden: Brill, 1962.

———. *Introduction to the New Testament*. Rev. ed. Trans. H. C. Kee. NTL. London: SCM, 1975.

Lacocque, A. *Le Livre de Daniel*. CAT. Neuchâtel: Delachaux, 1976.

———. *The Book of Daniel*. Trans. D. Pellauer. London: SPCK, 1979.

Lake, Kirsopp. *The Earlier Epistles of St. Paul: Their Motive and Origin*. London: Rivingtons, 1911.

Lambrecht, Jan. 'Thanksgiving in 1 Thessalonians 1–3'. In *TC*, ed. R. F. Collins, 183–205. BETL. Louvain: Leuven University Press, 1990.

Lampe, G. W. H. *A Patristic Greek Lexicon*. Oxford: Clarendon, 1961.

Lang, Friedrich. 'Σαίνω'. In *TDNT*, ed. G. Kittel and G. Friedrich, 7:54–6. 10 vols. Trans. G. W. Bromiley. Grand Rapids: Eerdmans, 1964–76.

Langevin, Paul-Emile. 'Le Seigneur Jésus selon un texte prépaulinien, 1 Thess 1, 9–10'. *ScEccl* 17 (1965): 263–82, 473–512.

'L'Intervention de Dieu, selon 1 Thess 5, 23–24'. In *TC*, ed. R. F. Collins, 236–56. BETL. Louvain: Leuven University Press, 1990.

Laub, Franz. *Eschatologische Verkündigung und Lebensgestaltung nach Paulus: Eine Untersuchung zum Wirken des Apostels beim Aufbau der Gemeinde in Thessalonike*. BU. Regensburg: Friedrich Pustet, 1973.

1. und 2. Thessalonicherbrief. NEchtB. Würzburg: Echter, 1985.

'Paulinische Autorität in nachpaulinischer Zeit (2 Thes)'. In *TC*, ed. R. F. Collins, 403–17. BETL. Louvain: Leuven University Press, 1990.

Lautenschlage, Markus. 'Εἴτε γρηγορῶμεν εἴτε καθεύδωμεν. Zum Verhältnis von Heilgung und Heil in 1 Thess. 5, 10'. *ZNW* 81 (1990): 39–59.

Lecompte, Cesar. *I Thessalonicienzen*. VB. Kampen: Kok, 1983.

II Thessalonicienzen. VB. Kampen: Kok, 1985.

Leeuven, Jacobus Adrian Cornelius van. *De brievan an de Thessalonicensen*. KVHS. Kampen: Kok, 1923.

Légasse, Simon. 'Paul et les Juifs d'après 1 Thessaloniciens 2, 13–16'. *RB* 104 (1997): 572–91.

Les Epîtres de Paul aux Thessaloniciens. LD. Paris: Cerf, 1999.

Lenski, R. C. H. *The Interpretation of St. Paul's Epistles to the Colossians, to the Thessalonians, to Timothy, to Titus and to Philemon*. Minneapolis: Augsburg, 1961.

Levene, D. S. *Religion in Livy*. SMBCB. Leiden: Brill, 1993.

Levinskaya, Irina. *The Book of Acts in its Diaspora Setting*. BAFCS. Grand Rapids: Eerdmans, 1996.

Lewis, Charlton T. and Charles Short. *A Latin Dictionary*. Oxford: Clarendon, 1896.

Liddell, Henry G. and Robert Scott. *A Greek–English Lexicon, with a Revised Supplement*. Rev. edn. Oxford: Clarendon, 1996.

Liebeschuetz, J. H. W. G. *Continuity and Change in Roman Religion*. Oxford: Clarendon, 1979.

Lightfoot, J. B. 'The Church of Thessalonica'. In *Biblical Essays*, ed. J. B. Lightfoot, 251–69. London: Macmillan, 1893.

Notes on the Epistles of St. Paul from Unpublished Commentaries. London: Macmillan, 1895.

Saint Paul's Epistle to the Galatians. Reprint of 10th edn. London: Macmillan, 1896.

Lillie, John. *Revised Version, with Notes, of the Epistles of Paul to the Thessalonians*. New York: American Bible Union, 1856.

Lectures on the Epistles of Paul to the Thessalonians. New York: R. Carter, 1860.

Lindars, Barnabas. 'The Sound of the Trumpet: Paul and Eschatology'. *BJRL* 67 (1985): 766–82.

Lindemann, A. 'Zum Abfassungszweck des zweiten Thessalonicherbriefes'. *ZNW* 68 (1977): 35–47.

Littleton, Harold Elijah, Jr. 'The Function of Apocalyptic in 2 Thessalonians as a Criterion for its Authorship'. Ph.D. diss., Vanderbilt University, 1973.

Lohfink, Gerhard. *Die Himmelfahrt Jesu: Untersuchungen zu den Himmelfahrts- und Erhöhungstexten bei Lukas*. SANT. Munich: Kösel, 1971.

Löhr, Gebhard. '1 Thess 4:15–17: Das "Herrenwort"'. *ZNW* 71 (1980): 269–73.

Lohse, E. *Paulus. Eine Biographie*. Munich: C. H. Beck, 1996.

Longenecker, Bruce W. *Eschatology and the Covenant: A Comparison of 4 Ezra and Romans 1–11*. JSNTSup. Sheffield: JSOT, 1991.

Longenecker, Richard N. 'Ancient Amanuenses and the Pauline Epistles'. *New Dimensions in New Testament Study*, ed. R. N. Longenecker and M. C. Tenney, 281–97. Grand Rapids: Zondervan, 1974.

'The Nature of Paul's Early Eschatology'. *NTS* 31 (1985): 85–95.

Galatians. WBC. Dallas: Word, 1990.

Louw, Johannes P. and Eugene A. Nida. *Greek–English Lexicon of the New Testament based on Semantic Domains*. 2 vols. New York: UBS, 1988.

Lövestam, Evald. *Spiritual Wakefulness in the New Testament*. Trans. W. F. Salisbury. LUÅ. Lund: Gleerup, 1963.

Lucchesi, E. 'Précédents non bibliques à l'expression néo-testamentaire: "Les temps et les moments"'. *JTS* 28 (1977): 537–40.

Luck, G. *Arcana Mundi: Magic and the Occult in the Greek and Roman Worlds*. Baltimore: Johns Hopkins, 1985.

Lüdemann, Gerd. 'The Hope of the Early Paul: From the Foundation-Preaching at Thessalonika to I Cor. 15:51–57'. *PRS* 7 (1980): 195–201.

Paulus und das Judentum. TEH. Munich: Kaiser, 1983.

Paul, Apostle to the Gentiles: Studies in Chronology. Trans. F. S. Jones. London: SCM, 1984.

'Ein Fälscher am Werk: das Schicksal des Ersten Thessalonicherbriefs in seiner "Interpretation" durch den zweiten Thessalonicherbrief'. *TG* (1996): 32–9.

Heretics: The Other Side of Early Christianity. Trans. J. Bowden. London: SCM, 1996.

Lueken, Wilhelm. *Michael. Eine Darstellung und Vergleichung der jüdischen und der morgenländisch-christlichen Tradition vom Erzengel Michael*. Göttingen: Vandenhoeck & Ruprecht, 1898.

Der erste Brief an die Thessalonicher. SNTG. Göttingen: Vandenhoeck & Ruprecht, 1917.

Der zweite Brief an die Thessalonicher. SNTG. Göttingen: Vandenhoeck & Ruprecht, 1917.

Lührmann, Dieter. 'The Beginnings of the Church at Thessalonica'. In *Greeks, Romans and Christians*, ed. D. L. Balch, E. Ferguson and W. A. Meeks, 237–49. FS A. Malherbe. Minneapolis: Fortress, 1990.

Lünemann, Gottlieb. *Critical and Exegetical Handbook to the Epistles of St. Paul to the Thessalonians*. Trans. P. J. Gloag. CECNT. Edinburgh: T. & T. Clark, 1880.

Lust, J., E. Eynikel and K. Hauspie. *A Greek–English Lexicon of the Septuagint*. 2 vols. Stuttgart: Deutsche Bibelgesellschaft, 1992, 1996.

Luterbacher, F. *Der Prodigienglaube und Prodigienstil der Römer*. Reprint of 2nd edn. Darmstadt: Wissenschaftliche Buchgesellschaft, 1967.

Lütgert, Wilhelm. 'Die Volkommenen im Philipperbrief und die Enthusiasten in Thessalonich'. BFCT 13 (1909): 547–654.

Luz, Ulrich. *Das Geschichtsverständnis des Paulus*. Munich: Kaiser, 1968.

Lyons, George Leroy. *Pauline Autobiography: Toward a New Understanding*. SBLDS. Atlanta: Scholars, 1985.

'Modeling the Holiness Ethos: A Study based on First Thessalonians'. *WesTJ* 30 (1995): 187–211.

MacBain, Bruce. *Prodigy and Expiation: A Study in Religion and Politics in Republican Rome*. Brussels: Latomus, 1982.

McCarter, P. K. *II Samuel*. AB. Garden City, N.Y.: Doubleday, 1984.

McCrystall, A. 'Studies in the Old Greek Translation of Daniel'. D.Phil. thesis, University of Oxford, 1980.

MacDougall, D. W. 'The Authenticity of II Thessalonians with special reference to its Use of Traditional Material'. Ph.D. thesis, University of Aberdeen, 1993.

Mach, Michael. *Entwicklungsstadien des jüdischen Engelglaubens in vorrabbinischer Zeit*. TSAJ. Tübingen: Mohr, 1992.

McKane, William. *A Critical and Exegetical Commentary on Jeremiah*. ICC. Edinburgh: T. & T. Clark, 1986.

McKay, K. L. *A New Syntax of the Verb in New Testament Greek: An Aspectual Approach*. SBG. New York: Peter Lang, 1994.

McKelvey, R. J. *The New Temple: The Church in the New Testament*. OTM. Oxford: Oxford University Press, 1969.

McLay, Tim. 'The Theodotion and Old Greek Texts of Daniel'. In *Origen's Hexapla and Fragments*, ed. A. Salvesen, 231–54. TSAJ. Tübingen: Mohr, 1998.

MacMullen, Ramsay. 'A Note on Roman Strikes'. *CJ* 58 (1963): 269–70.

Roman Social Relations 50 B.C. to A.D. 284. New Haven: Yale University Press, 1974.

Paganism in the Roman Empire. New Haven: Yale University Press, 1981.

McNicol, Allan J. *Jesus' Directions for the Future: A Source and Redaction-History Study of the Use of the Eschatological Traditions in Paul and in the Synpotic Accounts of Jesus' Last Eschatological Discourse*. NGS. Macon, Ga.: Mercer, 1996.

Magnien, P. M. 'La Résurrection des morts. D'après la première épître aux Thessaloniciens. Etude exégétique sur 1 Th. IV, 13–V, 3'. *RB* 4 (1907): 349–82.

Malherbe, Abraham J. '"Gentle as a Nurse": The Cynic Background to I Thess. ii'. *NovT* 12 (1970): 203–17.

'Exhortation in 1 Thessalonians'. *NovT* 25 (1983): 238–56.

Social Aspects of Early Christianity. 2nd edn. Philadelphia: Fortress, 1983.

'Paul: Hellenistic Philosopher or Christian Pastor?' *ATLAP* 39 (1985): 86–98. Also in *AThR* 68 (1986): 3–13.

Paul and the Thessalonians: The Philosophic Tradition of Pastoral Care. Philadelphia: Fortress, 1987.

'"Pastoral Care" in the Thessalonian Church'. *NTS* 36 (1990): 375–91.

The Letters to the Thessalonians. AB. New York: Doubleday, 2000.

Manson, Thomas W. 'St. Paul in Greece: The Letters to the Thessalonians'. *BJRL* 35 (1952–3): 428–47.

274   Bibliography

Marshall, I. Howard. *The Gospel of Luke: A Commentary on the Greek Text.* NIGTC. Exeter: Paternoster, 1977.

Acts. TNTC. Leicester: IVP, 1980.

1 and 2 Thessalonians. NCBC. London: Marshall, Morgan and Scott, 1983.

'Election and Calling to Salvation in 1 and 2 Thessalonians'. In *TC*, ed. R. F. Collins, 259–76. BETL. Louvain: Leuven University Press, 1990.

Kept by the Power of God. Rev. edn. BTCL. Carlisle: Paternoster, 1995.

Marshall, Peter. *Enmity in Corinth: Social Conventions in Paul's Relations with the Corinthians.* WUNT. Tübingen: Mohr, 1987.

Martin, D. Michael. *1, 2 Thessalonians.* NAC. Nashville: Broadman & Holman, 1995.

Marxsen, Willi. *Introduction to the New Testament: An Approach to its Problems.* Trans. G. Buswell. Oxford: Blackwell, 1968.

'Auslegung von 1 Thess 4, 13–18'. *ZTK* 66 (1969): 22–37.

Der erste Brief an die Thessalonicher. ZBK. Zurich: Theologischer, 1979.

Der zweite Thessalonicherbrief. ZBK. Zurich: Theologischer, 1982.

Mason, A. J. 'The Epistle to the Thessalonians'. In *A Bible Commentary for English Readers,* ed. C. J. Ellicott, 8:127–70. 10 vols. London: Cassell, 1902.

Mason, John Philip. *The Resurrection according to Paul.* Lewiston, N.Y.: Edwin Mellen, 1993.

Masson, Charles. *Les Deux Epîtres de Saint Paul aux Thessaloniciens.* CNT. Neuchâtel: Delachaux et Niestlé, 1957.

Mattern, Lieselotte. *Das Verständnis des Gerichts bei Paulus.* ATANT. Zurich: Zwingli, 1966.

Maurer, Christian. 'Σκεῦος'. In *TDNT*, ed. G. Kittel and G. Friedrich, 7:358–67. 10 vols. Trans. G. W. Bromiley. Grand Rapids: Eerdmans, 1964–76.

Meade, D. G. *Pseudonymity and Canon: An Investigation into the Relationship of Authorship and Authority in Jewish Early Christian Tradition.* WUNT. Tübingen: Mohr, 1986.

Mearns, Christopher L. 'Early Eschatological Development in Paul: The Evidence of I and II Thessalonians'. *NTS* 27 (1980–1): 137–57.

Meeks, Wayne A. 'Social Function of Apocalyptic Language in Pauline Christianity'. In *Apocalypticism in the Mediterranean World and the Near East,* ed. D. Hellholm, 687–705. Tübingen: Mohr, 1983.

The First Urban Christians: The Social World of the Apostle Paul. New Haven, Conn.: Yale University Press, 1983.

Menken, M. J. J. 'The Structure of 2 Thessalonians'. In *TC*, ed. R. F. Collins, 373–82. BETL. Louvain: Leuven University Press, 1990.

'Paradise Regained or Still Lost? Eschatology and Disorderly Behaviour in 2 Thessalonians'. *NTS* 38 (1992): 271–89.

2 Thessalonians: Facing the End with Sobriety. NTR. London: Routledge, 1994.

Merk, Otto. *Handeln aus Glauben: Die Motivierungen der paulinischen Ethik.* MTS. Marburg: Elwert, 1968.

'1 Thessalonicher 4, 13–18 im licht des gegenwärtigen Forschungsstandes'. In *Wissenschaftsgeschichte und Exegese,* 404–21. BZNW. Berlin: de Gruyter, 1998.

Merklein, Helmut. 'Der Theologie als Prophet: Zur Funktion prophetischen Redens im theologischen Diskurs des Paulus'. *NTS* 38 (1992): 402–29.

Metzger, Bruce M. 'Literary Forgeries and Canonical Pseudepigrapha'. *JBL* 91 (1972): 3–24.

The Text of the New Testament: Its Transmission, Corruption, and Restoration. 3rd edn. Oxford: Oxford University Press, 1992.

A Textual Commentary on the Greek New Testament. 2nd edn. Stuttgart: Deutsche Bibelgesellschaft, 1994.

Meyer, Ben F. 'Did Paul's View of the Resurrection of the Dead Undergo Development?' *TS* 47 (1986): 363–87.

'Paul and the Resurrection of the Dead'. *TS* 48 (1987): 157–8.

Michaelis, Wilhelm. 'Der 2. Thessalonicherbrief kein Philipperbrief'. *TZ* 1 (1945): 282–5.

'Μιμέομαι κτλ.'. In *TDNT*, ed. G. Kittel and G. Friedrich, 4:659–74. 10 vols. Trans. G. W. Bromiley. Grand Rapids: Eerdmans, 1964–76.

Michaels, J. Ramsey. 'Everything that Rises Must Converge: Paul's Word From the Lord'. In *To Tell the Mystery: Essays on New Testament Eschatology*, ed. T. E. Schmidt and M. Silva, 182–95. FS R. H. Gundry. JSNTSup. Sheffield: JSOT, 1994.

Michel, Otto. 'Μνημονεύω'. In *TDNT*, ed. G. Kittel and G. Friedrich, 4:682–3. 10 vols. Trans. G. W. Bromiley. Grand Rapids: Eerdmans, 1964–76.

Miller, S. R. *Daniel*. NAC. Nashville, Tenn.: Broadman & Holman, 1994.

Milligan, George. *St. Paul's Epistles to the Thessalonians*. MC. London: Macmillan, 1908.

Mitchell, Margaret M. 'Concerning περὶ δέ in 1 Corinthians'. *NovT* 31 (1989): 229–56.

Moffatt, James. 'The First and Second Epistles of Paul the Apostle to the Thessalonians'. In *The Expositor's Greek New Testament*, ed. W. Robertson Nicoll, 4:1–54. 4 vols. New York: Hodder & Stoughton, 1897.

'2 Thessalonians iii.14–15'. *ExpTim* 21 (1909–10): 328.

Moltmann, Jurgen. *Theology of Hope: On the Ground and the Implications of a Christian Eschatology*. London: SCM, 1967.

Montgomery, James A. *A Critical and Exegetical Commentary on the Book of Daniel*. ICC. Edinburgh: T. & T. Clark, 1927.

Moo, Douglas J. 'The Case for the Posttribulation Rapture Position'. In *The Rapture: Pre-, Mid-, or Post-Tribulational?*, ed. R. R. Reiter, 171–211. Academie Books. Grand Rapids: Zondervan, 1984.

The Epistle to the Romans. NICNT. Grand Rapids: Eerdmans, 1996.

Moore, A. L. *The Parousia in the New Testament*. NovTSup. Leiden: Brill, 1966.

1 and 2 Thessalonians. CB. London: Thomas Nelson, 1969.

Morris, Leon. 'ΚΑΙ ΑΠΑΞ ΚΑΙ ΔΙΣ'. *NovT* 1 (1956): 205–8.

1 and 2 Thessalonians. Rev. edn. TNTC. Leicester: IVP, 1984.

The First and Second Epistles to the Thessalonians. Rev. edn. NICNT. Grand Rapids: Eerdmans, 1991.

Morton, A. Q. and James McLeman. *Paul, the Man and the Myth*. London: Hodder & Stoughton, 1966.

Mosse, Claude. *The Ancient World at Work*. Trans. J. Lloyd. ACS. New York: Norton, 1969.

Moule, C. F. D. *An Idiom Book of New Testament Greek*. 2nd edn. Cambridge: Cambridge University Press, 1959.

Moulton, H. K. 'Tired of Doing Good?' *BT* 26 (1975): 445.

Moulton, James Hope and George Milligan. *The Vocabulary of the Greek Testament Illustrated from the Papyri and Other Non-Literary Sources*. London: Hodder & Stoughton, 1930.

Mulder, M. J. and H. Sysling, eds. *Mikra: Text, Translation, Reading and Interpretation of the Hebrew Bible in Ancient Judaism and Early Christianity*. CRINT. Philadelphia: Fortress, 1988.

Müller, Peter. *Anfänge der Paulusschule: Dargestellt am zweiten Thessalonicherbrief und am Kolosserbrief*. ATANT. Zurich: Theologischer, 1988.

Müller, Ulrich B. *Prophetie und Predigt im Neuen Testament: Formgeschichtliche Untersuchungen zur urchristlichen Prophetie*. SNT. Gütersloh: Mohn, 1975.

'Apocalyptic Currents'. In *Christian Beginnings: Word and Community from Jesus to Post-Apostolic Times*, ed. J. Becker, 281–329. Trans. A. S. Kidder and R. Krauss. London: Westminster/John Knox, 1993.

Munck, Johannes. *Paul and the Salvation of Mankind*. Trans. F. Clarke. London: SCM, 1959.

'1 Thess i. 9–10 and the Missionary Preaching of Paul: Textual Exegesis and Hermeneutical Reflections'. *NTS* 9 (1962–3): 95–110.

Christ and Israel: An Interpretation of Romans 9–11. Trans. I. Nixon. Philadelphia: Fortress, 1967.

Munro, Jill M. *Spikenard and Saffron: A Study in the Poetic Language of the Song of Songs*. JSOTSup. Sheffield: JSOT, 1995.

Munro, Winsome. *Authority in Peter and Paul: The Identification of a Pastoral Stratum in the Pauline Corpus and 1 Peter*. SNTSMS. Cambridge: Cambridge University Press, 1983.

Muraoka, Takamitsu. *Hebrew/Aramaic Index to the Septuagint, Keyed to the Hatch–Redpath Concordance*. Grand Rapids: Baker, 1998.

Murphy, Roland E. *The Song of Songs*. Hermeneia. Minneapolis: Augsburg Fortress, 1990.

Murphy-O'Connor, Jerome. *Paul the Letter-Writer: His World, his Options, his Skills*. GNS. Collegeville: Liturgical, 1995.

Paul: A Critical Life. Oxford: Clarendon, 1996.

Nebe, Gottfried. *'Hoffnung' bei Paulus: Elpis und ihre Synonyme im Zusammenhang der Eschatologie*. SUNT. Göttingen: Vandenhoeck & Ruprecht, 1983.

Neil, William. *The Epistles of Paul to the Thessalonians*. MNTC. London: Hodder & Stoughton, 1950.

Nepper-Christensen, Poul. 'Das verborgene Herrenwort. Eine Untersuchung über 1. Thess 4, 13–18'. *ST* 19 (1965): 136–54.

Newton, Michael. *The Concept of Purity at Qumran and in the Letters of Paul*. SNTSMS. Cambridge: Cambridge University Press, 1985.

Neyrey, Jerome H. 'Eschatology in 1 Thessalonians: The Theological Factor in 1:9–10; 2:4–5; 3:11–13; 4:6 and 4:13–18'. In *SBLSP 1980*, 219–31.

Nicholl, Colin R. '1 Thess. 4:15–17 as an Agraphon'. MA thesis, Trinity International University, 1996.

'Michael, the Restrainer Removed (2 Thess. 2:6–7)'. *JTS* 51 (2000): 27–53.

Nicholson, E. W. *Jeremiah 1–25*. CBC. Cambridge: Cambridge University Press, 1973.

Nigdelis, P. M. 'Synagoge(n) und Gemeinde der Juden in Thessaloniki: Fragen auf Grund einer neuen jüdischen Grabinschrift der Kaiserzeit'. *ZPE* 102 (1994): 297–306.

Nock, A. D. 'Greek Magical Papyri'. In *Essays on Religion and the Ancient World*, ed. Z. Stewart, 1:176–94. 2 vols. Oxford: Clarendon, 1972.

North, J. 'Diviners and Divination at Rome'. In *Pagan Priests: Religion and Power in the Ancient World*, ed. M. Beard and J. North, 51–71. London: Duckworth, 1990.

O'Brien, Peter T. *Introductory Thanksgivings in the Letters of Paul*. NovTSup. Leiden: Brill, 1977.

Oepke, Albrecht. "Ἐνίστημι'. In *TDNT*, ed. G. Kittel and G. Friedrich, 2:543–4. 10 vols. Trans. G. W. Bromiley. Grand Rapids: Eerdmans, 1964–76.

Die Briefe an die Thessalonicher. NTD. Reprint: Göttingen: Vandenhoeck & Ruprecht, 1970.

Okeke, George E. '1 Thessalonians 2:13–16: The Fate of the Unbelieving Jews'. *NTS* 27 (1980): 127–36.

'The Context and Function of 1 Thess. 2:1–12 and its Significance for African Christianity'. *AJBS* 2 (1987): 77–88.

Okorie, A. M. 'The Pauline Work Ethic in 1 and 2 Thessalonians'. *DBM* 14 (1995): 55–64.

Olbricht, Thomas H. 'An Aristotelian Rhetorical Analysis of 1 Thessalonians'. In *Greeks, Romans, and Christians*, ed. D. L. Balch, E. Ferguson and W. A. Meeks, 216–36. FS A. J. Malherbe. Minneapolis: Fortress, 1990.

Omanson, Roger L. 'Comings and Goings in the Bible'. *BT* 46 (1995): 112–19.

Orchard, J. B. 'Thessalonians and the Synoptic Gospels'. *Bib* 19 (1938): 19–42.

Otzen, P. '"Gute Hoffnung" bei Paulus'. *ZNW* 49 (1958): 283–5.

Palmer, Darryl W. 'Thankgiving, Self-Defence and Exhortation in 1 Thessalonians 1–3'. *Colloq* 14 (1981): 23–31.

Papazoglou, F. 'Macedonia under the Romans'. In *Macedonia: 4000 Years of Greek History and Civilization*, ed. M. B. Sakellariou, 192–207. GLH. Athens: Ektodike Athenon, 1983.

Pate, C. Marvin. *The Glory of Adam and the Afflictions of the Righteous: Pauline Suffering in Context*. New York: Edwin Mellen, 1993.

The End of the Age has Come: The Theology of Paul. Grand Rapids: Zondervan, 1995.

Pax, E. 'Beobachtungen zur Konvertitensprache im ersten Thessalonicherbrief'. *SBFLA* 21 (1971): 220–62.

'Konvertitenprobleme im ersten Thessalonicherbrief'. *BibLeb* 13 (1972): 24–37.

Pearson, Birger A. '1 Thessalonians 2:13–16: A Deutero-Pauline Interpolation'. *HTR* 64 (1971): 79–94.

The Emergence of the Christian Religion: Essays on Early Christianity. Harrisburg: Trinity Press International, 1997.

Peel, Malcolm Lee. 'Gnostic Eschatology and the New Testament'. *NovT* 12 (1970): 141–65.

Peerbolte, L. J. Lietaert. *The Antecedents of Antichrist: A Traditio-Historical Study of the Earliest Christian Views on Eschatological Opponents*. SJSJ. Leiden: Brill, 1996.

'The κατέχον/κατέχων of 2 Thess. 2:6–7'. *NovT* 39 (1997): 138–50.

Perelman, Chaim and L. Olbrechts-Tyteca. *The New Rhetoric: A Treatise on Argumentation.* Trans. J. Wilkinson and P. Weaver. Notre Dame: Notre Dame University Press, 1969.

Pesch, Rudolf. *Die Entdeckung des ältesten Paulus-Briefes. Paulus – neu gesehen: Die Briefe an die Gemeinde der Thessalonicher.* Freiburg: Herder, 1984.

Peterson, Erik. 'Die Einholung des Kyrios'. *ZST* 7 (1930): 682–702.

'Ἀπάντησις'. In *TDNT*, ed. G. Kittel and G. Friedrich, 1:380–1. 10 vols. Trans. G. W. Bromiley. Grand Rapids: Eerdmans, 1964–76.

Peterson, Robert J. 'The Structure and Purpose of Second Thessalonians'. Ph.D. diss., Harvard University, 1967.

Plevnik, Joseph. 'The Parousia as Implication of Christ's Resurrection: An Exegesis of 1 Thess 4, 13–18'. In *Word and Spirit*, ed. J. Plevnik, 199–277. FS D. M. Stanley. Willowdale: Regis College, 1975.

'1 Thess 5, 1–11: Its Authenticity, Intention and Message'. *Bib* 60 (1979): 71–90.

'The Taking Up of the Faithful and the Resurrection of the Dead in 1 Thessalonians 4:13–18'. *CBQ* 46 (1984): 274–83.

'Pauline Presuppositions'. In *TC*, ed. R. F. Collins, 50–61. BETL. Louvain: Leuven University Press, 1990.

Paul and the Parousia: An Exegetical and Theological Investigation. Peabody, Mass.: Hendrickson, 1997.

Plummer, Alfred. *A Critical and Exegetical Commentary on the Second Epistle of Paul to the Corinthians.* ICC. Edinburgh: T. & T. Clark, 1915.

A Commentary on St. Paul's First Epistle to the Thessalonians. London: Robert Scott, 1918.

A Commentary on St. Paul's Second Epistle to the Thessalonians. London: Robert Scott, 1918.

Pobee, John S. *Persecution and Martyrdom in the Theology of Paul.* JSNTSup. Sheffield: JSOT, 1985.

Pope, Marvin H. *Song of Songs: A New Translation with Introduction and Commentary.* AB. Garden City, N.Y.: Doubleday, 1977.

Porter, Stanley. *Verbal Aspect in the Greek of the New Testament, with Reference to Tense and Mood.* SBG. New York: Peter Lang, 1989.

Idioms of the Greek New Testament. BLG. Sheffield: JSOT, 1992.

Porter, Stanley E. and Thomas H. Olbricht, eds. *Rhetoric and the New Testament: Essays from the 1992 Heidelberg Conference.* JSNTSup. Sheffield: JSOT, 1993.

Powell, Charles E. 'The Identity of the "Restrainer" in 2 Thessalonians 2:6–7'. *BSac* 154 (1997): 320–32.

Prat, Fernand. *The Theology of Saint Paul.* 4th edn. Trans. J. L. Stoddard. 2 vols. Washington, D.C.: Burns, Oates and Washbourne, 1942.

Procksch, Otto. '"Αγιος'. In *TDNT*, ed. G. Kittel and G. Friedrich, 1:88–110. 10 vols. Trans. G. W. Bromiley. Grand Rapids: Eerdmans, 1964–76.

Ramsey, W. M. *St. Paul the Traveller and the Roman Citizen.* Reprint: Grand Rapids: Baker, 1962.

Rawson, B. 'Family Life among the Lower Classes'. *CP* 61 (1966): 71–84.

Reese, James M. *1 and 2 Thessalonians.* NTM. Wilmington: Michael Glazier, 1979.

'A Linguistic Approach to Paul's Exhortation in 1 Thess 4:13–5:11'. In *SBLSP 1980*, 209–18.

Reicke, Bo. *Diakonie, Festfreude und Zelos, in Verbindung mit der altchristlichen Agapenfeier*. UUÅ. Uppsala: Lund, 1951.

'Thessalonicherbriefe'. In *Die Religion in Geschichte und Gegenwart. Handwörterbuch für Theologie und Religionswissenschaft*, ed. K. Galling *et al.*, 6:851–3. 3rd edn. 7 vols. Tübingen: Mohr, 1957–65.

Reid, Daniel G. 'The Christus Victor Motif in Paul's Theology'. Ph.D. diss., Fuller Theological Seminary, 1982.

Reinmuth, Eckart. 'Der erste Brief an die Thessalonicher', 'Der zweite Brief an die Thessalonicher'. In *Die Briefe an die Thessalonicher und an Philemon*, ed. N. Walter, E. Reinmuth and P. Lampe, 104–56. NTD. Göttingen: Vandenhoeck & Ruprecht, 1998.

Rensburg, Fika J. Janse van. 'An Argument for Reading νήπιοι in 1 Thessalonians 2:7'. In *A South African Perspective on the New Testament*, ed. J. H. Petzer and P. J. Hartin, 252–9. FS B. M. Metzger. Leiden: Brill, 1986.

Resch, Alfred. *Agrapha. Aussercanonische Schriftfragmente*. 2nd edn. TUGAL. Leipzig: Hinrichs, 1906. Reprint: Darmstadt: Wissenschaftliche, 1974.

Reumann, John. *Variety and Unity in New Testament Thought*. OBS. Oxford: Oxford University Press, 1991.

Richard, Earl J. *First and Second Thessalonians*. SP. Collegeville: Michael Glazier, 1995.

Richards, E. Randolph. *The Secretary in the Letters of Paul*. WUNT. Tübingen: Mohr, 1991.

Ridderbos, H. N. *Paul: An Outline of his Theology*. Trans. J. R. de Witt. Grand Rapids: Eerdmans, 1975.

Riesner, Rainer. *Paul's Early Period: Chronology, Mission Strategy, Theology*. Trans. D. Scott. Grand Rapids: Eerdmans, 1997.

Rife, J. M. 'Some Translation Phenomena in the Greek Versions of Daniel'. Ph.D. diss., University of Chicago, 1931.

Rigaux, Béda. *L'Antéchrist et l'opposition au Royaume messanique dans l'Ancien et le Nouveau Testament*. Dissertationes ad gradum magistri in Facultate Theologica consequendum conscriptae. Paris: Gabalda, 1932.

Saint Paul: Les Épîtres aux Thessaloniciens. EBib. Paris: Gabalda, 1956.

The Letters of St. Paul. Ed. and trans. S. Yonick. HSL. Chicago: Franciscan Herald, 1968.

'Tradition et rédaction dans 1 Thess. V.1–10'. *NTS* 21 (1975): 318–40.

Rinaldi, P. G. *Le Lettere ai Tessalonicesi*. Milan: G. Daverio, 1951.

La Sacra Bibbia: Daniele. Turin and Rome: Marietti, 1962.

Rist, Martin. 'Pseudepigraphy and the Early Christians'. In *Studies in New Testament and Early Christian Literature*, ed. David Aune, 75–91. FS A. P. Wikgren. NovTSup. Leiden: Brill, 1972.

Roberts, J. H. 'The Eschatological Transitions to the Pauline Letter Body'. *Neot* 20 (1986): 29–35.

Roberts, Mark David. 'Images of Paul and the Thessalonians'. Ph.D. diss., Harvard University, 1992.

Robinson, D. W. B. *Jesus and His Coming: The Emergence of a Doctrine*. London: SCM, 1957.

'II Thess. 2:6: That which Restrains or that which Holds Sway?' In *SE II*, ed.
F. L. Cross, 635–8. TUGAL. Berlin: Academie, 1964.

Roetzel, Calvin J. *Judgment in the Community: A Study of the Relationship between Eschatology and Ecclesiology in Paul*. NovTSup. Leiden: Brill, 1972.

'1 Thess. 5:12–28: A Case Study'. In *SBLSP 1972*, 2:367–83.

Rohland, J. P. *Der Erzengel Michael: Arzt und Feldherr, zwei Aspekte des vor- und frühbyzantinischen Michaelskultes*. BZRGG. Leiden: Brill, 1977.

Romanuik, K. 'Les Thessaloniciens étaient-ils des paresseux?' *ETL* 69 (1993): 142–5.

Rongy, H. 'L'Authenticité de la seconde épître aux Thessaloniciens'. *REL* 21 (1929): 69–79.

Roosen, Antoon. *De Brieven van Paulus aan de Tessalonicenzen*. HNieT. Rome: Roermond, 1971.

'Das Zeugnis des Glaubens in 1 Thessalonicher 1, 6–10'. In *In Libertatem Vocati estis (Gal. 5:13)*, ed. H. Boelaars and R. Tremblay, 359–83. SM. Rome: Academia Alfonsiana, 1977.

Ross, J. M. '1 Thessalonians 3.13'. *BT* 26 (1975): 444.

Rossano, Piero. 'A che punto siamo con I Thess. 4,13–17?'. *RevistB* 4 (1956): 72–80.

'Preliminari all'esegesi di 1 Tess. 2, 1–12'. *BeO* 7 (1965): 117–21.

Rostovtzeff, M. *The Social and Economic History of the Hellenistic World*. Oxford: Clarendon, 1941.

The Social and Economic History of the Roman Empire. 2nd edn. Oxford: Clarendon, 1957.

Rowland, Christopher. *The Open Heaven: A Study of Apocalyptic in Judaism and Early Christianity*. New York: Crossroad, 1982.

Ruiz, J. M. G. 'La incredulidad de Israel y los impedimentos del Anticristo segun 2 Tes 2.6f.'. *EstBib* 10 (1951): 189–203.

Russell, R. 'The Idle in 2 Thess 3:6–12: An Eschatological or a Social Problem?' *NTS* 34 (1988): 105–19.

Rusten, E. Michael. 'A Critical Evaluation of the Dispensationalist Interpretation of the Book of Revelation'. Ph.D. diss., New York University, 1975.

Sabatier, Pierre, ed. *Bibliorum Sacrorum Latinae versiones antiquae: seu vetus Italica, et Cæteræ quæcunque in Codicibus Mss. & antiquorum libris reperiri potuerunt*. Rheims: Reginald Florentain, 1743.

Sæbø, M. 'יוה.' In *TWAT*, ed. G. J. Botterweck and H. Ringgren, 3:559–86. 10 vols. Stuttgart: Kohlhammer, 1970–2002.

Sagot, Solange. 'Le "Cantique des Cantiques" dans le "De Isaac" d'Ambroise de Milan'. *Recherches Augustiniennes* 16 (1973): 3–57.

Sanday, W. and A. C. Headlam. *The Epistle to the Romans*. ICC. Edinburgh: T. & T. Clark, 1896.

Sanders, E. P. *Paul and Palestinian Judaism: A Comparison of Patterns of Religion*. NTL. London: SCM, 1977.

Paul, the Law, and the Jewish People. Minneapolis: Fortress, 1983.

Sanders, Jack T. 'The Transition from Opening Epistolary Thanksgiving to Body in Letters of the Pauline Corpus'. *JBL* 81 (1962): 348–62.

Sandnes, Karl Olav. *Paul – One of the Prophets? A Contribution to the Apostle's Self-Understanding*. WUNT. Tübingen: Mohr, 1991.

Saunders, Ernest W. *1 Thessalonians, 2 Thessalonians, Philippians, Philemon.* Atlanta: John Knox, 1981.

Schade, Hans-Heinrich. *Apokalyptische Christologie bei Paulus: Studien zum Zusammenhang von Christologie und Eschatologie in den Paulusbriefen.* GTA. Göttingen: Vandenhoeck & Ruprecht, 1981.

Schenke, Hans-Martin and Karl Martin Fischer. *Einleitung in die Schriften des Neuen Testaments.* 2 vols. Gütersloh: Mohn, 1978–9.

Schippers, R. 'Pre-Synoptic Tradition in 1 Thessalonians II 13–16'. *NovT* 8 (1966): 223–34.

Schlatter, A. *Die Briefe an die Thessalonicher, Philipper, Timotheus und Titus.* SENT. Stuttgart: Calwer, 1950.

Schlier, Heinrich. *Der Apostel und seine Gemeinde. Auslegung des ersten Briefes an die Thessalonicher.* Freiburg: Herder, 1972.

Schlueter, Carol J. *Filling up the Measure: Polemical Hyperbole in 1 Thessalonians 2.14–16.* JSNTSup. Sheffield, JSOT, 1994.

Schmid, J. 'Der Antichrist und die hemmende Macht (2 Thess 2, 1–12)'. *TQ* 129 (1949): 323–43.

Schmidt, Andreas. 'Erwägungen zur Eschatologie des 2 Thessalonicher und des 2 Johannes'. *NTS* 38 (1992): 477–80.

Schmidt, D. '1 Thess. 2:13–16: Linguistic Evidence for an Interpolation'. *JBL* 102 (1983): 269–79.

'The Authenticity of 2 Thessalonians: Linguistic Arguments'. In *SBLSP 1983*, 223–34.

'The Syntactical Style of 2 Thessalonians'. In *TC*, ed. R. F. Collins, 383–93. BETL. Louvain: Leuven University Press, 1990.

Schmidt, J. E. C. 'Vermuthungen über die beiden Briefe an die Thessalonicher'. In *Bibiothek für Kritik und Exegese des Neuen Testaments und älteste Christengeschichte 2.3*, 380–6. Hadamar: Neue Gelehrtenbuchhandlung, 1801. Reprinted in Wolfgang Trilling, *Untersuchungen zum zweiten Thessalonicherbrief*, 159–61.

Schmidt, N. 'The Son of Man in the Book of Daniel'. *JBL* 19 (1900): 22–8.

Schmidt, Paul Wilhelm. *Der erste Thessalonicherbrief, neu erklart, nebst einem Excurs über den zweiten gleichnemigen Brief.* Berlin: Georg Reimer, 1885.

Schmiedel, P. W. *Thessalonicher, Korinther.* HKNT. Freiburg: Mohr, 1892.

Schmithals, Walter. 'Zur nachpaulinischen Herkunft des zweiten Thessalonicherbriefes'. *ZNW* 44 (1952–3): 152–6.

'Die Thessalonicherbriefe als Briefkompositionen'. In *Zeit und Geschichte*, ed. E. Dinkler, 295–315. Tübingen: Mohr, 1963.

'Die historische Situation der Thessalonicherbriefe'. In *Paulus und die Gnostiker: Untersuchungen zu den kleinen Paulusbriefen*, 89–157. Hamburg: Herbert Reich Evangelischer, 1965.

'The Historical Situation of the Thessalonian Epistles'. In *Paul and the Gnostics*, 123–218. Trans. J. E. Steely. Nashville: Abingdon, 1972.

Schmitz, Otto. 'Παραγγέλλω, παραγγελία'. In *TDNT*, ed. G. Kittel and G. Friedrich, 5:761–5. 10 vols. Grand Rapids: Eerdmans, 1964–76.

'Παρακαλέω, παράκλησις'. In *TDNT*, ed. G. Kittel and G. Friedrich, 5:773–99. 10 vols. Trans. G. W. Bromiley. Grand Rapids: Eerdmans, 1964–76.

Schneider, Johannes. 'Παρέρχομαι'. In *TDNT*, ed. G. Kittel and G. Friedrich, 2:681–2. 10 vols. Trans. G. W. Bromiley. Grand Rapids: Eerdmans, 1964–76.

Schnelle, Udo. 'Der erste Thessalonicherbrief und die Entstehung der paulinischen Anthropologie'. *NTS* 32 (1986): 207–24.

Schoedel, W. R. 'Polycarp's Witness to Ignatius of Antioch'. *VC* 41 (1987): 1–10. 'Polycarp, Epistle of'. In *ABD*, ed. D. N. Freedman, 5:390–2. 6 vols. Garden City, N.Y.: Doubleday, 1992.

Schonfield, Hugh J. *The Song of Songs*. London: Elek, 1959.

Schoon-Janssen, Johannes. *Unstrittene 'Apologien' in den Paulusbriefen: Studien zur rhetorischen Situation des 1. Thessalonicherbriefes, des Galaterbriefes und des Philipperbriefes*. GTA. Göttingen: Vandenhoeck & Ruprecht, 1991.

Schubert, Paul. *The Form and Function of the Pauline Thanksgivings*. BZNW. Berlin: Töpelmann, 1939.

Schulz, Anselm. *Nachfolgen und Nachahmen. Studien über das Verhältnis der neutestamentlichen Jüngerschaft zur urchristlichen Vorbildethik*. SANT. Munich: Kösel, 1962.

Schütz, John Howard. *Paul and the Anatomy of Apostolic Authority*. SNTSMS. London: Cambridge University Press, 1975.

Schweitzer, Albert. *The Mysticism of Paul the Apostle*. Trans. William Montgomery. 2nd edn. London: A. & C. Black, 1953.

Schweizer, Eduard. 'Der zweite Thessalonicherbrief ein Philipperbrief?' *TZ* 1 (1945): 90–105.
A Theological Introduction to the New Testament. Trans. O. C. Dean. London: SPCK, 1992.

Scott, J. Julius. 'Paul and Late-Jewish Eschatology – A Case Study, I Thessalonians 4:13–18 and II Thessalonians 2:1–12'. *JETS* 15 (1972): 133–43.

Selwyn, E. G. *The First Epistle of St. Peter. The Greek Text with Introduction, Notes and Essays*. 2nd edn. London: Macmillan, 1946.

Shires, Henry M. *The Eschatology of Paul in the Light of Modern Scholarship*. Philadelphia: Westminster, 1966.

Siber, P. *Mit Christus Leben: Eine Studie zur paulinischen Auferstehungshoffnung*. ATANT. Zurich: Theologischer, 1971.

Simpson, John W., Jr. 'The Future of Non-Christian Jews: 1 Thessalonians 2:15–16 and Romans 9–11'. Ph.D. diss., Fuller Theological Seminary, 1988.
'The Problems Posed by 1 Thessalonians 2:15–16 and a Solution'. *HBT* 12 (1990): 42–72.

Sirard, L. 'La Parousie de l'Antéchrist, 2 Thess 2.3–9'. In *Studiorum Paulinorum Congressus Internationalis Catholicus*, ed. C. Amato, 2:89–100. Rome: Pontifical Biblical Institute, 1963.

Slotki, J. *Daniel, Ezra and Nehemiah*. London: Socino, 1951.

Smith, Abraham. *Comfort One Another: Reconstructing the Rhetoric of 1 Thessalonians*. LCBI. Louisville, Ky.: Westminster John Knox, 1995.

Snyder, Graydon F. 'A Summary of Faith in an Epistolary Context: 1 Thess. 1:9, 10'. In *SBLSP 1972*, 2:355–65.

Soden, H. von. 'Der erste Thessalonicherbrief'. *TSK* 58 (1885): 263–310.

Söding, T. 'Der erste Thessalonicherbrief und die frühe paulinische Evangeliumsverkündigung. Zur Frage einer Entwicklung der paulinischen Theologie'. *BZ* 35 (1991): 180–203.

South, James T. *Disciplinary Practices in Pauline Texts*. Lewiston, N.Y.: Edwin Mellen, 1992.

Spicq, Ceslas. 'Les Thessaloniciens "inquiets" étaient-ils des paresseux?' *ST* 10 (1956): 1–13.

Theological Lexicon of the New Testament. 3 vols. Trans. J. D. Ernest. Peabody, Mass.: Hendrickson, 1994.

Staab, K. 'Die Thessalonicherbriefe'. In *Die Thessalonicherbriefe, die Gefangenschaftsbriefe und die Pastoralbriefe*, ed. K. Staab and J. Freundorfer, 7–63. RNT. Regensburg: Friedrich Pustet, 1965.

Stacy, R. Wayne. 'Introduction to the Thessalonian Correspondence'. *RevExp* 96 (1999): 175–94.

Steele, E. Springs. 'Jewish Scriptures in 1 Thessalonians'. *BTB* 14 (1984): 12–17.

Stephens, D. J. 'Eschatological Themes in 2 Thess. 2:1–12'. Ph.D. thesis, University of St Andrews, 1976.

Stephenson, A. M. G. 'On the Meaning of ἐνέστηκεν ἡ ἡμέρα τοῦ κυρίου in 2 Thessalonians 2, 2'. In *SE IV*, ed. F. L. Cross, 442–51. TUGAL. Berlin: Akademie, 1968.

Stepien, J. 'Autentycznosc listów do Tessaloniczan'. *ColT* 34 (1963): 91–182.

Still, Todd D. *Conflict at Thessalonica: A Pauline Church and its Neighbours*. JSNTSup. Sheffield: Sheffield Academic Press, 1999.

'Eschatology in the Thessalonian Letters'. *RevExp* 96 (1999): 195–210.

Stott, John. *The Message of the Thessalonians: Preparing for the Coming King*. BST. Leicester: IVP, 1991.

Stowers, Stanley K. *Letter-Writing in Greco-Roman Antiquity*. LEC. Philadelphia: Westminster, 1986.

Strack, H. L. and G. Stemberger. *Introduction to the Talmud and Midrash*. Ed. and trans. M. Bockmuehl. Edinburgh: T. & T. Clark, 1996.

Strack, Hermann L. and Paul Billerbeck. *Kommentar zum Neuen Testament aus Talmud und Midrasch*. 5 vols. Munich: C. H. Beck, 1922–61.

Strobel, A. *Untersuchungen zum eschatologischen Verzögerungsproblem auf Grund der spätjüdisch-urchristlichen Geschichte von Habakuk 2.2ff*. NovTSup. Leiden: Brill, 1961.

Stuckenbruck, Loren T. *Angel Veneration and Christology*. WUNT. Tübingen: Mohr, 1995.

Stürmer, Karl. *Auferstehung und Erwählung: Die doppelte Ausrichtung der Paulinischen Verkündigung*. BFCT. Gütersloh: Bertelsmann, 1953.

Sumney, Jerry L. 'The Bearing of a Pauline Rhetorical Pattern on the Integrity of 2 Thessalonians'. *ZNT* 81 (1990): 192–204.

Theissen, Gerd. *The Social Setting of Pauline Christianity: Essays on Corinth*. Trans. J. H. Schütz. Philadelphia: Fortress, 1982.

Thomas, Robert L. 'I and II Thessalonians'. In *EBC*, ed. F. E. Gaebelein, 11:229–337. 12 vols. Grand Rapids: Zondervan, 1978.

Thompson, E. 'The Sequence of the Two Epistles to the Thessalonians'. *ExpTim* 56 (1944–5): 306–7.

Thompson, J. A. *The Book of Jeremiah*. NICOT. Grand Rapids: Eerdmans, 1980.

Thrall, Margaret E. *A Critical and Exegetical Commentary on the Second Epistle to the Corinthians*. ICC. Vol. 1. Edinburgh: T. & T. Clark, 1994.

Thurston, Bonnie Bowman. *Reading Colossians, Ephesians, and 2 Thessalonians: A Literary and Theological Commentary*. Reading the New Testament. New York: Crossroad, 1995.

Thurston, Robert W. 'The Relationship between the Thessalonian Epistles'. *ExpTim* 85 (1973–4): 52–6.

Tomasino, Anthony J. 'Daniel and the Revolutionaries: The Use of Daniel Tradition by Jewish Resistance Movements of Late Second-Temple Palestine'. Ph.D. diss., University of Chicago, 1995.

Tov, Emmanuel. 'Die griechischen Bibelübersetzungen'. In *ANRW II, 20.1*, ed. H. Temporini and A. Haase, 121–89. Berlin: de Gruyter, 1987.

The Text-Critical Use of the Septuagint in Biblical Research. 2nd edn. JBS. Jerusalem: Simor, 1997.

Townsend, John T. 'II Thessalonians 2:3–12'. In *SBLSP 1980*, 233–46.

Travis, Stephen H. 'The Place of Divine Retribution in the Thought of Paul'. Ph.D. thesis, University of Cambridge, 1970.

Trilling, Wolfgang. *Untersuchungen zum zweiten Thessalonicherbrief.* Leipzig: St Benno, 1972.

Der zweite Brief an die Thessalonicher. EKKNT. Zurich: Benzinger; Neukirchen-Vlujn: Neukirchener, 1980.

'Literarische Paulusimitation im 2. Thessalonicherbrief'. In *Paulus in den neutestamentlichen Spätschriften: zur Paulusrezeption im Neuen Testament*, ed. K. Kertelge, 146–56. QD. Freiburg: Herder, 1981.

Troeltsch, Ernst. *The Social Teaching of the Christian Churches.* Vol. 1. Trans. O. Wyon. HSP. London: Allen & Unwin, 1931.

Trudinger, Paul. 'The Priority of 2 Thessalonians Revisited: Some Fresh Evidence'. *DRev* 113 (1995): 31–5.

Turner, N. A. *A Grammar of New Testament Greek. III. Syntax.* Edinburgh: T. & T. Clark, 1963.

Turrado, L. *Biblia commentada VI – Hechos de los Apostoles y Epistolas paulinas.* BAC. Madrid, 1965.

Uprichard, R. E. H. 'An Examination of the Early Date Hypothesis for the Writing of 1 Thessalonians, with Particular Reference to Development in Paul's Theology'. Ph.D. thesis, Queen's University of Belfast, 1976.

'Exposition of 1 Thessalonians 4, 13–18'. *IBS* 1 (1979): 150–6.

'The Person and Work of Christ in 1 Thessalonians'. *EvQ* 53 (1981): 108–14.

Vaccari, Albertus. *Cantici Canticorum: Vetus Latina translatio a S. Hieronymo ad Graecum Textum Hexaplarem Emendata.* Rome: Edizioni di Storia e Letteratura, 1959.

Valmin, Natan. *Arbete och slaveri i antiken.* NK. Stockholm, 1937.

Vanhoye, A. 'La Composition de 1 Thessaloniciens'. In *TC*, ed. R. F. Collins, 73–86. BETL. Louvain: Leuven University Press, 1990.

Verhoef, Eduard. 'The Relation between 1 Thessalonians and 2 Thessalonians and the Inauthenticity of 2 Thessalonians'. *HvTSt* 53 (1997): 163–71.

Vielhauer, P. *Geschichte der urchristlichen Literatur: Einleitung in das Neue Testament, die Apokryphen und die Apostolischen Vater.* De Gruyter Lehrbuch. Berlin: de Gruyter, 1975.

Vokotopoulou, Julia. *Guide to the Archaeological Museum of Thessalonike.* Athens: Kapon, 1996.

Vom Brocke, Christoph. *Thessaloniki – Stadt des Kassander und Gemeinde des Paulus.* WUNT. Tübingen: Mohr, 2001.

Vos, Craig Steven de. *Church and Community Conflict: The Relationships of the Thessalonian, Corinthian and Philippian Churches with their Wider Civic Communities.* SBLDS. Atlanta: Scholars, 1999.

Vos, Geerhardus. *The Pauline Eschatology*. 3rd edn. Grand Rapids: Eerdmans, 1930.

Wallace, Daniel B. *Greek Grammar Beyond the Basics: An Exegetical Syntax of the New Testament*. Grand Rapids: Zondervan, 1997.

Walters, P. *The Text of the Septuagint, its Corruptions and their Emendations*. Ed. D. W. Gooding. London: Cambridge University Press, 1973.

Waltke, Bruce K. and M. O'Connor. *An Introduction to Biblical Hebrew Syntax*. Winona Lake, Ind.: Eisenbrauns, 1990.

Wanamaker, Charles A. 'Apocalypticism at Thessalonica'. *Neot* 21 (1987): 1–10.

——— *The Epistles to the Thessalonians: A Commentary on the Greek Text*. NIGTC. Grand Rapids: Eerdmans, 1990.

Ward, Ronald A. *Commentary on 1 and 2 Thessalonians*. Waco: Word, 1973.

Warfield, Benjamin B. 'The Prophecies of St. Paul. I – 1 and 2 Thessalonians'. *The Expositor* 3rd series 4 (1886): 30–44.

Watson, Duane F. 'Michael'. In *ABD*, ed. D. N. Freedman, 4:811. 6 vols. Garden City, N.Y.: Doubleday, 1992.

Weatherly, Jon Allen. 'The Authenticity of 1 Thessalonians 2.13–16: Additional Evidence'. *JSNT* 42 (1991): 79–98.

——— *1 & 2 Thessalonians*. CPNIVC. Joplin, Mo.: College Press, 1996.

Weber, C. P. 'המה'. In *TWOT*, ed. R. L. Harris *et al.*, 1:219–20. 2 vols. Chicago: Moody, 1980.

Weima, Jeffrey A. D. *Neglected Endings: The Significance of the Pauline Letter Closings*. JSNTSup. Sheffield: JSOT, 1994.

——— 'The Pauline Letter Closings: Analysis and Hermeneutical Significance'. *BBR* 5 (1995): 177–98.

——— '"How You Must Walk to Please God": Holiness and Discipleship in 1 Thessalonians 4:1–12'. In *Patterns of Discipleship in the New Testament*, ed. R. N. Longenecker, 98–119. McNTS. Grand Rapids: Eerdmans, 1996.

——— 'An Apology for the Apologetic Function of 1 Thessalonians 2:1–12'. *JSNT* 68 (1997): 73–99.

Weiss, Bernhard. *Biblical Theology of the New Testament*. 2 vols. Trans. D. Eaton. CFTL. Edinburgh: T. & T. Clark, 1893.

Weiss, Johannes. *Das Urchristentum*. Ed. R. Knopf. Göttingen: Vandenhoeck & Ruprecht, 1917.

——— *Earliest Christianity: A History of the Period A.D. 30–150*. 2 vols. Trans. and ed. F. C. Grant. HT. New York: Harper, 1959.

West, J. C. 'The Order of 1 and 2 Thessalonians'. *JTS* 15 (1914): 66–74.

White, J. L. *The Form and Function of the Body of the Greek Letter: A Study of the Letter-Body in the Non-Literary Papyri and in Paul the Apostle*. SBLDS. Missoula: SBL, 1972.

Whiteley, D. E. H. *Thessalonians in the Revised Standard Version with Introduction and Commentary*. NClarB. Oxford: OUP, 1969.

Wichmann, Wolfgang. *Die Leidenstheologie: Eine Form der Leidensdeutung im Spätjudentum*. BWANT. Stuttgart: Kohlhammer, 1930.

Wikgren, A. P. 'A Comparative Study of the Theodotionic and Septuagint Translations of Daniel'. Ph.D. diss., University of Chicago, 1932.

Wilcke, H.-A. *Das Problem eines messianischen Zwischenreiches bei Paulus*. ATANT. Zurich: Zwingli, 1967.

Wilckens, Ulrich. *Die Missionsreden der Apostelgeschichte: Form- und traditionsgeschichte Untersuchungen*. WMANT. Neukirchen-Vluyn: Neukirchener, 1961.

Der Brief an die Römer. EKKNT. Neukirchen-Vluyn: Neukirchener, 1978–81.

Wiles, Gordon P. *Paul's Intercessory Prayers: The Significance of the Intercessory Prayer Passages in the Letters of St. Paul*. SNTSMS. Cambridge: Cambridge University Press, 1974.

Williams, David J. *1 and 2 Thessalonians*. NIBCNT. Peabody, Mass.: Hendrickson, 1992.

Wilson, R. McL. *Gnosis and the New Testament*. Oxford: Blackwell, 1968.

Winter, Bruce W. 'The Entries and Ethics of Orators and Paul (1 Thessalonians 2:1–12)'. *TynBul* 44 (1993): 55–74.

Seek the Welfare of the City: Christians as Benefactors and Citizens. FCCGRW. Grand Rapids: Eerdmans, 1994.

Witherington, Ben. *Jesus, Paul, and the End of the World*. Exeter: Paternoster, 1992.

Paul's Narrative Thought World. Carlisle: Paternoster, 1994.

Witt, Rex. 'The Egyptian Cults in Ancient Macedonia'. In *Ancient Macedonia I*, 324–33. Thessaloniki: Institute for Balkan Studies, 1970.

'The *Kabeiroi* in Ancient Macedonia'. In *Ancient Macedonia II*, 67–80. Thessaloniki: Institute for Balkan Studies, 1977.

Wohlenberg, Gustav. *Der erste und zweite Thessalonicherbrief*. KNT. Leipzig: Deichert, 1903.

Woude, A. S. van der, ed. *The Book of Daniel in the Light of New Findings*. BETL. Louvain: Leuven University Press, 1993.

Wrede, W. *Die Echtheit des zweiten Thessalonicherbriefs untersucht*. TU. Leipzig: Hinrichs, 1903.

Wright, N. T. *The Climax of the Covenant: Christ and the Law in Pauline Theology*. COQG. Edinburgh: T. & T. Clark, 1991.

Wrzól, J. 'Sprechen 2 Thess 2, 2 und 3, 17 gegen paulinischen Ursprung des Briefes?' *WS* 1 (1906): 271–89.

Die Echtheit des zweiten Thessalonicherbriefes. BibS(F). Freiburg: Herder, 1916.

Wuellner, Wilhelm. 'The Argumentative Structure of 1 Thessalonians as *Paradoxical Encomium*'. In *TC*, ed. R. F. Collins, 117–36. BETL. Louvain: Leuven University Press, 1990.

Yoder Neufeld, Thomas Raye. '*Put on the Armour of God'*: *The Divine Warrior from Isaiah to Ephesians*. JSNTSup. Sheffield: Sheffield Academic Press, 1997.

Zahn, Theodor. *Einleitung in das Neue Testament*. 2nd edn. 3 vols. Leipzig: Deichert, 1900.

Introduction to the New Testament. 3 vols. Trans. J. M. Trout, M. W. Jacobus and C. S. Thayer. From the German 3rd edn. Edinburgh: T. & T. Clark, 1909.

Zerwick, Maximilian. *Biblical Greek Illustrated by Examples*. Rome: Pontifical Biblical Institute, 1963.

INDEX OF PASSAGES CITED

D Dead Sea Scrolls

F Christian and non-Rabbinic Jewish literature

INDEX OF MODERN AUTHORS

INDEX OF SUBJECTS